With compliments from

[illegible]

Jan. 14, 2006

Collected Works of
Professor B.R. Grover Vol. 1

Land Rights, Landed Hierarchy and Village Community During the Mughal Age

Collected Works of
Professor B.R. Grover Vol. 1

Land Rights, Landed Hierarchy and Village Community During the Mughal Age

Edited by
Amrita Grover
Dr. Anju Grover Chaudhary
Dr. J C Dua

With an Introduction by
Satish Chandra

Originals
(an imprint of Low Price Publications)
Delhi-110052

Distributed by
D.K. Publishers Distributors (P) Ltd.
4834/24, Ansari Road, Darya Ganj,
New Delhi-110002
Phones: 51562573, 51562575, 51562578
e-mail: dkpd@del3.vsnl.net.in
visit us at: www.dkpd.com

First Published 2005

ISBN 81-88629-26-X (Vol. 1)

Published by
Originals
(an imprint of Low Price Publications)
A-6, Nimri Commercial Centre,
Near Ashok Vihar Phase-IV, Delhi-110052
Phones: 27452453
e-mail: lpp@nde.vsnl.net.in
visit us at: www.lppindia.com

Printed at
D K Fine Art Press P Ltd.
Delhi-110052

PRINTED IN INDIA

Dedicated to the Memory of my
Esteemed Brother
Professor B.R. Grover

Amrita Grover

About the Author

Professor B.R. Grover, former Chairman of the Indian Council of Historical Research, with an academic and administrative career spanning more than 55 years, has left an indelible mark as one of India's most eminent and dedicated historians. He has left behind a massive wealth of historical research based on original Persian, Urdu, Ottoman Turkish and English sources. Known for doing intensive research in the archives and libraries of India, several European countries and the United States of America, Professor Grover had carved out a distinct position for himself as a moving encyclopaedia of source material on agrarian history of the Mughals, especially the land revenue administration.

Upon his death on May 10, 2001, the then Prime Minister Atal Behari Vajpayee paid him a rich tribute, stating: "He would always be remembered for his formidable legacy of excellence, erudition, and dedication to historical research and academic administration." Dr. Murli Manohar Joshi, then Minister of Human Resources and Scientific Research, paid him a personal homage and called him a real "Karma Yogi". He said, "He lived like a Yogi and died like a Yogi." Former Vice President of India, Justice Hidayatullah, had also applauded him for his research. His colleagues described him as "a man of sterling qualities of head and heart"; and "a dynamic and objective head of country's premier historical Institute who has left a rich legacy of his outstanding achievements in the world of historical research," among other things.

Born on February 10, 1923, Professor Grover started his career in teaching in 1946 in Lahore and later taught at the University of Punjab and various universities in Delhi until 1974, including Delhi University, Jawahar Lal Nehru University and Jamia Milia Islamia, where he also served as head of the Department of Indian History and Culture. In 1974, he was called upon to join as Director cum Member-Secretary of the newly established Indian Council of Historical Research (ICHR), a premier historical research Institute, where he served from 1974 to 1985 as Director and was later appointed as Chairman in 1999. For his long association with ICHR, his colleague, Prof. A.R. Khan, wrote in his obituary: "On account of his long association with the Council and the services rendered by him to it, Professor Grover became an institution by himself and he and the Council became a synonymy, as the latter came to be identified, both in India and abroad, with Professor Grover, even when he was not holding any office in the Council."

Initially having received training at Paris under the auspices of UNESCO for the promotion of history as a means of international understanding, Professor Grover wrote and published books in British history. Later, because of his deep interest in the study of original sources and his proficiency in Persian language, his research interests shifted to the medieval period of Indian history. His interest later widened to the study and research in regard to the social, cultural and economic impact of the Indian immigrants in West Asia and East European countries. As an avid researcher, Professor Grover wrote and published copiously on various aspects of the Mughal Agrarian System, Patterns of Rural Trade, The Concept of Village Community and a host of other topics. His writings, mostly published in prestigious journals, like the journals of the Delhi School of Economics and the proceedings of various conferences, became nodal points for the scholars of his generation. His published writings in *The Indian Economic and Social History Review, Proceedings of the Indian Historical Records Commission, Indian Archives, Proceedings of the Punjab History Conference, Punjab Past and Present* and *The Proceedings of the Indian History Congress,* among others, brought him national and international recognition. At an early stage of Professor Grover's career, Prof. M.M. Pearson of Pennsylvania University, U.S.A., wrote about his Mughal Agrarian writings as "...an impressive start...brilliant, which makes fundamental contribution in this area." Prof. C.A. Bailey of Cambridge University, complimented him for "comprehensive listing of materials" and "excellent bibliographies."

Because of his expertise in historical manuscripts/documents and objects, Professor Grover was nominated by the Government of India for several honorary positions such as member of the Indian Historical Records Commission, member of the Historical Documents Purchase Committee of the National Archives of India, member of the Committee on Preservation and Development of Cultural Heritage of Delhi, and an expert member of the Verification Committee of National Museum, India. Professor Grover was also a member of the Publication Committee of the "Comprehensive History of India". For the Indian History Congress, he served intermittently as a Joint Secretary, a Treasurer and Sectional President (Medieval India). Professor Grover also edited the well-known Time Capsule in 1978, and advised the Government to display it in the National Museum instead of inserting it again underground. He also served on the Editorial Board constituted by the Government of India for the production of documentaries on "Freedom Struggle for India's Independence, 1984-2001." Under this scheme, more than 75 documentaries were published by the Films Division, Ministry of Information and Broadcasting.

Professor Grover represented India at several international organizations, including UNESCO in 1951; Indian delegate to West Germany, 1957; delegate to the International Conference in History, Bucharest, 1980; delegate to the International Conference on the Bulgarian Studies, Sofia, 1986; and delegate to the World Archaeological Congress, Croatia, 1998, among others. Besides participating in numerous Indo-European cultural exchange programmes, presiding over innumerable regional/national/international seminars and conferences and contributing papers to various national/international seminars and conferences, he also lectured widely in West Germany (1957), Bulgaria (1986), Zagreb (1998), UK (1998), Holland (1998), and United States (1998 and 2000).

Professor Grover received several honours and awards for his historical research. For his writings on Georgi Dimitrov, the "Role of the Indian Immigrants in the Culture and Economy of the West Asian and East European Countries During the Medieval Age," and "The Social, Religious and Agrarian Aspects in East Europe, especially Bulgaria under the Ottoman-Turkish Rule (14th-19th centuries)," he was awarded Georgi Dimitrov Gold Medal by the Peoples Republic of Bulgaria. For his work on Punjab History, Professor Grover was awarded Saropa Roll of Honour by the Punjabi University, Patiala, in 1996. A life-long scholar of medieval and Islamic India, Professor Grover again came in limelight in 2001 when (upon the demolition of Buddhist statues at Bamiyan by the Taliban government), his expert opinion was sought by the Indian media to determine whether there was any parallel between Bamiyan and Ayodhya.

As a distinguished historian and a scholar with an integrated and scientific approach to the analysis of the historical process, Professor Grover, being a liberal thinker, was a great believer in the social cohesion and national integration in India and made an immense contribution in this regard.

Introduction

Professor B.R. Grover was an indefatigable researcher who based his work on original sources, mainly Persian. The quantity and quality of his published work, and his devotion to learning has been admired immensily by academicians and his friends.

During the period that Professor Grover was working, there was a deep interest in the land revenue system and the rights of various sections – the state, the *jagirdars*, the *zamindars*, and different categories of cultivators. Part of the problem had been created by the early British administrators due to their failure to understand the meaning of various Indian revenue terms and expressions, and the nature of the society these terms reflected. There was also an attempt on the part of the British rulers to arrogate to the colonial state many of the rights and privileges traditionally enjoyed by different sections. Much of the debate revolved around the nature of *zamindari* rights and the position of the cultivators, including what came to be called "the village community". It has needed the work of a whole generation of Indian historians to try to overcome some of the confusion, and to arrive at a better understanding of the revenue system and its working during medieval times. Professor Grover was an active participant in this quest. Many of the papers brought together in this volume are a testimony to his contribution to it.

History is a developing science, and the research work of one generation becomes the basis for the research work of another generation. Such a process has to be seen both in a critical and a positive manner – critical about some of the assumptions or notions of the earlier generation of historians, and positive in recognizing their contribution. Historical debate in India has now shifted from understanding terms, procedures and forms of administration in pre-British times to the question: How did they affect different sections of society? Did they permit any growth, and if so, what was the nature and extent of the growth, and who benefited from it? A lot of work, using documentary sources, and adopting new methodologies would be needed to answer some of these questions. An understanding of the nature of the Indian village community was a key factor in this debate. As long as the Indian village was seen as a closed unit—economically self-sufficient and administering itself through a *panchayat* which claimed to own or control land—a paradigm which had been put forward by the early British administrative historians, and uncritically accepted by the early Indian historians and nationalist leaders, the question of growth in such a closed society hardly arose. The writings of Professor Grover on the nature of village society and its functioning, the nature of the *panchayats*, and their relationship with land-holding in the village, and in the assessment and collection of land-revenue, as also putting forward evidence which questioned the economic isolation or self-sufficiency of the Indian village played a crucial role in arriving at a new understanding. That the Indian village was *not* economically isolated but participated actively in the developmental problematic affairs is now being loudly proclaimed by a section of western historians, as if this was their "discovery". Thus, they are not prepared to comprehend or acknowledge the contribution of earlier Indian historians. Unfortunately, it has also become fashionable among a section of young Indian historians to refer to the works of western scholars in preference to those of Indian historians, both because the works of the former are more easily available and because it is somehow considered more prestigious to do so. The publication of Professor Grover's papers will, I hope, play a role in correcting this distortion or bias.

At the end, I would like to commend the efforts of Amrita Grover, Anju Grover Chaudhary and J.C. Dua in bringing together the widely scattered papers of Professor B.R. Grover on medieval revenue-administration, village revenue documents, the nature of *zamindari* and *taluqdari* rights, etc. This will be of benefit to both scholars and young historians.

Satish Chandra
Former Chairman
University Grants Commission

New Delhi
8 August, 2004

Preface

Mughal history is a field that has fascinated scholars and students of history for at least four hundred years. In particular, the study of the agrarian set up has attracted many a scholar. Numerous books and articles have been and continue to be written by several scholars about the nature of land rights, land revenue administration, agrarian system, classification of land and the concept of village community, etc. during the Mughal period.

This is not just another book on Mughal history providing anecdotes or description about the land revenue/agrarian system of the Mughal age. Rather, it is a critical analysis of the said topics, subjects based on an in-depth study of original Persian and Urdu documents and manuscripts of the Mughal period. Professor Grover has left behind a very large number of writings on the above subjects. Some of them were published in the national and international journals while many have remained unpublished. A wealth of information and analysis on the said topics is being presented in ***The Collected Works of Professor B. R. Grover***, of which this is the first volume.

Professor B. R. Grover, a distinguished scholar of Mughal history, was well-versed in Persian, Urdu, Punjabi and English. His writings are all based on original sources and documents relating to the agrarian structure of the medieval Indian society in coordination with the chronicles and various other categories of contemporary sources. At the time Professor Grover wrote these articles, many of these documents and terminologies were not fully deciphered. Moreover, he believed that "in order to appreciate the rights of the land owners and other classes of the agriculturalists during the Mughal age, it is imperative to understand the contemporary concept of ownership and varying rights, privileges and interests in land." In early 1960s, Professor Grover was the first scholar to break new grounds on the study of land rights and the concept of village community, etc. His writings thus reflected an in-depth understanding of various aspects of agrarian life during the medieval age.

Some of the most important articles being published in this Volume include (i) Nature of Land Rights in Mughal India; (ii) The Concept of Village Community in North India during Mughal age and the pre-British Era; (iii) An Integrated Pattern of Commercial Life in the Rural Society of North India during the 17th-18th Centuries; (iv) Nature of *Dehat-i-Ta'aluqa* (Zamindari Villages) and the Evolution of *Ta'aluqdari* System during the Mughal Age; (v) The Evolution of the *Zamindars* and *Ta'aluqdari* System in Bengal (1576-1765 A.D.); (vi) Extension and Administration of the Irrigation System under Shah Jahan and Aurangzeb; (vii) Classification of Agrarian Land under Akbar; (viii) Agrarian Problems of the 18th Century Eastern India—a Reappraisal; (ix) *Raqba-Bandi* Document of Akbar's reign and (x) Some Rare Persian Manuscripts and Documents on India (16th-18th centuries) in the German Libraries.

In this analytical and conceptual book on various aspects of land revenue administration and agrarian life in North India during the medieval age and early British period, Professor Grover has challenged the concepts of most of the 19th century British and Indian writers which have traditionally been acclaimed until recently. For example, Professor Grover observed, among other things, that the view held by the European visitors to India in the 16th and 17th centuries that all land was owned by the State was due to their gross ignorance of the working of the *jagir* system. Upon an examination of the comparative land rights of each class in different categories of land system in vogue during the Mughal Age, Professor Grover noticed, among other things, that the question of the ownership of agricultural land in Mughal India had been "oversimplified by ascribing the ownership to one exclusive category of owners—the State or the zamindars". His conclusion was that in the Mughal Age, "The State never claimed the absolute and exclusive ownership of the agrarian land and definitely recognised the existence of private property in it." He also observed that the 19th century British writers exaggerated the role of the *panchayat* or the Village Council. According to Professor Grover, the village community stood for the landed interests of the *malikana* (land owner) and it was "the community of land owners (co-sharing *zamindari* families) that decided if they had to admit new cultivators in the village."

The concept of village community in North India during the Mughal age and the pre-British era was also misperceived by the British and some Indian writers. Professor Grover stipulated that "the picture presented by most of the 19th century British writers about the concept of the village community in the pre-British India, and which has been traditionally accepted by historians, needs a radical modification." He thus studied the concept of the village community in relation to tribal and clannish settlements as well as the *zamindari* rights and jurisdictions of the dominant clans and concluded that there were no communal lands owned by the village communities. In fact, they were "all owned by the State and were regularly entered in the village boundary records." He also challenged the concept that the villages in North India were completely self-sufficient units. According to him "the village was essentially linked with the local markets and the *qasbas*."

In analysing the land revenue administration, the nature of *zamindari* and evolution of *Ta'aluqdari* system during the Mughal age, among other things, Professor Grover examined the original contemporary source material in Persian, Urdu, Ottoman Turkish as well as regional languages. Based on the original archival evidence covering the 17th and 18th centuries, Professor Grover found that hitherto "British and some Indian administrators/ scholars had not taken any comprehensive historical view of the social evolution of *Ta'aluqdar* class in Awadh and other parts of North India." For example, according to him, the two terms—"Zamindar and *Ta'aluqdar* are not synonymous because a *taaluqdari,* compared to *zamindari,* had a lower territorial jurisdiction and status," and "the *zamindari* system was drifting towards a hierarchical pattern of rights in many ways." He also concluded that "zamindars of the villages formed a regular part of the land revenue administration and a *zamindari* class with vested and landed interests formed an agency for the collection of revenues practically all over North India even in the well-settled regions," and "the main interest of the Mughal government was to realise the land revenue rather than to convert the *zamindari* villages into *riyati* (villages that were not under the cognisance of the zamindars).

Another major contribution of Professor Grover was in the area of agrarian problems of the 18th century Eastern India and the classification of agrarian land under Akbar. He found that "most of the works on agrarian problems undertaken by the English administrators, administrators/scholars and historians from the closing years of the 18th century down to the recent times have relied largely on controversial revenue literature comprising the official memoranda, minutes, official reports and private correspondence." In the chapter on "Classification of Agrarian Land Under Akbar," Professor Grover gave an extensive description of the way the agrarian land was classified under Akbar's reign which continued throughout the Mughal age. According to him, "Shah Jahan and Aurangzeb also used the same classification of agrarian land (with some modifications) used under Akbar's reign. In the chapter, "*'Raqba-Bandi'* Documents of Akbar's Reign," Professor Grover discussed the original *Raqba bandi* (i.e. measurement and area statement) documents of the year 1001 *Fasli*, i.e. 1591-92 A.D. of Akbar's reign, that he personally discovered in the Secretariat Records Office, Patna. These are the earliest of such archives in the field of land revenue literature of the Mughal age. These important documents bring out the main traits of the documentation of the *pargana* 'Record-of-Rights' based on the survey of land and also illustrate some new aspects of the local organisation for the land administration in Akbar's reign.

The chapter on "An Integrated Pattern of Commercial Life in the Rural Society of North India during the 17th and 18th Centuries," deals with commercial patterns governing rural society and links the latter with the urban, inter-provincial and foreign trade and commercial setup. Not much attention to this topic had been given previously because of the comparative paucity of contemporary sources as well as practical difficulty in the technique of research since the original sources available in Persian and local languages in the 17th and 18th centuries could not be deciphered by many research scholars. With the belief that a proper scrutiny of regional records can result in a reliable picture of the commercial set-up and business transactions of the rural society in various regions of North India during the 17th – 18th centuries, Professor Grover examined the records from the Rajasthan Archives as well as papers of private families with the National Archives of India including several ledgers and documents comprising correspondence among the merchants in the Rajasthani language and found that contrary to the popular belief, "trade with neighbouring countries, especially Central Asia and the Middle Asian countries, was a continued feature throughout the 17th, 18th and 19th centuries."

In the chapter on 'The Extension of Irrigation System and the Administration of the Canal Works in the Punjab during the

Mughal Age,' Professor Grover challenged Moreland's and other scholars' position that there was no development of the irrigation and canal systems worth the name in Mughal India. Professor Grover, upon researching the original Persian sources, concluded that "the Mughal government was keenly interested in the extension of irrigation facilities to the cultivators for the development of agricultural economy."

During his research endeavours, Professor Grover came across some rare Persian manuscripts and documents on India covering 16th and 18th centuries, a description of which is included in the Chapter on "Rare Persian Manuscripts and Documents on India." These documents throw some light on the social and economic conditions as well as the administrative system of North India from the late 16th to the late 18th centuries. These rare documents, including "Ravaet", written in 996 A.H./1587-88 A.D., "Ain-i-Akbari" of Abul Fazl, "Naisisui Muassar" by Alaud Daula bin Hussaini, written in 973 A.H./1565-66 A.D., and "Dasturulaml", written in the 3rd regnal year of Aurangzeb's reign/1659-60 A.D., are discussed in the above chapter.

For his research, Professor Grover visited several libraries throughout India, many countries of Europe, the U.K. and the United States of America. He utilised original manuscripts and documents available in the Libraries and Archives of Delhi, Himachal Pradesh, Rampur, Aligarh, Rajasthan, Patiala, Amritsar, Lucknow, Calcutta, Patna, Hyderabad, Madras and Jaipur in India; British Museum and Indian Office Library, London; State Library, Berlin (East) Marburg and Tubingen Libraries (West Germany); Universistatsbibliothek of Bonn; Bayerische Statsbibliothek, Munchen (Bavarian State Library) Munich; Westdeutsche Bibliothek (ethemalige Preussiache Staatsbibliothek), and Bibliotheque Nationale, Paris, in Europe; and the Library of Congress and Smithsonian Institution in Washington D.C., U.S.A.

The articles in this volume were (earlier) presented by Professor Grover at various national and international conferences/seminars dealing with Mughal history. Some of these papers published in this present volume have also been frequently quoted by the leading historians for the last four decades.

As most of these chapters consist of papers presented at various conferences on similar topics, there may be some repetition. The editors did not consider it desirable to make any changes since this is a collection of Professor B.R. Grover's original writings. The views expressed in these writings are those of Professor B.R. Grover.

The editors hope that this posthumous collection of Professor B.R. Grover's work will prove to be a valuable source material for the students of Mughal history.

The editors are indebted to Professor Satish Chandra, a distinguished historian and former Chairman of UGC for having spared his valuable time to write an Introduction to this volume. The editors also express their sincere thanks to Original Publishers (an imprint of Low Price Publications) for such a fine job in publishing this book with remarkable efficiency.

Amrita Grover
Dr. Anju Grover Chaudhary
Dr. J. C. Dua

Table of Contents

Chapter 1

Nature of Land Rights in Mughal India

The concept of proprietary rights in agrarian land and the nature of various types of land tenures in Mughal India has been an extremely vexed problem for the Indian administrators, jurists and economic historians ever since the later half of the eighteenth century. The problem was highlighted by the British administrators when confronted with the entrenched position of the zamindars and the various other classes of assignees after the assumption of the Diwani rights in Bengal in 1765. In their well-known controversy over the rights of the State versus the zamindars and other assignees, extremely divergent views were expressed by Warren Hastings, Sir Phillip Frances, Mr. James Grant, Sir John Shore and Lord Cornwallis before the introduction of the Permanent Settlement in Bengal in 1793. The important portions of their respective minutes were brought together by W.K. Firminger in his introduction to the Fifth Report from the Select Committee of the House of Commons on the Affairs of The East India Co. (1812).[1] In support of their contention, each one of the above participants in the controversy tried to base his conclusions on the original position of the various assignees and the working of the land system during the Mughal age from the reign of Akbar down to the later Mughal period. Much less known hitherto, a huge analytical revenue literature in the Persian language, equally controversial in content, was prepared by expert Indian *Munshis* and revenue officials to provide background material for the above-mentioned discussion. Equally important commentaries in Persian on the working of the land system during the Mughal age were written by independent revenue experts. Most of this material produced by the Indian writers has been well preserved in the State Library, Berlin[2], and some copies are available in the British Museum as well.

Paper read at *Indian Economic History Seminar*, Delhi, April, 1961 and published in *IESHR*, i, 1963, pp. 1-23

The main controversy initially hinged on the question as to whether during the Mughal age the ownership of land was vested in the State or the zamindars of various categories and completely kept the rights of the *ryots* out of the picture. As the British rule gradually extended to the different portions of India, in the course of the 19th Century, different types of land systems were encountered. Eminent British revenue experts, Sir Thomas Munro and Mountstuart Elphinstone in the Madras Presidency, Holt Mackenzie in the Ceded and Conquered Provinces in Northern India, Robert Pringle and George Wingate in *Bombay Deccan*, R.M. Bird, James Thomason, John Thornton in the North Western Provinces, A. Seton, C.T. Metcalfe, T. Fortescue in the Assigned Territory of Delhi, Lawrence Montgomery, Edmonstone, Thornton, Sir Richard Temple in the Punjab[3]—challenged the judiciousness of the Permanent Settlement and the entire question acquired a new complexion. The problem now came to be viewed from three angles—the rights of the State, the position of the zamindars and other assignees, and, finally, the rights of the various classes of the ryots. To this was added the equally controversial question—whether the land revenue in India had been a land tax or a rent. Consequently, the nature of the Settlements effected in different provinces based on the prevalent local conditions became diversified. The controversy regarding the nature of land-rights in pre-British India was long kept alive. The Report of the Indian Taxation Enquiry Committee (1924-25) quotes as many as 38 contradictory expert opinions expressed by the members of the Governor-General's Council, Provincial State Regulations, the Despatches exchanged between the Provincial Governments and the Court of Directors, the judgments of the Privy Council and the High Courts in India, Indian Famine Commission, Members of the Board of Revenue, eminent jurists and historians.[4] The problem was once again discussed at length by Prof. Kosambi in 1956 and Dr. Tara Chand[5] in 1960.

In this paper, I have attempted to analyse the land rights of the various classes in the Mughal age mostly on the basis of the original contemporary source material.

I. The question of the ownership of the agricultural land has so far been oversimplified by ascribing the ownership to one exclusive category of owners—the State or the zamindars and the assignees or the ryots—without probing into the comparative land rights of each class in the different categories of land-system in vogue during the Mughal age.

The view upheld by the European visitors in India in the 16th and 17th centuries that all land was owned by the State[6] was based on their gross ignorance of the working of the *jagir* System. Though both in theory and practice, the State was the proprietor of all the jungles and unreclaimed land for agrarian purposes, it did not possess any proprietary rights in the absolute sense over the vast cultivable lands already in hereditary possession of the various classes of *riaya*. Any fresh transfer of a jungle land or an unclaimed *Banjar* land to the *riaya* or a certain category of the zamindars was always accompanied by a *de facto* possession embodying in it a clear title to proprietorship so long as the land remained under cultivation.[7] *Ain-i-Akbari* stresses the claim of ownership of the pioneer cultivator on the waste land appropriated by him.[8] In case such a land became waste by being left uncultivated for long, it reverted to the State under certain proviso restoring the proprietary title of the State and could again be transferred to the *ryots* on the usual conditions.[9] The State claimed a share in the produce of the land rather than title to its proprietorship. In its chapter on '*Rowai Rozi*' (the means of Subsistence), the *Ain-i-Akbari* categorically recognises the proprietary title to the land in the various classes of the cultivators. It states, "It is evident that in all cultivated areas, the possessors of property are numerous, and they hold their lands by ancestral descent, but through malevolence and despite, their titles become obscured by the dust of uncertainty and the hand of firmness is no longer stretched above them. If the cultivator holds in awe the power of the Adorner of the Universe and the Elixir of the living, and the merchant turns back from evil designing and reflect in his heart on the favour of the Lord of the World, the development of divine grace, his possessions would assuredly be approved of wisdom. Thus the virtue of property lies in the pledge of intention, and a just ruler, like a saltbed, makes clean the unclean, and the evil good. But without honest co-adjustors, abundant accessories of State and a full treasury, even he could effect nothing and the condition of subserviency and obedience would lack the bloom of Discipline."[10] Further, in the same chapter, *Ain* explicitly mentions the land revenue as tax on the property of the subjects. It states, "In every kingdom, Government taxes the property of the subject over and above the land revenue and this they call *Tamghah*.... In short, what is imposed on cultivated lands by way of quit-rent is termed *Mal* ...Extra collections over and above the land tax, if taken by revenue officers, are *Wajuhat*; otherwise they are termed *Furuaat*."[11] Aurangzeb's *Farman* to Mohammad Hashim clearly mentions the proprietary title of the *ryots* with full rights of mortgage and sale.[12] This is equally supported by the contemporary documents.[13]

II. The nature of land-rights of various classes can be best appreciated in relation to their holdings in a village which comprised land both under *abadi* (habitation) and cultivation. *Ain* gives different names to the cultivators of the soil, viz., *Kashawarz, Dehkan, Ryots,*[14] whereas other sources and revenue literature of the Mughal times mentions them as *Riaya, Raiya* and *Muzariah.*[15] The term *Riaya* or *Raiyat* would stand, in general, for all kinds of agriculturists owing land revenue to the State as tax on the cultivated lands under possession. As such, the term *Riaya* or *Raiyati* was also used in contrast to the recalcitrant cultivators (*Mutmarid* or *Zor Talb*) who refused to pay revenues to the State. Of the revenue paying class known popularly as *Riaya,* a still further technical distinction was made between the land owners with proprietary rights and the tenants (*Muzarian*) holding lands from the former. So strictly from the technical viewpoint, the term *Riaya* connected the peasant-proprietors as well as such of the zamindar families who owned personal lands subject to the payment of land revenue.[16] A minute examination would show that the nature of the title to the holdings were different for the different classes of agriculturists. Thus, the cultivators in a village could be divided into two main categories, (a) *Riaya* and (b) *Muzarian,* i.e., tenants holding lands on terms stipulated in the *Patta.* The fact that these two types of holdings were distinct from each other is corroborated by the *Ain.*[17] The *Riaya* itself comprised two categories of agriculturists: the *Khudkashta* or *ryots* who cultivated their own land and a second group who had the right to rent out their land.

A *Khudkashta* cultivator was a peasant-proprietor with his holding and residential house situated in the same village. He tilled land of his own with the help of his family members and would not further rent out the land to any tenant. His holding was hereditary and he had full rights in land for the purposes of its transfer, mortgage and sale, though such transactions were, of course, extremely rare.[18] Even though the cultivation of all arable lands was the settled policy of the State, if, due to any adverse circumstances affecting the cultivator, any portion was left uncultivated, it was not subject to assessment and payment of land-revenue. The *Ain* in its Instructions to the *Amal Guzar* states, "Let him (*Amal-Guzar*) learn the character of every husband man, and be the immediate protector of that class of our subjects. Let him endeavour to bring the waste lands into cultivation, and be careful that the arable lands are not neglected....If a husbandman cultivates a less quantity of land than he engaged for, but produces a good excuse, let it be accepted."[19] As late as the early 19th century, Mountstuart Elphinstone in his "Reports on the Territories conquered from the Peshwa", after collecting full information on the tenures of land from the Collectors commented, "The result of those reports and of my own inquiries is, that a large portion of the *ryots* (*Meerassees*) are proprietors of their estates, subject to the payment of fixed land-tax to the Government; while their property is hereditary and saleable, and they are never disposed while they pay their tax, and even then they have for a long period (at least thirty years), the right of reclaiming their estate on paying the dues of Government."[20]

(b) The second class of *riaya* was that of *riaya Pahi-Kasht* or popularly known as *Pahi-Kashtkar*. He was a peasant proprietor but his holding was in a different village from that of his residence.[21] *Ain,* in its chapter on 'Instructions to *Amal Guzar*', directs, "He should strive to bring waste lands into cultivation and take heed that what is in cultivation fall not waste....Should there be no wasteland in a village and a husbandman be capable of adding to his cultivation, he should allow him land in some other village."[22] So a cultivator could have dual capacity, a *Khud Kashtkar* in his own village and a *Pahi-Kashtkar* in another one. But even as *Pahi-Kashtkar*, he had the same full rights in the land as was vested in a *Khud Kashtkar*.

The third category of *Riaya* was that of *Muqarari Riaya*.[23] Such *riaya* also had hereditary ownership of land vested by the State. [24] He had full rights of transfer, mortgage and sale of land.[25] After reserving a holding for his personal cultivation, he could give his spare land on *ijara* (contract) to the *mustajir* (revenue farmer) or give it on a purely temporary lease to the *mustajir* or on terms of *patta* to the tenants.[26] But in either case, he had the direct responsibility of payment of land revenue to the State.[27] He was subject to assessment even if the land was not brought under cultivation.[28]

Muzarian Tenants

As further explained, the zamindars possessed personal lands, both self-cultivated and those rented out to the tenants for cultivation. Similarly, the *Madad-i-maash* assignees could reserve some portions of the lands for self-cultivation and would pass on the rest to the tenants. Thus the *Muqarari-Riaya*, the zamindars and the *Madad-i-maash* assignees had the right to give their spare lands to the tenants known as *muzariahian* who also had hereditary title to the land.[29] In such a case, the ownership of land was split between the *riaya* which acted as the landlord owning full responsibility of payment of land revenue to the State and the *muzariah*, who tilled the land with full rights of hereditary possession so long as he paid the rent to the landlord and wished to retain the land.[30] The latter would retain a fixed share in the produce of the land as stipulated in the unalterable terms of the *patta*.

Usually, in the *Madad-i-Maash* lands, the tenant was entitled to half the share in the produce of the land under his tillage.[31] But in case of a tenant working on the land of the *riaya*, his share might vary a little depending, of course, on the nature of the soil, means of irrigation available, and the incidence of the State demand. All the same, it must have been sufficient for the subsistence of his family, failing which he could not have possibly worked on the land. Thus the landlord (*riaya*), after meeting the State demand, the tenant's share and the expenditure involved on the maintenance of the land, especially on the means of irrigation, would keep the balance (*malikana*) as his profit from the produce of land rented to the tenants.

The relationship between the State and the *riaya* and that between the latter and their tenants has to be viewed, not in terms of modern concepts but in the context of the agrarian conditions prevalent during the age. The availability of abundance of waste arable land for cultivation and jungle land to be rendered arable[32] as against a comparatively small population available for its tillage,[33] rendered the position of the tillers of the soil quite lucrative and sought-after. In this context, there was neither a chance nor the practice to dispossess either the *Riaya* or the tenants from their established hereditary rights.[34] So long as the *riaya* paid land revenue to the State and the tenant gave rent to the landlord (*riaya*), their respective positions were unchallengeable. Where land was sublet by the *riaya* to the tenants, more or less equal rights and privileges were enjoyed by the two classes, and the latter being far less in number, would neither be ejected nor overexploited. Zainuddin Khawf, Babur's historian, remarks that in Hindustan, "Most of the subsistence of the people is on agriculture.....of the *riaya* and the *kardan* (i.e. tenants and assoçiates working on the land), no distinction is made, whatsoever, between them (regarding their position and rights) and the former by themselves far exceed the latter in number.[35]

Though the two classes were bound to each other by mutual dependence and identical interests in the produce of the land, this would by no means strengthen the relationship between the two. A few documents of the reigns of Jahangir and Shah Jahan show that in the *Madad-i-Maash* land, at times the tenant refused to make regular payment of the rent to the landlord who had to resort to legal action for the recovery of the arrears in rent.[36] Though the State machinery helped the landlord in the realisation of the rent from the tenant, it did not dispossess the latter. It afforded protection to the respective rights of both the classes. It also provided relief to the *riaya* and the tenants in case the arable land was left uncultivated due to any natural calamity or personal hardship of cultivators.[37] In case of desertion of land on account of any hardship, Aurangzeb's *Farman* to Mohammad Hashim issues detailed instructions for making alternative provisional arrangements.[38] Even otherwise, the ownership of the hereditary *riaya* or the title of the hereditary tenants was by no means jeopardized as they could always reclaim the land for cultivation, whenever capable of doing so.[39]

The established rights in land of each of the above classes, *Riaya Khud Kasht, Riaya Pai Kasht, Riaya Muqarari* and the *Muzarian* (tenants) were fully safeguarded and guaranteed both by practice and the State law.[40] *Ain,* in its 'Instructions to the *Amal Guzar*', enjoins the latter to see that the *Khud Kashta* land is not converted into *Raiyat Kashta.*[41] Jahangir issued an ordinance that the revenue officials of the *khalsa* and the *jagirdars* should not forcibly dispossess the *ryots* of their lands.[42] He also ordered that a *jagirdar* should not forcibly settle the men and cattle of other *parganas* in his own *jagir* and should rather endeavour to increase the agricultural produce only with the settled cultivators of his own *jagir Pargana.*[43] The Jaipur archives in the *pargana* and the *mauza* documents record the names and the revenue paid by each of the above classes.[44] A *Dasturulaml* of Shah Jahan's reign quotes *parwanas* for the protection of the rights of the *riaya* and the *muzarian* against any high-handedness of the *pargana* and the village officials.[45] Aurangzeb's *Farman* to Rasik Dass Karori issues detailed instructions for the recording of each class of land holders, *mustajirs* (revenue farmers), *riaya* and their *Muzariahian* (tenants) in every village.[46] It directs the officials to safeguard the rights of the *riaya, kushawarz* (cultivators) and *muzariahian* and to afford them all possible facilities with *taqavi* (agricultural loans) for augmenting the agricultural produce and bringing the waste arable land under cultivation.[47]

Having fully comprehended the position of the various classes working on the land in a village, it is easy to appreciate the nature of the title and rights of various other classes in the land created by the State.

All the arable and cultivated lands were divided into two main categories, the *khalsa* and *jagir*. The *khalsa* lands were administered directly by the State which dealt with the *riaya* of various types in the villages for the purposes of assessment and collection of land revenue. The *jagir* lands were assigned to various categories of assignees on different terms. It is not within the scope of this paper to discuss the details of the nature and working of the *jagir* system except to emphasize the relationship of the assignees with the land and its cultivators. In all assigned lands, the assessment work was done by the *pargana* and village officials in accordance with the State regulations.[48] All land revenue documents pertaining to the 'Record-of Rights' for the individual villages (*mauzas*) and the *pargana* as a whole were prepared by the officials as for the *khalsa* lands.[49] But the assignees had to employ their own officials and soldiers for the collection of land revenue in collaboration with the village and *tappah* officials, the *Muqaddam*, *Patwari*, *Chaudhari* and the *Qanungo*[50], *jagir* or *Tuyul*.[51] The *jagir* lands were assigned to *mansabdars*, both civil and military servants, in lieu of cash salaries in accordance with the regulations. Such assignments were conditional on service on the part of the assignee and not hereditary in character. They lasted so long as the assignee was in service and were escheated to the State on his death. As the *jagirdar* was transferred from one place to another, his *jagir* lands could revert to *khalsa* or be put in the category of *paibaqi* lands i.e. earmarked as neutral lands administered by the State officials till further assignment. Even during the course of normal assignment, a *jagirdar* could be put on '*Tankhwah*' basis, i.e. cash payment and his *jagir* could revert to the *khalsa*.

In such a category of assignment, the *jagirdar* was entitled to the collection of the land revenue from the *riaya* in his jurisdiction. He was not the owner of the land. The ownership and the rights of the *riaya* remained undisturbed and they paid the State demand to the village officials who, in turn, deposited it with the *Amil* of the *jagirdar*.

Madad-i-Maash **Grants**[52]:

These were the maintenance grants. Though *Ain* has described them under the title '*Siyurghal*', the chronicles, both for Akbar's reign and his successors, and the revenue literature of the 17th century have used the term *Madad-i-Maash*. *Ain* has explained various classes of persons entitled to such a grant. This financial assistance was given either in the form of grant of rent-free lands or assignation of revenue from land or a cash grant in the form of stipend (*wazifa*) or daily allowance (*rozina*). A full picture regarding the procedure and the State policy towards such grants can be constructed from *Ain-i-Akbari*, Badaoni's *Muntakhabut Tawarikh*, various *Dasturulamls* of the 17th century, Allahabad Records, the Jaipur Archives, the Ajmer documents of the *khadims* of *Dargah* Sharif and the scattered private family documents in the district of Ajmer. Prof. Sheikh Abdur Rashid has published some definitive articles on the '*Madad-i-Maash*' grants under the Mughals.[53]

Unlike the *jagir*, the *Madad-i-Maash* grants (except those for the *Qazis*, *Muftis*, *Sadrs* and *Muhtasibs* – the members of Judiciary) were not conditional upon the performance of any civil and military duties. As Prof. Rashid puts it, "Such a grant was in the nature of transference by the State of the right of collection of revenue and other cesses to the grantee. The State, however, reserved the right to cancel, resume, decrease, or extend the original grant. The land so granted was hereditary in character and immune from State dues as well as administrative interference.......These lands could be bequeathed but not sold or given away as gift."[54]

In the Allahabad documents, a copy of a *parwana* issued by Jumlatul Mulk Raja Raghunath, dated A.H. 1071, 3rd year of Aurangzeb's reign and a copy of *Farman* dated 15th *Rabi-ul-awwal*, 34th year of Aurangzeb's reign, provide us with details of regulations and procedure of *Madad-i-Maash* grants.[55] Similarly, for religious institutions, Jahangir's *Farmans* issued in favour of Dargah of Khwaja Moinuddin Chisti, Ajmer, dated 26th *Ramzan* A.H. 1027/16th September 1618 A.D. and 26th *Ramzan* A.H. 1028/6th September 1619 A.D., are significant for detailed information for such grants.[56]

In small holdings, the *Madad-i-Maash* grant was usually given from the waste arable land of the villages. But where the grants were large, a considerable portion would be given from a waste arable land and the balance from the cultivated land already in possession of the *riayat*. Though the assignment was hereditary in character, the claim of assignee over proprietorship was qualified by the nature of the land assigned. If the rent-free grant of land were waste arable, the onus of cultivation rested with the assignee. He would reclaim the land with the help of the tenant who, in their turn, would assume hereditary rights. The assignee was regarded as the absolute owner of the land which was further rented out to hereditary tenants usually on unalterable terms of *patta*.[57] As to the right of alienation, two-fold evidence is available from the Allahabad

Document, one for Aurangzeb's reign forbidding the right of alienation or sale, another of later Mughal age, recording the sale of such lands.[58] The Ajmer documents of the *khadims* (custodians) of Dargah Sharif and private family archives do not point towards any sale having been effected during the Mughal period till the end of Aurangzeb's reign.

As distinct from the rent free grant of waste-arable land, if the assignment comprised land already under cultivation with the *riaya*, the latter were left undisturbed with their established rights in land as already explained. Then the assignee was entitled only to hereditary claim for the collection of the land revenue from the *riaya*. The ownership of the land for all intents and purposes, continued to be vested with the *riaya* and the assignee had no right either for alienation or sale.

Mustajir* or *Ijaradar :[59] The State could give a portion from the *khalsa* land on *ijara* (contract) to a *mustajir* (revenue farmer) for a term of few years—3 to 4 as stipulated in the terms of *Patta*. The *Jagirdars* were entitled to pass on their land on *ijara* for a term of few years though a *jagir* under transfer would not be given on *ijara*. The Jaipur archives are replete with accounts of such transactions between the *jagirdars* and the *mustajirs*. The *Riaya Muqarari* could also give its land on *ijara*. The agreement-bond (*tamsak*) executed by the *mustajir* was regularly stamped by the Qazi and showed the assessed land-revenue along with the regular bi-annual or yearly installments to be paid by the *ijaradar* who was responsible for the collection of the land revenue through the village and *pargana* officials. The *ijaradar* was entitled to the difference (*takhfif*) in the amount of the land revenue collected and the annual instalments contracted under the terms of the *patta*. A reasonable amount of *takhfif* was earmarked for the *mustajir*. For every instalment paid, he would be issued a receipt (*Qabzal-wasul*) by the *jagirdar* or the State officials. For the non-payment of instalment, he could be proceeded against in accordance with the law. As in the case of assignment of *jagir*, the grant of *ijara* did not clash with the right of the various classes of *riayat* on the *ijara* land. The ownership continued to be vested in the *riayat* whereas the *mustajir* was entitled only to collection of land revenue and to enjoy the profit of difference under the terms of contract. The assessment work being already done by the State officials, he would undertake in the bond executed to fully protect the rights of the *riayat* on the land.

The Zamindars :[60] No term in the Mughal administrative system is perhaps more important as also more ambiguous and misinterpreted than the term 'Zamindar'. During the Mughal age, the institution of *zamindari* covered a variety of individuals with hereditary landed interests from the chiefs of the princely territories to petty intermediaries, as distinct from those of the *ryots*. It comprised officials and non-officials of varying status and importance determined by their respective positions and ranks. Though the system of *zamindari* was known to the Sultanate of Delhi and the independent States of the pre-Mughal era, in some respects, it was accepted by the Mughals as they found it, while in others it was sufficiently replenished with new features so that it could be incorporated in the military and revenue structure of the Mughal administration. Under the Mughals, it was evolved into a regular pattern of land revenue administration. The hitherto accepted belief in the threefold division of the lands into *khalsa*, *jagirs* and *zamindaries* has to be modified, as for the purposes of land administration, even the portions of *zamindari* territories were assignable either to the Mughal State officials or to the zamindars themselves in lieu of their services to the State. This is true of the Mughal administration from Akbar's reign down to the later Mughal times.

The hereditary ruling chiefs, entitled Rajas, Maharanas, Ranas, Rawats, Raos and Rais, were known as zamindars and their domains as *zamindaries*.[61] After their submission to the Mughal government, they were all enrolled in the circle of loyal zamindars' and were treated as State servants.[62] As such, though they were confirmed in their *zamindari* rights and privileges with extremely rare exceptions, they were essentially obliged to render military service to the State.[63] They were usually enrolled as *mansabdars* and were awarded *jagirs* as remuneration. Territorially, each *zamindari* consisted of two portions, named hereditary *Watan jagir* (patrimony) and the other territory under its jurisdiction. They had, of course, hereditary claim to the *Watan-jagir* and could be assigned the other portions of the *zamindari* in *tankhwah-jagir* in accordance with the *mansab* regulations. When not enrolled as a *mansabdar*, apart from confirmation in the *Watan jagir*, the zamindar acted as a revenue collector in the other territory of his *zamindari* and after the deduction of the collection charges, would pass on the revenues as *peshkash* either directly to the State or its assignees.[64]

Quite distinct from the chief zamindars, a varied class of petty zamindars existed throughout Mughal India. Ethnographically, a *zamindari* belonged either to a dominant ruling minority or to the majority of a tribe or clan. Such settlements were known to India for ages.[65] Founded on parochial socio-economic and political territorialism, fortified by the ethnic and historic traditions, the institution of *zamindari* found due recognition in the Mughal polity. Where hereditary chieftaincies or petty *zamindaries* did not exist, a similar artificial atmosphere was created on a miniature scale through the institution of the semi-official class of the zamindars.[66] Even though subject to regular State control in respect of assessment and realisation of land revenue, in course of time, this semi-official class tended to acquire landed and more or less hereditary interests in the *zamindari* territory. Thus underneath the supralocal Mughal imperialism and uniform administrative structure lay the *zamindari* territories and village communities resting essentially in the clannish social structure and caste system.

The nature of *zamindari* was, at times, also marked by provincial practices. A regional study of the subahs of Gujrat, Ajmer, Malwa and Oudh would bring out the main traits of the *zamindari* system. In Gujrat, apart from the Chief zamindars, other hereditary zamindars, with comparatively limited jurisdiction, were all confirmed by the Mughal government. Such a *zamindari* comprised either a full *pargana* or a few villages of a *pargana*. Various families, viz., Girasias, Rajputs, Kolis, Kathis, Jats, Jhadejas, Bakhirs, Koraishis, Rathors, Ahirs, Makwanas and Muslims, who had such ancient *zamindaries*, maintained *status quo* in the Mughal age. They all undertook to serve the State and pay the land revenue. They were given one-fourth of the *zamindari* territory known as *banth* or *watan*-villages (Patrimonious *jagir*) for their maintenance while revenues of the three-fourth of the territory named *talpad* were to be deposited in the State treasury.[67] Except the revenues of the *watan-jagir*, the zamindar was not entitled to the land revenue of the other territory (i.e. *talpad*), which, if not assigned to any other *jagirdar*, had to be paid in installments as *peshkash* to the Mughal State.[68] In respect of their obligations in lieu of the *banth* possession (*watan jagir*), such zamindars fell into two divisions, those holding a full *pargana* had to render military service with a fixed contingent while the holders of only a *taraf* (division of *pargana*) or a few villages in a *pargana,* paid *salami*, i.e., nominal quit rent for allegience.[69]

Practice varied from province to province. It is clear from the contemporary documents that in the *Subahs* of Ajmer (Rajasthan), Malwa, and Oudh, apart from the Chief zamindars, semi-official petty zamindars were appointed in the villages and the *parganas* with multifarious duties. The existence of such a category of zamindars can be traced throughout the Mughal age and in most of the Provinces. *The Rajasthan Archives*, Jaipur[70], brings out the following salient features of this class in the 17th Century.

Nature of Appointment and Office

(i) A zamindar would be appointed for one or few villages, at times for one or a few *parganas. zamindari* could be granted both in the *khalsa* and the *jagir* lands.

(ii) A person could apply for the grant of *zamindari* through a petition of *tajwiznamah* (proposal) of *zamindari* or the State could directly grant it to any person at its discretion.

(iii) Such a *zamindari* was granted for life depending on good behaviour and discharge of proper duties. Usually, heredity of succession was conceded subject to confirmation of the Monarch at every vacancy. At times, the Monarch set aside the hereditary claims and bestowed the *sanad* of *zamindari* on another person considered more deserving and numerous such examples of transfer of *zamindaries* can be found in the Jaipur Archives for the 17th century.

(iv) Such a zamindar was regarded as an official and the *zamindari* was not alienable or saleable by the grantee.

(v) At times, joint *zamindaries* were granted to two persons.

Obligations

On his appointment, a zamindar had to execute a bond (*Muchalka*) for the proper discharge of the following duties:

(i) Warning the inobedient *riaya* and to suppress the refractory persons responsible for the breach of law.

(ii) To keep a watch against the thieves and dacoits, to keep the highways and other routes in his jurisdiction safe for the passage of the travellers, officials and caravans.

(iii) Apart from the above duties concerned with law and order, he had important revenue duties. He had to help the *amin* and other *pargana* officials at the time of assessment of the *riaya* in his *zamindari*.

(iv) To help the State officials in the *khalsa* lands or the agents of the *jagirdar* in collaboration with the village officials, as the case might be, in the collection of the land revenue. At times, he had the direct responsibility for collecting the land revenue and passing it on to the State treasury or the *jagirdar*.

(v) To help the State officials in the discharge of their respective duties.

(vi) A zamindar could not move out of the jurisdiction of his *zamindari*.

Remuneration

(i) Grant of *zamindari* was always accompanied by conferment of *mansab* in *zat* and *sawar*. Any increase in the *mansab* would entail increase in the jurisdiction of the *zamindari*.

(ii) In lieu of his services, a zamindar was granted *jagir* in accordance with the regulations of the *mansabdari* system. As a matter of practice, the *jagir* was assigned within the territory of the *zamindari* and could not be transferred to any other person. There are also instances of grant of *nankar*, i.e., rent free land, to the zamindars.

(iii) A zamindar would, at times, be appointed a *thanedar* or *faujdar* depending on the territory under his jurisdiction. That would entail higher *mansab* and larger *jagir* in accordance with the schedule.

(iv) Apart from the responsibility of the realisation of the land revenue and depositing it in the State treasury or with the *jagirdar*, the zamindar had to pay fixed *peshkash* (tribute) in instalments to the State.

(v) A zamindar could also act as *mustajir* on the land of a *jagirdar* and, in that capacity, would pay regular installments to the *jagirdar* after keeping to himself the difference (*takhfif*) between the amount realised and that given to the assignee under the terms of the *ijara* contract.

The assignment of *zamindari* of this category did not create any title in the land except for the duties explained above. The rights of ownership of the various classes of *riaya* in the territorial jurisdiction of the zamindar were not affected. The zamindar under his terms of appointment was required to safeguard the established land rights and interests of the *riaya*.

There was another class of the zamindars who were never awarded any *mansab* but formed a regular part of the rural agrarian life and the Mughal land revenue administration. A zamindar was essentially responsible for the agrarian improvement of his *zamindari* and for assisting the *pargana* officials in the assessment and the collection of the land revenue. His *zamindari* jurisdiction could vary from numerous villages in a *pargana* to a single village though, at times, it could cover an entire *pargana*. Such zamindars invariably held the offices of *muqaddams* and the *chaudharies* of the villages in a *pargana*[71]. The *zamindari* was hereditary though confirmed by a royal *sanad*. A zamindar was not the proprietor of the lands of the *riaya* (peasant proprietors) and their tenants. In lieu of his services, he was entitled to *nankar* (remuneration in lieu of service)[72] and customary charges (entitled *Rasum-i-Zamindari* or *Haquq-i-Zamindari*) in the shape of a small portion of the State share in the revenues of the villages in his jurisdiction.[73] By the close of the 17th century, such *zamindari* rights (*Rasum-i-Zamindari*) and obligations acquired proprietary and alienable character[74] though for want of contemporary evidence, it cannot be stated with certainty whether such saleable *zamindari* rights existed under Akbar. Of course, apart from the above stated customary charges, a zamindar was always himself a land-owner and possessed proprietary and saleable rights on the personal lands developed by him.[75] His personal lands comprised both self-cultivated tracts (*Khud-Kashta*) and those passed on to the tenants on terms of a *patta*. Like any other *raiyat* in his *zamindari* jurisdiction, he had to pay land revenue to the State[76] for all his personal lands excepting those held in *nankar*. Of the lands passed on to the tenants, he charged *malikana* share over and above the State revenue. The incidence of the *malikana* rights varied according to the customary local practice.[77]

Apart from the above stated categories, another class of *zamindari* was created by the Mughal state. The state policy of the extension of agricultural land created a new class of colonisers. For the purposes of reclamation of land for agricultural purposes, a person could be sold a portion of a jungle and waste culturable land (*banjar*) at a very moderate price and initial assessment rates, developing into normal state demand after the development of the lands.[78] Only such persons with either surplus labour or greater material resources would cover larger areas for reclamation. The original measurement documents of fallow land under reclamation show that, comparatively speaking, the families of the *muqaddams* and the *chaudharies* in the villages, much more than the ordinary peasants, occupied the larger portion of the *banjar* land for reclamation.[79] Such a right of reclamation of large tracts of land also entailed with it *zamindari* and *biswadari* rights in land.[80] These dignitaries of rural life could also purchase undeveloped fertile culturable land from the State.[81] Private transactions amongst the zamindars themselves were quite tenable and common.[82] In case the state required privately owned agrarian land for the construction of a monument or other purposes, it had to purchase it from the zamindars and the private owners.[83] The zamindar as coloniser would further sublet the land thus acquired to the tenants who, in their turn, acquired hereditary possession of the land. Ordinarily, such a zamindar claimed a *malikana* (ownership share) in the produce of the land in possession with his tenants. The incidence of such *malikana* share depended on the regional customary practice.[84] The 18th century sources reveal that taking advantage of the disturbed political condition, the zamindars in the provinces of Bengal and Bihar increased the *malikana* share to 10 percent of the produce which seems to have prevailed in some of the other regions in North India. But for want of contemporary evidence, the exact portion of *malikana* share cannot be stated with precision for the 17th century. The zamindar had also the rights of transfer, mortgage and sale of the *zamindari* rights in the land. Many such sale deeds are available in the Rajasthan Archives, Jaipur, as also the Allahabad and Bihar State archives.[85] Invariably, such transactions did not affect the position of the tenants who continued with their hereditary rights on the land for cultivation established in accordance with practice.[86]

Thus it can be stated, in conclusion, that in the Mughal age, the state never claimed the absolute and exclusive ownership of the agrarian land and definitely recognised the existence of private property in it. The ownership of the land was vested in the hereditary *riaya* which had the rights of transfer, mortgage and sale. Such rights were also vested with the zamindars in respect of their personally developed lands and villages and were also vested in a new class of colonisers named zamindars. The class of tenants working on the land of the *riaya* or zamindars, had also hereditary possession of the land with unalterable terms of *patta*. The landless labourer required either for cleaning the jungle or during the harvest days was entitled to a share in the produce in accordance with the established practice in the village. No serfdom or villeinage[87] binding the peasant to the land is known to have existed during the Mughal age. The best quality agricultural land, especially the gardens or land in suburban area or a large composite block agricultural land[88] or urban land had saleable value[89] though agricultural land, in general, had not acquired the character of saleable commodity in the way it did in the late 18th and 19th centuries.

Abbreviations

1.	A.N.	=	*Akbar Nama.*
2.	Ain	=	*Ain-i-Akbari.*
	J. tr.	=	Jarrett's translation
3.	A.D.	=	Allahabad Documents.
4.	Aghnides	=	Aghnides, *Muhammadan Theories of Finance*, New York, 1916.
5.	A.Q.R.	=	*Asiatic Quarterly Review.*
6.	B.G.	=	*Baharistan-i-Ghaibi.*
7.	Berlin	=	State Library Berlin (East).
8.	Br. M	=	British Museum.
9.	B.N. Paris	=	Bibliotheque Nationale, Paris (France).
10.	B.Ind. Pers. text	=	Bibliotheqa Indica, Persian text.
11.	F.K.	=	*Farhang-i-Kardani*
12.	Col. Galloway, *'Observations on the Law and Constitution of India'*	=	*'Observations on the Law and Constitution of India – Observations on the law and Constitution of India – of the nature of the Ceded Tenures and the System of Revenue and finance as established by the Moohummdun Law and Mughal Government with an enquiry into the Revenue and Judicial Administration and Regulations of Police in Bengal.'* London, 1825.
13.	Hydbd.	=	Hyderabad-Deccan (India).
14.	I.T.E.C.R.	=	*Indian Taxation Enquiry Committee Report*, 1924-25.
15.	Kh.S.	=	*Khulasatu-s Siyaq*
16.	M.H.	=	Aurangzeb's *Farman* to Mohammad Hashim
17.	*Mirat*	=	*Mirat-i-Ahamadi.*
18.	M.I.	=	*Makhzan-ul-Ihetsab*
19.	M.U. Aligh.	=	Muslim University, Aligarh.
20.	N.A.I.	=	National Archives of India.
21.	R.A.J.	=	Rajasthan Archives, Jaipur.
22.	R.D.	=	Aurangzeb's *Farman* to Rasik Dass Karori.
23.	S.D.S.R.	=	*Selected Documents of the Reign of Shahjahan*, Published by *Daftar-i-Diwani*, Hyderabad-Deccan, 1950.

References

1. *The Fifth Report from the Select Committee of the House of Commons on the Affairs of the East India Company,* July, 1812, 2 vols. edited by W.K. Firminger, 1917 edition. Introduction Vol. I, pp. iii-li; *Firminger's Historical Introduction to the Bengal Portion of the Fifth Report on East India Affairs,* p. cci; James Grant's *Historical and Comparative Analysis of the Finance of Bengal,* dated 27th April 1786, Vol. II, p. 170; *Original Minutes of the Governor-General in Council,* 1776, with a plan for the settlement of the revenues of Bengal, vide Introduction, Chapters XXV-XXVI, Vol. I, pp. CCXVIII-CCCXVIII, Sir John Shore, Minute, dated 18th June 1789, "Respecting the Permanent Settlement of the Lands in the Bengal Provinces", Vol. II, Appendix No. 1, pp. 1-37, 61, 80, 83 and 106. Also cited in F. D. Ascolis, '*Early Land Revenue History of Bengal*' (Clarendon Press, Oxford, 1917), pp. 42-70. Other Minutes, *vide* Firminger, Vol. II pp. 478-510, 515-18, 734-36, 737-57; Minutes of Lord Cornwallis, *Ibid,* vol. II, pp. 510-15, 518-27, 527-50. Also, *Bengal Permanent Settlement Regulation I* of 1793. Also, Bihar Secretariat, Patna, "Letter from Mr. Becher to the Hon'ble President", dated 24-5-1769; "Letter from R. Adir, Collector, District Bhagalpur to Sir John Shore, President and Members of the Board of Revenue," Nos. 35, dated 16-7-1787; 42, dated 18-8-1987; 50, dated 7-9-1987; 51, dated 9-9-1787; 55, dated 1987; B.H. Baden-Powell, "Is the State the owner of all Land in India ?" *Asiatic Quarterly Review,* New Series-Vol. VIII, Nos. 15 and 16, July-Oct. 1894, pp. 1-20; James Mill, *History of British India,* Vol. V, Chaps. V & VI.
2. Some of the important Mss' of the State Library, Berlin (East) are '*Nuskha Hai Bar Kafiat-in Subah Behar ; Nuskha Majmauhat; Sawalat-i-Malik-i-Zamin Kiast as Mister John Shore; Dar Bab-i-Nuskha Sarusa Hukm, Tawarikh-i-Badshahan-i Hind az ibtda-i Shah Timur baghayat Shah Alam; Majmuha-i Mutfarika, Akhbar ul Sadiq dar Kafiat Bengala Darj Ast.*
3. See, for details, Eric Stokes; *The English Utilitarian and India* (Oxford University Press, 1959), pp. 81-139; *Records of the Delhi Residency and Agency* (1807-57), (Punjab Government Press Lahore, 1911), pp. 7-336; J.M. Douie, *Punjab Land Administration Manual,* Lahore (1930), pp. 8-18, 24-44 ; C.A. Elliot, *Chronicles of O'onao - A district in Oudh,* pp. 146-156; Also J. H. Joung, *Report on the Revenue Administration of the Lower Provinces,* for 1856-57; *The Revenue Hand Book; Official Papers, Manuscript*' vide *The Calcutta Review,* Vol. XXXII, Jan-June, 1859, pp. 308-34; R.C. Dutt, *The Economic History of India,* (Published by the Publication Division, 1960), Vol. I, pp. 97-139; 262-83; Vol. II, pp. 519-27, pp. 382-499, 558-726 and Vol. III.
4. *The Indian Taxation Enquiry Committee Report,* 1924-25, (1926) Vol. II, Appendix IV, 'A Compendium of opinion on the nature of the Indian Land Revenue', pp. 27-74 records the opinions of Sir Philip Frances; Mr. James Grant, Sir John Shore; Madras Regulations XXXI of 1802 ; Lieut. Col. M. Wilks; Despatch from the Court of Directors to the

Government of Madras - 1813, Board of Revenue, Madras - 1818; the Hon'ble Mountstuart Elphinstone; Mr. James Mill; Professor H.H. Wilson; Sir Thomas Munro, 1824; Colonel Galloway; Privy Council decision in Freeman vs. Fairlie; Colonel J. Munro; Mr. Willium Erskine; Despatch from the Madras Government to the Court of Directors, 1855; Letters from the Court of Directors to the Madras Government to the Court of Directors, 1855; Letter from the Court of Directors to the Madras Government, 1866; Mr. J.S. Mill; Rt. Hon'ble J. Wilson; Rt. Hon'ble Henry Fawcett; Privy Council Appeal in Gunga Gobind Mundal vs. The Collector of Twenty-four Pergunnahs and others; Sir George Campbell; Privy Council Appeal in Collector of Trichnopoly vs. Lekkamani and others; Sir Louis Mallet; Sir Henry Montogomery; Sir Erskine Perry; Sir Henry Maine; Sir Bartle Fyere; Lord Salisbury; Bombay High Court Judgement in Vyakunta Bapuji vs. Government of Bombay; Sir John Strachey; Mr. A.C. Burnell ; Indian Famine Commission (1880 A. D.); Mr. Sullivan; Professor Bastable; Col. Baden Powell; Madras High Court Judgement in Secretary of State for India vs. Penumecha Venkatapathiraju Garu and another; and Mr. Lionel Curtis, *Dyarchy* (1920).

5. D.D. Kosambi, *An Introduction to the Study of Indian History* (1956), pp. 351-70. Tara Chand, *Society and State in the Mughal Period,* Patel Memorial Lectures, Dec. 1960 (The Publication Division, Ministry of Information and Broadcasting, Government of India), pp. 33-36, 46-50.
6. "Eulogy of Father Jermone Xavier, S.J., a missionary in Mogor", tr. from Spanish by Rev. H. Hosten, S.J., *Journal and Proceedings of the Asiatic Society of Bengal,* New Series, Vol. XXIII, 121; Francois Bernier's *Travels in the Moghul Empire,* 1656-1668, Oxford University Press, 1934, pp. 211-12, 220-226.
7. *Ain-i-Akbari,* British Museum, Add. 7652, fol. 145a. *Jarrett* II, T. 54, also Ms. or. Oct. 113, Berlin, Fols. 1b-4a. The same view is upheld by B.H. Baden-Powell both for Ancient India and Mughal India though he has not quoted any contemporary Mughal source. See details in his Paper, " Is the State the owner of all Land in India?" *A.Q.R.,* July-October, 1894, pp. 4-8.
8. *Ain,* in its chapter on *Rowai Rozi* (Means of Subsistence), fol. 145a, J. 54, states, " Simple, innocent-minded folk, consider that there are no unappropriated wastelands and were they obtainable, it would be difficult to furnish the implements of cultivation, and if these could be had, the means of providing food which would enable them to labour, are not manifest. They can discover no mine to excavate, and if one were pointed out to them which had no owner, it would be extremely onerous to obtain a living therefrom". Ms. or. Oct. 113, Berlin fols. 1b. 4a, an early 18th Cent. Ms. while explaining the procedure of colonisation on a virgin, wasteland during the Mughal age clearly recognises the *de facto* as well *de jure* claim of the pioneer cultivator on land. Also see Dr. I.H. Qureshi. "The Ownership of Agriculture Land during the Muslim Rule in India," *J. I. H,* 1942, pp. 230-32.

9. Aurangzeb's *Farman* to Mohammad Hasim, printed in *Mirat-i-Ahmadi* (*Mirat*), Vol. I, pp. 268-270. Though the *Farman* theorises on the land revenue practice in India in terms of Islamic polity, all the same it vests the rights of ownership of land with the ryots and gives the details of the relationship between the State and the ryots. Also, Dr. I. H. Qureshi, *Ibid*, pp. 232-36.

10. *Ain*, fol. 145b; Jarret, tr., pp. 55-56. In a famous case from Kanara, the Bombay High Court (Sir Michael Roberts Westropp, C.J. and West, J. in Vyakunta Bapuji vs. The Government of Bombay, reported in Bombay High Court Reports, C Vol. CII, 1875. Judgement delivered by Westropp, C.J.) in a comprehensive judgement examined the genesis of the land rights based in various authorities since Manu and concluded, "This review of the authorities leads us to the conclusions arrived at also (after careful discussion of the question) by Professor H.H. Wilson, that the proprietory right of the Sovereign derives no warrant from the ancient laws or institutions of the Hindus and is not recognised by modern Hindu lawyers as exclusive or incompatible with individual ownership." H.H. Wilson, in his edition of Mill's *History of India,* comments on the history as having :"defects occassioned by incomplete materials" and as presenting inaccuracies both of fact and opinion" and in his continuation of the History, Vol. I, p. 294, ed. 1858, has criticised the views of the following who all assert that the rights of ownership of land were not vested in the cultivations.- James Mill, *op. cit.*, pp. 256-276; Abbe Duboi's *Description of the People of India*, p. 496; Grant's *Report on the Northern Circars and Revenue of Bengal;* and the Minutes of Lord Cornwallis, *Fifth Report;* Col. Munro's theory (Revenue Sel. 1. 94) that the private property has never existed in India except on the Malabar Coast; Board of Revenue's concurrence with Munro, *Ibid.* 486; Fortescue's opinion with respect to Western Provinces, Lord's Committee, 1830 Evid., Question 511; Col. Barnewell in Commons Committee, 1832, Evid. 1755; Prof. Wilson further comments, "Proprietary right is vested in the individual who first clears and cultivates the land, it is therefore referred to as colonisation; The King may occupy unclaimed or uncultivated lands, as well a subject: ... if there are appropriated by a subject, the king claims only the share of the produce assigned to him by law". Exactly the same view is held by Col. Galloway (*Observation on the Law and Constitution of India- of the nature of the Ceded tenures and the system of Revenue and Finance as established by the Moohummudun Law and Moughal Government with an enquiry into the Revenue and Judicial administrations and Regulation of Police in Bengal.* (London,1825), p. 191), with regard to Mughal India. He asserts that the School of Abu Hanifa was chiefly followed in Hindustan and that in conquered countries, the people paying the legal impost preserved their proprietary rights. William Erskine (*A History of India under Babar and Humayun,* Vol. I, p. 528, ed. 1854), upholds the same view and comments, " The rights of landed property were considerably different from those that prevail in the West. There were two separate and legal rights in the land, that of the *ryot* or

cultivator, who held it by hereditary succession; and that of the Government, which could justly claim a fixed share of the produce collected from villagers or smaller zamindars, or separate *ryots*." Also, see similar viewpoint of Privy Council Appeal in Gunga Gobind Mundul and others vs. the collector of the Twenty-four Pergunnaahs and others, reported in Moore's *Indian Appeal Cases*, Vol. VI, 1866-67, pp. 359-362.

11. *Ibid.*, fol. 148a; Ms. Hamilton I Berlin, fol. 124a; J. tr. p. 63.
12. *Mirat* I, pp. 268-270.
13. Allahabad Document (A.D.) no. 1180, dated 21-1-1643. Moreland thinks (vide *India at the Death of Akbar*, (London, 1920), pp. 96-97) that with the continuation of the traditional pattern of land tenures in Mughal India wherein two parties existed, the ruler and the subjects, the latter was required to pay a share of the produce of land to the former in return for the protection received. As the conceptual process of the disentanglement of private property from political allegience took place only in the 19th century, the question of ownership of land during the Mughal age did not arise. But this view in the light of the available archival evidence cannot be sustained.
14. *Ain*, fols. 142a, 143a-143b, Ms. Berlin, fols. 120a, 121a.
15. *Akbarnama* (A.N.) Br. M. OR 26, 207, Fols. 161b, 194a-194b; Ms. or quart 1822, Berlin, fols. 258b-260a, 310b-312a in its 27th and 30th years reforms by Todar Mal and Fatehuallah Shirazi respectively uses the terms *Riaya, Riayt*, and *Kashawarz*. Aurangzeb's *Farman* to Rasik Dass Karori (R.D.) serving as *Dasturulaml*. ms. or. Oct 113. J, Berlin, invariably mentions *Riaya, Riayt, Muzariah, Kashawarz* in their respective contexts.
16. See f.n. 76.
17. *Ain.*, Br. M. fol. 143b; Ms. Berlin, fol. 121a.
18. Rajasthan Archives, Jaipur (R.A.J.). Category no. 4, dated 4th *safar*, 8th R.Y. (Aurangzeb) 1668 A.D. records the sale of 7 *bighas* of land in village Pilmiptala, *pargana* Shahjahanabad for Rs. 70 and is duly signed by the parties, attested by witnesses in the court of the *qazi*; also case no. 7 regd. no. 1718, dated A.H. 1071/1661 A.D. records the deed of sale for a garden of 15 *bighas* in Village Khanpura, *pargana* Shahjahanabad, for Rs. 1000/-. The document bears the details of the transaction, signatures of the seller, attestation of *chaudharis* and *qanungo* and stamp of the *qazi*.
19. *Ain*, Br. M. fol. 142a; Ms. Berlin, fol. 120a, Jarrett's translation, p. 46 of the last sentence, "And if the husbandman cultivate less and urge a plausible excuse, *'let him not accept it'*" is wrong and contradictory in the context.
20. Elphinston's "Reports in the Territories conquered from the Peshwa, 25th October, 1819," *Bombay Judicial Selections, East India House Records*, Vol. IV, pp. 159, 160. A similar view was held by Lord William Bentick

who observed in his minutes, dated 26th September, 1832, " I have little hestitation in declaring my conviction that there is very generally all over India a description of *riayats* having a proprietary title in the lands cultivated by him. These *riayats* are termed *mirasidars, mirasi maurusi, Khudkasht, Kadim,* and have other designations. Those resident *riayats,* again, who may acquire a sort of possessory title by prescription, are called *Chapparbands, Jama' Jadid,* and other appellations." For Bentick's detailed views , see Paragraphs 35, 41, 42, 44 in *Selections from the Revenue Records of the North-Western Provinces Government,* 1821-23, p. 385.

21. R. A. J. 'Yaddasht Haqiqat Qalba Hai of Villages of Tappah Akbarpur, Pargana Riwari (Subah Delhi), dated A.H. 1067-1073/1656-1663 A.F., fol. 10b; also Ms. or, quart 258, Berlin, fol. 304b.
22. *Ain,* Br. M. fol. 142; Ms. Berlin, fol. 120a; J.tr. p. 46.
23. Ms. or. quart. 258, Berlin, fol. 304b.
24. M. H. *Mirat,* I, p. 270.
25. *Ibid.*
26. *Ibid.*
27. *Ibid.*
28. *Ibid.,* p. 269. In case, the owner of land, despite the assistance offered to him by the State, failed to cultivate or deserted it, the latter had the right to make provisional arrangements for getting the land cultivated by a *Mustajir* or a tenant of the owner. Also, see M.s or. quart. 258, Berlin, fol. 304b.
29. *Ibid;* The tenant was known as *muzariah* and the act of subletting the land by the owner was known as *muzariat* or giving the land on *Zira'at.* (*Ibid,* p. 269). Under the agreement *(patta),* the tenant after reserving a fixed proportion of the produce to himself, would hand over the balance to the owner of the land. Such a tenancy was also named as *mukhbrah* and the share of the owner was known as *malikana.* (Aghnides, p. 385).
30. That a tenant had hereditary possession of land is confirmed by an original document in R.A.J., a *parwana,* Reg. I, dated A.H. 1035 (20th March 1626 A.D.). The tenant , of his own, could surrender his rights of land after the expiry of the *patta* and could change his holding if he liked.
31. R.A.J. A *Razi Namah* (an agreement deed) case no. 2, dated 2nd *Rajab,* A.H. 1049 9th *Jeth,* 1696 *samat*/30th May 1639 A.D., duly stamped and executed in the court of the *qazi,* settles the dispute between Musamat Fateh Khatun and Nathu for the rent of a garden situated in Mauza Khanpura, *pargana* Haveli Delhi (*sarkar* and *subah* Delhi). It states that the garden under dispute was originally rented out by the claimant on the terms of half the share in the produce.
32. *Ain,* Br. M. fols. 145a; 142a; *Tarikh-i-Baburi* of Zainuddin Khawf Ms. Rampur, p. 155; *Babur Namah,* (tr. Beveridge) Vol. III, p. 487; Geleyseen

de Jongh (1629 A. D.), *J.I.H.* 1925, tr. Moreland, pp. 78-79; Ms. or. Oct. 113, Berlin fols. 1b-4a.

33. Moreland estimated (*India at Death of Akbar* ed. 1920, pp. 9-22) that in 1600 A.D., the population of India stood at one hundred million, less than 1/4th of what it is today. Dr. Tara Chand *(Society and State in the Mughal Period,* pp. 23, 48), estimates that in the 17th century, it was around 100 to 140 million. Prof. Percival Spear *(India : A Modern History,* Michigan, University of Michigan Press, 1961, p. 153) suggests that the population in India increased in the 17th century from 100 to 150 million.

34. Col. Galloway *(Law and Constitution of India,* p. 48, also vide *I.T.E.C.R.,* Vol. II, pp. 44-45) comments, " Where so much encouragement was required to take lands and cultivate them, we can hardly expect to see much on the law of ejectments. But there we see nothing at all, and although the Moohummudan law, which declares the property of lands to vest in the cultivators, allows the sovereign to eject a cultivator who does not cultivate, and give his lands to another, yet there is not a single word on that head in the whole of the instructions of Akbar to his revenue, or judicial, or fiscal officers."

35. *Tarikh-i-Baburi,* Ms. Rampur, p. 155.

36. R.A.J., *a parwana,* Reg I, dated A.H. 1035, directs the *mursaddis* of *pargana* Haveli, Delhi, to realise the rent of the garden of Musamat Fateh Khatun from Bhagwan Dass and to hand over the same to her. Another document, a *Razi Namah,* case no. 2, dated A.H. 1049, executed in the Qazi's court, deals with the settlement between the landlord and a tenant. See details vide f.n. 31. Also f.n. 30.

37. A.N.Br.M. fol. 331b; Berlin, fol. 259a; Br. M, fols. 142a 142b; Berlin fols. 120a-120b; *Khulasatu-s Siyaq* N.A.I. pp. 32; Br. M. OR. 2026, fol. 34b; *Makhzanul Ihtesab* Ms. Berlin, fols. 4b-5b; R.D.H. Ms. Or. Quart 259, Berlin, fol. 56a-56b; M.H. *Mirat* I. p. 270.

38. *Mirat,* I, p. 269.

39. *Ibid.*

40. Todar Mal's revenue regulations, 4th clause, A.N. Br. M. Add. 27, 247, fol. 332a; *Ain,* Br. M. fol. 143a, Berlin, fol. 121a; R.D. Ms. Or. Oct. 113, Berlin, fol. 1b-8a; M.H. *Mirat,* I, pp. 268-71. Also, Colonel Galloway *(Observations on the Law and Constitution of India,* pp. 126-141) after exhaustive scrutiny of the theory and practice of the Muslim land law in Mughal India, comments (p. 48; also, *I.T.E.C.R.* 1924-25, II. p. 45), "The soil was the property of the cultivator as much as it could be attached; and so can those of the first peer, holding by the firmest tenure of the English law. The right of the Indian husbandman is the right of possession and of transfer; and the rate of his land tax was fixed; often indeed the amount. In what respects, then, is his right of property inferior to that of the English land holder?"

41. *Ain, Ibid.*

42. *Tuzuk-i-Jahangiri,* Ms. Rampur, p. 10, tr. Rodgers p. 9.

43. *Mirat,* I., p. 187. 8th Clause of the regulations issues by Jahangir on his accession to throne. This differs from the version available in the Ms. of Jahangir's's *Memoirs.* But in the context, it can be accepted as quite reliable.

44. See. f.n. 21 & 79.

45. Ms. No Suppl. 482, B.N. Paris, fols. 157b-159ab; 161a, 165a.

46. Ms. Or. Oct. 113, Berlin, fols. 1b-8a.

47. *Ibid.*

48. M.I. fol. 4b-5b; *Balaristan-i-Ghaibi* no. Suppl. Pers. 252, B.N. Paris, fol. 61b; *Murraqat-i-Hassan,* No. 217 Rampur, p. 238; R.A.J. a *Dastak,* Misc. Persian Letters Reg. 623, dated A. H. 1117 (1705 A.D.); Also R.A.J. uncatalogued Pargana documents. *Farhang-i-Kardani* M.U. Aligh fol. 29a; Kh. S. no. 74, Sulam Collection M.U. Aligh. fol. 10a; R.A.J., the original *'Tumar Jamma'* (uncatalogued) documents comprising the assessment and realisation of land revenues and customs from Pargana Tonk in the *jagir* of Raja Bishan Singh for the Rabi crop of the year 1098 *Fasli* (1693 A.D.); Also *'Tumar Wasalat'* i.e., documents of realisation reg. no. 1371, dated 28th regnal year of Aurangzeb, *Fasli* year, 1090 (1683 A.D.); also, documents Misc. Persian Letters, Reg. no. 1165, dated A. H. 1104/1692-93 A.D.

49. *Ibid.*

50. A. N. Br. N. Add. 27, 247, fol. 332; *Maktubat-i-Khan Jahan,* fols. 63a-64a; *Mahzar-i-Shahjahani* by Yusuf Ibn Abu Qasim, *Namkin,* written in 1004 A.H./1634-35A.D. Published in Karachi, 1961, pp. 18, 32, *Riazul Vidad,* B.M.O.R. 1725, fols. 3b-4a, 11a, 24b; *Selected Documents of Shah Jahan's reign* (S.D.S.R.), Central Records Office Hyderabad (India) pp. 21, 23, 18; M.I. Berlin, fols. 6b-7a; R.A.J. case no. 93, dated 1091 A.H./1680 A.D. *Akhbarat,* Waqai *pargana* Othal Sarkar Ujjain (*subah* Malwa), Reg. No. 679, 15th *Jamada,* I, 49th R. Y. 117 and 775, dated 26th *Jamada* I and 19th *Jamada,* I, 49th R.U. 1117 A.H./1705 A.D. At times, the *Jagirdar's* revenues could be collected through the state agency and passed on to the *jagirdar* vide B.G. II., tr. Borah, p. 673.

51. The principles underlying the *jagir* assignment and its administration can be analysed from various chronicles, *dasturulamls,* S.D.S.R. and R.A.J. Of the scores of available references, only a few can be cited. *A.N.,* fol. 331b; 332b; Akbar's *farman,* dated 990 A.H./1582 *Makatib-i-Allami,* N.A.I. pp. 95, 104, 105, 107-109; B.G. B.N. Paris, fols. 101a-102b, 145b; tr. Borah, Vol. I., pp. 11-13, 29, 229, 310, Vol. II, pp. 518, 627-28, 633, 647, 663, 671, 673, 676, 705, 741, 747, 776; S.D.S.R. pp. 17, 21, 23, 33, 35, 64-65, 67-71, 74-78, 123-28, 147, 158, 176-177; *Mahzar-i-Shah Jahani,* pp. 18, 22, 32, 89-193; *Waqai Sarkar Ranthanbore,* Ms. Asafia Library Hydbd., Copy M.U. Aligh, pp. 4-5, 19, 27, 74, 85, 238-39, 240. *Siyaq Nama* Ms. 858 C.R.O. Hydbd., fols. 16b-18b. R.A.J. category no. 4, regd. no. 164, dated 17th *Ramzan* 1106 A. H./1690 A.D.; *Ibid,* reg. no. 1389, dated 1105 A. H./1693; regd. no. 149, dated 1693 A.D.; Vakil Reports, reg. no.

390/279, dated 29th *Zul-qada,* 35th R.Y./14th August, 1691 A.D.; reg. no. 369/239, dated 28th *Shaban,* 34th R.Y., 1101 A.H./17th May, 1690 A.D. reg. no. 947/627, dated 21st Safar, 38th R.Y. 1105 A.H./1694 A.D.; reg. no. 25/46, dated 20th *Muharram,* 25th R.Y. 1093 A.H./1691 A.D.; reg. no. 1096/800, dated 17th Safar, 48th R.Y. 1116 A.H./10th June 1704; reg. no. 1287/978, dated 16th Rajab, 30th R.Y. 1181 A.H./13th Oct. 1706; Misc. Pers. Letters, reg. no. 1157, dated 1100 *Fasli* year/1688 A.D.; reg. no. 732, dated 26th *Jamada* I 49th R.Y. 1117 A.H./15th Sept. 1705; reg. no. 708, dated 21st *Jamada* I 1117 A.H./10th Sept 1705; category no. 2, case no. 93, dated 1111 A.H./1699-1700 A.D.; *Akhbarat,* 30th *Jamada* II 49th R.U. 1113 A.H./ 24th Nov. 1701, reg. no. 688, dated 24th *Jamada* I, 49th R.Y. (Aurangzeb); also, f. n. 50.

52. For details, see *Ain.* Br. M. 7652, fols. 100b-101b; Blochmann I, pp. 273, 278-85; Badauni *Muntakhbbut-i-Tawarikh,* tr. Lowe, pp. 207-8, 282; *Tabaqat-i Akbari,* B. Ind. Pers. text II, p. 336; Akbar's *Farmans,* dated 27th Rabi 11 A.H. 986 (3rd July 1578 vide A.D. no. 24, dated *Ramzan* A.H. 972/April 1565 A.D. vide Archives, Dargah Hazarat Khwaja Moinuddin Chisti, Ajmer; Shah Jahan's *Farmans,* dated 15th *Ramzan,* A.H. 108/8th May 1629 vide Br. M. OR 11697, dated, 10th R.Y./1636-57 A.D. vide Archives, Dargah Ajmer, I; original *Farman,* dated 15th *Ramzan* 12th R.Y. A.H. 1048/20 Jan. 1639 A.D. vide no. B. 584. Records Office, Bihar, Patna; A.D. no. I, 3, 144, 154, 156, 157, 159, 160, 162, 180, 199, 789, 1177(1-2); also, F.K., Ms. 85/315 Abdus Salam Collection, M.U. Aligh, fols. 39a-40a.
53. Professor Sheikh Abour Rashid, " Siyurghal Lands under the Mughals:, *Sir. Jadunath Sarkar Commemoration Volume,* published by Punjab University (India), 1958, pp. 313-22; also, 'Madad-i Maash Grants under the Mughals', *Journal of Pakistan History Congress,* Session Rajshahi, 1961.
54. *Ibid.*
55. A.D. II no. 284 and nos. 53, 54, 56 respectively.
56. Archives, Dargah Ajmer.
57. R.A.J., vide F. ns. 30, 31 and 36; also a copy of a letter duly attested by Diwan Todar Mal, dated 19th *Jamada* II 7th R.Y. (Aurangzeb) and stamped by Qazi Abdul Fateh, dated 8th R.Y. (*Ibid*) vide Family Archives of Saiyyad Ali Khadim (custodian) of Dargah Ajmer.
58. A.D. nos. 1 and 218.
59. For the above description of *Ijara System* and details, see R.A.J. Misc, Official correspondence between the officials of Amber Chief and the Mughal officials in Aurangzeb's reign, reg. no. 84 O.H.R., dated 23rd *Safar* 39th R.Y. (Aurangzeb), reg. no. 50, 36th R.Y. A.H. 1103/1691-92 A.D. reg. no. 150, dated 22nd *Muharram* 1101. A.H./1689 A.D.; reg. no. 66, dated A.H. 1100/1694 A.D. also, Misc. Pers. Letters, case no. 135, dated 10th *Zul-hijja* 37th R.Y./1683 A.D.; reg. no. 506, dated 28th *Safar* 49th R.Y. 1117 A.H./1705; reg. no. 709, dated 21st *Jamada* I, 1117 A.D. 49th R.Y./1705 A.D.; reg. no. 1616, dated 2nd *Rabi* I A.H. 1117/

1705; reg. no. 800, dated 15th *Rajab* 49th R.Y. 1117 A. H./1705; reg. no. 1701, dated 8th *Jamada* I, 49th R.Y. 1117 A.H./1705, dated *Safar* 50th R.Y. 1706 A.D.; reg. no. 897 10th *Safar* 51 R.Y. Vakil reg. no. 830/493, dated 37th R.Y. 1693 A.D.; also, Category no. 2, reg. no. 1159, dateless; Also, A.D., nos. 885, dated 1672 A.D., 884; dated 1674 A.D.; 1231, dated 1699 A.D.

60. It is not proposed to discuss the details of the nature and working of the zamindar system in different regions of Mughal India but only underline broadly its relationship with land administration.

61. *Ain,* tr. J. II, pp. 237-40, 248-57.

62. B.G., tr. II, p. 517.

63. *Ibid,* I, p. 431.

64. *The Mughal Chronicles,* Rajasthan Archives, *Baharistan-i Ghaibi* and *Mirat-i Ahmadi* are full of such instances giving details or relationship between the Princely zamindar and the Mughal State. It is not intended to enter into detailed discussion on this topic.

65. For example, for Sarkar Sorath in Subah Gujrat, See *Ain,* II, *Antiquities of Rajasthan,* I., pp. 32-105; also Risley, H, *The People of India,* ed. 1908; Enthoven, R.E., *The Tribes and Castes of Bombay,* Vol I. & II, Ibbeston, *Panjab Castes,* Lahore, ed. 1916; Ghurye, G.S., *Caste and Class in India,* ed. 1937.

66. See f.n. 70.

67. *Mirat,* I. pp. 21, 173-74; *Ibid,* Settlement, pp. 228-29. Akbar's *Farman, Mirat,* I., pp. 172-73.

68. *Ibid.,* Supple., pp. 228-39.

69. *Ibid.,* Supple., p. 229.

70. Of the numerous documents available for Aurangzeb's reign, only a few can be quoted which mention the above noted features. R.A.J. *Akhbarat,* dated 1st, 10th, 24th, 28th *Zul hijja* 20th *Rabi* II, 3rd *Safar,* 10thR,Y. (Aurangzeb), dated 9th Rabi I, 13th R.Y.; reg. no. 1699, 25th *Zul-qada,* no. 1470/3 9th *Rabi* II, no. 530, dated 3rd *Safar,* 1557/1, dated 8th *Rajab,* 23rd R.T.; no. 1847, dated 11th *Rabi* II, no. 1790, dated 13th *Safar,* no. 1757/1, dated 9th *Muharram,* 24th R.Y.; Misc Pers. Letters, no. 42, dated A.H. 1101/1690, no. 371, dated A.H. 1105/1693; no. 853, dated A.H. 1117/1705; Category no. 4, no. 1622, dated 5th Rabi I.A.H. 1113/1701; Letters of Maharaja, ref. no. 964, dated A.H. 1108; no. 1311, dated 27th *Shawal* 47th R.Y.; Vakil Reports, no. 171/208, dated 20th Safar A.H. 1101/1689; no. 436/337, dated A.H. 1103/16th June 1692; no. 343/197, dated 15th *Shawal* A.H. 1100/1689 Rs. no. 829/492, dated 10th *Zul-qada* A.H. 1104/8th July 1693; no. 1050/722, dated A.H. 1110/7th April, 1699, dated A.H. 1115/1703; also, A.D. nos. 897 (1-2), dated 1684, 1196, dated 28-11-1672, 1205, dated 30-11-1677, 1224, dated 24-4-1689, 1216, dated 22-11-1681.

71. Akbar's Farman to Gopal Das (Thakur of Darbhanga) in Sarkar Tirhut (Subah Bihar), Aurangzeb's *Farman* to Mahinath Thakur of Darbhanga, dated 14th Rabi II 9th R.Y. vide, *Indian Historical records Commission Proceedings,* XXXVI, pp. 89-98; Jahangir's *Farman* concerning the *zamindari* and Chaudhari of some *Tappas* in Sarkar Monghyr, *subah* Bihar, vide *I.H.R.C.* XVIII, pp. 188-189; *Mahzar-i Shah Jahani,* p. 191; A.D. no. 1192 (Aurangzeb's reign), Ms. or. Oct. 113, J. Berlin.
72. R.A.J. '*Yaddasht Haqiqat-i Arazi Muwazna Pargana Riwari*' (*subah* Delhi), uncatalogued. Sheet No. 7 (Aurangzeb's reign); Aurangzeb's *Farman* to Mahinath Thakur of Darbhanga (*Ibid*); M.I. Berlin, fol. 74 b; Ms. Oct. 113, I, Berlin.
73. Akbar's *Farman* to Gopal Das of Darbhanga (vide f.n. 71); A.D. Nos. 782 and 1214 (Aurangzeb's reign); For customary emoluments *(Dastur)* for the Chaudhari, see M.I., Berlin, fol. 74 b and *Intkhab-i Dasturulaml,* Br. M. Add 6599. fols. 42b, and 53a which put 2.5% as joint emoluments of the Chaudhari and the Qanungo whereas F.K., Ms. M.U. Aligh shows 2.7 % as their joint customary charges. For customary charges *(Inam)* of *Muqaddams,* Ms. Br. M. Add. 6599, fols. 45a, 49 b, 53 a-53 b; M.I. Ms. Berlin, fol. 74 a show varying *Inam* changes 1.687% to 2.25% depending upon the practice of the villages. Also, see R.A.J.' *Mal-e-Jihat' Pargana* Riwari (*subah* Delhi), dated A.H. 1073, sheet no. 12.
74. See f.n. 86.
75. Akbar's *Farman,* dated 38th Ilahi year/A.H. 1001/1593 A.D. states that Gosain Vithalrai of village Jaitpura (near Mathura *Subah* Agra), purchased land from the zamindars (vide K.M. Jhaveri, Farman No. IV, fol. 13.); also f. no. 86.
76. *Mahazar-i Shah Jahani* p. 182; A.D. nos. 897, 1206 and 1223 (Aurangzeb's reign); Ms. Br. M. Add. 24,039, fol. 36 a; Ms. or. Oct. 113 J, Berlin.
77. See f. n. 84.
78. Ms. or. Oct. 113 Berlin, fols. 1a-4a. Baden-Powell, on the basis of the testimony of Muslim lawyers, conceded that the rights of land as acquired by "first clearing" on the part of "Such overload families (Zamindars) especially when they settled on , or extended their possessions into, wasteland which they themselves first cultivated, might combine in themselves both kinds of rights as first clearers and as overlords." Though Baden-Powell rightly points out that this right was also based on inheritance, he has failed to recognise any other class of the Zamindars as distinct from the 'ruling families or of conquering clans'. For details of Baden-Powell's views, see " Is the State the owner of all land in India?" *A.Q. R.,* July-Oct; 1894, pp. 5-6.
79. R.A.J., '*Yaddasht Haqiqat Arazi Mazruat wa Uftada Muwazai Pargana Riwari*', dated 1073 A.H./1662-63 A.D. Measurement records of agrarian land under cultivation and fallow land under reclamation for Haveli Riwari (Subah Delhi), fols. 1a-16b.

80. See f. ns, 83 and 85.
81. *Mahzar-i-Shah Jahani*, pp. 191-92.
82. See f.n. 85.
83. R.A.J., O.H. Records, *Kapat-dawara* Documents, serial no. 7, no. 177C Ph; Shahjahan's *Farman,* dated 26th *Jamada* II 1043 A.H./28th December, 1633, for purchasing land from Maharaja Jai Singh for the construction of Raj Mahal in Agra.
84. A.D. no. 299 (Aurangzeb's reign).
85. Only a few of the numerous available documents can be cited. R.J.A. category 4, reg. no. 1721, case no. 9, dated 7th Zul-hijja A.H. 1074/ 1664; A.D. No. 1192, dated 14-2-1669; no. 1215, dated 1-2-1681; no. 1222, dated 10-4-1688, no. 1224, dated 26-4-1689, no. 1227, dated 15-12-1695; Bihar State Archives, Patna, no. B-335, dated 22nd Jamada J.A.H. 1066/18th March, 1656 for giving of gifts; also see A.D. no. 1226, dated 28-8-1692; no. 1192, dated 14-2-1669.
86. Ms or. Oct. 113 Berlin, fols. 1a-4a.
87. Moreland (*India at the Death of Akbar*, pp. 90-91, 111-15) on the basis of the 19th century agricultural reports, contends that the rural population included a number of landless labourers and that village serfdom is an institution of old standing since pre-Akbar days and it continued as such throughout the Mughal age and later. Moreland, however, has failed to advance any contemporary evidence. In view of the positive evidence (vide f. ns. 21 & 79) for the absence of such a serville class in the 16th and 17th century Mughal India, his theory cannot be accepted. It seems that with the growing population and the consequent pressure on land, the serville class traceable in the 19th century came into existence much later. In the 9th century, Tod (I., p. 145, II, pp. 593-94) found in Rajasthan a class of cultivators named "*Bussie*, a term which embraces bondage amongst its synonyms, though it is the highest species of slavery... still strange to say, the condition includes none of the accessories of slavery; there is no task duty of any kind, nor is the individual accountable for his labour to anyone, he pays the usual taxes, and the only tie upon him appears to be that of a compulsory residence in his *Vas* (habitation)". In fact, *Bussies* were neither slaves nor serfs in the European sense. That such cultivators were peasants was a heritage from the medieval practice of the terms of the *patta* meant to inhibit unnecessary migrations, diminishing of agricultural produce and loss of revenue to the State. Also, see, Jahangir's Ordinance, vide f.n. 43.
88. R.A.J., Category No. 4, regd. no. 1718, case no. 7, dated 1661 A.D.; *Ibid*, reg. no. I, dated 1668 A.D.; reg. no. 5, dated 1686 A.D.
89. *Ibid.*, M.K. Records, Serial No. 32, No. 254 Ph, dated 21st Shaban A.H. 1109/22nd February, 1698; *Ibid*, Serial no. 35, no. 200 Ph, dated 29th Shaban A.H. 1114/7th Jan., 1703.

Chapter 2

The Concept of Village Community in North India during the Mughal Age and the Pre-British Era

The economic historians and sociologists have accepted the view that ever since ancient period, the village community remained one of the dominant features of the Indian rural life till the establishment of the British rule in India in the eighteenth-nineteenth centuries. Ever since the beginning of the nineteenth century to the present day, numerous reflections have been made on the concept of the village community. Looked from the point of view of modern historiography, the fact about the existence of the Indian village communities throughout the ages was for the first time brought to light by the British revenue administrators of the East India Company. During the debates of the last three decades of the eighteenth century, the most controversial issue hinged on the concept of land proprietorship on the part of the *zamindars* versus the state and the position of the land rights of the varying classes of the *riaya,* which were mostly ignored. It was only in the course of the nineteenth century that the British revenue administrators, with their experience of the land rights of the classes in the ceded and conquered provinces, that the judiciousness of the permanent settlement of Bengal was challenged and a keen academic interest was taken to review the position of land rights of the *zamindars* versus *riaya* prevalent in India before the inception of the British rule. It was at this stage that the concept of the Indian village communities was discovered. Based on the memoranda of the British Indian administrators, the Committee of the House of Commons, which enquired into East India Affairs in 1810, drew a general picture of ancient Indian revenue practices.[1] Similar position was also taken up by the Report of the Select Committee of the House of Commons

---

Paper read at the *Social and Economic History Seminar,* Institute of Advanced Studies, Shimla, 1966.

on the Affairs of the East India Company in 1832.[2] These Reports emphasised the role of the village community as a 'Corporation' or 'township' and that the inhabitants of India continued to live under 'this simple form of municipal Government' or 'a small republic' throughout the ages till the nineteenth century.

The concept of village community had great advocates in Charles Metcalfe,[3] James Mill,[4] Elphinstone[5] and Sir Henry Maine.[6] Metcalfe's statement about the tenacious character of the institution of village communities having been "little republics.... almost independent of any foreign relations and its unchangeable character despite all political upheavals and dynastic changes "Hindo, Patan, Mogul, Mahtratta, Sikh, English" is well known. He equally believed in the interdependent community character of the various classes of inhabitants living in a village. James Mill confirmed his belief in the concept of the village community as a 'Corporation'. In general, Elphinstone also agreed with the theory of the concept of the village community having persisted from ancient times till the nineteenth century. He also believed that during the "Mohometan" period, ordinarily the municipal institutions of villages with some local jurisdiction acted as a deterrent against the imposition of the theory of the Mahometen law upon the Indian life. Whatever his views on the past history, it must be conceded that Elphnistone was quite adept in the technique of sifting nineteenth century regional sources for arriving at conclusions. He approached the concept of the village community based on the nature of land tenures prevalent in a particular region. He asserted that there were regions in which the village communities did not exist while in others they did. He also maintained that not all the classes of functionaries lived in every village and that within the village community, the waste land was owned by the state rather than by the community.

The concept of the Indian village community received a fresh reorientation at the hands of Sir Henry Maine, the great jurist and sociologist. Basing his study on 'Comparative Method' for analysing the European and Indian societies, he formulated a regular theory about the Indian village communities. He looked upon the Indian facts through the spectacles of European theories about the German mark relating to ancient agricultural customs and forms of property in land by Von Maurer and the Russian Mir involving the ancient customs or redivision of the lands. He found the Indian community as "an organised self-acting group of families exercising a common proprietorship over a definite tract of land." This is expressed in the "double aspect of a group of families united by the assumption of common kinship, and of a company of persons exercising joint ownership over land." According to Maine, customs in India have always been sacred and perpetual which accounts for the continuance of the archaic institution of the village community as a living institution till the nineteenth century. Maine recognised that a village may acknowledge itself to belong to a larger group or clan and that a dominant family personally claimed a superiority over the whole brotherhood and even over a number of separate villages especially when villagers formed part of a larger aggregate tribe or clan. But in all cases, the village community was so organised as to be complete in itself. In case of composite villages with different castes and religions, the unity and structure of such village groups was artificial as they lived in different parts of the inhabited area. A village with descendants of the original colonisers and others distributed into well ascertained groups formed a brotherhood which was a sort of hierarchy, the degrees of which were determined by the order in which the various sets of families were amalgamated with the community. Maine further maintained that there were two types of village communities. In such parts of India in which the village community was more perfect and in which there were the clearest signs of original proprietary equality between all the families composing the group, the village authority was lodged with the Village Council (or 'Council of Village Elders or *Panchayat*') consisting of five members. The Village Council was not universally found.

There were villages wherein the customs and the disputes of the members of the community were decided by a single headman whose office was sometimes admittedly hereditary but at times elective, the choice being confined in practice to the members of one family and to the eldest male of the kindred unless specially disqualified. The village community in India was the source of a land law which defined the relations of one another of the various sections of the group, and of group itself to the government, to other village communities, and to certain persons who claimed rights over it. It may be pointed out that starting from his earliest writing on the Indian village communities in AD 1861 to his last publication on the subject in AD 1883, Maine went on modifying the rigidity of his theory.[7] Realising the fact that for a country so vast as India and peopled by various races, no general statement could be true without qualifications, Maine tried to be cautious but his main thesis on the concept of the Indian village communities remained the same.

Despite the high position that Maine enjoyed as the Law Member of the Governor General's Council, his findings were challenged by his contemporary revenue administrators.[8] The latter argued that Maine's communal concept of the village community was opposed to regional evidence and the first principles of the society in North India. Maine had mostly confused the nineteenth century communal *zamindari* estates, *pattidars* and *bhaiachara* land tenures with the communal concept of the village communities. This version was later on confirmed by Baden-Powell.[9] Some of the European sociologists contended that the views of Von Maurer on the ancient Teotonic mark and other writers on Russian Mir for considering them communal in character were proved incorrect by more intensive research.[10] As such, the very basic assumptions of Maine for finding similarities between them and the Indian village communities collapsed.

Notwithstanding the fact that the official memoranda of the academically serious minded revenue administrators, who sifted facts based on contemporary regional evidence in many a portion of North India, denied the more popular concepts of the village communities viz, the 'Republican', 'Panchayat', 'communal' in respect of land tenure and the complete self-sufficiency. The 20th century Indian traditional and nationalist schools of thought have accepted these characteristics of the village communities. Some of the eminent Indian scholars on Ancient India have confirmed the existence of such features of the village communities in the past[11] thereby leaving the onus to medieval India either to trace these characteristics in the medieval period or to account for their disappearance from the Indian rural life. While some of the modern economists[12] and nationalist historians hold the view that they disappeared because of the land revenue and economic policy of the British rule in India,[13] others believe that they disappeared under the impact of the centralised administration of the Muslim rule during the medieval age.[14]

Still another school of thought[15] holds that the process of extinction of the village communities started under the Muslim rule and was completed under the stress of the economic policy of the British revenue officers who failed to trace the village communities in many portions of North India in the pre-British era. A few of them doubted about their existence in these regions even in the past.[16] For such regions, where the perfect type of village communities in respect of land tenures did exist, they outrightly rejected Maine's thesis for the pre-British eighteenth-nineteenth centuries North India while at the same time they surmised that such characteristics may have been prevalent in the past in India.

Arthur Philips of Cambridge University and Officiating Standing Council to the Government of India attempted a socio-economic approach for the decline and disappearance of the village communities in India.[17] He contended that for the concept of the village community in respect of land tenures, one had to rely only upon the scanty nineteenth century available information for the Hindu Code of Manu which was of little help in this respect. At the same time, he believed that the relics of the nineteenth century village communities do show that the full-fledged concept of the village community did exist in Ancient India. He explained the phenomenon of the decline of the village communities on a twofold basis. Firstly, with the establishment of Muslim rule, the Islamic concept of centralised administration clashed with the Hindu 'autonomous' character of the village communities resulting in the ultimate compromise between the theory and fact of the Muslim administration. Under the Muslim rule, the hereditary character of the village officials like headmen, *patwaries* and above them *chaudharies*, etc. was conceded with status-quo though the state always claimed its prerogative to remove the above mentioned local officials at its pleasure or when they failed to discharge their proper functions. Secondly, the growth of the institution of *zamindari* led to the decline or disappearance of the village communities in the medieval age.

Philips surmised that during the ancient Hindu rule when the Rajas claimed full revenues of their states, the Headmen and the village community were left with greater autonomy for the fiscal administration of the villages which may have formed local political units. But after the establishment of the rule, when the Rajas were depressed as more zamindars acting as tax-gatherers entitled to perquisites, they encroached upon the rights of the Headmen and the autonomy of the village communities.

It is difficult to agree with Philip's views. It is not true to say that the theoretical concept of Islamic administration guided the state policy of the Muslim sultanates towards the position of the local semi-officials and the autonomy of the village communities, if at all in existence. The assertion of the state prerogative for confirming or setting aside the local hereditary semi-officials on grounds of recalcitrance or inefficiency was deemed to be an act of state administration. It is equally a doubtful presumption that the Hindu Chiefs, who were suppressed by the Muslim Sultanate, had not exercised or asserted these powers. Moreover, the hypothesis that the suppression of the Hindu Chiefs unto zamindars as landed intermediaries strangled the authomous character of the village communtities is untenable. The Muslim Chroniclers use the term zamindar in a general sense and they mention the Hindu Chiefs, independent, semi-independent, suppressed as well as landed intermediaries as the zamindars. Even though the term zamindar or *zamindari* came into vogue during the Turkish rule, it can be well maintained that the institution of *zamindari,* with its indigenous socio-economic features under the *bhumias,* can be traced in some of the portions of North India in early medieval period under the Hindu rulers. However, the institution of *zamindari* in its manifold aspects found acceptance during the Sultanate period and the Mughal age. Far from saying that the centralised administration of the Sultanate and Mughal rulers or the suppression of the Hindu Chiefs into landed intermediaries as zamindars led to the decline of the village communities in India, it can be well maintained that the type of village communities based on land tenures found in the nineteenth century was more traceable in the regions which had remained in complete suppression as a part of the Sultanate or Mughal rule than in such regions where the Sultanate or Mughal patterns of regular agrarian administration did not penetrate and the Hindu Chiefs continued to pay *peshkash* (tribute or regularly assessed revenues) to the Central government . The Hindu Chiefs of Orissa remained semi-independent during the Sultanate period and paid *peshkash* to the Mughal state. In his specialised study on Orissa, W.W. Hunter points towards the absence of the *zamindari* and the village community system.[18] In Orissa, a village lacked the corporate character and was merely a collection of families. There were other regions in North India, especially in Sub-Himalayan ranges under the Hindu Chief (*Zamindaran-Umda),* which were much less amenable to the Sultanate or Mughal patterns of administration known to the directly administered territories. [19] Still there were no signs of village communities in the nineteenth century.

In a country like India, no generalisation is possible. In Bengal wherein there were both Hindu and Muslim zamindars having been subjected by the Sultanate and Mughal rulers, village communities in the eighteenth century were practically non-existent.[20] In fact, the concept of village communities was governed by regional and tribal practices undergoing changes from time to time rather than by 'Hindu' or 'Muslim' patterns of government. In ancient and early medieval ages (pre-Turkish period), the tribal conquests by the Eres, the Gujars and the Rajputs[21] led to reshuffling in the imposition of clannish landed interests imposed on the settled villages, new relationship between the dominant clans with intermediary landed rights and the other cultivating families of other castes, the settlement of villages by the religious assignees and concentration of the professional non-agricultural casts adept in certain crafts in particular villages and on regional basis and trade routes.

During the Sultanate period, where the Hindu Chiefs were completely suppressed, they assumed the role of landed intermediaries as dominant clans of the rural society. In the course of a few centuries, the cadet members of the erstwhile ruling families were reduced to the position of petty zamindars. Many dominant clans accepted Islam and continued to possess *zamindari* rights. On the Turkish conquest, some of the Rajput families fled from the plains and set up new Chieftainships in Sub-Himalayan ranges of Rajasthan, Gujrat, Malwa and Awadh. They not only suppressed the erstwhile clans but colonised new villages. Some such Rajput states were at times invaded by the Muslim Sultans only for getting tribute and recognition of suzerainty yet their local socio-economic order remained unchanged. But the process of subduing the weaker Rajput clans as vassal chiefs through mutual warfare, at times fighting against the Muslim states of Delhi, Malwa and Gujrat, the suppression of lower caste Hindu tribes as well as Muslim tribe chiefs and communities continued throughout the medieval age till the emergence of these territories in the Mughal Empire under Akbar.

During the Mughal age, the concept of the village community depended upon the nature of prevalent land tenure and the relationship between the agricultural and non-agricultural population residing in a village. The old established villages *(Kadim)* were known as *Asli* whereas, those newly developed or having branched off from old villages were noted as additionally *(Izafa)* or *Dakhili* which were attached to the bigger *Asli* villages.[22] The villages which had been deserted due to any political or economic reasons were regarded as desolate *(Wiran)*. The cultivable lands and the revenues of the *Dakhili* villages were attached to the old *(Asli)* villages. The cultivators of the newly developed villages may continue to live in their old established villages or may live in the newly colonised villages *(Dakhili)* which, after a lapse of a few years, would be reckoned as full-fledged villages.

Under the Mughal assessment regulations, the newly developed lands and villages were assesssed on a comparatively moderate rate of assessment until they reached full maturity for normal assessment rates.[23] Apart from it, the villages assigned as revenue free grants in *madad-i-mash, muafi* and *waqf* were regarded as *aimma* villages. Practically all over North India, the villages were owned by the *zamindari* and peasant proprietor *riaya* families whereas, the non-proprietor cultivating *riaya* settled in the villages comprised the *muzarian* (the term applied both to contracting and occupancy cultivators) and the *paikashtkars.* (Short-term contracting cultivators usually living in the neighbouring villages rather than in the village of their holding).[24] The *aimma* villages (religious and maintenance grants) may be developed from waste cultivable lands by the revenue-free grantees or may compromise already settled villages inhabited by the above mentioned *riaya* families who would pay revenues to the assignees.[25] The villages which paid revenues to the state were categorized as *Dehattaluqa* and *Dehat-i-raiytri.* The *taluqa* villages paid revenues through the local semi-official governmental machinery like the *muqaddams,* the *chaudharies* and other specially appointed revenue officials.[26] Except for this difference, both the types of villages were inhabited by similar agricultural and non-agricultural classes.

The village population consisted of both agricultural and non-agricultural families though a small village may comprise merely agricultural population. The village boundaries were usually marked by geographical landmarks which were regularly entered in the village revenue records.[27] The village lands were mainly divided into two portions viz. under habitation *(abadi)* and the agricultural area.[28] The latter could be further divided into two categories under regular tillage and waste cultivable land. Of course, there were villages where the entire agricultural land was under plough though most of the villages also had waste cultivable lands which were developed by the zamindars and *muqadams* by letting out to *muzarian* and *paikashtakkars.* Besides that, there were also barren lands, grassy jungle tracts attached to the villages. The agricultural lands were also classified into various categories dependent upon various factors viz irrigated (through wells, *nalas* or a regular canal), unirrigated *(barani-* dependent on rainfall), nature of soil governed by various regional geographical factors, manured or unmanured and the distance of the agricultural fields nearer or farther from the village habitation.[29] The land nearer the villages were well-irrigated and well manured while those at a distance were left dependent upon rainfall *(barani)*.[30] The agricultural fields were surrounded by waste cultivable land, grassy tracts and jungles.[31]

The composition of agricultural population and the nature of land tenure may vary from one group of villages to another or at times from one village to another. During the medieval age, in the course of historical development, people belonging to varying tribes, clans and castes imposed and superimposed their *zamindari* rights on the settled villages and various new villages were developed by various cultivating clans and castes in different regions of North India. For the Mughal period under review, the *Ain-i-Akbari* and the contemporary revenue literature throw light on the nature of the land rights of various tribes and clans settled in different portions of North India.

According to Mughal law, the rights of the revenue paying (*raiyati*) land-owning *zamindari riaya* families, the ordinary peasant proprietor *riaya,* the *muzarain* settled in the villages whether belonging to the same clan or different cultivating clans and castes were confirmed acquiring an element of stability. The process of alienation of the *zamindari* and *muqaddam* shares was known all over North India.[32] Even when it is conceded that in the ancient period, the self cultivating *(khud kashta)* land owning families did not possess the right of alientation without the consent of the village community, such a right was definitely exercised in the sixteenth-seventeenth centuries. It seems that the original condition of transfer requiring the consent of the village community, if at all, it had existed during the ancient period, had ceased to be considered binding.[33] This consent became a tacit consent or with the absence of objection when urged by economic factors, the instances of alientation were frequent. Though some clannish settlements clung to preemption regulations, others were freely alienated to outsiders and even to persons of different religion. This continued to augment the hetrogenous ethnic and inter-communal character of the agricultural population in the villages throughout the seventeenth century.[34]

Apart from this, the state policy of extension of agricultural land implemented by the zamindars and the *muqaddams* of the village led to the settlement of the *muzarian* and *paikahhtkar* of different clans and castes which helped the process of composite ethnic settlements in the villages. There were regions where the clannish settlements governed by the law of pre-emption kept up the purity of the ethnic character of the *zamindari* and the landownership rights but in other regions, they came to be sufficiently reshuffled resulting in the composite ethnic nature of the village settlements. The available original documents relating to the *subahs* of Lahore, Delhi, Agra, Malwa, Awadh, Bihar and Bengal show that a considerable reshuffling of the *zamindari malkiyat* rights and *muqaddmi* rights took place during the seventeenth-eighteenth centuries. The same may have been true of the other *subahs* of North India. By and large, the agricultural population in the villages with multiple clans and castes and even of inter-communal character developed strong economic bonds so as to override religious prejudices. The agricultural classes developed identical economic interests so as to render the village as an integrated unit for agricultural production and as a revenue unit for agrarian administration.

On the agrarian side,[35] there were zamindars who acted as tax-gatherers, owned self-developed villages and lands which may be under self-cultivation or rented out to the *muzarian*. Similarly, the primary *zamindari* of the villages as self-cultivated *riaya* owned self-developed ancestral villages. Such *zamindari* may own villagers and lands on individual or co-sharing basis. Many of these families enjoyed *chaudhari* and *muqaddami* status. Their villages may be entirely self-cultivated or a few villages passed on entirely to *muzarian*. In others, the lands may be partly under self-cultivation and partly with the *muzarian*. Apart from these two clear cut classes viz the *zamindari* families and the *muzarian*, the lands in some of the *zamindari* villages may as well be owned by the peasant-proprietor *riaya* who were the descendants of the *zamindari* or *muqaddami* families and as cadet families did not enjoy any such designations. The *paikashatkars* may as well be settled by the *zamindari* families. The village could be owned by a single zamindar family or by multiple *zamindari* families on co-sharing basis. The holding of each family was reckoned in accordance with the regional method. The agricultural lands were always owned on joint *zamindari* and *muqaddami* shares even in such villages which were once owned exclusively by one or a few families. This was a continuous process till the seventeenth and eighteenth centuries.[36] Thus the villages with multiple shares owned on co-sharing basis by the *zamindari* and *muqaddami* families (termed *riaya*), ordinary peasant-proprietor *riaya* along with their occupancy and non-occupancy cultivating families came to constitute what were termed as the village communities in the early nineteenth century.

As a matter of fact, the concept of the village community in North India prevalent during the Mughal period rested on the rights and obligations of the cultivating families which in their own turn were essentially co-related with the nature of the land rights. A zamindar had the right of regulating occupancy both with regard to its personal lands and the waste or the deserted lands in the village. He had to keep up and extend the cultivation of agricultural lands. He owned the responsibility of payment of revenues to the state. Similarly, the simple peasant proprietor *riaya* possessed the right of self-cultivation and regulation of occupancy. The *muqaddami* families, whether belonging to *zamindari* cadre constituted the principal peasant proprietor *riaya* of a village and owned the responsibility of payment of revenue through the zamindar or the *pargana.*[37] The *zamindari* families and the peasant-proprietor *riaya* had the right to dig wells on their lands and this, in fact, has been a main trait of ownership of land in the Indian agrarian society. They could rent out wells to the *muzarian* who could dig their own wells only with the permission of the owners of land *(zamindari* families or peasant proprietor *riaya* as the case may be). More often, the *zamindari* families and the peasant proprietor *riaya* being old settlers possessed more central, well-developed and irrigated lands than the *muzarian* and the *paikashtkars.*[38] In case of desertion of land, a peasant proprietor *riaya* could always come back to the village and claim back the land as a matter of right.[39] The *muzarian* as contracting or occupancy *riaya* had to keep up the cultivation in accordance with the terms of the *patta.* Once the cultivators introduced by the zamindar in a village developed their own means of irrigation, especially by constructing water channels from the rivulets and ponds or sinking a well, they acquired occupancy rights. As they owned their settlement to the land owning families *(zamindari, muqaddami* and peasant-proprietor *riaya),* and paid revenues and *malikana* to them, they were deemed to be cultivating the lands with the former's consent *(Razamandi* or *Basalah).* [40]

The concept of village community emphasised both rights and obligations which had customary sanction and in practice, with the passage of time, acquired the validity of law. The *muzarian* owed the obligation not only for the payment of the revenues and *malikana* but they had to keep up the cultivation and undertake further development of land to their full capacity. At the beginning of cultivation of every seasonal crop *(kharif* or *rabi),* they had to give an undertaking for covering particular tracts of land for cultivation for which they were held liable for the payment of revenue. Only valid reason could exonerate them for not honouring the commitment in which case an alternative arrangement would be made by the zamindar or the *muqaddam* by passing on the land for cultivation to the *paikashtakars.* As the *muzarian* holding periodical tenures for the reclamation of lands always enjoyed concessional assessment rate in the first few years of cultivation, the Mughal State imposed restrictions against frequent migration of the *riaya.*[41] *However,* in view of the imposition of the condition for covering particular tracts of land for cultivation and restriction against frequent migration, it cannot be maintained that the *muzarian* were bound to the soil like the serfs or villains. Even occupancy *muzarian* could get an acquittal deed[42] from the landlords and could shift their interest of cultivation to other areas or a member of their family could go in for another profession in the urban centres. The freedom and the right to a profession was never denied.[43] A member of the cultivating families, whether *zamindari,* peasant proprietor *riaya* or *muzarian,* was always free to join army or some other vocation in the city. But it was extremely rare that the entire family would shift to some other profession.

Whether the *muzarian,* who were essentially immigrants to the village, were fully regarded as an integral part of the village community or not depended upon the village or the *pargana* customary practice (named as *Ravaj-i-Am* or *Dasturalaml* or *Hasbulamul).* It was not merely the long duration of their settlement in the village but even a short stay with full conviction on the part of the zamindar for their permanent settlement which may entitle them to full rights and obligations of the occupancy cultivators. What essentially mattered was the permanent residence within the village of their settlement. The *muzarian* had to pay regular cesses *(abwab)* to the State. They had as well to contribute through physical labour or otherwise towards the maintenance of irrigation channels (drawn from lakes, ponds, canals, beds of the main rivers, their tributaries and the streams as the case may be), and the construction of weirs *(bandhs).*[44]The customary practice of a village may consider them as an integral part of the village community but their special link with the *muqaddam* or engaging *zamindari* family was clearly marked. Apart from the payment of the *malikana* dues, they always enjoyed less privileges than those possessed by the *zamindari* and the peasant- proprietor *riaya.* Even though they could not be ousted for default of payment of revenue or for not having kept up the full cultivation in accordance with the seasonal agreement, in case of desertion they could not reclaim their holdings. It is very doubtful if during the Mughal age they had played a part in the management of the affairs of the village community. However, the nineteenth century sources reveal that in some of the villages of Rajasthan, *muzarian* (as occupancy *riaya)* possessed transferable rights of mortgage and sale of their holdings though in the other villages, the *muzarian* possessed their own wells but without any rights of mortgage or sale.[45] In the Punjab, such rights were exercised only by the *muqaddami* and *zamindari* families but otherwise the title of the hereditary *muzarian* to their lands was as perpetual as of the former.[46] This is true for most of the states of North India. Notwithstanding this, the *muzarian,* even as occupancy cultivators, seldom enjoyed any status in the management of the village communities. Such a status was neither given to the *paikashtkars* during the Mughal age or thereafter even though their lands were always assessed on reduced rates in comparison to the other cultivating families of the village.[47]

There were no communal lands owned by the village communities. So far as the sixteenth-seventeenth century documents reveal, it is difficult to trace such a concept of village community. Under the Mughal revenue regulations, all the cultivating families, whether in the co-sharing zamindar or other villages, were reckoned as *assamian*[48] and the assessment on the holdings of the land-owning *zamindari* or *riaya* families as well as their *muzarrain* was done directly by the Government assessment officers[49] attached. In various parts of North India, the *muzarian* would pay *malikana* to the land owner and the land revenue directly to the state.[50] In the *riayat,* in villages too, the assessment of revenue was done by the State and the *riaya* paid through the *muqaddams* and the *chaudharies* who enjoyed perquisites *(inam* and *dastur* respectively) for the discharges of their duties.[51]The Mughal State had as much direct relationship with the *muzarian* as with other *riaya* and under the revenue regulations, all agricultural facilities for *taqavi* loans and remissions of land revenue were equally affordable to both. There is no documentary evidence to show that during the sixteenth-seventeenth centuries, distribution of assessment over the various holdings and mutual adjustment amongst the co-sharing land-owning families on account of arrears of revenue was ever left to the village communities. Of course, the possibility of such a practice cannot be ruled out for such villages which were farmed out to the *mustajirs* or in the *gair-amli* areas which paid fixed revenues, were not subjected to the Mughal land revenue regulations. Some writers have associated *malba* and *kharch-i-deh*[52] as underlining some basic communal traits of a village community during the Mughal age. In fact, *malba* was a cess comprising common village fund for meeting the expenses on the entertainment of revenue accountants and touring revenue officials. This was declared as an illegal cess by Akbar[53] and there is documentary evidence to show that it was levied even as an illegal cess during the Mughal age. Of course, the practice of levy of *malba* is traceable in some regions of North India in the nineteenth century.[54] The term *kharch-i-deh* denotes incidental expenditure items relating to the rations of the *muqaddam* (while on duty), entertainment *(mahmani)*, entertainment of the *chaudhari (mahmani-i-chaudhari)*, rations for the merchants and expenditure incurred on the *Qunungo (Qanungoi)*, medicants *(faqiri)*, and servants employed during the crop seasons and realisations of revenue.[55]The *Kharachi-i-deh* never implied a common pool of the village *riaya* in a village community. The items of expenditure of the *kharach-i-deh* were debited to the state revenues. The accounts of the *kharach-i-deh* were regularly entered by the *patwari* in his documents and consolidated accounts in this respect for all the villages were maintained at the *pargana* level.

It cannot be argued that under the Mughal revenue law, the village waste lands, the pasture lands and the adjoining jungles belonged to the village community. In fact, they were all owned by the State and were regularly entered in the village boundary records. The zamindar or the *muqaddam* had to bring the maximum waste cultivable land under plough. This may be done by the *muqaddami* families themselves or by other cultivating *riaya*. A cultivating family with more capacity for further tillage could cover as much waste cultivable land as it could, but the approval of the zamindar and the *muqaddam*, who in this respect acted as the State representatives, was essential. Such reclaimed lands were governed by concessional rates of assessment. The *zamindari* families rented out such lands to the *muzarian* (tenants) on easy terms of fixed periodical assessment based on sliding scale.[56] The cultivating *riaya* of all categories in the village had a right to the usage of pasture land, wood from the jungle and piscary from ponds. But they were not a free usage. For these, the agriculturists had to pay regular nominal cesses *(abwab)* to the *zamindari* and *muqaddami* families.[57] These impositions were reckoned as regular and legal state cesses and were credited to the revenues *(Sair-o-Jihat)* of the villages and *pargana*. During Aurangzeb's reign, the extra charges on the gardens situated in the residential villages *(abadi)*, fees charged on the grass and the foul brought from the jungle charged by the *muqaddams* were forbidden in order to benefit the agriculturists.[58] Notwithstanding the issue of the order, it can by no means be asserted that these cesses were scrupulously avoided by the *jagirdars* and the semi-Government local revenue machinery. An original *farman* of Bahadur Shah I, dated AD 1710, concerning the *muqaddami* rights of a village in *pargana* Ajmer, *subah* Ajmer, declares the charges on the grass and foul from the pasture lands and jungles as illegal and forbids the *muqaddams* from further collection.[59] It is difficult to believe that these cesses continued to be abolished during the chaotic period of the eighteenth century. During the nineteenth century, in major portions of North India, the waste and the jungle lands were mostly at the disposal of the zamindar and the rights of user enjoyed by village community were extremely limited.[60]

During the Mughal age, the incidence of State share and the assessment rates on agricultural lands were not essentially associated with the concept of the village community. The state demand was fixed in accordance with a detailed classification of the agricultural land and a varying schedule of assessment rates was applied. Within the general pattern of state administration, some variation on a *subah* or a regional *pargana* level may be noticed but no differential scale of assessment was permissible in respect of privileged and non-privileged *riaya* in a village community. The *zamindari* and the *muqaddami* families were entitled to perquisites in lieu of revenue collection. But like any other *riayat,* they had to pay land revenue on all their personal lands except those held in *viam* or *naukar.* They were assessed on reduced scale on state demand on the newly developed lands and villages. In some regions, of course, this concession would apply to some of their personal lands as well. In fact, many a petty zamindar of a village or a portion thereof were never entitled to any other perquisites (i.e. *nakur* and *rasum)* but claimed only a reduction in the State demand on their personal lands as a concession. This was especially true of the petty zamindars paying their revenues through another zamindar. The concessional rates of assessment for the reclamation and development of fallen lands were also enjoyed by the *muzarian.* Such regions of north India where the *taaluqdari* system with hierarchical pattern of lauded intermediaries developed from the mid-seventeenth to the nineteenth centuries, the petty *zamindari* and *muqaddami* families were reduced to the status of peasant proprietor *riaya* who claimed concessional rates of assessment on their lands.[61] During the nineteenth century, these families claimed such privileges in the village communities.[62]

The relationship between the agricultural and other professional classes in a village may as well be examined. The nineteenth century sources refer to a well-established traditional concept of the village community in which the agricultural and other professional classes led an intergerated community life. This general trait of village community seems to have persisted throughout the medieval period. During the Mughal age, the *zamindari, muqaddami* and other cultivating families were entitled to take service from the menial part-time workers (known as *chakran* or *kamin)* who helped the agriculturists, especially at the time of the reaping of the crops. They were paid a fractional share of the crops called *rasum*. For the Mughal period, some Rajasthan documents refer to revenue free grants of land to petty *bhumias* whose main duty was to keep a watch on the crops of villages and to safeguard the interest of the agriculturists.[63]The village *patwari* (accountant), who was a semi-official functionary, acted as the representative of the *riaya* and recorded the income and expenditure of the village. The *patwari* had to help both the *amin* (Assessment Officer) and the *ryots* for field to field measurement and assessment done on the latter. The most important of the documents kept in his personal custody was '*Kaghaz-i-kham-i-Patwari*' popularly known as '*Kaghaz-i-Kham*' in which he daily recorded the realisations from the cultivators.[64]This always served as a check against any duplicate or excessive realisation from the cultivators. For his remunerations, he got a fixed percentage (one per cent according to *Ain-i-Akbari)* of the village revenues. Apart from this, the Mughal documents do not mention about any village worker. The staff for survey and measurement of land, the *gumashtas* (agents) and messenger *(gurzbardars)* and other servants of the local officials were not considered as a part of the village community. The available nineteenth century picture that the village community comprised the headman, accountant, watchman, moneylender, priest, astrologer (one of them acting as a school master), smith, carpenter, barber, potter, leather worker, tailor, washerman, physician, musician, minstrel and dancing girl is definitely overdrawn. During the Mughal age, the population of every village was neither so large nor did it accommodate all these professional classes. In fact, nor was it so during the nineteenth century. A sociological and anthropological study would show that instead of a family from every professional class living in a village, professional classes rather concentrated in particular villages.[65]

The contemporary Mughal revenue documents only mention the revenue units viz. a village *(mauza* or *quarya)* and a *qasba* comprising numerous villages and serving as the head quarters of a *tappah* or *pargana*. No light, however, is thrown on the internal social structure of a village. A newly developed village may be inhabited by only agricultural population which, for its other needs, would depend upon a neighbouring parent or big village. In a fully developed and old settled village, apart from the cultivating occupational communities, they served as the menials of the village and at the same time, supplied agricultural labour receiving fixed dues in the shape of a share of the produce of the fields.[66] Amongst the village menials, the scavenger castes (known in many portions of North India as *chamar* or *chura)* usually formed the lowest social class. The scavenging castes would perform scavenging work, take manures to the fields, cut grass, carry wood and bundles, make ropes, work in grass and reed, act as watchman, make and mend shoes, throngs for the cart, and whips other leather works, take the hides of all dead cattle and the flesh of all cloven footed animals. Some of the castes would also take to weaving work. Not all the *chamar* castes would perform scavenging work or take to all types of above mentioned vocations. Based on regional practice, certain castes performed certain jobs. But, by and large, they occupied predominant position amongst the agricultural labourers. The watermen *(bhishtis),* the cooks (oven keepers), boatmen (fishermen) with different castes performed their own vocations and many of them associated themselves with agricultural labour. The other village menials were the carpenters and blacksmiths (at times the *lohars* doing both the jobs) making wood materials for the husbandmen as well as making and mending all iron implements of agriculture. The potters *(kumhars)* supplied earthern vessels for household use and earthernware pots used on the Persian wheel (wherever in use), possessed donkeys on which they brought goods and grain from outside and distributed within the village. The washermen *(dhobis)* and barbers *(nais)* were also considered village menials in so far as they got customary charges from the produce. Except for big villages, a village may not be inhabited by all the above mentioned menial castes and occupational groups. Some may predominate in a few villages thereby making a group of neighbouring villages interdependent for such services. The dyers, tailors, *sunars (banayas* or *sarafs*) who were not themselves scholars as a teaching community and religious class usually lived in their own revenue-free villages (bestowed on them in *maafi* or *madad-i-maash).*

It cannot be maintained that the rigidity of the caste system precluded the lower caste from the possession of occupancy lands. The medieval concept of the dominant tribes and castes accepted the erstwhile agricultural tribes as *muzarian* unless they proved extremely recalcitrant and evaded payment of revenues. When the low caste non-Aryan or Aryan agricultural tribes of a particular region accepted the dominant *zamindari* rights of the conquering clans or of the officially appointed zamindars by the Mughal State, their land tenure rights were not disturbed. In fact, there is much regional variation on this respect. In regions like Chota Nagpur, Sub-Himalayan ranges and Orissa, the low caste non-Aryan agricultural classes maintained their *zamindari* and occupancy rights whereas in other regions of North India where the Aryans had dominated, they were reduced to the status of either *muzarian* or village menials' occupations. Such a situation persisted till the nineteenth century. It seems that during the course of the eighteenth century, the eruption of new dominant clannish and *zamindari* rights in various parts of North India and the politically chaotic situation affording fewer chances for employment in the urban centres led to the emergence of a regular servile landless labour class in various regions.

Thus it may be seen that during the Mughal age, the concept of the village community was mainly confined to the landed interests of the proprietors *(malikan)* of the agricultural lands and the villages. In general, it also comprised the landed rights and obligations of the *muzarian* and the other non-cultivated professional classes connected with a village. A village was essentially a territorial concept for agriculture and habitation as well as a unit of revenue administration. In fact, the concept of the village community must be studied in relation to the regional tribal and clannish settlements as well as the *zamindari* rights and jurisdictions of the dominant clans. This aspect is of vital importance. A *zamindari* family may own numerous villages. Its agricultural interests and pecuniary interests in lieu of *zamindari* rights were by no means confined to a single village. This may as well be true of *muqaddami* families in possession of multiple villages. Ordinarily, a *tappah* composed of various villages and forming a fiscal unit of a *pargana* was associated with a clan exercising dominant *zamindari* rights in its jurisdiction.[67] At times, a clannish settlement may cover more than one *tappah* and still more at times a full *pargana*.[68] The concept of *tappah* organisation was known practically all over North India. The families and sects of a clan possessed self-cultivating agricultural lands and would divide *zamindari* rights amongst themselves. The *zamindari* perquisites were enjoyed by the families of the *muqaddams, chaudharis, desais,* (only in Gujrat), *tappadars, kalantaram, sardars* and *arbaban* (in

Sindh) who were also the dignitaries of rural life and village communities settled on clannish basis.[69] These officers were mostly governed by the practice of primogeniture and direct line of descent. The cadet families not enjoying any of these offices were mere *zamindari* and peasant proprietor *riaya.* Even though the Mughal State asserted its prerogative for the dismissal of these semi-officials on grounds of inefficiency or evasion of payment of revenues, it had always to keep on mind the family claims for the appointment of a successor. The office of a village *muqaddam* was widely known but instances for the absence of *muqaddami* offices in certain villages are equally known when the duty of the revenue collection of the village would be performed by another member of the *riaya* and the revenues would be passed on to the *zamindari* family or to the *chaudhari* of the area. The link between the dominant *riaya (muqaddami* or *zamindari)* of a village and the same dominant clan of other villages in a *tappah* was essentially marked. The law of preemption was clannish in character and would operate similarly in the villages of the same clan in a *tappah* or in a *pargana.*[70] The obligation of the maintenance of irrigation-channels drawn, the lakes, canals, streams and river beds were basically a territorial and clannish concept, being the joint responsibility of the zamindars and *riaya*[71] even though it ultimately depended on the village community. The practice of communal *vesh* traceable in many a village in North India during the second half of the nineteenth century[72] involved periodical redistribution of land amongst various branches of clan on inter-village basis or the redistribution and readjustment of land within a single village or periodical exchange of certain ancestoral lands within a single family.

The ethnological and economic study of these tribes suggests how joint family proprietary notions of the medieval age descended from the communal rights of the tribe. It is quite conceivable that in view of the varying qualities of the soil with different facilities for natural irrigation from the hill streams or through flooding of the rivers in a particular region under the territorial jurisdiction of a clan, the holdings of the family were subjected to periodical exchange and the concept of the communal ownership of the tribe or clan was the norm. But with gradual improvement in land in particular villages and holdings of the families, both through human labour and the development of the artificial means of irrigation, the concept of ownership on the part of the severalty gradually gained ground. It is not intended to suggest that medieval age for this region had been the scene of political vicissitudes and clannish domination in the eighteenth century which may have brought about this practice into existence.

Similarly, in the early nineteenth century, in Bundelkhand villages, there was the practice of re-partition and redistribution of holdings amongst various households of the village in case the revenue assessment on different households would become inequitable due to division and sub divisions within the family or any other factor that led to the decline in the household resources. This is equally a primitive clannish trait rarely adopted by the households of families rather than a uniformly prevalent concept of a village community during the age under review. In conclusion, it may be stated that during the Mughal age, in matters relating to agricultural life, revenue administration and social behaviour, a village community was never a complete socio-economic entity. It was essentially an integral part of wider territorial and clannish settlements.

It is difficult to trace the concept of the 'Panchayat' System or a 'Council of the Village Elders' forming an integral part of the village community during the Mughal age. Of course, the *muqaddam* as the headman of the village and constituting the principal *riaya* of the village formed a link between the State and the village community. He safeguarded his personal landed interests as well as those of other cultivating families in the village.[73] Similarly, on a large scale in the *zamindari* villages forming the *malkiyat* of the primary zamindars, whether owned by a single *zamindari* family or by various *zamindari* family or by various *zamindari* families, the agricultural interests of the zamindars and the other cultivating families were considered to be integral and corporate in nature.[74] The *mandals, kalantars,* the *chandharis sardars, arbaban,* etc were equally considered to be guardians of the agricultural interests of the other *riaya* families, especially those of the *muzarain (raiyat-i-raiza).* It is evident from the sixteenth-seventeenth century documents that without the central control over them, in matters of assessment and distribution of revenues, they were more liable to act in self-interest and to the detriment of the ordinary cultivating families.[75] As a safeguard against it, the Mughal state stressed the assessment work and the inspection of the holdings under actual tillage to be undertaken by the *amin, shiqdar* in collaboration with the local semi-government revenue staff. Of course, the zamindars and the *muqaddams, chaudharis* and *Qanungos,* along with the other *riaya* always took a united stand against the tyranny and exploitation on the part of the *jagirdars* or the *madad-i-maash* assignees. The zamindars, *muqaddams,* land-owning *riaya* and the *muzarain* were all governed by the customary regulations of the village or the *pargana.* In fact, due to dearth of agricultural labour and with large holdings in the possession of the cultivating families, there were practically no disputes over the jurisdiction of the holdings of the cultivating *riaya* in a village. Such disputes were quite common over the demarcation of the holdings of the *madad-i-maash* (revenue-free) assigness. All such cases were settled by regular government staff viz. the *amin, shiqdar* in consultation with the local revenue machinery. Usually the arbitration was done by the *chaudharis and kanungos* in the presence of the *riaya* of the villages.

Apart from this, the disputes over inter-*muqaddami* and inter-*zamindari* over the villages were always settled by the Mughal state through its provincial and local revenue machinery.[76]

At the lower level, in concept, the interests of the agricultural community in the *zamindari* villages were integral in character but the place a village community would enjoy in such an agrarian set up would depend on the nature of the assertion of the control the zamindars would have upon other agricultural classes and this might vary according to the regional practice and the clannish character of the *zamindari* families. In the *raiyati* villages, the *zamindari* and other *riaya* families were more liable to Mughal control in respect of revenue administration than they were in the *taaluqa* villages. Ordinarily, within the *zamindari* set up, the co-sharers in the *zamindari* rights like the *sardaran, kalantaram, raisan* and *arbaban* were in their knowledge of local topography, regional and clannish customary practices, and the decisions relating to agricultural interests would be taken amicably. But in the event of conflict with regard to their own dominant shares for the enjoyment of such position and perquisites they were always referred to the higher Mughal authorities.[77] Akbar's *Farman* instructing the *madad-i-maash* families to construct a *chaupal* in the assigned villages is on record.[78] Such a practice must have been followed by the *zamindari* families in big villages under their jusrisdiction. The *zamindari* and the *muqaddami* families as well as other *riaya* would often meet in the village *chaupal* and discuss matters relating to the interests of the agricultural community.[79] The *chaupal* would as well serve as the venue for the castes groups for discussion and enforcement of the caste regulations. It is in this sense that the village community may be said to have existed during the Mughal age.

It may, however, be conceded that in matters of social behaviour, caste regulations governed the lives of both agricultural and non-agricultural population of the villages. At the same time, in economic sphere relating to trade and commerce, many regions in North India developed local guilds or corporations in which local representatives from a big village or group of villages were associated. The Rajasthan inscriptional and archival sources refer to *Panchas, Panchkul, Mandapika, Ghosthi* (or *Gosti*), *Sangh* and *Shershti* (of commercial groups) which clearly show the existence of the craft and mercantile organisations.[80] In view of the extraordinary expansion of inland and foreign trade and commerce in the sixteenth-seventeenth centuries and also the fact that, by and large, the villages of North India were regularly integrated with the *qasba* and the city markets,[81] there is every possibility that such commercial organisations representing the villages may have been equally known to some other parts of North India. During the Mughal age, the emphasis on the cash assessment of the crops, the escalation of the growth of the cash crops, and the development of the local rural commercial centres *(mandis)* led to the growth of money economy in rural life. A chain of villages was linked with the local *mandis* which, in their own turn, were well connected with the *qasba* and the city markets.[82]The village communities were by no means self-sufficient and isolated units.

It seems that in major regions of North India, in matters of agrarian structure, the character of the *zamindari* villages and the village communities underwent change during the course of the eighteenth century. The disintegration of the Mughal Empire, resulting in lack of conformity to the Mughal revenue regulations on the part of the zamindars, *taaluqdars* and the semi-government local officials, the extension of the *ijara* system with all its malpractices under a weak government, the impact of the Maratha revenue administration demanding fixed *mamla* from the regional governments and the chief zamindars, the continual tussle for physical and economic advantages between the newly established regional governments and their local zamindars, the change from the seasonal *(kharif* and *rabi)* land revenue assessments based on the produce of crops to periodically fixed assessment demands levied upon the chief zamindars and the village communities, the suppression of the petty primary zamindars by the powerful zamindars or zamindar cum *taaluqdars,* the acquisition of the *zamindari* rights by the newly erupted dominant clan and the suppression of the erstwhile *zamindari* rights specially in the north western regions of India, the continued process of mutations of the *zamindari* shares and the division and subdivision of the *zamindari* villages, the realisation of revenues based mostly on coercion, the chaotic intermissions in the midst of settled regional governments were the chief characteristics of the eighteenth century agrarian life. All these factors affected the socio-economic structure of the village communities. With the breakdown of the Central machinery of the Mughal Empire, the regional governments and the chief landed intermediaries were mainly concerned with the realisations of revenue from the primary zamindars whereas, the latter's clannish with territorial structure over the village communities essentially tended to draw to their shells. In some portions, the scope of operation of the village communities was extremely limited in character and they were governed through the agents *(gumashtas)* and family members of the local *zamindari* practices in the villages came to rest in land tenures based on communal *zamindari* estates, *pattidari* and *bhaichara*.

For the nineteenth century, different views on the concept of the village community have already been explained. As a matter of fact, the concept of the village community in the pre-British era was mainly based upon two aspects viz. the nature of *pattidari* and *bhaichara* land tenures on the one hand, and the relationship between the agricultural families and the low caste menial functionaries on the other. During the nineteenth century,[83] there were non-co-parcenary *zamindari* tenures, owned by individual families. In contrast to it, the *zamindari* tenures of communal type were those wherein the co-parcenary *zamindari* families held and managed the land in common. Whatever land the owners themselves cultivated, it was occupied by them as tenants of the community. Their rights were regulated by their holdings and the distribution of the profits. If the amount due from the *malikana* rights from his lands held by his non-proprietary cultivations *(muzarain, pai kashtkars* and other lease holders) was not sufficient to meet his State revenue demand, the balance would be met by the co-parcenary *zamindari* families in accordance with their respective shares.

Apart from the communal *zamindari* estates, the lands were also owned on *pattidari* and *bhaichara* basis. The *pattidari* estates were held on ancestral shares whereas villages in which other kinds of customary shares prevailed were called *bhaichara* . Though both the patterns of *zamindari* villages were governed by the law of pre-emption and joint responsibility of revenue payment in a *pattidari* tenure, the share regulated the revenue payable, in a *bhaichara* tenure, the revenue payable regulated the share. Both the *pattidari* and *bhaichara* estates were of perfect and imperfect nature while the distribution between the ancestral and customary shares was more superficial than real. In a perfect or complete *pattidari* tenure, the lands were divided and held in severalty by the different proprietors(*zamindari* families) according to ancestral or other customary shares, each family managing its own lands and paying its fixed share of the revenue, while all were jointly responsible in the event of any shareholder being unable to fufil the obligations for revenue payment. In incomplete or imperfect *pattidari* tenures, part of his land was held in severalty and part in commonalty, and the interests of the landowners in both corresponded to well-known customary shares. In perfect *bhaichara* tenures, all the lands were held in severalty. The customary shares, if they ever existed, had disappeared and each man's holdings or rather the portion of total revenue he paid, had become the sole measures of his rights and liabilities. An imperfect *bhaichara* was different from a perfect *bhaichara* estate in exactly the same way as an inperfect *pattidari* from a perfect *pattidari* estate.

It is, however, significant that the above mentioned different forms of tenure were not permanent as a village or an estate could easily pass from one class to another keeping the joint responsibility intact. A *zamindari* estate owned by an individual became communal when the sole owner died leaving it to his sons. If the latter effected a partition of any part of the joint property, it resulted in imperfect *pattidari*. The unequal improvement of different holdings and the sales and mortgages of land to outsiders rendered the system of paying revenue according to customary shares unsuitable. Thus the consequent assessment on the extent of cultivated land of different classes in each family possession, and not on its ancestral or customary shares, would render a *pattidari* estate into a *bhaichara* one. Moreover, the tendency to break up the communal *zamindari* lands into *zamindari* possessions held in severalty for payment of land revenue on separate individual family rather than on joint basis was on ever increase. It was rare to find a village where the entire land was held on communal basis and an ideal type of village community would prevail. Ordinarily, a portion of the village lands was held on communal *zamindari* basis whereas other portions held in severalty. Even in communal *zamindari* holdings, the occupancy *riaya* (*muzarain*) paid land revenue and *malikana* according to their respective holdings and for every occupancy, *muzaria* owned individual responsibility for payment. Thus, during the 19th century in North-West India, the village communities were generally large co-parcenary societies or corporations, each constituting a number of propreitors who either held the land in common, dividing what escaped of the rents when all charges had been paid or divided all their lands and each family collected and defrayed the rents and charges in severalty; or hold some of the lands of the same property in common and others severally.

With regard to land tenures, such were the main features of the village community prevalent, to a large degree, in Awadh and Uttar Pradesh (comprising the erstwhile Mughal territories of the Subahs of Awadh, Allahabad, Agra and a part of Delhi), Delhi and Punjab (formed after 1849-1858 comprising the territories from the erstwhile Mughal *Subahs* of Delhi, Lahore, Multan). Even within these territories, there were marked disparities and there were various regions which were not regulated by such land tenures. Similarly, such features were confined to some portions in Gujarat and to an extremely limited degree in Bengal. Orissa remained practically uninfluenced by such a concept of village community. The concept of the communal *zamindari* villages, the *pattidari* and *bhaichara* tenures has already been explained. During the Mughal age, the idea of the co-sharing land-owning families (known by various designations in different parts of India) in the village communities and the co-sharing landed intermediary families with their clear cut earmarked shares (division being based on regional indigenous methods) was well known. The co-sharing, land owning families paid revenues according to their shares and the co-sharing landed intermediaries enjoyed perquisites in accordance with their respective shares. But it is very doubtful if the practice of assessment of *jama* on the entire village as lump sum amount (here not in the sense of fixed assessment but after regular survey of the village holdings) left to redistribution by the co-sharing *zamindari* and land owning families in accordance with their shares and at the same time owning joint responsibility for the revenue payment by the co-shares from the *malikana* (gathered from the non-proprietary cultivating families) and the proprietary cultivating families) and perquisites (deducted from the state revenues) and making up the balance (if need be) for the payment of state revenues or redistributing the profit from the excess amount saved from the common pool of *malikana* and perquisites after having paid the state revenues did ever exist under the Mughal land revenue regulations.

If we accept this fact, such a phenomenal growth can be explained for various regions only in the socio-economic and political factors which operated mostly during the course of the eighteenth century. It seems that on the breakdown of the Mughal Empire, in such regions where the Mughal system of land revenue administration with regard to assessment methods was sufficiently modified or where the incidence of *malikana* (taken from the non-land owning cultivators) and the rate of perquisites enjoyed in lieu of revenue collection were highly raised as to tempt the primary *zamindari* and landed intermediary families, such features of land tenures and village communities were more marked. On the contrary, in such regions where either the chief zamindars (Rajas etc.) asserted their independence or the powerful local zamindars established firm hold on their local *zamindari* jurisdictions or the newly originated dominant castes and clans established their *zamindari* rights or the tribal trait for the assertion of the superior social and economic position of the dominant *zamindari* families (named as *malikana ala* in North-West portions of the Punjab after the British Conquest), such features were less pronounced.[84]

It is not possible to put forward any rigid theory for varying factors governing different regions and, at times, one strong socio-political factor cut across the others resulting in diversification in the land tenure system within the same province or territory. Notwithstanding recalcitrance on the part of the chief or powerful local zamindars, the Bengal administration under the Mughal Nawabs was quite assertive during the first half of the eighteenth century for the collection of its revenues. Of course the incidence of *abwab* and the extortion on the part of the local landed intermediaries and the habit of concealment of the actual holding under tillage by the *riaya* sufficiently increased. But there is sufficient contemporary evidence to show that the nature of land rights of *riaya* and landed intermediaries (like *chaudharis, talluqdars* and zamindars) as well as the basic methods of assessment remained the same as they had been during the seventeenth century. With the laxity of administration from the governorship of Mir Jafar in the second half of the eighteenth century, the landed intermediaries were less amenable to strict control of the Mughal revenue regulations and exploited the *riaya* with overassessment and illegal cesses. Far from developing a village community based on joint responsibility of the payment of state revenues, the principal *riaya* (*mandals* and *paramaniks*) evaded the revenue regulations and shifted the burden of assessment on the holdings of the ordinary and lower classes of the *riaya*.

In Orissa, the Rajas asserted a strong control over their territories and while collecting revenues, either through *jagirdars* or state servants, dealt directly with the headmen and other *riaya* of the villages. In Malwa and Rajasthan, the chief zamindars (Rajas) and the powerful local zamindars fought against each other for the acquisition of territories and *zamindari* villages and imposed suzerainty upon the less powerful local zamindars. They assigned their kinsmen (zamindars and *bhumias* etc.) and collected revenues through the assignees and state servants from the village headmen. But the local practices of assessments, the rates of *malikana* and prequisites (*rasum wa dastur*) continued as before. It does not seem that the fixation of *mamla* by the Maratha government upon the revenues of the local chiefs affected the village land revenue practices.[85] By and large, the concept of land tenures governing the village community did not develop in Rajasthan. Some of the territories of Gujarat felt a strong impact of the Maratha administration. The Rajput princes in Saurashtra, Kutch and high-land Gujarat maintained their old setup by paying tribute to the Marathas. In the plains also, the *kolis* of the Mawasi (recalcitrant) villages rose as a dominant caste and paid lump sum amount (*ghasdana*) as revenue whenever forced to pay. These regions kept up the dominant *zamindari* rights without being effected by the *pattidari* land tenure. This marked the emergence of the dominance of the *pattidars* as a caste from the other members of their *kunbi* tribe.[86] In the *Senja* villages, the *desais* contracted for payment. These village communities were prevalent mostly in the *narwadari* village governed by the *patidars*.

In eighteenth century Awadh,[87] the introduction of the periodically fixed assessment by the Lucknow Government and the rise in the incidence of *malikana* and perquisites were conducive to the growth of the co-sharing community features. But the revenue regulations of Nawab Saadat Ali Khan (AD 1798-1814) tried to create as much contact between the Lucknow Government and the cultivating *riaya* as possible, which would have a sickening effect upon the communal *zamindari* and *pattidari* tenures. But after the death of Saadat Ali Khan, their enforcement remained a pious wish. In Uttar Pradesh[88] and Delhi territories,[89] several parallel social strata constituted the village community. The main features were the enjoyment of *malikana* and perquisites and joint responsibility of payment of revenues by the village *zamindari* families viz. *pattidars*, *thokaedars* and *behriwars*. In Punjab,[90] in the eastern and the central regions, the village communities were much organized but they were rather rare in the South West Punjab. In Multan, the concept of property and the revenue to be paid thereupon was governed by the ownership of wells and the lands attached to them. Every owner owed individual responsibility of payment. This was a legacy from the Sikh rule. North Western Punjab and Hazara districts were governed by dominant *zamindari* principles and no concept of village community entered their agrarian structure. The *jirga* and the *hamsaya* system worked on different principles. Notwithstanding the prevalence of the *Vesh* system on a limited scale, the *Pattan* tribes remained under the domination of the zamindars. In eastern Punjab, Kangra district and the hill territories never developed village communities.

It may also be observed that the nineteenth century British writers exaggerated the role of the *panchayat* or the village council. The village community stood for the landed interests of the *malikana* (land owners). The community of the land owners (co-sharing *zamindari* families) decided if they had to admit new cultivators in the village. The relations between the agricultural community and the non-agricultural professional and menial castes have already been explained. The interdependence of the village agricultural and non-agricultural caste groups also formed the main prop of the nineteenth century village community practically all over North India.

Nor were the villages in North India complete self-sufficient units. A village was essentially linked with the local markets and the *qasbas*. In various regions of North India, there was a high degree of monetization. The assessment in cash for various crops (*zabti and naqdi*) was widely prevalent and even assessment was done basically in *batai* or *kankut* that was commutable in cash. Of course, the determination of state share in kind was quite spread over. Many a village exported cash crops in increasing quantities. In the end, it may be suggested that the picture presented by most of the nineteenth century British writers about the concept of the village community in pre-British India, which has been traditionally accepted by historians, needs a radical modification.

References

1. *The Fifth Report from the Select Committee of the House of Commons on the Affairs of the East India Company,* July 1812, 2 vols., ed. By W.K. Firminger, 1917 ed.

2. *The Report of the Select Committee of the House of Commons on the affairs of the East India Company.* dt. 16th August 1832. Also, in *Report of the Select Committee of the House of Lords (1830) in the evidence of Col. Briggs,* 4137.

3. *Charles Metcalfe's Minutes* dt. 7th November 1830 vide Appendix No. 84 to the *Report of the Select Committee of the House of Commons, 1832.* (vide f.n.2), *Selections from the Government Records,* Vol. I, p. 446.

4. James Mill, *The History of British India,* Vol. I Chapter V, p. 247, Vol. IV, Chapter III, pp. 1-23.

5. Mountstuart Elphinstone, *The History of India,* 2 Vols. London, 1841, 9th edition, London, 1916 with Notes and Additions by C.B. Cowell, Chapted II, pp. 66-87, 472-77.

6. H.S. Maine, *Village Communities in East and West,* published in 1871. See London edition, 1895, pp. 103-239; also Maine, *Early History of Institutions,* ed. 1874, pp. 81-83, 221.

7. H.S. Maine, *Ancient Law,* 1861, pp. 261-64, Minutes by Sir H.S. Maine, 1862-69 with a note on Indian Codification, dt. 17th July, 1879, Calcutta, 1890; *Village Communities in the East and West, Early History of Institutions*' (vide f.n.6). his last work was a Paper published in the "Nineteenth Century", and reprinted in his book *Early Law and Custom,* 1883, pp. 240. In *Early History of Institutions,* Maine contested his own earlier "Theory of Village Community" based on Kinship. He also came to believe that property in land had grown up though its outlines were not clear and that the periodical redivisions of the domain had become a mere tradition while it was practiced among the ruder portions of the race.

8. For Punjab, See Prinsep's *Punjab Theories,* dt. 26th October 1866 vide *Minutes by H.S. Maine,* 1862-69 (vide f.n.7), No. 51, pp. 99-103; for Awadh, See comments by Mr. Charles W. Mc Minn who was entrusted with the preparation of the *Government Gazetteer of Oudh,* which was later on completed by W.C. Benett, 'Gazetteer of the Province of Oudh', III, pp. 583-84. Even earlier writers like R.M. Bird and James Thomason had differed from the versions of Charles Metcalfe and the memorandums embodied in the *Reports of the Select Committees (1812 and 1832) of the House of Commons.* See details for R.M. Bird vide 'Fourth Report from the Select Committee on Indian Affairs, 1852-53', Vol. XXVIII-Question no. 5576; James Thomason's 'Directions from Settlement Officers', 1844, para 99, 105-106; 'Despatches and Minutes of Hon'ble James Thomason, 2 Vols. Calcutta, 1856 and 1858, Despatch No. 8, paras 6-8'.

9. B.H. Baden-Powell, *The Land System of British India*, Oxford, 1892, Vol. I, pp. 104-78.
10. See details vide W.J.Ashley's *Introduction to 'the Origin and Property in Land'*, by De Conlanges (1890) tr. by Margaret Ashley, 2nd edition, London, 1927, pp. VII-XIVIII.
11. K.P. Jaiswal, *Hindu Polity*, 3rd edition, p. 15, Pramathanath Banerjee, *Public Administration in Ancient India*, p. 289; A.S. Altekar, *Village Communities in Western India*, p. 23; R.K. Mookerji, *Local Government in Ancient India*. Their views have been followed up by nationalist writers. See John Mathai, *Village Government in British India*, pp. 1-29; S.V. Samant, *Village Panchayats* pp. 1-12.
12. S.C. Gupta, *The Village Community and its Disintegration in U.P in the late 18th and early 19th Century*, vide Report, pp. 58-71, All India Seminar on Indian Economic History, Delhi, 1961; *Agrarian Relations and the Early British Rule in India*, pp. 1-42, 52-55, 169-204.
13. Jawaharlal Nehru, *Discovery of India*, 4th Edition. pp. 261, 320-21, *Report of the Congress Village Panchayat Committee*, A.I.C.C. New Delhi, 1954, pp. 10-11. Dr. B.R. Ambedkar quoted the well known Minute of Sir Charles Metcalfe (vide f.n.3) in the Indian Constituent Assembly on 4.11.1948.
14. B.P. Vaish, *Panchayat Raj in U.P.*, pp. 13-14; Also Arthur Phillips vide f.n. 17.
15. B.M. Bhatra, *Disintegration of Village Communities*, pp. 77-78 vide 'Report of the All Indian Seminar on Indian Economic History,' Delhi (f.n.12).
16. R.Richards, *India*, 2 Vols. London, 1828, Vol. I, p. 587; Vol. II, 285, 289-91.
17. Arthur Philips, *Land Tenures of Lower Bengal*, Calcutta, 1876, pp. 40-148.
18. W.W. Hunter, *Orissa*, Vol. II, p. 206.
19. See f.n. 90.
20. See f.nos. 17a 83.
21. Also see R.S. Sharma, 'Feudal Elements in the Pala and Prathihara Polity, 750-1000, *Asian History Congress'*, New Delhi, 1961;' Land Grants to Vassals and Official in North India (1000-1200)', *Journal of Economic and Social History of the Orient*, IV, pp. 88, 90-91, 94, 'Land Rights in Early Medieval India' *(c.* AD 500-1200).
22. *Raqbabandi* documents of the villages and *tappahs* of *Pargana* Bhagalpur (*subah* Bihar), S.C.R.O., Patna. See details vide my Paper on'*Raqbabandi* documents of Akbar's Reign', *I.H.R.C.*, Chandigarh Session, 1961. Also *Khulasatu-t-Siyaq* (AD 1703), (Abbreviation-Kh.s.). N.A.I., pp. 27-28, Ms. M.U. Aligarh, Sulaman Collection, no. 74, fols. 13b-14a.

23. *Ain-i-Akbari* (Abbreviation *Ain*) British Museum, (Abbreviation -Br.M.) Add 7652, fols 150a-151b; Ms. Hamilton Berlin, fols. 126b-127a; *Akbar Nama* (abbreviations-AnN.). Br.M.Add. 27, 247, fol. 331b; R.A.J. 'Yaddasht-i-Haqiqat; Arazi-i-Mazruat wa Uftada', of *Pargana* Riwari, *Subah* Delhi, 1037 AH. AD 1662-63, *Ibid., a Yaddasht* of Aurangzeb's reign.

24. See details vide my Paper on 'Nature of *Dehat-i-Taaluqa* (*zamindari* Villages) and the evolution of the *Taaluqdari* System during the Mughal Age', *The Indian Economic and Social History Review,* Delhi, Vol. II, No. 2, April, 1965, pp. 166-77; Vol. II, No. 3, July, 1965, pp. 259-88.

25. Also see my Paper, 'Nature of Land Rights in Mughal India, '*The Indian Economic and Social History Review,* Vol. I, No. I, July-September, 1963, pp. 8-9.

26. Rajasthan Archives Jaipur (Abbreviation-R.A.J.) '*Yaddasht-i-Dehat-i-Mazria* (i.e. the list of cultivated villages) of Pargana Dadakar (Sarkar Alwar Subah Agra), Aurangzeb's reign; *Siyaq Nama* (AD 1694-96), no. 858, C.R.O. Hyderabad, fols. 28b-29b. Also see my paper on 'Nature of *Dehat-i-Taaluqa*' vide f.n. 24.

27. R.A.J. Uncatalogued Muawazas' documents; Also see f. nos. 37, 47-49; *Makhzannl Ihetsab* (Abbreviation-M.I.) (Aurangzeb's reign), Berlin, fols 8b-25b. The boundary of every village was marked through a *Chaknama.* A number of *Chaknamas* are available in the Allahabad documents of the 17th-18th centuries as well as with the madadments of the *Khadims* (custodians) of *Dargah Sharid* , Ajmer. A full record of the measured, both culturable and unculturable areas was maintained in a document named *Taqsim.*

28. *Ibid.;* also f.n. 22.

29. See details vide my Paper on, ' Agrarian Classification of Land under Akbar', *I.H.C.,* Aligarh Session, 1960, pp. 198-209.

30. '*Nuskha Hai Bar Kafiat-i-Subah Bihar*', Ms. Berlin (18th Century).

31. *Ibid.;* also f.n. 27.

32. Allahabad Documents (abbreviation-A.D.) no. 1196, dt. 28-11-1672; no. 1200, dt. 7.2.1676; no. 1221, dt. 19.5.1688. R.A.J. Category 4, regd. No. 1721, case no. 9, dt. AD 1664; Also See 'Nature of Land Rights in Mughal India', (vide f.n. 25) pp. 14-15, f.n.86.

33. The Consent of the co-sharers was needed A.D. nos. 332, dated 15.10.1620; 435, dt. 11.10.1698; 51, dt. 6.3.1701.

34. For sale of the *zamindari* villages by the Hindu zamindars to the Muslims, See A.D. nos. 317, dt. 2.2.1586; 1194, dt. 28.11.1672 and 9.1.1996; 1227, dt. 15.12.1695; For the sale of *Muqaddami* rights, AD 1183dt. 14.3.1653, Also S.C.R.O. Patna, 13-335, dt. 27.2.1656; For the sale of *zamindari* village by Muslims to the Hindu zamindars, See A.D.

nos. 1180, dt. 21.1.1643; 1200, dt. 7.2.1676; 1226, dt. 28.8.1692 (Hiba Nama); for the sale of village by the Muslims to other Muslim families, See A.D. No. 1199, dt. 1676; 893, dated 1679; for sale by Hindus to Hindus of other Caste, R.A.J. regd. no. 1721, case no. 9, dt. AD 26.6.1664; R.A.J., M.K. Records, no. 99, 235 Ph. dt. 7.7.1719.

35. See details in my paper on 'Nature of *Dehat-i-Taaluqa*' vide f.n. 24.

36. *Ibid*.-

37. R.A.J., '*Yaddasht Jamawasil baqi mowazah Pargana*' dt. 1101 A.H./1690-91 A.D., category no. 636 (Aurangzeb's reign) relating to Pargana Dooti Sanchar; regs. no. 65, dt. A.H. 1105/1693 A.D. relating to Pargana Jullunder (Subah Lahore).

38. Copies of lease deeds dt. 19.6.1626 and 3.5.1731 vide Archives of Sayyid Sarfaraz Ali, Khadim Dargha Sharif, Ajmer, Also *Darr-al-Ulum* (1688-89), Bod. Oxford, fol. 909.

39. Ms. Suppl. 482, *Bibliotheque Nationale*, Paris. See details vide my paper on "The Position of Desai in the Pargana Administration of Subah Gujrat under the Mughals', *I.H.C.*, Delhi Session, 1961, pp. 152-55. f.nos. 20-21.

40. A.D. no.329 (Sarkar Lucknow, *subah* Awadh). Such practice continued in Rajasthan and Punjab till the 19th century. *Cavendish Enquiries* (AD 1829-Persian Vols. Record Office, Ajmer), fols. 228a-229b., James Douie, *Punjab Settlement Manual* (published in 1889), Lahore, 4th edition, 1930, pp. 52-111.

41. See f.n. 39.

42. See f.n. 38.

43. Read the passage of *Ain-i-Akbari* in its chapter on Rowai Rozi in this context. (AIN, Br.M. Add. 7652, fol. 1459), Jarrett, tr. II, p. 54.

44. *Mahza-i-Shah Jahani*, pp. 17-18, 191-92. *Letters of Balkrishan Brahaman* (Late Shah Jahan "and early Aurangzeb" reign), Ms. Br. M. Add. 16859, fols. 108a-109a.

45. *Cavendish Enquiries*, fol. 153a (Village Hothah, *pargana* Ramsar, District Ajmer). However, in *pargana* Masuda, the hereditary *muzarian* possessed their own well but no rights of mortgage and sale of agrarian lands *(Ibid.*, fol. 4a-4b).

46. See various Settlement Reports quoted by James M. Douie *(op. cit.)*, pp. 52-111.

47. R.A.J.'*Yaddash-i-Haqiqat Qalba hai Muwazai Pargana Riwari*', dt. AD 1656-57, fol. 10b, 22a-22b.

48. R.A.J. uncatalouged documents. '*Yaddashi-i-Haqiqat Qalba hai Muwazai Pargana Riwari*', dt. A.H. 1073/AD 1661-62, Also Kh. S. (N.A.I.), pp. 25-27.

49. Under Akbar and Jahagir, the assessment was done by the Karori and Bitkchi (*Ain*, Br. 14, Add. 7652, fols. 142-144b) or a specially deputed officer (vide *Baharistan-i-Ghaibi*, Bibliotheque Nationale, Paris, fols. 61b, 284b). From the reign of Shah Jahan, the assessment was done by the *amin* and his staff. See Kh. S. N.A.I., pp. 32-33. M.,I. Berlin, fols. 4b-5b, *Nigar Nama-i-Munshi*, Ms. Pers. e. I. Bod, Oxford, fols. 99b-102a, A.D. nos. 897 (1-2), dt. 1684; nos. 218, dt. 28.2.1687; no. 1223, dt. 19.11.1688.

50. R.A.J., *Jama Kharch* (Income and Expenditure) *Pargana* documents of *Paragana* Riwari dt. 1665-66. Documents of income of the villages (*Amadani-i-Fotah Muwazai*) of *pargana* Fatahbad, *Rabi* Crop, *Jamada* II, A.H. 1092/ June 1682, *Nigar Nama-i-Munshi*, Bod. Oxford, fols. 127a-128b, "Aurangzeb *Farman* to Rasik Das Karori vide Ms. Or Oct. 113J, Berlin, fols. 2a-4a.

51. See details of my paper vide f.n. 24.

52. Tappan Ray Chaudhuri, 'The Agrarian System of Mughal India', vide *Enquiry*, New Series, Vol. II, No.1 (Old series, No. 10), Spring 1965, pp. 98-101.

53. A.N. Br. M. Add 27, 247, Todar Mall "27th R.Y." reforms, fol. 332b, Fatah Ulllah " 30th R.Y." reforms vide Ms. Add 26, 207, fol. 194b., M.S., p.14.

54. James Douie, *Punjab Settlement Manual, (op. cit.)* pp. 48-51 has quoted various reports from the Ceded and Conquered Provinces and the Punjab.

55. Kh. S., N.A.I. pp. 61-63., Ms. M.U. Aligarh fols. 27a-28b.

56. *Nigar Nama-i-Munshi*, N.A.I. fols. 74b-75a., *Durr-al-Ulum*, Bod. Oxford, fol. 90a.

57. M.I., Berlin, fols. 5b-6b., Also my paper on "Nature of *Dehat-i-Taaluqa*" vide f.n. 24.

58. *Zawabit-i-Alamgiri*, Ms. 2336, C.R.O. Hyderabad, pp. 101-103., *Intkhab-i-Dasturnlaml-i-Alamgiri*, Br. M.Add 6598, fols. 189a-190a.

59. An Original *Farman* dt. AD 24th March 1710 concerning the *Muqaddami* rights and abolition of *Jizya, Begar* and other cesses in village Anna Sagar *Pargana* and *Subah* Ajmer, Preserved in the private Archives, Patel family, Ajmer.

60. Baden Powell, I, pp. 128-29., James M. Douie vide f.n. 46.

61. See my paper on 'Nature of *Dehat-i-Taaluqa*', vide f.n. 24.

62. *Cavendish Enquiries, pargana* Ramsar, fols. 153b-154a, *pargana* Binai, p. 3. Jonathan Duncan Revenue Selections, dt. AD 1794, Vol. I, p. 169.

63. R.A.J. Uncatalogued documents ("Aurangzeb" reign).]

64. *Ain*, Ms. Berlin, fols. 120b, 126b, A.N. Br. M. Add 27, 247, fol. 331b, M.I. Berlin, 4b-6b.

65. See f.no. 22.

66. For Punjab, see Denzil Ibbetson, *Punjab Castes*, Lahore, 1916, pp. 266-338. For Bengal, Arthur Philips (vide f.n. 17), pp. 1-40. For United Provinces, see early 19th century sources quoted by S.C. Gupta, *Agrarian Relations and Early British Rule*, pp. 1-25 and also vide f.n. 12.

67. See *Raqbabandi Documents of Akbar*, reign and the 18th century documents vide f.n. 22.

68. *Ibid.*

69. See details in my paper on 'Nature of *Dehat-i-Taaluqa*', vide f.n. 24, also Elliot, C.A.'Chronicles of Oonaol', pp. 29-85.

70. The *Cavendish Enquiries* in the district of Ajmer reveal that the village practice and the tribal custom also played a determining factor for the exercise of the rights of mortgage and sale. At times, within the same villages, a cultivating caste might exercise alienable rights while others might not. See fols. 4a-b, 7a-b, 149a, 153a-154a, 228a-b. Also see C.L. Tupper, *Punjab Customary Law*, Vol. I, Introduction, pp. 1-98.

71. See f.n. 44.

72. For details, see Mr. Thorbun's 'Vesh in Marwat', Bannu District, and Beekett's paper on 'Vesh in Sawat' vide *Punjab Gazetteer Supplement*, 27th March 1873 and 27th November 1873 respectively. Also Fryer's *Settlement Report on Dehra Ghazi Khan*, 1875, Paras 215-220, pp. 32-34; Majpr Wace's *Settlement Report on Hazara District*, 1874, Paras no. 60, 64, pp. 109, 111; Bellew's *Report on the Yusuf Zais*, 1864, pp. 194-200. also C.L. Tupper *(op. cit.)* Vol. II, District Peshwar, p. 15; District Multan, p. 25; District Rawal Pindi, pp. 27-28; District Sialkot, p. 32; District Gurgaon, a letter from Mr. Wilson, Assistant Settlement Officer, District Gurgaon dt. 16th March, 1880, pp. 42-43.

73. See f.n. 30 and the revenue literature of the Berlin Library, noted in my paper vide f.n. 25.

74. Ms. Or. Fol. 234, Berlin; fols. 9b-10a; Ms. Or. Oct. 113, Berlin, fols. 1a-4a; Ms. Berlin vide f.n.30.

75. Kh. S., N.A.I., pp. 28-29; Ms. M.U. Aligarh fols. 14a-15a also see my paper on 'The Position of Desai in the *pargana* administration of *subah* Gujrat under the Mughals', vide. f.n.39.

76. All this picture is very clear from the Rajasthan Archives and the Allahabad Documents of the 17th century. Also M.I., Berlin, fols. 4b-6b.

77. Vide R.A.J.

78. Vide AD.

79. Such a picture is available from the Rajasthan paintings.

80. These inscriptions cover from the 12th to the 17th centuries. See *Epigraphica Indica,* Vol. VIII, p. 27; Jain Inscriptions, I, nos. 837-47, pp. 206-15, I, No. 877, p. 217, I, no. 804, p. 198, I, no. I, p. 232, I. No. 879, pp. 233, I, 217, I, no. 726, p. 173. Mandapika has been used as customs house or toll house, *Panchas* and *Panekul* as corporate organisations of the towns, *Gosti* as managing committee of a Corporate organisations of the towns, Gosti as managing committee or a corporate body or merchant community, *Sangh* as a union and *Shershiti* as the leader of the commercial groups.

81. See the documents relating to *mauzas* (villages), *tappahs* and *Mahals* (as commercial centres and *mandis* of specialised commodities) of *Pargana* Bhagalpur (18th century) attached to the *'Raqbabandi'* documents of Akbar' reign, S.C.R.O., Patna, vide f.n. 22.

82. Also see Satish Chandra's "Some Aspects of Growth of Money Economy in India during the Seventeenth Century:, *Asian History Congress*, New Delhi., 1961.

83. See W.C. Bennet, 'Gazetteer of the Provinces of Oudh' *(op. cit.)* and Settlement Reports quoted by James Douie *(op. cit).*

84. W.W. Hunter, *Orissa*, II, p. 206.

85. *Cavendish Enquiries (op. cit).*

86. Aso see A.M. Shah, 'Political System in Eighteen Century Gujrat', *Enquiry*, Vol. I, No.1 (Old Series No. 7), Spring 1964, pp. 83-95.

87. W.C. Bennet, *Gazetteer of the Provinces of Oudh, op. cit.; The Dastur ul aml* of Saadat Ali Khan.

88. See various Settlement Reports vide S.C. Gupta, *op. cit.*

89. See detail vide T. Fortescue, Esquire, Civil Commissioner Delhi, to Holt Machenzie, Esquire, Secretary to the Government in Territorial Department, dt. Fort William, 28th April 1820, *'Report on the Revenue System of the Delhi Territory'*, 1820.

90. See details in the Assessment and the Settlement Reports of the various districts of the Punjab. Also James Douie, *'Punjab Settlement Manual'*, pp. 52-111.

Chapter 3

An Integrated Pattern of Commercial Life in the Rural Society of North India During the Seventeenth and Eighteenth Centuries*

I

Recent trends of historical research on the economic history of India have already made considerable progress on the analysis of Indian commercial life in the pre-British era, with special reference to aspects like the process of urbanization, the role of commercial classes in cities, and the nature and extent of inland and foreign trade. But not much attention has been paid to the commercial pattern governing rural society and to linking the latter with the urban inter-provincial and foreign trade and commercial set-up. The lack of proper importance attached to this subject may be partly ascribed to the comparative paucity of contemporary sources as well as the desire to trace the history of business in India in the light of economic developments in the European countries during the pre-industrial age.

The problems and the methods of the study of the social and commercial history of India *vis-a-vis* pre-industrial Europe are quite different. This is both because of the difference in the extent of contemporary source-material as well as the variation in the stages of socio-economic development. The source-material of seventeenth-eighteenth-century European societies on the growth of cities, and the role played by business communities in ports, cities and rural areas, is very vast. With the development of new research techniques and the computation of data on a country-wise or regional scale, it is possible to attempt generalization and theorization about socio-

---

* *Indian Historical Records Commission*, Proceedings of the thirty-seventh session, Vol. xxxvii (Delhi, 1966).

economic problems. Despite some parallelism, the vastness of the Indian subcontinent offers regional variations because of the diversity in the geographical situations and the habits of the tribal peoples settled in different regions. Moreover, in medieval Indian history, the socio-economic and political forces had diverse effects on the growth of different regions. The scattered source-material is equally unproportional in relation to time and areas. For some regions, ample source-material is forthcoming, which shortens the timegap for gathering consecutive information while for others, the data is sufficiently time-gapped, and for still others, practically no source-material exists.

The abundance or paucity of the available source-material with regard to time and area is bound to affect methodology in the technique of research so as to avoid sweeping generalizations. Moreover, there is an essential difference in the European *vis-a-vis* Indian concepts of the nature of urbanization in pre-industrial society. Except for the main cities, which had some rural features and were surrounded by rural areas, Indian towns (*qasbas*), unlike their European counterparts, showed more rural than urban features. Another factor responsible for insufficient attention paid to the commercial history of India has been the practical difficulty in the technique of research; research scholars are tempted to rely on direct evidence gleaned from the accounts of travellers, chronicles, geographical accounts and official records of foreign companies operating in India, than to scrutinize varying categories of regional sources in Persian and the local languages available for the seventeenth-eighteenth centuries.

II

The sources available for the history of business and rural commercial life are two-fold. Firstly, there are sources which give a general description of the commercial life of the whole of north India or particular parts thereof. Secondly, regional sources provide us with a detailed insight into the commercial pattern.

a) In the first category are included chronicles, provincial and regional histories, geographical treatises, the accounts of foreign travellers, official records of the European companies and the correspondence of their officials. Of the already well-known sources, the following deserve special notice: *Ain-i-Akbari, Mahzar-i-Shah Jahani, Khulasat-ul-Tawarikh* by Sujan Rai Bhandari, *Hadiqat-ul-Aqalim* by Murtaza Hussain Allah Yar Usmani Belgrami, *Mirat-i - Ahmadi, Riyaz-us-Salatin, Muntakhab-ul-Lubab* by Khwafi Khan,

Tarikh-i-Muhammad Shahi, Firaqi's *Waqai Alam Shahi*, *Siyar-ul-Mutakhirin*, *Safar Nama-i-Anand Ram Mukhlis*, and *Tarikh-i-Gorakhpur*, the accounts of foreigners like Sebastien Manrique, Bernier, Tavernier, Manucci, Walter Hamilton, Twining, Grose, Alexander Hamilton, Verelst, Bolts, Vansittart, Pennant, Raper, Valentia, Hodges and Forster; the English and the Dutch Factory Records, and the 'Letters Received' from the servants of the companies; the correspondence of the officials of the English East India Company; and the Persian correspondence.[1] The main information available from these sources relates to the general description of commercial life in the provinces, specialized crafts and industries in the urban centres, and the nature and extent of foreign trade. The description of inland rural trade and the conducting of business transactions is incidental and has to be gleaned from the implied meanings in the statements offered. It is very rarely that descriptions of the prevalence of certain crops and crafts in the villages and *qasbas* have been grouped along with the main cities of the same province. However, it may be reasonable to ask that, whenever the description of particular crafts and industries is available for the main cities of only the province, whether any commercial relationship between such cities and the rural *qasbas* of the same province can be established in this respect.

(b) A better picture of the rural commercial life and business transactions is available from the regional sources.[2] As the income to the State from the non-agricultural products levied in the village or a local *mandi* (market) was included under the heading of *sair-jihat*, the village, *tappah* and the *pargana* revenue documents essentially contain much information in this respect. At the same time, documents are available which exclusively relate to State policy towards the local *mandis* and *katras* (commercial centres or markets), the movement of commodities from one *pargana* to another, and the activities of the trading classes in the local *katras*. All this information can be collected from the Rajasthan Archives, covering the *Subahs* of Ajmer, Malwa, Agra and Delhi; papers of private families with the National Archives of India relating to various *subahs* of North India and the late eighteenth-century archives preserved in the Secretariat Records Office, Patna (Bihar). The Record offices of Bikaner, Kotah and Udaipur and the libraries in Udaipur, specially (Vidyapeeth Collection, Udaipur) possess manuscripts, *Bahis* (ledgers) and documents (viz. *kharitas*, *ruqqas*, *tehris*, etc.) comprising correspondence among the merchants in the Rajasthani language contains information on the activities of merchant's loans, private debts, rate of interests, and the various commodities involved in business transactions, etc. Interesting information is available on the working of craft and mercantile organizations which exerted control over the production and sale of goods and also established contact with craftsmen in the *qasbas* and cities and exercised control over them. These organizations were recognized by the State and they regulated the trade and industry of the area. They had regular contracts with the *banjaras* who helped to maintain internal and external trade by carrying goods from one place to another. Thus, it can be asserted that with a proper scrutiny of regional records, it is possible to construct a reliable picture of the commercial set-up and business transactions in the rural society of different regions of North India during the seventeenth-eighteenth centuries.

III

The concept of village self-sufficiency has been well exploded. In fact, in a vast country like India with a great diversity of geographical and topographical conditions as well as varying degrees of socio-economic development, it is basically incorrect to talk of an 'Indian village' in general terms, for the stage of economic development of a village may differ from one *Subah* to another and may even vary from one region to another within a *Subah*. Villages generally grew cash crops and excessive grain crops for export to the local *mandis* or *qasbas;* they also responded to the regional prices and their economy was well integrated with that of the *qasbas* and cities. Only villages in the background regions maintained traits of self-sufficiency and a subsistence economy. Regional archives point towards the interdependence of groups of adjacent villages on the local *mandis,* both for commercial crops and non-agricutural products. Within a *pargana* or a larger territory, a few commercial centres named *mahals* or *katras* served as links between villages and *qasbas*. The *qasba,* apart from serving as the administrative headquarters of the *pargana,* was also the main commercial centre of the rural areas. However, today if there is a strict line of demarcation between the rural and the urban areas in medieval Indian society, a *qasba* with its jurisdiction over *tappahs, katras* and villages was more a part of the rural society than an urban centre. Certain big villages (*muwazai-i-kalan*), *katras* and *qasbas* were known for established *mandis* dealing with grain crops, commercial crops as well as goods and animals. Contemporary evidence points to the establishment of regular *katras* in the *subahs* of Malwa and Ajmer (Rajasthan) and the prevalence of the *mahals* (here in the commercial sense) in Bihar, which served as markets in the rural areas.[3] It was equally true of the other regions of North India though the local names for such markets varied in accordance with the local dialects. These commercial centres served as *mandis* where the rural population could sell their surplus agricultural and industrial goods for regional consumption as well as export to the main cities. Similarly, the rural population would purchase from these *mandis* such commodities not available locally and which were imported from the other *mandis* of the cities. Moreover, grain crops assessed in kind were collected by the official revenue staff (of either the *khalisa* administration or the *jagirdars* as the case may be) and transported to such *mandis* for sale to the merchants (*beoparis*).[4] Depending on the nature of the regional products, some *mandis* specialized in certain commercial crops or other goods. Ordinarily, the *katras* or the *qasbas,* which served as the local *mandis,* were connected with the other villages and the nearest main city through regular means of communication and indigenous road-works. Similarly, in the riverine regions, the villages and the *mandis* were connected with the rural areas either through roads or canals.[5] Many a village fell on the land trade routes or on the bank or near the rivers and waterways which served as the commercial depots for the traders.[6]

Apart from this, it was an old established Indian practice for the central villages surrounded by a group of small feeding villages to hold weekly or fornightly local *mandis* where goods were bartered or purchased by the agriculturists or artisans. Certain villages were known for religious or cultural fairs which equally served the purpose of the local markets.[7] At times, temporary *mandis* were established at open places (known as *hauts* or *peeth* or *peth*) on the bank of a river or near sacred places during religious fairs.[8] These places were not regular villages or towns but they acquired the status of seasonal mandis on a permanent basis.

The occupational and artisan classes were concentrated in the villages which were well-connected with the local *mandi* and the main *qasba* by roads. A small village may only comprise of an agricultural population but a big village may be inhabited by certain occupational castes as well.[9] A village may be dominated by the artisans of a particular occupational caste like the carpenter-cum-blacksmith or the goldsmith or the weaver or the dyer or the scentmaker or the potter or the shoe-maker. Such a village would be known for the craftsmanship of its dominant occupational caste and would also serve the needs of the surrounding villages. The craftsmen usually sold their goods in their residential-cum-shop premises. Production was carried on by them with their own tools and equipment on an individual basis. They usually bartered their services or goods. The occupational workers rendering services to the agriculturists were entitled to the customary share from the crops of the *riaya* and a few of them even got some land in *inam*.[10] In various regions, there were settled tribes who took to agriculture and the breeding of animals like horses, camels, oxen, buffaloes, cows, sheep and asses, etc – the latter traded in animals. They also paid the land revenue and cesses (*sair*) on sale of their goods in terms of animals rather than in cash.[11] There were also vagrant tribes moving from one place to another in search of good grass and some cultivable land. They took to agriculture as well as grass products.[12] In the regions where no cultivable land was available, such tribes took to fishing and cutting grass to sell and paid lump-sum revenues (*sair*) to the State. Certain Gujar tribes adept in cattle-rearing and the sale of milk moved from one jungle to another, and at times had seasonal movements from the plains to the hilly areas and back. They also paid lump-sum revenues (*sair*) to the State.[13] Some of these Gujars purchased and sold petty articles en route their seasonal movements.

The commercial pattern of a *qasba* ran on different lines. The Rajasthan Archives give a fairly reliable picture about commercial life in the *qasbas* of Rajasthan and Malwa.[14] In a *qasba,* normally different craftsmen lived in separate streets. Each craft and trade was concentrated in a separate street where the craftsmen had residential houses, workshops and shops. This may also have happened in big villages where a few occupational craftsmen lived in concentrated pockets. Thus, in the *qasbas,* the shops of the cloth dealers, thread workers, dyers, tailors, perfume sellers, potters, shoe-makers, washermen, basketmakers, ironsmiths, oil-pressers, painters, bangle manufacturers, barbers, utensil-manufacturers, physicians, confectioners, grocers, retail shopkeepers, goldsmiths, jewellers, *sahukars, sarafs,* arm-manufacturers were ordinarily located in different lanes. In the main *qasbas,* which constituted the headquarters of the chief zamindars (rajas etc.), many shops dealing in cloth, armaments, scents, fruits, garlands, betels, bangles, sweets, etc. would be located on the main street of the *qasbas*. A number of artisans, such as arm-repairers, painters, wood-workers, leather-workers, oil-pressers, wine-manufacturers and shoe-makers would have their shops in the side lanes. This pattern of commercial life may have been true only of the big *qasbas* and may not have been applicable to all the regions of north India. The concept of commercial life in a *qasba* was essentially governed by the geographical situation, the commercial importance of the *qasba* and the population residing therein. However, the tendency of businessmen and craftsmen of the same trade to have consecutively adjacent shops in these lanes was quite widespread.[15]

The profession of artisans and occupational castes was mostly hereditary, and this helped in acquiring proficiency in the art to an admirable degree.[16] Different castes took to different occupations. In trade and commerce, many regions in North India developed local guilds or corporations with which local representatives from a big village or group of villages were associated. The Rajasthan sources refer to *panchs, panchkul, mandapika, ghosthi* (or *gosti*), *sangh* and *shershti* (or commercial groups) which clearly show the existence of craft and mercantile organizations.[17] In view of the extraordinary expansion of trade and commerce—inland and foreign in the sixteenth-seventeenth centuries and also the fact that, by and large, the villages of north India were regularly integrated with the *qasba* and the city markets, there is every possibility that such commercial organizations representing the villages may have been equally known in some other parts of north India. They had some control over the production and sale of the products as well as the conduct of the craftsmen. Eighteenth-century Bengal documents show that in rural society the *mundles, chaudharis* and zamindars had as much jurisdiction over craftsmen and regulation of local trade as over agriculture and land revenue.[18] The artisans of different professions, i.e. the weavers, bricklayers, smiths, braziers and handicraftsmen were incorporated into their respective bodies, one in each *pargana*. They elected a *chowdree* (*chaudhari*) or chief to represent them, and the *mundels*, i.e. *muqaddams* of every *pargana* rendered monthly accounts to the zamindars (in Bengal) in respect of every artificer residing within their limits. The *chaudharis* were supposed to inform the zamindar about the just and the true rates of all types of labour, and the rate per day of all types of labourers and artificers were fixed. These details and those of the shopkeepers were recorded in the zamindar's ledgers. All artificers were to be licensed. While introducing these regulations, the English East India Company thought that it was reviving the old system of the village communities. Besides that, at the *qasba* level, there were *bazar panchayats* which took voluntary decisions relating to commercial matters.[19] The mercantile organizations and the *bazar panchayats* made voluntary charitable contributions to religious institutions or holy persons either by levying a tax on the sale of articles or by a cess per shop in a particular village or a *qasba*. At some places, these organizations exercised a tight control over the services in the temples. At times, they also contributed to public welfare for the construction of wells and roads. The guilds were recognized by the state. They regulated trade and industry of the area and looked into the payment of state taxes and customs duties (*sair-jihat*) levied on commercial goods in accordance with scheduled rates. In fact, the *chaudhari* of a *mandi* served as the link between local businessmen and the state.[20] The *chaudhari* was responsible for the payment of the revenues and worked under the supervision of the *amin wa darogha-i-sair*.[21]

The trading communities had a network of establishments in the rural and urban commercial centres, thereby linking the rural commercial life both with the urban and international trade. Apart from wealthy merchants settled in the main cities and ports, known as *sahus or sahukars* and *kothiwalas* (bankers) – who carried on import and export business on a large-scale and are quite well-known – there were merchants of varying financial levels settled in the *qasba* who indulged mostly in inland trade, though a few of them also carried on foreign trade. In a large *qasba*, the shops of the merchants surrounded by those of the *banjaras* (caravan merchants) were located in the central street. The agents of wealthy city merchants and foreign trading companies were in contact with the brokers (*dalals*) and the local *qasba* merchants to acquire the necessary commodities. The Rajasthan Archives mentions the names of several merchants who were engaged in trade both within Rajasthan and on an inter-provincial basis.[22] Their agents purchased grain, cash crops as well as industrial goods from the villages, small *qasbas* and rural *mandis*. They sold these commodities at a profit for consumption within Rajasthan and to export to other provinces. Similarly, they supplied outside commodities to small *qasbas* and villages. These merchants, through their agents, provided raw material to the weavers, gold and coppersmiths, glass manufacturers in the *qasbas*, and the villages where artisans worked on the 'putting out' system. Though working on an individual basis was well-known, a considerable number of weavers, dyers and washers worked on the 'putting out' pattern. Thus, craftsmen and the artisans worked both on personal as well as 'putting out' basis. In the latter system, the Indian merchants and the foreign trading companies which procured industrial goods kept a good deal of margin for their profits. The merchants (*saudagaran* or *beoparis*) or their agents would even purchase or sell goods at the individual village level.[23] In riverine regions connected through waterways, the merchants had a network of establishments and agents at various village-ports and inland villages inhabited by various tribes and clans. They imported and exported goods on a large-scale. Seventeenth-century documents show that in certain regions people viewed visiting *beoparis* (merchants) as village guests who served the essential needs of the village community.[24] They were entertained at the expense of the village revenue and the cost of rations for their entertainment during their stay in the village was debited to seasonal state revenues. This relieved the villagers of the responsibility of taking to and bringing from *mandis* the goods they needed. The merchants had all the apparatus of transportation for this purpose. The margin of profit could not have been large enough to exploit the rural population; otherwise the concept of treating the *beoparis* as village guests could not have existed.

In every province there were mercantile castes who, except for hawking or peddling, carried on mercantile and commercial transactions. These mercantile castes were known by different names in different provinces. Every mercantile caste operated in a certain region with their territorial jurisdiction more or less marked. The territorial beats of these commercial castes were based on inherited custom and business. Trade in liquor and vegetables and traffic in cattle were carried on by the occupation castes who were considered comparatively inferior in social status to the other mercantile communities. In South Rajasthan and other such regions where agricultural occupation was not possible, there were pastoral tribes of varying grades who specialized in the breeding and rearing of different kinds of animals and birds.[25] They took to the breeding of animals like cows, oxen, horses, camels, sheep, and goats, and rearing hawks, parrots and other birds which were sold to the nobility or other well-to-do classes in the main *qasbas* and cities. In Rajasthan, the Malani tribe[26] bred cows, oxen and horses; the Rebaris[27] bred camels; and the Gayaris[28] reared sheep and goats. Some of the inferior tribes specialized in catching birds and animals from the jungles, which were then sold in the markets. The names of the seventeenth-century pastoral and animal breeding tribes are available for the *subahs* of Thatta, Lahore and Delhi.[29] Apart from this, there were peddling castes which specialized in certain merchandize commodities – petty peddlers and hucksters moving from one village to another. They sold rope, grass mats, petty hardware, earthenware such as pipe-bowls, images meant for decoration and for children, *pan*, betelnuts, etc. A few among the peddling castes were also engaged in cattle trade and traffic in small merchandize on a large-scale. A few among the mendicant class too acted as roving merchants.[30] The vagrant and gipsy tribes with varying occupations, manufactured and carried with them articles to sell such as grass, ropes, straw and reeds, matting, coarse sacks for pack animals, and grass brushes used by weavers.[31] They also reared animals like sheep, goat and camel which were then sold. While staying near the villages, they were also employed to do earthen work, fishing, diving and sinking wells.

The rural mentality was to export commodities to the main *qasbas* and cities. The rural areas supplied food, commercial crops and industrial goods to army camps and cities. Wherever army camps were stationed, the grain prices of the area rose considerably.[32] During normal times too, regions with surplus grain crops exported them to the deficit regions and even to foreign countries.[33] In Bengal, people lived on rice and fish and were not used to wheat, which was exported to southern India, the Portuguese possessions on the western Indian coast, and abroad. Bengal also exported sugar and wheat to Gujarat. Bengal herself imported wheat from Bihar for further export. Kerala received opium, sugar and rice from Bengal by sea. The provinces of Bihar and Agra imported sugar and rice from Bengal. Gujarat imported foodgrains from the *subahs* of Malwa and Ajmer and rice from Malabar and the Deccan. Above all, the rural areas producing cash crops developed a high degree of commercial sense for production. Cotton, sugarcane, oilseed crops (barring ground nut), dye-yielding crops were grown practically all over the country. Though indigo was cultivated in the *subahs* of Multan, Lahore, Delhi, Malwa, Allahabad and Awadh, it was a highly valued commercial crop grown in Sehwan (*subah* Thatta), Bayana and Doab (*subah* Agra), Mewat (*subahs* of Agra and Ajmer), and Sarkhej (*subah* Gujarat). The indigo of these places was sent to all parts of India and abroad. Agra indigo acquired world fame. Opium was grown in the *subahs* of Ajmer, Malwa and Bihar. It was in demand all over India. Bengal imported it from Bihar and sent it to Kerala and abroad by sea. Mewar (*subah* Ajmer) and Malwa opium was in great demand in China, South East Asia, Arabia and Persia. Tobacco introduced in India in the early seventeenth-century was grown all over India and was consumed both in rural and urban areas. The commercial policy of the Mughal state gave utmost impetus to the growth of cash crops.

With the expansion of the Mughal empire in the sixteenth-seventeenth centuries, the growth of services, both military and civil at the centre and in the provinces, and the heavy expenditure of the State, posed new problems. The State needed large revenues which was possible only with a dynamic approach for an increased agricultural output and highly developed trade and commerce. In the course of the late sixteenth and seventeenth centuries, both inland and overseas trade increased rapidly which had a great impact on the agricultural development as well as rural and urban prosperity. The need to feed the heavily populated urban centres, the growing population of the commercially developed rural areas and *qasbas* and the military camps led to an ever increasing inter-regional and inter-provincial dependence on foodgrains. Cash crops like indigo, sugarcane, cotton, oilseeds and opium were in heavy demand for export, as finished industrial products to foreign markets. All this tended to break the parochial village outlook of producing crops for mere self-consumption and local supply. An Indian village in the developed regions no longer lived in economic isolation. These changes led to an increase in the land under cultivation and in the volume of agricultural produce. This not only increased the land revenue and the income from the imposition of sale and customs duties, but also earned a favourable balance of trade. The indigo of the province of Agra was in great demand with foreign merchants and trading companies. The indigo business was so lucrative that the Mughal state started giving monopoly of its sale to the contractors (indigo farmers).[34] The Mughal state even financed the contractor for purchasing indigo from the various local *mandis* and entered into an agreement with the latter, keeping its stipulated share in the profit of the sale proceeds. It also offered quite reasonable terms to the indigo farmers who, in case of little profit, would be obliged to return only the State loan. The indigo farmer had the monopoly on sale of indigo to local merchants and foreign trading companies. This resulted in the rise of the indigo price and greater returns for the State.

Apart from this, the fact that the English and the Dutch East India Companies always competed with each other in purchasing indigo for their foreign markets was equally conducive for the rise in price. Whenever there was a good indigo crop of fine quality, wealthy Indian merchants liked to keep up the price by withholding stock for clearance in the ensuing year. The Indigo cultivator was also very alive to the fluctuation in its price and the international demand. This is well illustrated by an incident over the indigo price of AD 1633.[35] In that year, the rights of indigo sale were farmed out by the Mughal state to an Indian contractor. Due to the Deccan wars, the Parsi merchants refrained from purchasing the Deccan goods and concentrated on the purchase of the Agra indigo. Consequently, the indigo price shot upto Rs 50 per (*Akbari*) maund.

In fact, this price was much higher than that in the preceding or following years. Ordinarily, the English and Dutch East India Companies preferred to purchase Agra indigo (here too the Koel, i.e. Aligarh rather than Bayana indigo) to the indigo of other regions. In the face of such a high price of Agra indigo, the English and Dutch Companies felt reluctant to purchase it. The English Company even considered the possibility of acquiring direct farming rights from the Mughal state but gave up the idea due to the practical difficulty of dealing with Indian merchants. Ultimately the two Companies, namely the English and the Dutch, thought of reaching a mutual agreement of abstaining from indigo purchases. As the proposal was initiated at Surat, indigo cultivators of the Agra province, fearing a slump in the market in the ensuing year, immediately uprooted their indigo plants and cultivated other crops instead. Other sources equally reveal how conscious the indigo and melon-growing villages in the territory of *Subah* Thatta were of the importance of the export of their commodities to other regions and the international market.[36]

Trade in the industrial products of many a region of north India was well-established. Most villages and *qasbas* in the *subahs* of Bengal, Orissa, Bihar, Allahabad, Agra, Delhi, Lahore, Sindh and Kashmir produced a variety of piece goods.[37] The regions of Allahabad manufactured cotton cloth known as *jhonah* and *mibrkul*, which was exported to Agra, Delhi and other places. Cotton and silk-weaving were done by peasant families or the landless class during the season. They combined agriculture and weaving. Apart from this, there were the *chamar* castes who took to leather-working, tanning and weaving. Even though they did wholetime weaving jobs and thought themselves socially upgraded as against the scavengers, they were by and large considered village menials. They worked in lieu of a fractional share in the produce of the cultivators, though a few *chamar-julaha* castes worked as paid artisans. Technically speaking, in the social hierarchy a weaver (known as *julaha* or *tanti* or *paoli*) was an artisan rather than a village menial. The *julaha* as a wholetime weaver belonged to a low caste, both amongst the Hindus and the Muslims. He was paid by the piece rather than by customary dues. The *julahas* were concentrated in certain villages and *qasbas*. They worked both as an individual and on a 'putting out' system. Though cotton was woven practically all over India, the provinces of Bengal, Awadh, Lahore and Sindh exported large quantities of cloth. Various qualities of coarse cotton were woven in Assam and Bengal. The provinces of Agra and Bihar received raw silk and textiles from Bengal. Agra also imported cotton and cotton textiles from Gujarat and Khandesh. Silk was produced largely in Assam, Bengal, Awadh, Sindh and Kashmir. The provinces of Bihar, Agra and Gujarat imported raw silk from Bengal. Despite the fact that Gujarat imported silk from a long-distance, it had a large-scale silk weaving industry and exported its products to other parts of India. Similarly, the *subahs* of Agra (Fatehpur Sikri), Lahore, Kashmir and the western coast had a highly developed silk-weaving industry.

The industrial products of commercial regions in many a province of north India were exported to other places. Kashmir manufactured and exported silk cloth, shawls, blankets, woollen cloth on a large-scale and of various fine varieties, wooden articles and paper; Sindh – silk cloth, cotton textiles, skin-hides, wooden articles, ivory bangles, gumlace and saltpetre; Lahore – cotton textiles, shawls, blankets and paper (especially in Sialkot and the surrounding villages); Delhi – shawls, blankets, utensils of copper, brass and other types, paper, *huqqa* (for smoking) and glass vessels; Agra – utensils of copper, brass, wooden articles and paper; Allahabad – (especially in the Jaunpur Sarkar) wooden articles, glass vessels, paper, gumlace and needle; Malwa – clothweaving; Awadh – saltpetre, gumlace; Bihar – (especially in *Sarkar* Monghyr) wooden articles, glass vessels and other domestic utensils, saltpetre, paper, gumlace, iron articles like grid irons, sauce pans, forks and knives; Bengal – muslin, cotton textiles, woven silk, woven jute cloth and mats; Assam – silk weaving. The Himalayan regions manufactured woollen cloth of various varieties, animal skins, gums, timber, fuel, herbs and fruits. Many of these articles were produced in other hill regions and forests which covered a considerable portion (nearly half) of north India. Gujarat occupied an extremely important position in Indian commerce and was known for cotton textiles and silk weaving. Silver was scarce in India. Gold and silver were imported as bullion in exchange for agricultural and industrial products.[38] Ornaments of gold, silver and metals were made all over the country. Iron was extracted in plenty from surface ores and melted in small furnaces near mining sites practically all over India (except the western coast). The agricultural and industrial implements made of wood and iron were manufactured in all the provinces. Copper and various types of precious stones were available in Rajasthan. Copper was a State monopoly and was exported to other regions of India.[39]

Sixteenth-seventeenth-century sources reveal that unlimited quantities of salt were procured from rock salt at Khukra, Kheora near Shamsabad, and at other places in Sind Sagar Doab (known as Sindhi Salt), *subah* Lahore.[40] There were salt pits in Thatta (*subah* Sindh). The Sambar lake and other salt lakes in the deserts of *subah* Ajmer produced a large quantity of salt.[41] These regions supplied salt all over north India at a very cheap and reasonable price. Salt was scarce in Bengal and was imported from long distances.[42] The State imposed a regular *abwab* (cess) on the production of the salt and had a regular government machinery for its collection.[43] The revenue from salt was usually farmed out to salt contractors.[44] In these regions, a large number of the rural population was employed to extract salt and transport it to the local *mandis*. Salt extraction was undertaken by the professional castes. The *alasha-khash* people worked at Kheora and Sindh Sagar *doab*, whereas the *nunias* were experts in extracting salt from nitrous soils.[45] Salt formed an extremely important item of the rural trade. It was transported to distant places by *banjaras*. Apart from this, there is ample evidence to show that in the seventeenth-eighteenth centuries, animal production was luxurious and cheap.[46] There was plenty of cattle wealth, *ghee* and butter in all the regions of north India. Butter of high quality was produced in Sindh and Multan, both for home consumption and export to other regions. Agra, being a great commercial centre, imported butter from places along the Jamuna and the Ganges right upto Bihar and Bengal. Thatta (Sindh) bred and exported horses of good quality. During the eighteenth-century, the main commercial classes which operated on an inter-provincial basis were the *Multanis*, the *Banias*, *Poggyahs* (merchants with turbans from the north-western regions), *Sheikhs, Pathans, Kashmiris, Sannasses, Bettees, Sahukars* and *Beoparis*, all of whom had *dalals* (agents) spread over in the rural and urban centres.[47] They sold their own regional goods and procured goods from other regions on the 'putting out' system.

Goods from one place to another were taken by *kafilas* (caravans) by the wealthy class of merchants known as *banjaras*, who maintained supplies between the different parts of the country and to the seaports for export to foreign countries.[48] The *banjara* community operated both on short and long-distance routes transporting goods on fixed charges. They specialized in carrying salt, foodgrains, butter and a few other articles. The *manori* tribe specialized in transporting food-grains and salt. The *banjaras* carried armed guards with them. On behalf of the state, the zamindars of the regions were required to ensure their free passage in their respective *zamindari* jurisdictions.[49] As the *banjara* class kept up the supply pipeline from one place to another and hazarded a great risk on the insecure routes, they were well respected in society. Whenever a caravan reached a village or a *qasba*, it was received with great warmth. The chief zamindars (*Zamindaran -i-Umda*) often offered robes of honour to *banjara* chiefs on their safe arrival in their territories.[50] Similarly, the other *kafilas* carrying iron, indigo and other industrial goods moved from one place to another. The cost of road transportation was quite high. On an average, for grain transportation it would cost nearly annas 6½ to annas 10 per maund for 100 miles, thereby raising the price of grain per maund by 37.4 per cent to 61.8 per cent (on late-seventeenth-century freight rates and prices).[51] The cost of sugar transportation was nearly half. On long-distances, the imported articles from Kabul to Delhi or Agra would cost nearly four to eight or nine times, depending upon the article, and for grains (wheat etc.) from Agra to Surat nearly four times the original cost. Sugar, iron and salt cost half or even less than foodgrain transportation. As the rural commercial import and export ran mostly on short-distance routes, the transportation charges of foodgrains and other articles were much less. Moreover, the zamindar families carried their goods to the local *mandis* nearby in their own bullock carts. All over north India, the indigenous means of land communication were *kaccha* roads, which were developed. Ordinarily, there were trees on both sides of the road and regular places of halt were provided. At every stop, there was a *sarai* (a pavilioned resthouse) with trees, wells, tanks and other amenities around it. Sometimes provisions were also available for cattle. On important roads, pillars indicating distance in terms of *karohs* (a *karoh* is about 2 to 2.5 miles) were fixed at regular distances. Bridges were constructed over rivulets and large-scale ferry bridges over the main rivers. Though Sher Shah is well-known for having constructed a few new roads,[52] the *kaccha* roads interlinking the villages, *qasbas* and cities are known to have existed throughout the medieval period.[53] The local chiefs (*Zamindaran-i-Umda*), the other zamindars, the wealthy Hindu merchants and philanthropists, the commercial guilds and temple organizations, all helped in the construction and maintenance of these roads and *sarais*.[54] The usual means of transport were bullock carts. In some regions, for instance the semi desert or hilly tracts, depending on local practice, other means of communication were quite common. Asses, drome daries, horses, mules, hill ponies, goats and porters were used for transportation.[55] Sometimes, the *banjaras* followed the known pilgrimage routes.[56] They usually avoided the rainy season.

Apart from land routes, goods were also transported through the rivers. As inter-river navigation on a large-scale was well-established, goods were transported to long-distances both on a provincial and inter-provincial basis.[57] The goods were transported not only from one main city on a river bank to another, but the villages and the *qasbas* situated near the rivers equally benefited from this transport system, both for purposes of export and import. The Indus river system connected the rural areas, the main cities of the *subah* of Lahore, Multan, Sindh and Kashmir. The Jamuna-Ganges river system connected *subah* Delhi to Bengal. The Brahmaputra connected Assam and the hilly regions with Bengal. The tributaries and the various waterways attached to the main rivers mostly served the rural areas. There was great commercial traffic through river navigation. This was because of the fact that the cost of maintenance of cargo-boats was much less, as against ox-driven carts, and the freight charges of riverborne goods were much cheaper in comparison to road transportation. On long-distances, the cost of road transportation of cotton goods per maund was nearly 66.66 per cent higher than river transportation, but the insurance rates of the former goods were nearly less than a quarter (around 22.72 per cent) as against water insurance.[58] However, the cost of water transport on short-distance routes in the rural regions was very little. This was also a quicker means of transport. Big boats and ships for commercial transportation were built in the provinces of Kashmir, Thatta, Lahore, Allahabad, Bihar, Orissa and Bengal.[59] The seasons were the determining factors for land and river traffic. River navigation was operated by boatmen who belonged to the *mallah* caste.[60] Commercial navigation as well as the boat and shipbuilding craftsmanship absorbed a vital section of the rural population. Boats of various kinds and shapes were constructed for commercial purposes. In certain jungles, special kinds of trees were grown for boat wood. Boat bridges were built over the rivers. The Mughal state maintained its own fleet of boats in all riverine regions for the purpose of transporting goods and armies for internal warfare against recalcitrant chiefs and tribes.[61] In fact, in the riverine tracts, it was obligatory on the part of local zamindars who accepted the Mughal sovereignty to keep a fleet of boats for the transportation of royal goods and armies.[62] This was a part of an agreement which entitled the zamindars to a conditional *jagir* for the maintenance of boats. The same policy was followed by eighteenth-century regional governments towards rural zamindars.

The *bharawala* firms were given the contract for carrying goods for inland, provincial and inter-provincial trade.[63] There was considerable rural banditry, especially in the regions inhabited by the wild or recalcitrant tribes. In order to cover the risk against rural banditry, the *bimawala* (insurance) companies with headquarters in the main cities had agents and small establishments in rural areas, i.e. *mandis, katras* and *qasbas*. These companies insured the transported goods and animals both in the period of peace and trouble at specified rates. However, the insurance of land-transported goods extended to a limited number of articles. Grain, salt, wood and cattle were seldom insured. Only valuable goods like opium, iron, sugar, spices, bullion and jewels were insured. The insurance companies also undertook to pay the custom duties *en route* and the insurance rates covered these charges as well. Surprisingly, even the conditions in the troubled regions or the chaotic eighteenth-century political situation did not normally disturb commercial operations or caravan merchants. Recalcitrant tribal chiefs *en route* were more concerned with the exorbitant custom duties they realized, and with the regular supply of goods for their own benefit, than with violent robbery. This, of course, led the *hundiwala* or *bharawala* firms to charge high insurance premium and transportation rates from the owners of merchandise.[64] The *sahukars* kept themselves in touch with political developments in the region that they operated. There were even news reporters to their patron Chief.[65] *Bima* companies insured goods carried by road or riverborne traffic. Though the freight rates of riverborne goods were cheaper, the insurance fee was higher in comparison to road transportation as the risk on river transport was much greater because of the chances of loss to heavily laden cargo-boats. In abnormal times too, a regional revolt for instance, the insurance rates on the land routes were higher because of the great risk involved. Many a *bima* company kept in their employ carts for road transport and a large number of boats and boatmen, along with armed guard. At the same time, safeguards were taken against carrying cash money in rural areas and on hazardous trade routes. The practice of money payment by means of *hundis* was widely operative in the business circles during the seventeenth-eighteenth centuries. A *hundi* was a written order of promise to pay the amount at sight or after a stipulated period. *Hundis* were drawn by *sarafs* who, after deducting a nominal discount (of nearly 1 per cent), would direct their agents or counterparts at the destination of a trader to make the payment. Lakhs of rupees were remitted like this. *Sarafs* in the *qasbas* had established contacts with *sarafs* in the main cities and ports. Traders carried on much of their business through *hundis*. The *hundis* were drawn by merchants to raise money for the payment of purchased goods. The discount in such cases varied from place to place, ranging between I per cent to 10 per cent during the seventeenth-century.[66] *Hundis* which covered the risk of loss or damage of goods in transit were known as *jokhami hundis*. At times, the *hundiwalas,* on contract to convey goods at a discount, paid the necessary freight charges and the custom duties levied *en route*.[67] Local *sarafs* and *mahajans* acted as bankers. They advanced loan on interest which amounted to 1 per cent to 4.68 per cent per annum in the *qasbas* and upto 5.8 per cent in the cities.[68] For urgent borrowings, compound interest called *badotra* was charged.[69] In the towns, houses could also be mortgaged. The *qasba sarafs* would also advance loans to agriculturists, but it seems that in some regions, prior state permission was necessary for it.[70] The *chaudharis* who belonged to the *zamindari* class[71] and the temple priests[72] would also advance money on loan. In a big village, it was the *mahajan* (or *zargar*) who was a shopkeeper and also helped in commuting village crops in kind into cash at the scheduled rates for the purposes of revenue assessment.[73] For the latter service, he was entitled to a customary share from the *riaya*. In some regions, the moneylenders (*zargaran*) developed agricultural interests.[74] They would take the land for purposes of development on temporary lease on a sharing basis from revenue-free assignees (*aima*) and *jagirdars*. But this was a malpractice and, as such, was not encouraged by the Mughal government.[75] It does not seem that the village *mahajan* acted as a usurer. It was the zamindar family or the local revenue officials who managed the transportation of grain or commercial crops for sale in a local or *qasba mandi*.[76] In the developed regions, agents of the *beoparis* would purchase the crops or industrial goods at the village level.[77] As a matter of fact, during the seventeenth-eighteenth centuries rural India had a strong middle class, both upper and lower. Apart from the affluent rural zamindar families and dignitaries like *chaudharis, tappadars, desais* (in Gujarat and Deccan), *sardaran* (the landed chiefs), *arbaban* (in Sindh) and *taluqdars* who acted as the landed intermediaries[78] and a few of them also as moneylenders[79] and revenue-free assignees (*aima*), there was the rural commercial class of different types. There were the *sarafs, mahajans,* goldsmiths and jewellers, the merchants (*saudagars* and *beoparis*), the *banjaras* and caravan contractors settled in the rural *mandis, katras* and *qasbas*, who constituted the upper rural middle class. The petty merchants (*beoparis*), the brokers (*dalals*) in the *ganj* and the *mahal* (i.e. market), and the *chaudharis* getting fixed commission on the sale and purchase of goods and merchandise, the manufacturers, the artisans, the technicians and the village *mahajans* (*zargaran*) all formed the lower middle class. A few of the business families, especially the moneylenders, started showing interest in the acquisition of agricultural and even *zamindari* rights.

During the Mughal age, the State imposed customs duties (*mahsul*) on imported goods and other cesses of various kinds on arts and crafts manufactured by artisans.[80] Cesses imposed on sale and purchase in the rural *qasba* markets covered commodities like articles of food, grains, commercial crops, oil, cloth, skin, medicine, horses, camels, other animals and birds. Under the revenue headings of State income, all these cesses formed a part of *sair-jihat* and *sair-ul-wajah*.[81] Notwithstanding the fact that Akbar abolished various miscellaneous cesses (*baj, tamgha* and *zakat*),[82] transit duties known as *rahdari* and *zakat* (amounting to 2½ per cent) on the merchandise continued to be collected.[83] Jahangir abolished *zakat* on transit goods, river tolls and some other miscellaneous cesses which were being realized by the *jagirdars* in their territories.[84] Later, Aurangzeb abolished transit duties (*rahdari*) on gram and vegetables which were being levied per ass-load or cartload or per maund.[85] Levy of some of the cesses (*zakat* and *rahdari*), declared illegal, continued in practice in various parts of the empire throughout the seventeenth-eighteenth centuries.[86] However, strict orders were issued by the government to the local officials to refrain from charging *rahdari* from traders moving in the deficit regions.[87] Aurangzeb fixed *mahsul* on merchandise at 2½ per cent *ad valorem* on the goods carried by the Muslim merchants and 5 per cent on the goods of the Hindu merchants.[88] But after his death (AD 1707), the local administration illegally raised the *mahsul* duties to 10 per cent and 15 per cent on the goods of Muslim and Hindu merchants respectively.[89] In 1711, Bahadur Shah ordered the compliance of rules framed under Aurangzeb.[90] Seventeenth-century sources reveal that the *mahsul* duties were collected both in cash and kind. In the rural areas, merchants usually paid in kind. It seems that notwithstanding the general royal regulations there were regional schedules (*Dasturalamal-i dharat* or *Dastur dharat*) with varying rates on different commodities of production brought into the market.[91] In the riverine areas, *mahsul* was levied per boat with specified rate for every kind of merchandise brought by boat.[92] An empty boat was exempted from the payment of *mahsul*. Duties were levied both on the merchants and the customers.[93] In territories far from the central or provincial seats of governance, much depended upon the discretion of the *jagirdars* and the rates of *mahsul* varied from one *jagirdar's* tenure to that of another.[94] An honest *jagirdar* considered it his duty to encourage merchants and artisans to import goods and imposed reasonably light customs, but an unscrupulous *jagirdar* would charge very high duties.[95] The Mughal state regulated trade and commerce.[96] A *jagirdar* or a *khalisa* officer would adopt a conciliatory attitude towards fairminded merchants and artisans, but he would impose a penalty in the shape of double duties upon the merchandise of traders and artisans who violated regulations and indulged in blackmarketing.[97] The provincial or local administration fixed prices of foodstuff on a regional scale.[98] The fixing of prices was governed by the principle of local supply and demand. In a region where a particular commodity was in excess, its import was forbidden and the commodities in excess were diverted to other regions.[99] For droughtstriken areas or regions with certain deficit commodities, special facilities were provided to traders. In order to keep down the prices, they were afforded unrestricted movement and were exempted from *mahsul* duties.[100]

The rural commercial set-up in the eighteenth-century practically ran on the same lines as during the seventeenth-century. The presumption that Farrukh Siyar's *Farman*, issued in 1717 to the East India Company, and the intermittently chaotic situation created by foreign invasions (Nadir Shah's in 1739 and Ahmad Shah Abdali's campaigns culminating in the final battle of Panipat in 1761) and internal political disturbances – all ruined Indian cottage industries and commercial life is not fully borne out by the vast contemporary regional evidence available for north India. It is true that the grant of permission to the English to carry on duty-free trade in Bengal and Gujarat on the annual payment of Rs 3000 was a huge revenue loss to the government.[101] But this did not disrupt commercial life in the countryside and urban centres. The seventeenth-eighteenth-century sources are well linked up and give a co-ordinated picture of commercial trends. Of course, some changes occurred in the pattern of production of some commercial crops. The export of indigo and sugar declined owing to competition with the West Indies, but the important regions known for it in the seventeenth-century retained their importance. The regional position of commercial crops and industrial goods was by no means static during the seventeenth-eighteenth centuries. Though the growth of indigo in many provinces was well-known even earlier, it acquired real international importance during the seventeenth-century. The cultivation of indigo was extended to the Deccan and East Coast, while Bengal indigo also came into prominence. By the end of the seventeenth-century, indigo was exported even from Bengal.[102] During the sixteenth-century, paper was manufactured in the *Subahs* of Lahore and Bihar, but by the end of the seventeenth-century it was also manufactured in Awadh.[103] During the sixteenth-century, opium was grown in Rajasthan, Malwa and Allahabad, but in the course of the seventeenth-century, its cultivation was extended to the *Subahs* of Bengal and Bihar.[104] During the sixteenth-seventeenth centuries, Bengal had been deficient in salt, which had to be imported from great distances. But during the eighteenth-century, Bengal managed to manufacture salt of its own and even exported to the other regions.[105]

During the eighteenth-century, the ruination of the Mughal nobility and the aristocracy resulted in lack of patronage for industrial goods. But this affected the State-owned *karkhanas* located in the cities rather than rural commercial production. Owing to political upheavals and chaotic intermissions, there was considerable reshuffling in the territorial jurisdictions of local chief and zamindar families. Many an upstart zamindar family acquired new rights upon the ashes of old families. But this did not affect the consumption or patronage of the indigenous rural production since the newly established zamindar families patronized the local craftsmanship as the old families had done.[106] The Marathas, Jats, Gujars, Rohillas, Afghans and Sikhs did considerable damage to property and caused great insecurity to life.[107] In the affected regions, mercantile communities suffered and the prices of foodstuffs went up.[108] Cotton and silk-weaving as well as other industries suffered due to the scarcity of raw material. At times, this resulted in the flight of the weaving class.[109] Insecurity regarding the goods in transit led to an increase in the rate of interest on loans (even upto 12 per cent p.a.) and also accounted for the increase in the rate of discount on the *hundis,* the freight charges and the insurance fee for the transportation of goods.[110] All the same, the disruption caused by marauding activities referred to above was temporary in nature and affected limited regions. Once the inroads subsided and they were successful in establishing their own *zamindaries* and chieftainships, they were equally interested in restoring law and order and normal commercial life in their respective territories. However, eighteenth-century sources highlight other disquieting features which had crept into commercial life. The worst aspect was a lack of enforcement of official Mughal practices in the regulation of trade and commerce. In Mughal territories and across regional governments, the imposition of exorbitant cess (*abwab*) on merchandise in transit was a growing phenomenon.[111] The local administration imposed *rahdari* and also enhanced the rate of *mahsul* on goods. Some regional governments framed their own trade regulations and levied exorbitant *mahsul* duties.[112] The minting of coins by independent rulers led to a multiplicity in the currency system.[113] At times, *baniyas* established their own mints.[114] The currency of spurious coins in the markets adversely affected trade and industry.[115] Sometimes, merchants were exposed to vexatious demands due to the multiplicity of custom houses within a single province. At times, the merchants, in turn, violated trade regulations. In regions where no strong control was exerted over them, they unduly enhanced the prices of their goods; local weavers and artisans were unable to get foodstuffs at reasonable prices.[116] In Bengal, Bihar and Orissa, English East India Company officials resorted to the enforcement of the 'putting out' system in a high-handed manner which harmed the local rural trade.[117] This equally contributed to decline in the quality of the manufactured goods. The monopolistic attitude of the East India Company, which ruled out competition with other traders (even Indian merchants), left artisans and craftsmen at the mercy of agents (*gumashtas*) of the Company. The middlemen (*dalals*) and pykes were often chastised for not procuring goods at the stipulated rates. Wherever possible, the *dalals* themselves resorted to corrupt practice, paying much less than was due to the manufacturers, and keeping a high margin of profit on sale of articles to customers. This adversely affected the Indian silk and cotton industries in these regions.

All these features marked a definite deterioration in the commercial life of India, in comparison to conditions in the seventeenth-cenury. It was more marked in the second half of the eighteenth-century than in the earlier phase. However, this was by no means a uniform phenomenon, as the extent of normality or decline in rural commercial transactions varied in the different regions of north India. Commercial decline was confined only to certain regions. Moreover, a greater strain was felt by the urban commercial centres and inter-provincial trade than by people engaged in rural commercial life. The rural commercial output and its set-up for import-export remained integrated in Mughal territories, and various other independent or semi-independent regional governments under the chief zamindars (*rajas* etc.).[118] Even though these abuses operated in the rural areas of these regions in varying degrees, they remain only incidental and secondary in the decline of rural commercial life. The real causes which led to the decline of cottage industries and upset the commercial pattern of rural society of India were the Industrial Revolution in Europe, and the reaction of Industrialized European society upon Indian trade and commerce during the later decades of the eighteenth-century and nineteenth-centuries. Even before the Industrial era, the English government was particular to protect its cotton industry at home. By Acts of British Parliament in 1700, 1720 and 1765, the use of printed or dyed calicoes was prohibited, and the British government imposed high duties on foreign ships which exported Indian cotton and silk manufactures.[119] After the Industrial Revolution, England was keen to sell its own manufactured industrial goods. This greatly affected the demand for Indian goods in European markets.

Apart from this, after the introduction of the Indian railways during the nineteenth-century, the changed pattern in the means of communication equally affected the Indian rural commercial set-up. Though the impact of all these factors upon the Indian rural economy is undeniable, it is still doubtful if rural commercial production and the cottage industries were ever strangulated. The argument of an ever-increasing decline of cottage industries and handicrafts during the course of the eighteenth and nineteenth centuries has been mostly exaggerated. Trade with neighbouring countries, especially Central Asia and the Middle Asian countries, is a continued feature throughout the seventeenth, eighteenth and nineteenth centuries.[120] The misuse of English political authority in India as a part of British colonial policy and the competition of the Indian trade with the French and the Dutch trade in South East Asia[121] did affect Indian foreign trade, but it gave a new turn to the internal trade. The local rural commercial production found new avenues in provincial markets within the subcontinent, which greatly compensated the comparative loss of foreign trade with respect to handicrafts and cottage industries.[122] Notwithstanding the harassment caused to artisans during the eighteenth-century in Bengal, Bihar and Orissa by officials of the English East India Company, as well as the tussle between local merchants and the agents (*gumashtas*) of the East India Company for the priority of claims over the producing class and consuming markets, British policy became more practical for the sustenance and regulation of trade in the Indian subcontinent. With the gradual consolidation of British rule in India during the course of the nineteenth-century, internal trading rules were enforced for the regulation of local and inter-provincial trade and commerce, which helped rural commercial trade to recover from the strains it had suffered during the chaotic period of the eighteenth-century.[123]

References

1. For detailed annotation, see the notes that follow.
2. *Ibid.*
3. For *Katras in Subah* Malwa, see *Hukam* of Nur Jahan, dated seventeenth *Bahman*, 19 R.Y., Jahangir/1623-4, confirming and narrating the duties of Jagjiwan Das s/o Mathura Das in the office of the Qanungo in *Sarkar* Chanderi, *Subah* Malwa. The document is from the personal collection of Shri Jagmohan Lal Mathur of Udaipur, acquired by the National Archives of India. Also see S.N. Mukhlis, p. 47. For *mahals* as commercial centres, see *Farhrist-i-tappajat pargana Bhagalpur*, dated *Fasli* AD 1179/1771, Secretariat, Central Record Office, Patna. These documents are attached to the *Raqbabandi* documents of Akbar's reign. Though the nature of these two documents is different, the identical names of the villages, *tappahs* in the *pargana* show how the practice of noting down the names of the commercial centres (*mahals*) in the *pargana* was inherited from the Mughal age. For a detailed discussion on the importance of the documents, see my papers "Raqbabandi Documents of Akbar's Reigns" in *The Indian Historical Records Commission Proceedings*, Vol. 1961, pp. 55-60. For *ganjs*, see *Ibid.* and C.P.C., Vol. viii, (1788-89), pp. 241-3, relating to Awadh and the territories of the English East India Company. For rural markets and marts in the hilly regions, see Traill, pp. 192-6.
4. Raj Archives Misc. "Persian Letters to State Officials and to the Officers at the Mughal Court," regd. no. 57, dated AH 1104, 37th R.Y., Aurangzeb/AD 1693, gives a detailed account of the sale of grain crops at Kobahar, *qasba* Toda Bhim, *Subah* Akbarabad, by the *mutsaddis* of the *jagirdar* to the merchants (*beoparis*).
5. MS. Jahani, pp. 18-19, 62, 65-6, 145, 172 and 186-7. The eleven *parganas* of Sehwan (*Subah* Thatta) were well connected through a river and canal system. Four rivers passed through *pargana* Narun. There were four navigational canals (*Guzar*) in Sehwan which connected the rural areas. Also for Thatta, see Hamilton, Vol. I, pp. 71-9. For other regions, see Hodges, pp. 26 and 43. This has been a common sight in India until recently, especially in regions which are not well connected with the main *pakka* roads or the railway system.
6. *Ibid.* Also see Valentia, Vol. I, pp. 90, 181 and 194; Traill, pp. 192-6, giving details of rural manufacturers and markets in Rohilkhand and Kumaon; and Hodges, p. 33.
7. Sujan Rai, pp. 35-6 and 66-9; Chaturman Saksenas *Chahar Gulshan*, compiled and edited by Chander Bhan Kaist Saksena, AH 1173/AD 1759-60; MS in Abdus Salam Collection, no. 62/292, Muslim University, Aligarh, fols. 24b- 88b; Firaqi, p. 136; Traill, pp. 140-55, 193, 195 and 216-17; and Pennant, Vol. II, p. 283. For commercial transactions effected in a religious town like Hardwar, see Raper, pp. 450-6.

8. *Ibid.* Also, Hamilton Walter, *Geographical, Statistical Description of Hindoostan and the Adjacent Territories* (London, 1820), Vol. I, p. 38; and Traill, pp. 216-17. This practice has continued in the rural areas till today.

9. An original *Farman* of Bahadur Shah I, dated 23rd *Muharram*, 4th R.Y., AH 1122/24 March AD 1710, while narrating the *muqaddami* rights of village Annasagar (*pargana* and *subah* Ajmer), refers to both agricultural and non-agricultural residents, including professional castes in the village. Of the latter, only two castes, i.e. scent-manufacturers (*attars*) and greengrocers (*baqals*), are mentioned. Also, see *Cavendish Enquiries* by Honble Richard Cavendish, the Superintendent and Political Agent of Jodhpur and Ajmer etc. (AD 1829-31). The enquiries were related to District Ajmer and based on a village and pargana-wise survey. They were written in Persian and the volumes are available at the District Records Office, Ajmer. Cavendish Enquiries gives details of the agricultural and non-agricultural classes of all the villages and parganas in District Ajmer. The references on the subject in *Waqai-Ranthambore* (AD 1678-80), MS. 2242, Asafiya Library, Hyderabad, and the other revenue literature of the seventeenth-eighteenth centuries, correspond with the names of the professional castes mentioned in the Cavendish Enquiries. Also see Long, Vol. I, p. 97; Hodges, p. 27; and Valentia, Vol. 1, p. 207.

10. *Siyaqnama* (AD 1694-96), MS. No. 858, Central Records Office, Hyderabad, fols. 6a-14a; Br. Mus., Add. Mss. No. 6603 (Yasin's Glossary) for 62a; *Dasturulamls* no. 676, Central Record Office, Hyderabad, fols. 7b-8b (most of the description is of the Deccan). For Punjab, see Denzil Ibbetson, *Punjab Castes* (Lahore, 1916), pp. 266-338. For Bengal, see Arthur Phillips, *Land Tenures of Lower Bengal* (Calcutta, 1876), pp. 1-40.

11. Sujan Rai, pp. 14-15, 36, 44, 75 and 80 (general description of various regions). For Rajasthan, see Raj Archives, *dastak*, dated 11 Rajab AH 1124/AD. 1712, in Persian Documents, Register 11, no. 525 (North West Rajasthan), and *Vat Sangrah*, fol. 24, which mentions many pastoral classes of *gayaris* in South Rajasthan. For Sehwan (*subah Thatta*) tribes like Baloch and Sanriha etc., see MS. Jahani, pp. 59-60, 69, 85 and 134. Valentia, Vol. I, p. 222.

12. *Ibid.* For the migratory habits of the zamindars of the southern *parganas* of Kumaon who indulged in petty trade of the regional products, see Traill, p. 193.

13. Sujan Rai, pp. 63 and 74 (for *subahs* of Multan and Gujarat). The Gujars settled in the *subahs* of Lahore, Delhi and Ajmer (Rajasthan) were in this trade till recent times.

14. Sujan Rai, pp. 2&-33. The following throw light on the *qasbas* in Rajasthan; regarding Udaipur *qasbas*, Man kavi, *Rajvilas* (Hindi), V.S. 1734-1737/1677-78 to AD 1680-81, Canto II, vv, 92-136, Saraswati

Bhandar Library, Udaipur; regarding Jodhpur *qasbas*, the *Abhayavilas* (Rajasthan), fol. 17; Bikaner *Gazal* (Rajasthani) in Nahata collection, Bikaner, VS. 1765/AD 1708-09, Verses 4-5, 11-8, 27-8, 38, 44-5 and 57-8; and Jaisalmer *Gazal* (Rajasthani) in Nahata collection, Bikaner, VS. 1822/AD 1765-66, Verses 70-5.

For the commercial set-up in the *qasbas* of the other territories of north India during the seventeenth century, see Sujan Rai, pp. 28-83; for the eighteenth century, Valentia, Vol. I, pp. 84, 115 and 194, Traill, pp. 146, 149 and 195-6 and Raper pp. 497-8 and 528.

15. For the eighteenth century, *Ibid*. This is still the practice in many a *qasba* in the rural areas of Punjab.
16. *Waqiyat-i-Baburi*, Bibliotheque Nationale, Paris, MS. Pers. 260, fol. 360; *Ain-i-Akbari* (tr. Blockmann), Vol. I, pp. 93-6. *Bernier's Travels*, trs., A. Constable (London, 1916), Vol. I, p. 259.
17. *Epigraphia Indica*, Vol. VIII, p. 27, and *Jain Inscriptions*, Vol. I, Nov. 726, 837-847 and 879. These inscriptions cover the period from the twelfth to the seventeenth century. *Mandapika* refers to corporate organizations in towns, *gosti* to a managing committee of a corporate body or merchant community, *sangh* to a union, and *Shershti* to a leader of the commercial groups.
18. Lon. Vol. I, para 240, p. 97, proceedings, 7 April 1757.
19. Vide official order dated 25th *Ramzan* 14th RY., Muhammad Shah, AH 1141/AD 1730 communicating the decision of the *panchayat* of the *bazar* of *qasba* Mohiuddin (*sarkar* Bari Doab, *subah* Lahore). From this, it is seen that *panchayat* levied one tanka (Alamgiri) on each shop as voluntary religious donation to Gosain Hira Nath of the Jogi family of Jhakpar (Tehsil Pathankot, District Gurdaspur, Panjab). The family documents are in the possession of the Panjab University, Chandigarh. I am obliged to Dr J.S. Grewal of Panjab University for having drawn my attention to the document.
20. *The English Factories in India* (1618-21), ed. W. Foster (Oxford, 1906-7), pp. 198, 269 and 273-4.
21. Raj Archives, Misc. Persian Letters, no. 249 (Aurangzeb's reign) and no. 355 (25th RY. of Aurangzeb, AH 1093/AD 1682).
22. Raj Archives, *Dastur Komwar* (based on *toji* records), Vol. xv, fol. 85, dated V.S. 1799/AD 1742-43, and *bhandar* no. 16, *basta* no. 6, V.S. 1821, 1842, 1855-56 and 1863/1764-65, 1785-86, 1798-1800, and AD 1806-1807. Letter from Hira Chand to Rai Chand, dated 1st bright-half) *Kartika*, V.S. 1754-/6 October AD 1697, in the Vidya Pith Collection, Udaipur (the Old Deposited Records of the State Archives, Udaipur). Amar Singh II's patta to Devadatta, dated 3rd (dark half) *Posh*, V.S. 1763/10 January AD 1707. The above documents give the names of the Gujarati, Malwai, Punjabi and Kashmiri merchants settled in

Rajasthan. Raper, pp. 497-8, mentions that in Kumaon (Srinagar and Almora) the petty shopkeepers served as agent to great *sahukars*, merchants and banking houses engaged in the sale and exchange of merchandise and coins in Najibabad and the Doab.

23. Sujan Rai, pp. 43 and 77. Bahadur Shah I's *Farman* of AD 1710 referred to in note 9 above gives details of the transactions of the *beoparis* (merchants) engaged in purchasing scent etc. from village Annasagar (*pargand and subah* Ajmer), Raper, *Ibid.*, Traill, p. 196, states that in Tarai and even in the hilly region of Kumaon, the Zamindars were in contact with the merchants of Rampur and the other towns of Rohilkhand. They had established local *mandis* and marts. Only in the isolated regions, were the Zamindars who indulged in trade obliged to sell their goods at a low price. However, *Kuth* and other tighter articles were carried by hackeries, buffaloes and *tatoos*. *Kuth* was prepared by the people of the Dom caste on the putting-out system.

24. *Khulasatu-s-Siyaq* (AD 1703), MS. NAI, pp. 61-3.

25. See note 11 above. Also Raj Archives, P.C., Register V. Letter No. 1587, dated 10th *Zulqada* AH 1107/11 June AD 1696. Many such tribes lived in the forests around Gagron.

26. Fol. 46 of *Raj Villas* (Hindi), V.S. 1734-37/1677-78 to AD 1680-81, MS. No. 354, Saraswati Bhandar Library, Udaipur, gives the physical features and tribes of Mewar.

27. *Jaitpur Bahi*, dated V.S. 1726/AD 1669-1670, Raj Archives. Also, *bhandar* no. 1, *basta* no. 57, *nathi* (i.e. attached documents) no. 13, all of V.S. 1815/AD 1758-59, Raj Archives.

28. See note 11 above.

29. Br. Museum, Add. Mss. No. 16859, *Arzidasht-i-Muzaffar Khan*, fols. 2a-4a, 115a and 120b, and letters of Jalal Hissari and Balkrishan Brahman, fols. 28b, 52a-b and 56 (Shah Jahan's reign). Sujan Rai, pp. 17, 60 (Thatta) and 63 (Multan). In Thatta, there were hereditary itinerant fisherman and graziers. Pennant, Vol. I, p. 35. The province of Lahore was known for horse studs. Cross breeding with Persian and Arabian horses was practised for the further improvement of the breed. The *subah* of Lahore supplied the best cavalry to the Mughal state. For details, see *Ibid.*, p. 41. In Tyroot (*subah* Bihar), there were breeding studs of horses of different breeds i.e. Arabs—Tazzies, Turkoman, English, Persian and the cross of these breeds, Valentia, Vol. I, p. 22.

30. Raper, pp. 450-2 and 456-7. A large number of Gosains indulged in commercial and agricultural pursuits. Various Hindu pilgrims to the cultural and religious fairs carried on petty trade.

31. See note 11 above. For nineteenth century Punjab, see Denzil Ibbetson, *Punjab Castes*, pp. 271-90.

32. Raj Archives, *Akhbarat*, dated 15th *Muharram* 36th RY. Aurangzeb/8 October 1692, quotes the price of grains in the camp of Prince Kam Baksh. Wheat: Re. 14 seers; and rice: Re. 15 seers. Various other examples can be quoted.

33. *Ain-i-Akbari*, Hamilton MS., Tuebingen University (W. Germany), fols. 150b-242b and Sujan Rai, pp. 28-83.

34. W. Foster (ed.), *The English Factories in India (1630-33)* (Oxford, 1906-07), pp. 324-5.

35. *Ibid.*

36. MS. Jahanj, pp. 211-12. Pennant, Vol. I, pp. 31-7. Exports from Multan to Persia included cotton, sugar, opium, brimstone, galls, camels and bows.

37. *Ain.i-Akbari*, Hamilton MS., Tuebingen University (W. Germany), fols. 150b-242b. Sujan Rai, pp. 28-83. Raper, Vol. XI, pp. 450-540. Traill, pp. 192-6 (Kumaon manufactures) and p. 226 (exports from the Kumaon hills to the plains). Long, Vol. I, p. 250 (Bengal). Pennant, Vol. I, pp. 50, 71. 79 and 80. Pennant, Vol. II, p. 272 (silk in Assam) and pp. 228-31 and 233 (saltpetre, opium, salt, tobacco and rice in Bihar). Valentia, Vol. I, p. 231 (indigo in Bengal) and pp. 77-8 (silk industry in Bengal). Hodges, p. 27 (handloom industry in Bihar). Hamilton, pp. 71-9 (Thatta).

38. John Van Twist. "A General Description of India (AD 1638)" in Brij Narain, *Indian Economic Life* (Lahore, 1929), pp. 56-67. Under the Indian regulations, the export of gold and silver from India was forbidden. For details regarding the favourable balance of trade, see *Ibid.*, and Balkrishna, *Commercial Relations between England and India (1600-1757)* (London, 1924), pp. 37 and 208.

39. *Ain-i-Akbari*, Br. Museum, Add. Mss. No. 7652, fol. 243a, *Haft Alqim*, Bibliotheque Nationale, Paris, MS. Suppl. Pers. 357, fol. 38b (Bengal). Raj Archives, *Akhbarat*, dated 3rd *Muharram* 10th R.Y. of Aurangzeb, 25 June AD 1667 (*subah* Patna) *Ibid.*, no. 1683, dated 29 *Ramzan* 24th R.Y. of Aurangzeb/12 October AD 1681 states that the discovery of silver in a village of *pargana* Badhnaur (*subah* Malwa) brought an income of rupees one lakh per year. Sujan Rai, pp. 11, 36, 45, 47 and 49, Traill, pp. 157-8 and 188 (copper iron, lead, coarse mica, sandstone and rock crystal in Kumaon). Raper, p. 511 (Dhanpur copper mines were farmed out for rupees four thousand). Long, Vol. I, p. 210 (AD 1760) and p. 250 (AD 1761) (export of iron and stone plates from Ballasore to Calcutta). Pennant, Vol. I, pp. 18 and 41 (metals and gold in the Punjab), Also, Tod, Vol. II, p. 157.

40. *Ain-i-Akbari*, Br. Museum, MS. 7652, fols. 261a-b. Sujan Rai, pp. 75. Salt was extracted in the *subahs* of Gujarat and Thatta, *Ibid.*, pp. 58-9.

41. *Ibid.*, p. 55.

42. *Ain-i-Akbari*, Br. Museum, Add. Mss. No. 7652, fols. 261a-b.
43. Raj Archives, *Akhbarat,* dated 28th *Zulqada* 24th R.Y. Aurangzeb/20 Dec. 1680 mentions the appointment of Abdul Qadir as the *amin-i-namk* and *faujdar* of *Shamsabad* (*Subah* Lahore), nos. 4449/1, dated 18 *Rabi* I, 23rd R.Y. of Aurangzeb/18 April AD 1680 and no. 1451/1, dated 20 *Rabi* I, 2 R.Y. Aurangzeb, *Rabi* I, 24 R.Y. of Aurangzeb/9 April AD 1681. Sujan Rai, pp. 55, 58, 59 and 75.
44. *Ain-i-Akbari*, Br. Museum, Add. Mss. No. 7652, fol. 261a-b, states that merchants purchased Sindh Sagar salt at half to two dams a *man* (maund) and paid duty of one rupee for every 17 *mans* to the state. Also, Sujan Rai, *Ibid.*
45. Sujan Rai, pp. 75. The *zamindari* of the salt mountains at Kheora and Sindh Sagar belonged to the Janjohia tribe settled in the *parganas* of Chahak, Nandna, Makhiala etc. The salt mountain was also known as *Janjohia* after the name of the tribe. For *nunias*, see Lieut, Col. James Skinner, *Tashrih al-Agwam* (AD 1825), Br. Museum, Add. Mss. No. 27, 255, fols. 354-b-356a. Also, Duncan Records, Vol. II, pp. 12-13; Tod, Vol. II, p. 133.
46. Linschoten states, 'an Ox or a Cow is there to be bought for one *Larijin*, which is as much as a half a *Gilderne*, sheep, Hens, and other things after the like rate'. *The Voyage of John Huyghen Van Linschoten of the East Indies from the Old Translation of 1598*, Vol. I (tr. Arthur Coke Bumell) (London, 1885), pp. 94-5. Thus the price of an ox or a cow in Bengal in the late sixteenth century was 7½ annas. For the abundance of cattle, see Sujan Rai, pp. 14-15, 17, 36, 44, 48-9 and 80-2. Hamilton, Vol. I, pp. 73 and 75-7 (Thatta). Pennant, Vol. II, pp. 239-40 (native horses, tatoos, mules, oxen and buffaloes). According to MS. Jahani, p. 85, in the seventeenth century, some of the tribes in Sehwan (*subah* Thatta) paid even the land revenue in terms of cattle.
47. Bolts, pp. 200 (for merchants operating in Bengal, Bihar and Orissa). Verelst, pp. 113-47. Hodges, pp. 80. Pennant, Vol. I, p. 38 states that the *Banias* or merchants and bankers of Multan had settlements in all the commercial towns of India. They sent colonists for a certain number of years to the trading towns of Arabia and Persia. They had establishments from Astrakans to the interior parts of the Mughal Empire. Foster, Vol. II, pp. 259-67. Also see N.A.I., Foreign Deptt. Miscellaneous, Ch. 12, pt. I, *Short account of the Nouputtee Mahajans of Benaras*, pp. 13-18. The mercantile classes i.e., *sahukars* and *sarafs* etc. settled in Central India and Malwa since the sixteenth century and established their firms and territorial beats for commercial operation, John Malcolm, *A Memoir of Central India Including Malwa etc.* (London, 1823), Vol. II, pp. 159-65.
48. Peter Mundy, *Travels* (London, 1914), Vol. II, pp. 95-6. Travernier, *Travels in India* (London, 1926), pp. 32-3. Even in the nineteenth century,

Tod (Vol. II, p. 132) noticed that salt was transported in *tandas* (caravans) of 40,000 head of oxen from Sambher Lake to distant places. Hamilton, Vol. I, pp. 71-5. Raper, pp. 450-4, G.H. Barlow in his letter dated 27 May 1787 to Lord Cornwallis noted that merchants owning goods did not transport them on their own but passed them on to Carriers or *Hundiwalas* who contracted for their transportation and for payment of customs en route, *Duncan Records*, Vol. II, pp. 71-5.

49. For details of the functions of the Zamindars, see my paper on 'Nature of Land Rights in Mughal India' in *The Indian Economic and Social History Review*, 1963, no. I, pp. 10-I5. Hamilton, p. 73.

50. Hamilton, pp. 72-4.

51. For the details of the freight charges from Agra to Surat on camel-back, see Hague's letter dated 5th October 1620 in *The English Factories in India* (1618-21), pp. 47, 51 and 73-4. In AD 1656, the *banjaras* carried saltpetre from Agra to Surat and the cost came to nearly Rs 2.7 per *man* (*man-i- Shahjahani*) vide *The English factories in India* (1655-60), p. 63, and also Travenier, p. 29. The rates varied according to the commodities, safety *en route* and the season. For transportation in Kumaon in the eighteenth century, see Traill, pp. 194-5. In the hilly regions, transportation was costlier as goods were carried over the hills by coolies. Merchandise cost 50 per cent to 75 per cent over and above the purchase price in the plains. Also, *Purchase*, Vol. IV, pp. 268-9. Richard Steel and John Crowther (AD 1615) noted that the merchants operating between Lahore and Asfhan (Persia) charged nearly Rs 120-30 per camel load of pepper and spices. This included the cesses charged at various places. A caravan consisted of nearly twelve to fourteen thousand camels and supplied goods to the villages, *qasbas* and the cities that were on the way.

52. Abbas Sarwani, *Tarikh-i-Sher Shahi*, India Office, MS. No. 218, the 219, fol. 109a. *Waqiat-i-Mushtaqi*, Br. Museum. Add. Mss. No. 11, 633, fol. 50a. *Tarikh-i-Daudi* (Aligarh, 1954), p. 217. Sujan Rai, pp. 323-7.

53. For the maintenance of roads, road pillars, plantation of trees, *chaubutras* and halting placcs, *sarais* and bridges on the rivulets and *nalas* during the eighteenth century, see Raper, pp. 452-4, 507 and 558; Hodges, 9-28; S.N. Mukhlis, pp. 13, 16 and 106; Firaqi, p. 35; and Valentia, Vol. I, pp. 123-4, 130 and 181.

54. Purchas, Vol. IV, p. 268. Richard Steel and John Crowther (AD 1615) noted the existence of *sarais*, provisions for men and horses etc. after every six or seven *krohs* on the way from Agra to Lahore. *Saris* were built by Kings and rich men in commemoration of their dear ones. Valentia, Vol. I, pp. 80-1 and 194. Valentia pays tribute to the Mughals for the proper maintenance of roads, *sarais*, wells etc. but regrets that of late (i.e., in the later part of the eighteenth century), the local

zamindars, even when they were paid large allowances, were not attending properly to the repair of bridges and roads after the monsoons. Also, Traill, pp. 141-2. Long, Vol. I, para 12 (Despatch to the Court, dated 27 January 1748) and para 31. These despatches suggest that in Bengal, it was the traditional duty of the local merchants to look after the repair of roads. As the merchants declined to do it, the East India Company advanced money which was to be repaid out of '*the merchants' accounts current*.'

55. For details regarding the means of transport, see Pennant, Vol. I, p. 35 (camels in Thatta), 99-100 (oxen and hackeries in Gujarat) and 101 (sheep in Goa); Pennant, Vol. II, pp. 239-40 (horses, ponies, mules and oxen); Hodges, pp. 31, 34 and 109 (bullocks, hackeries and horses); Valentia, Vol. I, pp. 70-I and 240; S.N. Mukhlis, pp. 9, 39 and 106 (palanquins and carts); Firaqi, pp. 3l, 56, 74 and 111 (oxen and camels); and Raper, pp. 642-63 and 529 (hill-ponies called *gunts, char singhas* and *chha-singhas, Sura gai*, i.e., cow used for carriage and riding).

56. Raper, pp. 457-8.

57. *Ain-i-Akbari*, Vol. I, (Blochmann), pp. 289-92 and 389. Purchase, Vol. IV, p. 268 (AD 1615). Sujan Rai, pp. 10, 43-4, 59, 77, and 80. Hamilton, Vol. I, pp. 75-7. Hodges, pp. 23-43, gives a detailed description of different types of boats for different purposes, i.e. for passengers and different kinds of goods. A special type of construction and weight was kept up for a boat meant for a particular purpose. Hodges, pp. 38-9, refers to special types of boats constructed for carrying cotton. Twining, pp. 125-8, refers to a journey by boat from Bengal to Monghir, underlining the importance of the Ganges as a cheap and expeditious means of transport. Goods were carried along the Gogra to the Ganges and from thereon transported on larger boats to Calcutta. Valentia, Vol. I, pp. 90-222. Firaqi, pp. 74, 79, 122, 127 and 140; Raper, p. 479.

58. For freight rates in respect of riverborne goods in AD 1639 from Agra to Multan and Multan to Thatta, see *The English Factories* (1637-41), pp. 135-6.

59. For details, see *Ain-i-Akbari*, Vol. I, (Blochmann), pp. 389, 555 and 563; *Tuzuk-i-Jahangiri* (tr. A. Rodgers), pp. 298, *Tarikh-i-Tahiri*, Br. Museum, OR. No. 1685, fols. 58a-b; Peter Mundy, *Travels*, Vol. II, pp. 87-8; Thomas Bowrey, *A Geographical Account etc.* (AD 1669-1679) (Cambridge, 1905), p. 225; Sujan Rai, pp. 323-7; and Hodges, pp. 75-6.

60. S. N. Mukhlis, p. 105. The boatmen in various parts of north India were usually Kashmiris.

61. See note 57 above, Also, Mirza Nathan, *Baharistan-i Ghaibi* (Jahangir's reign) MS. Suppl. Pers. 252, Bibliotheque Nationale, Paris, fols. 2b-4b. For special boats maintained by the English East India Company, see Hodges, pp. 38-9 and Valentia, Vol. I, p. 185.

62. *Ibid*. SN. Mukhlis, pp. 12-13, 15, 24, 95-6 and 99-100. The zamindars were to provide boats on the *ghats* of the rivers from Dacca to Calcutta for the crossing of the troops of the English East India Company. Long, Vol. I, p. 398.

63. Sujan Rai, p. 25. The author gives details of the procedure of the *hundi* system. The *sarafs* had their agents at important commercial places, especially within a beat of 200 leagues. The *sarafs* got their commission and the system worked most satisfactorily. Sujan Rai praises the commercial integrity of the Indian set-up. Also, Raper, pp. 451 and 497. The areas of commercial operation mentioned by Raper extend from Kabul and Kashmir to Bengal. The premium charged by the *sarafs* and their agents on bullion, coinage and exchange on outside coinage ranged from 1½ per cent to 2 per cent.

64. Malcolm, Vol. II, pp. 93-4. In Malwa itself, there were insurance companies at Ujjain, Indore and Mandesore operating since generations throughout Malwa, Gujarat, Deccan and North India. Also, Tod, Vol. II, pp. 501.

65. N.A.I., *Akhbar* No. 185, O.R. dated l8th *Jamada* II, AH 1211/19 January AD 1797.

66. *Ibid*. Tavernier, Vol. I, pp. 36-7. *The English Factories* (1637-41), p. 84.

67. Sujan Rai, p. 25. C.P.C., Vol. VIII, pp. 241-2 (in Awadh and the English East India Company's territories). *Duncan Records*, Vol. II, pp. 10-11.

68. *Bahi of Sarakji*, Saraswati Bhandar Library, Udaipur, documents, dated 22nd (dark half) *Phalguna*, V.S. 1838/20 March AD 1778 and 1st (bright half); *Chaitra*, V.S. 1835/29 March AD 1778, fols. 248a-263b.

69. *Ibid*. Letter, dated 14th (bright half) *Kartika*, V.S., AD 1866/1809, no. 1, File No. 4.

70. Patta, dated 3rd (dark half) *Posh*, V.S. 1763/10 January AD 1707 in Old Deposit Records, State Archives Udaipur, no. 163 (3).

71. Document V.S. 1729/AD 1672-73 in Vidya Pith Collection, Udaipur.

72. Raper, p. 536. The *mahants* of some of the temples of Ajmer (Rajasthan) are still in possession of documents showing rate of interest on the loans given by them to the latter. The priests of the Badrinath temple lent money to the Rajas of Srinagar (Kumaon) and kept two to three villages as security against the repayment of loan which was never paid and the revenues of the villages remained under constant pledge.

73. *Siyaqnama*, MS. No. 858, Central Record Office, Hyderahad, fols. 6a-14a and *Dasturulaml* no. 676, fols. 7b-8b.

74. M.S. Jahani, p. 180. Though this practice can be traced in Bhakkar and the two *sarkars* of Chakarhala and Nasirpur (*subah* Thatta), it may have developed in other regions as well.

75. *Ibid*.

76. Raj Archives. "Misc. Persian Letters," regd. no. 57, dated AH 1104/ AD 1693. Also, Sujan Rai, pp. 43 and 77. Traill, pp. 193-6. The zamindar families themselves were engaged in trade and commerce and set up their *mandis* and marts.

77. *Khulasatu-s-Siyaq* (AD 1703), MS. in N.A.I., pp. 61-3. Traill, pp. 193-6.

78. For details, see my paper entitled 'Nature of *Dehat-i-Taaluqa* (*zamindari* villages) and the Evolution of the *Taaluqdari* System during the Mughal Age' in *The Indian Economic and Social History Review*, Vol. II, no. 2 (April 1965), pp. 166-77, and Vol. II, no. 3, (July 1965), pp. 259-288.

79. Vide Note 64 above.

80. *Ain-i-Akbari*, Br. Museum, Add. Mss. No. 7652, fol. 150b. *Ain-i-Akbari*, Hamilton, Berlin, fol. 127a. *Arzdasht-ha-i-Muzaffar Khan*, Br. Museum, Add. Mss. No. 16859, fol. 103b. Raj Archives, *Yaddasht mal-o-Jihat Wa Sair-a-Jihat*, Sohkhar *Pargana*, dated AH 1069/AD 1658-59, and *Pargana* Riwari (*Subah* Delhi). Sujan Rai, pp. 11, 36, 43-4, 56, 59, 75, 79 and 80.

81. *Ibid*.

82. *Akbarnama* (tr. by Beveridge) (Calcutta: Bib, Ind., 1897-1921), Vol. II, pp. 33-4, and Vol. III, p. 437, *Insha-i-Allami*, MS. Orient. Oct. 1140, Berlin, fols. 47a-48a. *Tarikh-i-Akbari* alias *Tarikh-i-Qandahari* (Rampur, 1962), pp. 32-3.

83. MS. Jahani, p. 186.

84. *Jahangir Nama*, MS., Rampur, F. 172, p. 9, and *Memoirs of Jahangir*, English tr., A. Rogers and Beveridge (London, 1909), pp. 4 and 47, MS. Jahani, p. 186, states that even though *zakat* was abolished by Jahangir, ½ *seer* of the commodity carried by boat were levied in the riverine tracts in Sehwan.

85. *Zawabit-i-Alamgiri*, MS. 2336. Central Record Office, Hyderabad, pp. 101-3. *Mirat-i-Alam*, (AD 1666), MS. 51, Muslim University, Aligarh, fols. 138b and 181a. *Ain Bakht*, MS., Muslim University, Aligarh, 84/ 314, fol. 21lb. *Mirat-i-Ahmadi*, Vol. I, pp. 258-9.

86. Khwafi Khan, Vol. II, pp. 88-90. Shihabat Din Tatlish, *Fathiya-i-Ibriya* (AD 1663) (continuation), MS. Or. 589, Bodleian Library, Oxford, fols. 109b-111a. Raj Archives, *Akhbarat*, no. 1495/2, dated 5th *Jamada* 1, 23rd R. Y. Aurangzeb/3 June AD 1680 and no. 1563, dated 14th *Rajab* 23rd RY. Aurangzeb/10 August AD 1680; and Maharajas Letters, no. 1066, dated 10th *Ramzan* AH 1116/6 January AD 1705.

87. The references quoted from *Akhbarat*, Raj Archives, in the preceding note, and *Akhbarat*, dated 25th Safar 13th R.Y. Aurangzeb/14th July AD 1670.

88. *Mirat-i-Ahamdi*, Vol. I, pp. 258-9, 264—5 and 298-9. Khwafi Khan, Vol. II, p. 88.

89. Raj Archives, *Akhbarat* No. 1636, dated 5th R.Y. Bahadur Shah 16th *Ramzan* AH 1123/17 October AD 1711.

90. *Ibid.*

91. MS. Jahani, p. 172.

92. *Ibid.*, pp. 146-7, 172, 182 and 186-7. Valentia, Vol. I, pp. 217-8 and 225.

93. *Ibid.*, pp. 172 and 186-7

94. *Ibid.*, pp. 146-7, 151, 172 and 186.

95. *Ibid.*

96. Vide Notes 73-8 above. Also, Sujan Rai, p. 11.

97. M.S. Jahani, p. 145 (territory of Sehwan). Like tbe division of the agricultural *riaya* and the zamindar classes into *raiyati* (revenue paying) and recalcitrant (*sarkash* or *zortalb*), the author divides the merchants into two classes viz. *raiyati* (revenue paying and law abiding) and *sarkashi.* The latter violated regulations and indulged in black marketing.

98. *Ain-i-AKbari*, Br. Museum, Add. Mss. No. 7652. fols. 143a-b. M.S. Jahani, pp. 172 and 186. Raj Archives, *Nirkhbazar*, Kohi *Pargana* dated 11th bright half margashirsha V.S. 1785/1 December AD 1728. For the fixation of tbe local rates, see Raj Archives document, dated 25th *Jamada* II, 44th R.Y. Aurangzeb/7 December AD 1700. For the daily reports sent by the *Karori* of the *ganj* to the Central Court, see Raj Archives, Misc. Persian Letters, regd. no. 355, 25 *Jamada* II, 44th R.Y. Aurungzeb/7 December AD 1700, *Ibid.*, dated 27 *Muharram*, 44th R.Y. Aurangzeb/14 July AD 1700.

99. Raj Archives, letter of 5th *Jamada* II, AH 1127/8 June AD 1715 and letter of, dated 13th *Rajab* AH 1127/15 July AD 1715.

100. Raj Archives, *Akhbarat*, dated Safar 13th R.Y. Aurangzeb/June-July AD 1670.

101. *Farman* of Emperor Farrukhsiyar, dated 4th *Safar*, 5th R.Y./18th January 1717. A copy of the original *Farman* in Persian with translation in Surman's Diary, India Office Records, Home Series, Vol. LXIX, pp. 130-1. Also, a photostat copy of the latter in S. Bhattacharya, *The East India Company and the Economy of Bengal from* 1704 *to* 1710 (London, 1954), p. 234.

102. Twining, pp. 86: Calwa, a village on the bank of river Ganges had a flourishing commerce in grain, and near it were some indigo works. Indigo plantations were also run by Englishmen near Hooglie. Valentia, Vol. I, p. 231 (Report, dated 4 October 1802).

103. Sujan Rai, p. 34. Pennant, Vol. II, p. 318, refers to Indian paper used at Calcutta for printing purposes. Apart from paper manufacture in North India at Sialkot, Farrukhahad, Kashmir, Khairpur, Haunpur

and Gaya, its manufacture was becoming quite common in Southern India too.

104. Grose, Vol. I, p. 122. Pennant, Vol. II, pp. 228-30. Vatentia, Vol. I, p. 90.

105. *Hafi Aqlim*, Bibliotheque Nationale, Paris, fol. 38b (salt was extracted from grass and vegetation). Verelst, p. 114 (manufacture of salt at certain seasons by manufacturers on putting-out basis) and Appendix, p. 59. Long, Vol. I, para 979 (Select Committee, 4 August 1767), states that zamindars were engaged in making salt on their lands with the help of artificers. The merchants procured salt from the zamindars at the village level, and a record of the salt produced was maintained. Also, N.A.I. *Akhbars* (Persian), no. 224 OR 5. 8 (c), dated 30 July 1777, and no. 225 OR 5, 81(d), dated *Ibid*. However, Sindhi salt was also imported to Bengal in English ships, *Akhbar* No. 231 OR 5, dated 5 September AD 1777. Verelst, Appendix, pp. 59, *Duncan Records*, Vol. II, pp. 12-13. G.H. Barlow noted that despite the fact that Bengal salt was sold in Awadh at the cheap rate of Rs. 3½ to Rs. 4 per maund, it was not considered of good quality and the Sambhar salt was preferred. Barlow suggested the removal of the custom duties on salt in order in bring down further the price of the Bengal salt so as to procure for it a larger market.

106. The palaces of Patiala, Alwar and Bharatpur built during the eighteenth century contain numerous works of art and craftsmanship.

107. S.N. Mukhlis, pp. 69 and 82 (damage done by the Rohillas). Verelst, pp. 125-7 and Appendix, pp. 111 (Rohillas and Sikhs). Raper, pp. 453-4. Poll tax on travellers attending religious fairs and the heavy duties levied on cattle and merchandise by the Marathas. C.P.C., Vol. VIII, para 234, p. 97 (pillage by the Sikhs, Mewatis and Marathas). *Firaqi*, pp. 33, 48, 50, 64-5, 72-3, 90-1, 117, 121, 124, 126-7, 135 and 142 (Sikhs, Gujars, Marathas, Jats and Rohillas). N.A.I., *Akhbars* Nos. 186 OR 186, dated 6th *Rajab* AH 1211/20 January 1797; no. 187 OR 61, dated 11th *Rajab* AH 1211/22 January 1797; no. 189 OR 63, dated 27th *Jamada* II/22 January 1797 (Sikhs); no. 195 OR 84, dated 28 January 1797 (Gujars); and no. 91 OR 418, dated 9th *Zulqada* AH 1201/1 September 1787 (Rohillas).

108. N.A.I. *Akbar* No. 95 OR 422, dated 10th *zulqada* AH 1201/1 September 1787 (rise in price due to pillage by the Gujars). Twining, pp. 100. Pennant, Vol. II, p. 273. Foster, Vol. I, p. 261. Raper, p. 953, Grose, pp. 78-93. Grose comments that due to the atrocities of the Marathas, even the Hindu merchants especially the *Banyas* and Brahmins, preferred to live under a Moorish Govemment or any other Government. Surat was crowded with Hindu merchants and mechanics.

109. Long, para 87, p. 32. The Despatch to the Court, 18 September 1752, states that the weavers and washermen ran away from Jugdea in Bengal.

110. *Bahi of Sanakji*, Saraswati Mahal Library, Udaipur, nos. 260, 264, 267-8, dated 2nd dark half of *Phalguna*, V.S. 1834/20 March AD 1778 and 1st bright half of *Chitra*, V.S. 1835/29 March AD 1778 mention the rate of interest at 1 per cent or a *takka* per rupee per month. Also, Bolts, pp. 157-8 and Raper, pp. 451-2.

111. Khwati Khan, Vol. II, p. 90. Long, Vol. I, p. 27 (Consultations, dated 30 May 1751) and p. 119 (letter to the Court 27 Februay 1758). *Duncan Records*, Vol. II, pp. 25-31. Grose, Vol. I, pp. 99-100. Foster, Vol. I, pp. 191-2.

112. *Ibid.*, C.P.C., Vol. VIII, pp. 175-6, letter, dated 31 May AD 1788 (Benaras, Bengal and Bihar); pp. 241-3, letter, dated 3 August 1788 (Awadh, Bengal, Bihar and Orissa); and pp. 85-6, letter, dated 29 February 1788, Raper, pp. 453—4. Foster, Vol. I, pp. 268 and 347-8 and Vol. II, p. 88, Duncan Records, Vol. II, pp. 16 and 19.

113. Long, Vol. I, pp. 211-12 (Proceedings, dated 14 April AD 1760), and p. 242. C.P.C., Vol. VIII, p. 29. Bolts, pp. 157-8 and 203-6. Foster, Vol. II, p. 38, Hamilton, Vol. II, p. 497.

114. Bolts, pp. 203-6,

115. *Ibid.*, pp. 158 and 206. Grose, Vol. I, pp. 282-3. G.W. Forrest, *Selections from Letters* etc. (London, 1870), Vol. II pp. 101-2.

116. Khwafi Khan, Vol. II, pp. 395-6. Long, Vol. I, p. 40 (Consultation, 11 December 1752) and p. 57 (Consultation, 24 April 1755).

117. Long, Vol. I, p. 250 (January 1761) and pp. 276-7 (Proceedings, 7 June 1762). Bolts, pp. 73-4 and 190-200. Verelst, pp. 58 and 84-90, *Duncan Records*, Vol. II, pp. 3-9.

118. Traill, pp. 146-7, 149-50 and Appendix, pp. 192-6. C.P.C., Vol. VIII, pp. 241-3 (letter, dated 3 August 1788). Also, Notes 35-47, 53, 59a and 95-8.

119. Taylor, *Letters on India etc.* (London, 1800), p. 164. William Milburn, *Oriental Commerce*, Vol. II (London, 1858), pp. 250-2. D. Macpherson, *The History of European Commerce with India* (London, 1812), p. 282. Balkrishna, *Commercial Relations between England and India*, 1600-1757 (London, 1924), pp. 308-10; N.K. Mishra, *The British Parliamentary Act of 1700 and The Textile Industry of India* (Poona: Proceedings of the Indian History Congress, 1963), pp. 554-61.

120. Raper, p. 530. Mir Ahmad, *Tawarikh-i-Kalan Kashmir* (AD 1834-37). MS. M/829, State Archives, Patiala.

121. Long, Vol. I, p. 119 (Letter to the Court, 27 February 1758).

122. See, Notes 5-7, 29-30, 38, 41, 58, 95-8, and 110-112.

123. For example, see, B.H. Baden Powell, *Economic Products of the Punjab* (Lahore, 1872), and J.L. Kipling's, '*The Industries of the Punjab*' in *The Journal of Indian Art*, no. 20, October 1887, London, pp. 25-40.

ABBREVIATIONS USED IN THE NOTES

Ain-i-Akbari (Tr. Blochmann)	*Ain-i-Akbari* (Tr. by Blochmann), vol.1.
Bolts	William Bolts, *Considerations on Indian Affairs* etc. (London, 1772).
Br. Museum, Add. Mss.	British Museum, *Additional Manuscripts.*
C.P.C.	*The Calendar of Persian Correspondence*, National Archives of India, New Delhi.
Duncan Records	A. Shakespear, *Selections from the Duncan Records*, 2 Vols. (Benaras, 1873).
Firaqi	*Waqai-Alam-Shahi* by Kanwar Prem Kishore Firaqi (ed. Imtiaz Ali Khan Arshi) (Rampur, 1949).
Foster	George Foster, *A Journey from Bengal to England etc.* (London, 1798).
Grose	John Henry Grose, *Voyage to the East Indies etc.* (London, 1766).
Hamilton	Alexander Hamilton, *New Account of the East Indies etc.*, 2 Vols. (London, 1930).
Hodges	William Hodges, *Travels in India During the Years, 1780-83* (London, 1793).
Khwafi	Khwafi Khan, *Muntakhabal Lubab* (AD 1731). Persian Text, Bib. Ind. Calcutta, AD 1860-1874.
Long	John Long, *Selections from unpublished Records of Government for the years 1748-67 relating mainly to the social condition of Bengal with a map of Calcutta in 1784*, Vol. 1 (Calcutta, 1869).
Mirat-i-Ahmadi	Ali Muhammad Khan, *Mirat-i-Ahmadi* (AD 1761). Persian text. 2 Volumes and a Supplement. Baroda, 1927-28 and AD 1930.
M.S. Jahani	*Mahzar-i-Shah Jahani* (AD 1634) (ed. by Yusuf Mirak) (Karachi, 1961).

N.A.I.	National Archives of India, New Delhi.
Pennant	Pennant, *A View of Hindoostan, Eastern Hindustan*, 2 Vols. (London, 1798).
Purchas	Samuel Purchas, *Purchas, His Pilgrims*, Hakluytus Posthumus, IV (Glasgow, 1905).
Raj Archives	Rajasthan Archives, Jaipur (now transferred to Bikaner).
Raper	Capt. F.V. Raper, *Narrative of a Survey for the Purpose of Discovering the Sources of the Ganges – . Brief Survey of the Ganges*, Asiatic Researches, XI (Calcutta, 1810).
S.N. Mukhlis	*Safar Nama-i-Anand Ram Mukhlis* AH 1164/ AD 1751 (ed. Sayyid Azhar Ali) (Rampur, 1946).
Sujan Rai	Sujan Rai Bhandari, *Khulasatu-i-Tawarikh* (AD 1695-96) (ed. by Zafar Hasan) (Delhi, 1918).
Todd	James Todd, *Annals and Antiquities of Rajasthan*, 2 Vols. (London, 1914).
Traill	G.W. Traill's, *Statistical Sketches of Kumaon*, Asiatic Researches, Vol. XVI (Calcutta, 1928).
Twining	Thomas Twining, *Travels in India etc.* (London, 1893).
Valentia	George Viscount Valentia, *Voyages and travels in India, Ceylon, etc. (1802-6)*, 3 Vols. (London, 1809).
Verelst	Harry Verelst, *A View of the Rise, Progress and the Present State of the English Government in Bengal* (London, 1772).
Waqiyat-i-Baburi	*Waqiyat-i-Baburi*, Bibliotheque Nationale, Ms. Paris. Suppi. Pers. 260, Fol. 360a-Babar's Memoirs, Beveridge, III.

Chapter 4

Nature of *Dehat-i-Ta'aluqa* (Zamindari Villages) and the Evolution of the *Ta'aluqdari* System During the Mughal Age*

During the Mughal period, the primary zamindars or the villages were never awarded *mansabs* but formed a regular part of the land revenue administration. It is evident from the Mughal documents that a *zamindari* class with vested landed interests formed an agency for the collection of revenues practically all over North India, even in the well-settled regions. In fact, for the purposes of collection of revenues, the villages in a *pargana* were entrusted to the zamindars, the *chaudharis* and other Government officials specially associated with particular villages with responsibility for full realisation.[1] They were, of course, helped by the normal *pargana* and village revenue machinery. In the revenue documents pertaining to the record-of-rights, the villages under the cognisance of the zamindars were known as *taaluqa* (i.e. *zamindari*) villages and others were recorded as *riayati*.[2] In a *taaluqa* village, a zamindar had no direct control over the assessment made by the *pargana* officials on his own lands and those of the *riayats* in his territorial jurisdiction. The assessment was effected on the individual holdings of the cultivators as well as on the zamindar's self-cultivated (*khudkashta*) lands. The zamindar thus represented the interests of both the state and the agricultural community.

Published in *IESHR*, ii, no. 3, (1965), pp. 166-77; 259-88.

* After the completion of this paper, the present writer came across Dr. S. Nurul Hasan's paper on 'The Position of the zamindars in the Mughal Empire', read at the 26th International Congress of Orientalists, New Delhi, January, 1964 and subsequently published in Vol. 1, No. 4 of *The Indian Economic and Social History Review*. Dr. S. Nurul Hasan has made a good general analysis of the various classes of the zamindars in the Mughal period. The present writer regrets to say that he was not able to draw upon Dr. Hasan's article.

Though the revenues of both the *taaluqa* (*zamindari*) and the *raiyati* villages were assessed by the State,[3] the ultimate responsibility for the collections rested with two different categories of officials. In the *taaluqa* villages where the zamindars owned revenues on their personal lands, the *riaya* and the tenants would normally pay through the *muqaddam* of the village and the *chaudhari* of the area who would deposit the revenue in the treasury (*fotah khana*) or entrust it to the assignee in an assigned territory.[4] The zamindars were usually themselves the *muqaddams* and more especially *chaudharis* in a *pargana*.[5] Even when they did not hold these offices, they could make collection from the *raiyats* through the village officials and their own *gumashtas* and deposit the assessed amount in instalments with the State officials.[6] At times, even in a *zamindari* territory, the collections were made by a specially deputed *pargana* official (*mutsaddi*) with the help of *muqaddam* and the *gumashtas* of the zamindar and the accounts were finally settled with the zamindar concerned.[7] But in any case, the zamindars were held finally responsible for the full realisation of the assessed revenues in their territories and had to make good the Government loss on account of arrears of land revenue.[8] The performance of a *zamindari* service (*khidmat-i-zamindari*) was regarded as an official service to the State.[9] On the other hand, the raiyats of the *raiyati* villages paid revenues either directly to the state treasury (*fotah khana*) or through the village revenue officials and the *chaudharis* who were responsible for the collection of the revenues.[10] The 17th century documents reveal that even *raiyati* villages were included in the collection charge (*amal or batarafdari*) of *pargana* and village officials with full responsibility for the realisations. The expenses of the collection charges of these officials were met from the collected revenues of the *pargana*.[12] In either case, the *pargana* revenue officers had full jurisdiction and authority for the realisation of revenues from both the *zamindari* and *raiyati* villages.[13]

It appears that the institution of zamindars and *zamindari* villages was inherited by the Mughal administration from the past and the Mughal achievement mainly lies in the fact of having reduced such zamindars to revenue paying *malguzars*. The *zamindari* jurisdiction could range from an entire *pargana* to a part of a village. Many of these *zamindari* villages had been settled on a tribal and clan basis. And with the extension of agricultural lands, fresh settlements took place even in the course of the 16th and 17th centuries in various regions of North India.[14]

The zamindars were the leading men of the clans and tribes. In the old settled villages, the ancestors of the *zamindari* families belonged to the conquering clans or were introduced by the state for revenue collection and the maintenance of law and order, or were the pioneer colonizers of the settlements.[15] During the Mughal age, the *zamindari* families held vast tracts of personal lands in their *taaluqa* villages[16] and exercised *zamindari* rights over the agrarian lands of the *riaya*. As both the zamindars and the *riaya* had the right to rent out lands to the tenants, a *taaluqa* village comprised all the three classes, zamindars, *riaya* and the tenants (*muzarian*). In respect of their personal lands subject to revenue payment, the *zamindari* families were also considered as a part and parcel of the *riaya*. The revenue paying and the obedient zamindars of the *taaluqa* villages were named *zamindaran-raiyati* in contrast to the recalcitrant (*zortalb*) zamindars.[17] The *riaya* other than the *zamindari* families may have been introduced by the zamindars themselves as pioneer settlers under their *zamindari* jurisdiction.[18] In the early stages of settlements, the *riaya* in a village may have belonged to the same clan or caste as the dominant *zamindari* family as was the case in some regions of North India even in the 17th century.[19] The contemporary sources also give instances where the *riaya* and the tenants in a village belonged to other clans and castes.[20] Thus in the *taaluqa* villages, the zamindars belonged to certain dominant families and clans and enjoyed an admitted social and economic superiority over a large body of men constituting the *riaya* and the tenants of the lesser known castes who cultivated the greater parts of the lands.[21] The juxtaposition of dominant families and clans and of a miscellaneous collection of inferior tribes is a marked feature of most of the *zamindari* villages. The proportion of the agricultural lands in the possession of the *zamindari* families and the *riaya* respectively varied from village to village or region to region. In the process of conquest, it often happened that the conquering clans established their *zamindari* jurisdiction over the old villages and developed their own agricultural lands but the holdings and land rights of the *raiyat* were usually continued subject to the payment of land revenue. The conquering clans acquired the *zamindari* status along with its rights over the suppressed villages and reduced the original zamindars of these villages either to depressed zamindars or virtually to *riaya*.[22] In such old settled villages, the cultivating *raiyats* of a single or multiple clans and castes continued to hold the bulk of the agricultural lands. The extermination of the former cultivators was a rare step, and during the Mughal age such a policy was adopted only against extremely recalcitrant tribes.[23]

Apart from this, when the State appointed new zamindars in old settled villages, the hereditary rights were maintained, and their lands[24] were usually more extensive than the *zamindari* lands. In the newly colonised villages, it often happened that the members of the *zamindari* family divided most of the land amongst themselves and the *riaya* belonging to other castes were introduced for the development of the remaining land.[25] In course of time, many of the descendants of the *zamindari* family were themselves reduced to the status of the *riaya* paying revenues through the head of the family clan, i.e., the zamindar. In the *riayati* villages also, the *riaya* and their tenants often did not belong to the same castes or clans. In fact, such villages too were inhabited by a variety of castes and clans. As the growth of the villages depended upon historical, ethnic and geographical factors, it is very difficult to draw a rigid line of demarcation between the *zamindari* and the *riayati* villages in any region or a *pargana.*[26] It seems that there was no rigid permanent division either because during the Mughal age any *riayati* village could be entrusted to a zamindar and treated as a *taaluqa* one.[27] On the contrary, despite the recognition of more or less hereditary *zamindari* rights, a *taaluqa* village could under certain circumstances be placed under the direct charge of the *khalsa* administration and the State officials of the *pargana* for the realisation of the revenues.[28] The main interest of the Mughal Government was to realise the land revenue rather than to convert the *zamindari* villages into *riayati* ones. Ordinarily, the *riayati* settlements were docile and revenue paying whereas, the *zamindari* settlements could be turbulent unless forced to pay revenue. Thus it suited the Mughal policy to employ the hereditary institution of *zamindari* so long as the zamindar accepted the responsibility and exerted his influence on the people of his territory for the payment of the state revenues. Far from converting the *zamindari* into *riayati* villages, at times the Mughal Government, in order to ensure regularity of revenue collection, created new *zamindaris* over the hitherto non-*zamindari* villages.[29] This was done as a matter of expediency if any of the influential persons from the *riayati* villages showed recalcitrance,[30] or else the state might award fresh *zamindaris* to such persons who had deserved it.[31] Many a time, a zamindar held the *zamindari* and *chaudhurai* rights over his *zamindari* villages and at the same time acted as the *chaudhari* for some of the adjacent *riayati* villages.[32] As such, he held multiple official status and was entitled to remuneration from different sources. But in the record-of-rights, the *taaluqa* and the *riayati* villages were always shown separately along with their respective realisations and the remunerations of the *chaudhari*.[33]

Of the *zamindari* territory, a full *zamindari* or its portion could form a part of the *khalsa* or *paibaqi* and could be given in *tankhwah jagir* to a *mansabdar* or in *madad-i-maash* and *aimma* to the revenue grantees.[34] In any case, the revenues of *zamindari* villages were assessed by the *amin* or his representative (*gumashta* or *mutsaddi*)[35] with the help of the *pargana* officials.[36] At the time of assessment, the *amin* would take into confidence the zamindars of a *pargana* who would accompany him from village to village and acquaint him with the condition of the *ryots* and their agricultural fields.[37] They could recommend the deserving *ryots* for the grant of agricultural loans and suggest ways and means for the betterment of the condition of the peasants and the increase in the agricultural production.[38] The zamindar had to attest the assessment document (*siyah tashkish*).[39] Notwithstanding the ultimate responsibility of the zamindar for the revenue realisations, the *ryots* could make the payment through the official revenue machinery of the village and the local *pargana*.[40] In case of any unjust assessment by the *pargana* revenue officers and an overpayment by an assessee, the latter could make representation to the higher authorities and realise the excess amount from the zamindar who could later on finalise the accounts with the *pargana* administration.[41] For any arrears in land revenue, the zamindar was responsible to the *karori* (when in *khalsa*)[42] or the *jagirdar* (when in *tankhwah jagir*),[43] the *thanadar* and the *faujdar* of his division.[44] The latter were vested with military powers to realise revenues from a recalcitrant zamindar.[45] In case of repeated recalcitrance and evasion of payment of revenues, a zamindar could be removed from office and his *zamindari* could be conferred on another person.[46] But there is no documentary evidence to indicate the practice of auctioning the *zamindari* of a defaulting zamindar or attachment of his personal lands.[47] Of course, a defaulting zamindar unable to pay the state revenues from his normal resources was often obliged to sell his *zamindari* villages in part or full in order to pay the arrears to the Government.[48] As most of the *zamindari* territories were held as ancestral inherited properties, a zamindar could always sell his shares in the *zamindari* villages mostly to his own brethren[49] or at times even to outsiders[50] to clear the arrears. The zamindar was himself a landowner and possessed proprietary and saleable rights on the personal lands developed by him.[51] His personal lands comprised both self-cultivated tracts (*khudkashta*) and those rented to the tenants on terms of a *patta*. Like any other *raiyat* in his *zamindari* jurisdiction, he had to pay land revenue to the state for all his personal lands[52] excepting those held in *nankar*. It is, however, apparent that even in the 17th century, though the majority of the zamindar families were also a cultivating class on the *khudkashta* lands, in various regions there was a strong tendency on the part of the zamindars owning large *zamindari* territories and personal lands to live simply on the perquisites of the *zamindari* rights and the rent gathered from the tenants in occupation of their personal lands.[53] This was especially true of the families of the *muqaddams, chaudharis,*[54] *desais*[55] (only in Gujarat and Deccan), *tappadars,*[58] and *arbaban* (in Sindh)[57] who were the dignitaries of rural life and owned *zamindari* villages. Here was an anticipation of the future absentee landlordism. In his relationship with his *ryots*, a zamindar had to induce them to pay revenue regularly and possessed coercive powers to suppress the defiant cultivators. He commanded his own small local militia of footmen (*piyada*) and horsemen (*sawars*)[58] and shouldered all the duties of the preservation of law and order as already noted for the previous category of an ordinary Mansabdar-zamindar. A resourceful zamindar possessed even a little *kacha* fortress (*qilhacha*).[59] The expenditure of his small number of soldiers was always met from his own remunerations and as a customary charge from the collected revenues of a village.[60] It was never imposed as an extra cess upon the agriculturists.

In lieu of his services, a zamindar was entitled to *nankar*, i.e., rent-free grant of land and customary charges named *yasum-i zamindari* and *haquq-i-zamindari*. In fact, the right to *zamindari*, even though hereditary, was always conditional upon service to the state. A zamindar was essentially considered as an official for the realisation of the revenues and their regular payment to the state treasury. As such, his remunerations were equally conditional upon the performance of the services to the State. A recalcitrant zamindar could forfeit both his *zamindari* and the remunerations attached to it. But later on, if any of his sons or descendants assured the government of his allegiance and regular payment of the revenues, he was restored to his ancestral *zamindari* and its remunerations. As a revenue paying zamindar, he claimed *nankar* as a matter of right though the amount of remunerations would vary in proportion to the extent of the *zamindari*, its revenues and the services to be rendered by the zamindar. The *nankar*, when given as land in a village or as a full village or still more, was nothing but a *maafi jagir* involving exemption of the payment of the revenues of such lands on the part of the zamindars.[61] The *nankar* lands were regularly assessed by the State and in the revenue documents showing income (*jama*) were recorded as *nankar* along with other categories of *jagir* grants involving exemption from revenues.[62] The assignment of the *nankar* was made within the jurisdiction of a *zamindari*. In various parts of North India, the *nankar* instead of being given as land grant assumed the shape of payment in kind (grain) or cash known as the *rasum-i-zamindari*.[63] In the non-*zamindari* villages (i.e. *riayati*) the remunerations of the *chaudharis* and the *qanungos* were usually termed as *nankar*,[64] though in some regions they continued to be termed *dastur*[65] (i.e. customary rights). Thus, the customary pecuniary rights (*rasum*) of the zamindars like the remunerations of their counterparts in the *chaudharis* of the *raiyati* villages formed a fractional portion of the State revenues of the villages under his jurisdiction. The incidence and the mode of payment to the zamindar equally depended upon the local practice and was fixed in cash per *bigha* of agricultural land or in kind (based on *bhaoli*) per maund of produce for the grain crops and percentage in the cash crop collections. For a territory in *subah* Bihar, Akbar's *farman* mentions the customary rights of the *chaudhurai* cum *qanungoi* of the non-*zamindari* territory fixing 1 *tankah* (a copper coin) per *bigha* of agrarian land as *chaudhurai* and ¼th *tankah* per *bigha* as *qanungoi* for the lands assessed in the jurisdiction of the *chaudhari*.[65] Later on the same family was conferred *zamindari* rights over its *chaudhurai* territory by a *farman* of Aurangzeb's confirming the traditional customary *rasum* (mentioned above) as well as granting *nankar*[67] (*jagir* land).

In various other regions, the 17th century sources reveal that a *chaudhurai* and *qanungoi* was fixed at 2.5% of the collections (2% for *chaudhurai* and 5% for *qanungoi*).[68] At the same time, a *sanad* of Jahangir's reign concedes the *chaudhurai rasum* of 4.5% upon the waste lands to a *zamindari* family in *pargana* Kahalgaon, *sarkar* Monghyr, *subah* Bihar.[69] Another *sanad* early in Shah Jahan's reign grants a gift (*inam*) of *piscary* rights to the same family.[70] As regards exclusively *zamindari* rights, the later sources in Rajasthan put the *rasum* at 2.5% of the collections (1 *seer* against every maund for the collection in kind and 2.5% for the cash crops) as the traditional charge on the revenue collections.[71] It is, however, significant that the zamindar invariably acted as the *chaudhuri* of his *zamindari* villages and the *rasum* of the *zamindari* and the *chaudhurai* were identical and the zamindar could not charge separate rights for his two-fold status within the *zamindari*.[72] Of course, he could hold *nankar* as *jagir* land from the state in addition to the *rasum*.[73] In this context, it is very reasonable to presume that the incidence of the *rasum* known for a *chaudhari* in non-*zamindari* villages during the Mughal age was equally applicable to the *zamindari rasum* in the *taaluqa* villages. This practice is confirmed by the above mentioned *farmans* of Akbar and Aurangzeb for the territory in *sarkar* Tirhut, *subah* Bihar[74] and the later sources available for Rajasthan.[75] A petty zamindar, who held no *chaudhurai* rights and paid his revenues through a big zamindar cum *chaudhari*,[76] could claim more or a less the same *rasum* if he did not hold any *jagir* in *nankar*. In any case, the pecuniary rights of the zamindars, viz., *nankar* and *rasum*, were always deducted from the revenues realised as the State share from the *ryots*.[77] They never formed any additional burden upon the *ryots* who paid only the normal land revenue and the legitimate cesses. Like the *inam* of the *muqaddams* and the *nankar* of the *chaudharis* in the non-*zamindari* villages, the zamindar could, of course, collect his *rasum* in advance from the *ryots* which was always adjusted at the time of the harvest and the realisation of the revenue.[78] In the revenue documents, the *nankar* (when in cash) and the *rasum* were always shown as items of expenditure against the income (revenues) of a *pargana* and the State was entitled only to the net realisations (*hal-i-hasil*).[79]

Apart from the customary *nankar* and *rasum* in lieu of services, a zamindar always claimed a fractional quit rent (*Haq or Haquq-i--Zamindari*) from tbe *riaya* in lieu of his *malkiyat* (*i.e.*, ownership rights for revenue collection only) over the *zamindari* villages.[80] The pecuniary right of *Haq-i-Zamindari* (known as *malikana*) formed a fractional charge upon the gross produce of the *riaya* and could be collected both in kind and cash.[81] This charge was always over and above the normal land revenue and the other legitimate cesses. For the Mughal period, it is not possible to say exactly what percentage of the gross produce was taken as *Haq-i-Zamindari*. We only know that as a nominal quit rent, it depended on the customary practice and could vary from region to region and at times from village to village. However, the later sources show that in some regions of North India, the incidence of ownership quit-rent paid to the zamindar varied from 1.25% (1/80th portion as ½ seer in every maund) to 1.75% (Rs. 1-l2As. for every hundred rupees) and 2.17% (1/46th share).[82] In any particular region, the rate during the Mughal age could not have exceeded the one prevalent in the mid-I9th century when agrarian practices in the *zamindari* villages were still based on old Mughal notions. Most probably, such quit rent rate was rather lower in the 17th and early 18th centuries. During the Mughal age, even when a *zamindari* village was assigned in rent-free grants *viz. altamgha, maafi, madad-i-maash, aimma* etc., the grantees, though exempted from all collection charges from local officials, had in many regions to pay *Haq-i-Zamindari* to the zamindars in accordance with the regional practice.[83] The grantees could pay it as the fixed fractional share or in some places in the shape of further assignment of a portion of their rent-free lands to the zamindars.[84] A faithful and deserving zamindar was granted a tube of honour (*saropa*) or reward (*inam*) in cash in lieu thereof after the asessment of the crops[85] and at times could also be granted *inam jagir*[86] or *madad-i-maash* lands. [87] On the other hand, both as a result of displeasure with a zamindar and on grounds of administrative expediency, the State could suspend a zamindar and convert his *zamindari* territory into *sir-i-hasil* or *khas tehsil* whereby the revenue realisations were entirely entrusted to the *khalsa* administration.[88] Even though the *zamindari* operation was in abeyance in the *sir-i-hasil* teritory, the zamindar was not divested of his pecuniary rights of ownership and was entitled to nominal quit-rent (*Haq-i-Zamindari*) in the form of some fixed percentage of the realisations from the *zamindari* villages.[89] The zamindar could not charge this incidence on his own personal lands for which he paid full land revenue.[90] The above-mentioned *Haq-i-Zamindari* was in lieu of the recognition of the zamindar's rights of *malkiyat* (ownership rights) over the *zamindari* villages for the collection of the revenues.[91] Thus even when his authority for the revenue collection was suspended, the state had the moral responsibility for the maintenance of his family and did not deny him *Haq-i-Zamindari* (ownership dues).[92] But during this period, he had no claim on the *nankar* or *rasum* which were paid only for active *zamindari* service.[93] It seems that in the course of the 18th and early 19th centuries in extensive regions of North India, the customary *zamindari* dues *viz. nankar, rasum, haquq* etc. were compounded into 1/10th of the share of the total revenue collection known as the *malikana* rights.[94] There is no contemporary evidence to show that a zamindar could charge *malikana* dues amounting to 1/10th of the revenues in any territory of North India during the Mughal age till the end of Aurangzeb's reign. According to an 18th century source, it was during the disturbed political conditions prevalent in the later Mughal period that the zamindars, taking advantage of the situation, claimed the *malikana* share of 10% of the revenue collections in most of the regions of North India.[95] The Mughal Government, concerned with the realisation of the uncertain revenues, was constrained to recognise this practice.[96] Notwithstanding this development, many regions in the North India stuck to the original practices of *nankar* (rent free land) and *rasum-i-zamindari* fixed at 2.5% of the total revenue realisation.[97] Apart from the usual perquisites, at times, a zamindar was assessed on a reduced scale of state demand on some of his personal lands,[98] more especially on the newly developed lands and villages.[99] A zamindar would undertake to pay fixed reduced rates (per *bigha* in case of *naqdi* assessment) to the State and was in a position to make profit on the yield even if he rented the lands to the tenants[100] or to the *paikashtkars*.[101] In fact, many a petty zamindar of a village or a portion thereof were never entitled to any *nankar* or *rasum* but claimed only a reduction in state demand on their personal lands as a concession.[102] This was especially true of the petty zamindars paying their revenues through another superior zamindar.[103]

During the Mughal age, a zamindar undertook to collect the land revenue (*mal-o-jihat*) as well as the legal cesses – both agrarian and non-agrarian (*sair-o-jihat*) from the *ryots* under his jurisdiction. He could not impose any extra *zamindari* cess as distinct from a legal State cess. After retaining his own legitimate remunerations, he had to deposit all realisations with the State officials.[104] Though the problem of irregular cesses (*abwab-i-mamnua*) recurred continually throughout the Mughal age, these were imposed more frequently by the *tankhwah-jagirdars* than by the local zamindars.[105] It is only during disturbed political conditions of the 18th century that in some of the provinces, the zamindars imposed their own *zamindari* cesses which were rather irregular and previously unknown.[106]

As regards the nature of the relationship of the zamindar to the agrarian lands in the *zamindari* villages, he was not the proprietor of the lands of the *riaya* (peasant-proprietors) and their tenants. However, the contemporary Mughal documents mention a zamindar as the *malik, i.e.*, owner or landlord of a *taaluqa* village.[107] As such the zamindars always considered themselves as the *maliks* of their *zamindari* territories and exercised rights of *malkiyat* over them. It is this fact which becomes the root of trouble and controversy during the English administration in Bengal and other territories in the late 18th and 19th centuries.[108] But it should be clearly understood that in this context, the term *malik* does not denote absolute proprietor with private rights of ownership in the soil or the agrarian lands of the *zamindari* villages. On the contrary, the cultivators or the *riaya* with proprietary rights over the agrarian lands could alone be designated as the *maliks* of the soil (*zamin*).[109]

The twofold aspect of the nature of the proprietary rights (*malkiyat*), – those of the zamindars over the *taaluqa* villages and of the *riaya* over the soil or agricultural lands in the same village, – has to be distinctly borne in mind. Undeniably, the *zamindari* families as the chief cultivators also owned personal lands quite distinct from those of the *riaya* in their *taaluqa* villages and both the classes, the zamindars and the *riaya* claimed proprietary titles to their respective lands.[110] A zamindar could alienate his personal land over which he exercised both *zamindari* and *biswadari* rights.[111] The *riaya* in the *taaluqa* villages always claimed heritable and transferable rights on their agricultural lands.[112] However, though the perpetual occupancy rights of the resident-cultivators (*riaya-i-khudkasht*) were fully respected during the Mughal age, the transferable rights were always circumscribed by the social and tribal customs of the *riaya* in a village[113] as well as the extent of saleable value of the agricultural land in a particular region. Moreover, the agricultural land was always held on a joint-family basis and for any sale transaction, the consent of all the co-partners was essential[114] and the transaction could take place only within the family regulations. In fact, in a predominantly agricultural country like India where much depends upon artificial irrigation and in a state of society wherein agricultural land had not acquired the character of a marketable commodity in the modern sense, the attributes of proprietary rights depended upon the development of the land especially through the sinking and the maintenance of the wells and digging of the water-channels from the rivulets, innundation canals, tanks and ponds. The *riaya* who developed their lands through the construction of the wells or the maintenance of the water-channels from the rivulets[115] and ponds etc. or by building embankments on land dependent on hill torrents or breaking up waste lands always[116] claimed proprietary title to their lands. Such a notion of proprietorship lingered in various portions of North India even till the 19th century.[117] Such of the *riaya* or the occupancy tenants who did not possess any wells of their own and used rented wells always claimed only occupancy rights over the lands.[118] In case of need, the *riaya* might claim financial assistance (*taqavi* etc.) from the State through the zamindars for the digging of the wells or the development of the lands,[119] but the zamindars had no powers of interference in the management of the cultivated holdings of the *riaya*.

The zamindars had, of course, the powers to introduce new cultivators for the extension of the agricultural lands,[120] providing for the cultivation of the deserted land[121] or on the holding of the *riaya* and the tenants where the line of inheritance became extinct.[122] The zamindars exercised full discretion for the choice of the new settlers in a village and could give the lands to whomsoever they pleased. The new settlers always derived their right of settlement from the zamindars. If the new settlers were permitted to dig their own wells and develop their own means of irrigation, in due course they and their descendants could claim heritable proprietary rights on the lands.[123] In the villages developed exclusively by the *zamindari* families, whenever the cultivators outside the *zamindari* circle were introduced on the lands, they always owed their right of settlement or those of their forefathers to the zamindars.[124] In villages, such *riaya* and tenants owing their own original settlements or those of their forefathers to the zamindars and paying the land revenue through the latter were technically known to be cultivating their agricultural lands with the sanction (*razamandi* or *basalah*) of the zamindars.[125] This technical language simply implied that the cultivators would pay the revenues only through the zamindars who would enjoy their customary perquisites (*rasum* and *haquq*) thereupon.[126] It never meant that the *riaya* or the *muqaddams* were simply tenants-at-will, liable to be ejected if the zamindar withheld his sanction for the further cultivation of the lands. Once the cultivators introduced by a zamindar in a village acquired occupancy rights and developed their own means of irrigation, especially by digging a well, they could not be ejected.[127] In an agrarian society, with scarcity of agricultural labour on the one hand and the Mughal state's pressure on the zamindars for the maximum cultivation of the agricultural lands on the other, the question of ousting of the cultivators or withholding the formal sanction (*razamandi*) does not arise. In practice, the *riaya* with self-developed means of irrigation always claimed heritable proprietary title and the hereditary tenants had always had occupancy rights on the land. Only the tenants holding periodical tenures or purely temporary *pahikashtkars* did not claim such rights. From the official view point, the tenant's distinct status was always recognized and like the *riaya,* they were reckoned as regular *asamian,*[128] *i.e.,* persons subjected to assessment and liable for payment of land revenue. The assessment on the holdings of the tenants was always done by the State.[129] In various parts of North India, the tenants would pay rent to the landlord and the land revenue directly to the State.[130] The Mughal state had as much direct relationship with the tenants as with the *riaya* and under the revenue regulations, all agricultural facilities for *taqavi* loans and remissions of land revenue were equally afforded to both.[131] For want of any contemporary evidence, the exact incidence of the land rent (*malikana*) cannot be ascertained; we only know that it formed a fractional share of the gross produce and depended on the regional practice.[132] The hereditary tenants usually possessed their own wells and, like the *riaya,* were responsible for the maintenance of artificial means of irrigation.[133] In case a tenant got an already constructed well on his lands from the landlord, he had to pay separate customary rent for it. An early 18th century document relating to a village in *pargana* and *subah* Ajmer puts the annual rent of a *kacha* (unlined) well at Rupee one (1/-) having been paid by the tenants to the landlords ever since the later half of the 17th century.[134] Such rent would vary from one region to another and would be undoubtedly lower for a low-cost *kacha* well as also in those regions in North India which had much greater rainfall than in an arid territory like Rajasthan.

Apart from the hereditary tenants, even periodical tenures were known to the Mughal age. It is known from the late 17th century documents that for the purposes of reclamation, the landlords would often rent out the fallow lands to the tenants.[135] The lands may have been rendered fallow due to fall in the water level of the wells[136] or innundations[137] or because it was beyond the physical capacity of the families of the landlords to till all the lands in their occupation. As the Mughal state did not allow the agricultural lands to become *banjar*, it afforded concessional rates of assessment under the reclamation regulations. The landlords were allowed to rent out lands to the tenants on easy terms of assessment, viz., application of sliding scale rates for the first five years, fixed assessment for the next five years and normal rates of assessment only after the expiry of ten years.[138] Thereafter, the tenants would hold the land on a perpetual lease, if they so chose.[140] It was always the responsibility of the landlords to keep up the cultivation of the agricultural lands or else the State would step in to provide for the cultivation of the fallow lands with the help of the tenants. In the *zamindari* villages, it was the special responsibility of the zamindars to reclaim the fallow lands and hence they leased out the *banjar* and jungle lands to the tenants either on periodical or perpetual leases.

An hereditary tenant or a tenant with a periodical lease on easy terms of assessment could not be ejected from his holding so long as he paid a regular rent to the landlord. The 19th century *Cavendish Enquiries* on the agrarian condition in District Ajmer (erstwhile *sarkar* and *subah* Ajmer) conducted after the British occupation in Rajasthan show that in some of the villages even hereditary tenants possessed the traditional transferable rights of mortgage and sale of their holdings.[141] But in view of the fact that such transactions were rather rare in the 17th century, no verdict can be given on this aspect for the latter period. However, the occupancy rights of the hereditary tenants are fully confirmed by the contemporary documents.[142] An occupancy tenant could surrender his tenancy rights of his free choice and for that he had to sign an acquittance deed stating that he had left the land of his own will, and would not advance any further claim on the land when leased out by the landlord to another tenant.[143] As the tenants holding periodical tenures for the reclamation of lands always enjoyed concessional assessment rates in the first few years of cultivation, the Mughal State did not like the frequent migration of the tenants either.[144] Apart from it, though a *paikashtkar* (non-resident cultivator) with a permanent holding in the village of his *paikasht* might claim proprietary title to land,[145] a purely temporary or periodical *paikashtkar* could not claim such rights. The scarcity of good uncultivated land in his own village and the abundance of it in the one to which he proceeded was the main cause of the *pahikasht* in a village. At the same time, there were villages where the *riaya* or the zamindars could not bring their entire holdings under cultivation owing to scarcity of agricultural labour on the part of the members of their family or their tenants, permanently or temporarily. Such families would also give their lands to non-resident cultivators either just for a season (one crop)[146] or for a year (both the crops) or for a few years.[147] In such circumstances, the *pahikashtkar* entered into a contract for a fixed period stipulated under the terms of a *Patta* and would not claim any rights of ownership on the land.[148] Similarly, a zamindar might give waste cultivable land of a village to the non-resident cultivators if the lands could not be fully covered by the *riaya khudakashta* or the resident hereditary tenants. A *pahikashtkar* had to provide for his own plough, cattle and seeds,[148] but under the state revenue regulations prevalent practically all over North India, the *pahikashtkar* was always assessed on reduced rates in comparison to the *riaya khudkashta* and the hereditary tenants.[150] Thus financially, a *pahikashtkar* was in an advantageous position and this served as a bait for the physical exertion involved on the part of his family for having either two different holdings in separate villages or a single holding in a village other than his native one. This equally prevented the wastage of land and consequently loss of revenues. With such a dual status in two different villages, a *pahikashtkar* could simultaneously fall under the jurisdiction of two separate *zamindaries*.

So far one can see a zamindar's proprietary title to a *taaluqa* village was quite distinct from the proprietary right to the agricultural lands therein which were claimed both by the *zamindari* families and the *riaya*. However, a zamindar could claim certain nominal customary cesses from the *riaya* for the grass or the fuel taken from the adjoining jungle and could also impose piscary charges. But all such impositions were reckoned as regular and legal state, cesses and they were credited to the revenues (*sair-o-jihat*) of the villages and the *pargana*.[151] They never formed a part of the private income of the zamindar. A zamindar as the *malik* of the *zamindari* villages stood in the same relation to a village as a *muqaddam* known as the *malik* of a village.[152] Such *malkiyat* implied rights of ownership for the collection of the State revenues rather than proprietary title to the soil or the agricultural lands in the *zamindari* territory or a village.[156] It carried with it a position of authority in the tribe or a village. As perquisites of such *malkiyat*, a zamindar was entitled to *malkiyat* rights, *viz., rasum* and *haquq* (when escheated to direct *khalsa* administration, *i.e., sair-i-hasil*). Thus the *zamindari* perquisites were considered as malkiyat and along with the *zamindari* acquired a hereditary, transferable and proprietary character. In the greater part of North India, a zamindar possessed absolute private rights to alienate his *zamindari* lands whence he collected revenue along with his perquisites. Similarly, a *muqaddam* of a village could also sell out *muqaddami* rights over the *riaya* of a village. The 17th century and early 18th century documents dealing with the sale and gift deeds covering the *subahs* of Awadh, Bihar and Bengal mention the zamindars as *maliks* (owners) and refer to various sale transactions of the *zamindari* villages[155] which affected the *malkiyat* rights for the revenue collection and the customary perquisites attached to them. Such a sale transaction would transfer a *zamindari* village or a portion thereof indicating the exact boundaries of the village or its transferred portion with a claim on the wells, means of irrigation, trees and the *riaya* living in it.[156] Some transactions covering the sale of a village might exclude particular holdings of specified *riaya*[157] or certain named tombs and mosques etc.[158] Evidently a sale of a *zamindari* transferred the zamindar's claim on the *riaya* for the revenue collection and the customary charges thereupon rather than the agricultural lands of the cultivators. Notwithstanding the sale of a *zamindari* portion regarded as *malkiyat*, the absolute proprietary rights of the different strata of the *riaya* on their respective lands were neither involved in the transaction nor disturbed. In fact, the *malkiyat* and the *malikana* rights of a zamindar were not incompatible with the absolute proprietary rights of the *riaya*. Dr. Irfan Habib appears to have misunderstood the nature of the *malkiyat* rights of the zamindars and his statement that the proprietary rights of the zamindars and those of the *riaya* were mutually exclusive is not consistent with certain facts available to us.[159] The rights of *malkiyat* of a zamindar in a village co-existed with the *malkiyat* rights of the *riaya* over their lands. The *riaya* could not be ejected by a zamindar who possessed no *malkiyat* rights over the agricultural soil of the former. The occupancy tenants could not be dispossessed either and the Mughal state protected the rights of even such tenants as took periodical leases of the deserted wells and the lands attached to them in a village.[160]

Apart from the above categories, there were *zamindari* villages developed by the zamindars (also known as *dehat-i-taaluqa*) wherein the *zamindari* rights as well as the ownership of the soil and the agricultural lands were exclusively claimed by the *zamindari* families. It often happened that the members of the pioneer *zamindari* family divided the lands amongst themselves and each man brought what he could under cultivation without regard to any regular shares. Each became full proprietor of his holding but had to pay *haq-i-zamindari* to the Chief of the tribe or family. Most of the agrarian lands in such villages were cultivated by the *zamindari* families on joint family basis though the share of each individual member was always earmarked in accordance with the law of inheritance.[161] In case, for the purposes of reclamation of land, the members of the *zamindari* family introduced outsiders as *riaya* with a right to sink their own wells, the latter could as well claim proprietary rights on the payment of the quit-rent of *haq-zamindari*. A zamindar always possessed the right to create under-tenures. But the introduction of *riaya* from outside would change the nature of *dehat-i-taaluqa* and would modify the character of a *dehat-i-taaluqa*. Ordinarily, the zamindar families would not introduce the *riaya* class on their lands but the spare land, if any, would be leased out to the tenants or purely temporary *pahikashtkars*.[162] The Mughal state, guided by the policy of extension of agricultural land, always recognised the rights of this class of pioneer cultivating families and colonisers.[163] For reclamation of land for agricultural purposes, a person could be granted a portion of a jungle and waste culturable land (*banjar*) on most moderate terms of assessment rates.[164] Such a right of reclamation of large tracts of land also entailed with it *zamindari* and *biswadari* rights in land.[165] These dignitaries of rural life could also purchase waste culturable land from the State.[166] Private transactions amongst the zamindars themselves were quite tenable and common.[167] In case the State needed privately owned agrarian land for the construction of a monument or other purposes, it had to purchase it from the zamindars and the private owners.[168] The zamindar had the rights of transfer, mortgage and sale of the *zamindari* rights in the land.[169] Such transactions did not affect the position of the tenants who continued to enjoy either their hereditary rights or their rights as short term lease-holders.[170]

Any man of substance who undertook to develop large tracts of jungle or *banjar*[171] land was made into a zamindar through a royal sand.[171] The evolution of such *zamindari* rights was a landmark in the Mughal agricultural development policy which was followed till the end of Aurangzeb's reign and even thereafter. These *zamindari* grants had an important impact on the rural economics and created a class of hereditary land owners of substance. Such landowners invested capital in agriculture, leased out land and also employed agricultural labourers,—a development which was not without advantages to the agrarian life of the community. It attracted enterprising families in the agricultural community who could also command the services of a body of tenants. The fact that the zamindars themselves were also cultivators (*khudkashta*) and with their tenants undertook full responsibility for the development of land proved helpful to agricultural progress. It relieved the pressure of population in some areas and led to the growth of new villages. The clearance of the jungles helped the Mughal administration's efforts to suppress the recalcitrant agricultural tribes and enabled the latter to settle as revenue paying peasants under the leadership of a zamindar. Where the development of the villages was tribal in character, it afforded opportunity for transporting bodily the tribal communities and this led to a speedy development of the area concerned.[172] A zamindar had both vested interests in and sufficient leisure to look after the development of his lands and could exercise influence with the local administration for getting the *taqavi* loans for himself and his tenants. At the same time, he could put pressure on his tenants so that no portion of the land remained uncultivated. A zamindar could also be trusted to have an adequate knowledge of local geography required for the extension of irrigation.[173] This pattern of agricultural economy worked smoothly as long as the

Mughal revenue department was strong enough to administer it and as long as there was a demand for leasehold lands. With the disintegration of the Mughal state in the 18th century and the growth of population and pressure on land in the 19th century, the position became confused in different regions of North India and created extremely difficult problems for the British administration,

Thus it is clear that even the *zamindari* villages (*dehat-i-taaluqa*) were of two types: first those where the zamindars exercised *zamindari* rights but the agricultural lands were owned both by the *riaya* and the zamindars themselves with rights to rent out their personal lands to the tenants; and secondly, such self-developed villages as were owned exclusively by the *zamindari* families with similar rights for renting the lands to the tenants. As the development of the new villages depended on the local geographical factors and the situation with regard to the tribes and castes, the proportion of villages developed exclusively by the zamindars varied from province to province and region to region. In some provinces or regions, they were very numerous and in others, much less so. Except for the difference in the nature of the title to the agricultural land, the zamindar's right in the two types of the *zamindari* villages discussed above were identical. In both the cases, the zamindars engaged for the payment of the State revenues, receiving in return the customary *rasum*, exercised alienable *zamindari* rights and above all were governed by the same laws of inheritance. Even in such *zamindari* villages as were not affected by the sale transactions, the zamindars' shares were continually divided and subdivided simply because of the laws of inheritance. The petty shareholders in a single village thus belonged generally to the same clan descended from the same ancestral stock.[174] As a result of such fragmentation of the *zamindari* shares, gradually in both types of *zamindari* villages, the petty zamindars began to pay the revenues through a superior representative zamindar.[175] In a few generations, the petty zamindars in villages developed by the zamindars were bound to be reduced virtually to the status of peasant-proprietors though their customary rights would still be recognised in the form of a reduction in revenue assessment. This was equally true of the petty *zamindari* families in the *zamindari* villages of mixed character in respect of their personally owned lands. It cannot be stated with certainty if such a stage had already been reached in any of the villages towards the close of the 17th century because during the Mughal age even the petty zamindars continued to hold the *zamindari* title regardless of the size of their shares in the *taaluqa* villages.[176] But the reduction of the petty *zamindari* shares to peasant-proprietorship holdings on a large scale certainly took place towards the close of the 18th and the beginning of 19th century.[177] This accounts for the existence of the ancestral villages jointly owned by the *bhaiachara* communities in the early 19th century in some parts of North India where the petty *zamindari* families lost the *zamindari* status except for holding petty shares in the villages subject to a reduced revenue demand.[178] On the other hand, in some other parts of North India, despite a similar development, the old *zamindari* titles and status lingered on.[179] This varied development explains the differences in the findings of the English revenue experts in the late 18th and the 19th century with regard to the different provinces.

The Taaluqdars

For the *subahs* of Awadh and Bengal, the late 17th century documents record the existence of a class of *taaluqdars* acting as intermediaries like the zamindars. Literally speaking, *taaluq* or *mutaliqa* just meant 'pertaining to' and could be freely associated with the territories of the *tankhwah jagirdars*,[180] *khalsa* officers,[181] zamindars[182] and *ijaradars*. But in the technical territorial sense, the term *taaluq* or *taaluqa* seems to have connoted only a *zamindari* territory.[183] In the *Ain's* detailed revenue tables of the *mahals* of *subah* Bengal, some of the *mahals* are mentioned as *taaluqa* and some of the *taaluqdars* are described as independent.[184] The *Ain* does not record these terms for any other *subah*. Besides, it mentions the existence of the zamindars in Bengal as in the other *subahs* and mentions their castes in the *mahal* tables.[185] It cannot be stated with certainty if the *Ain* identifies *taaluqdars* with the zamindars and *bhuyas* but it is clear that the *taaluqs* or the *mahals* of the *taaluqdars* were in the nature of *zamindari* territories. Evidently, the term *taaluqdars* were known to Bengal under Akbar or even in the pre-Akbar era but it cannot be traced in the revenue literature for any of the other *subahs* under Akbar. In Bengal too, with the consolidation of the Mughal rule late in Akbar's reign and under Jahangir, the *taaluqdars* no longer remained independent and were brought within the Mughal pattern of *zamindari* and revenue regulations.[186] It is equally known from the 17th century Rajasthan Archives and the administrative manuals that even in other provinces of North India, *taaluqa* villages[187] or at times even *taaluqa parganas* were associated with the *zamindari* territories.[188] Thus the term *taaluqa* in the territorial sense was associated as much with a zamindar as with a *taaluqdar*. At the same time, it is evident from the revenue literature of the second half of the 17th and 18th centuries that even though they also belonged to an intermediary class, technically the *taaluqdars* were always distinct from a proper zamindar.

For *subah* Awadh, the 17th century Allahabad documents show that a person might exercise *zamindari* rights[189] or *taaluqdari* rights or the same person might be zamindar for some villages and *taaluqdar* for others but his *taaluqa* would comprise both categories of villages.[190] This fact raises doubts as to whether the two terms zamindar and *taaluqdar* were synonymous. The 18th and early 19th century documents of Awadh always differentiate between the zamindars and the *taaluqdars.*[191] For the *subah* of Bengal, the revenue literature of the 18th century not only insists on but even offers adequate explanation of the difference in the status of the two classes. According to this evidence, a *taaluqdari,* compared to *zamindari,* had a lower territorial jurisdiction and status.[192] This is in line with the 17th century tradition in Bengal.[193] The act of *zamindari* lay in the payment of revenues (*malguzari*) to the state; a zamindar was always confirmed by a royal *sanad* and paid nominal *peshkash* to the State.[194] On the other hand, a *taaluqdar* with a large *taaluqa* would assume the role of a zamindar when he paid the revenues of his territory directly to the state but, by and large, the petty *taaluqdars* paid the revenues of their *taaluqas* through a superior zamindar-cum-*chaudhari* who acted as the representative.[195] Such a zamindar paid the revenues not only of his own *zamindari* but even of the petty *taaluqas* of the *taaluqdars* under his jurisdiction. His *zamindari* was reckoned to cover both his personal *zamindari* and the petty *taaluqas.* However, he possessed no rights of sale or mortgage of the *taaluqdaris* under his jurisdiction. A zamindar in Bengal, unlike one in North India, could not alienate the title of *zamindari* but could sell only his rights over *panj taaluqa* (*i.e.* rights over revenue collection) and *chaudharai* rights along with the relevant perquisites.[197] Ordinarily, the hereditary charitable grants, *viz., debottars, brahmottar, mehtran* and grants to the medicants (*fakirs*), were not affected when a zamindar sold *taaluqa* village and the holders of such grants retained their rights under the purchaser now entitled the taaluqdar.[198] Except when otherwise stipulated in his *taaluqdari patta,*[199] a *taaluqdar* possessed alienable rights and could sell the *taaluqdari* title.[200] Except in the case of the *taaluqa* villages colonised and developed by the *taaluqdar* himself[201] a *taaluqdar* was not the owner of the soil or the agricultural lands of the *riaya* and his proprietary rights in a *taaluqa* were exactly of the same nature as the zamindar's rights over his *zamindari.* But unlike a zamindar or a *chaudhari*, he was not entitled to *nankar* as *maafi jagir* from the state but possessed both customary rights of *rasum* as well as malikana.[202] He claimed *malikana* only when the *taaluqa* was declared *sair-i-hasil*.[203] Ordinarily, a *taaluqdar* did not have an ancient claim to the *taaluqa* and the majority of the *taaluqas* were established after they were purchased from the original *taaluqdars*.[204] The extensive sale transactions of the I7th and 18th centuries established a large class of petty *taaluqdars*. A person who did not hold any *zamindari* from the State but purchased *zamindari* rights of a few villages or a village from the original zamindar was known as *taaluqdar*.[205] Ordinarily, the sale or mortgage of the petty *zamindari* shares would take place without the prior sanction of the Government but in the case of transactions involving large *zamindari* shares, formal sanction of the Government was generally solicited and always granted by the state.[206] The purchaser of a *zamindari* property comprising *taaluqa* villages would hold the *zamindari* title only when confirmed with *zamindari* rights by the state for the direct payment of the revenues to the latter. The essential criterion of *zamindari* lay in the recognition by the state through an issue of a *zamindari sanad* and a *taaluqdar* of a few villages, unless confirmed by a royal *sanad* in the *zamindari* rights, could not be designated as a zamindar.[207] According to Muhammad Reza Khan, revenue consultant to the Governor-General in Council[208] (l789 A.D.), there were different categories of the zamindars and the *taaluqdars*.[209] A *zamindari* might be an ancient one covering territories colonised and developed by the zamindars or might have been purchased or granted as a gift by the state or created through the award of a royal *zamindari sanad*. A colonising zamindar could alienate tracts of waste culturable land to persons entitled *taaluqdars* who, after having developed the land, might exercise the *malkiyat* rights in it for sale or gift but would pay the revenues to the state only through the zamindar. A purchaser of *taaluqa* villages from a *taaluqdar* or a zamindar acquired similar *malkiyat* rights but would have to pay the revenues through the original zamindar. But if a zamindar granted a *taaluqdari patta* to any one in respect of villages and lands already under cultivation, the *taaluqdar* would enjoy such *malkiyat* rights only if these were specifically transferred to him according to the terms of the *patta*. A *taaluqdar* who paid direct revenues to the state was named *huzuri* whereas a *taaluqdar* who paid through a zamindar was described as *muskuri*.

The above mentioned analysis of *taaluqdari* rights in the *subah* of Bengal does not apply strictly to the other *subahs* of North India. It seems that in Awadh, Allahabad and other portions of North India, wherever the *taaluqdari* system existed, the position of a *taaluqdar* was basically different from that in Bengal. A *taaluqdar* was a zamindar who engaged with the State for the payment of the revenues of his own *zamindari* villages as also of various other petty *zamindaries* under him.[210] The revenues were assessed by the State and the *taaluqdar* was subject to all the rules and regulations binding a zamindar for the payment of revenues to the State.[211] By himself, a *taaluqdar* might be a powerful zamindar or, more usually, a small and influential zamindar, but in either case, he assumed the role of a superior zamindar who was not only responsible for the payment of revenue for his own *zamindari* villages but also acted as a channel for the revenue payment of the inferior zamindars who did not deal directly with the Government.[212] Similarly, in joint *zamindari* villages, one of the co-sharers who acted as representative for the collective payment of the revenues, was known as a *taaluqdar*.[213] But when a zamindar and a *taaluqdar* had under them villages paying equal amounts of revenue, the former invariably enjoyed a better income and a higher status.[214] It is, however, significant that where such a system of *taaluqdari* came into being, three parallel claims, by no means mutually incompatible, were established on the *taaluqa* villages and their agricultural lands. Both the *taaluqdars* and their dependent zamindars belonged to intermediary classes in hierachical order whereas the *riaya* were the owners of the soil. The dependent zamindars by no means surrendered their transferable *malkiyat* rights over their *zamindari* villages but only shared their perquisites (*rasum* and *haquq*) with the *taaluqdars* and the details of such apportionment would depend upon the local practice. Even though such *taaluqdari* rights tended to become hereditary, there is no documentary evidence for the 17th century to show that a *taaluqdar* possessed any transferable proprietary rights of sale or mortgage over the *zamindari* villages of the dependent zamindars within his *taaluqa*. He possessed such rights only on his personal *zamindari* villages, some of which he might have purchased, and the same rights continued to be vested with the dependent zamindars in respect of their respective shares in the *zamindari* villages.[215] Thus a *taaluqdar*, when mentioned as the *malik* of the *taaluqa* comprising his own *zamindari* and dependent *zamindari* villages, was entitled to only a share in the perquisites of the dependent zamindars and, as such, both the intermediaries claimed parallel rights of *malkiyat* over the *zamindari* villages.[216] Like a zamindar, a *taaluqdar* might own his personal lands in his *taaluqa* but neither he nor his dependent zamindars could claim proprietary rights in the soil and the agricultural lands of the *riaya* under them.[217]

The documents of the latter half of the 17th century dealing with *subah* Awadh show that the *taaluqdari* villages were by no means consolidated into regular and compact *taaluqdari* estates though they are tending fast towards such a development.[218] The payment of revenues by the inferior zamindars through a *taaluqdar* was purely voluntary based on mutual convenience, though, in due course, the relationship acquired a customary force. It is known from the later sources that in a territory of *subah* Allahabad, as late as the early 19th century, many inferior zamindars paid their revenues through a *taaluqdar*, others directly and still others only at times through a *taaluqdar*.[219] For the Mughal period, there is no evidence to show that a *taaluqdar* was ever appointed by the State and, as such, the *taaluqdari* rights were not based on a royal *sanad*. All the same, the Mughal State did confirm and recognise the *taaluqdari* rights of an individual.[220] In some portions of North India, especially Bengal, a person who did not hold any ancient *zamindari*, but purchased a few *zamindari* villages, was also known as a *taaluqdar*.[221] The laws of inheritance and the nature of the proprietary rights governing the *zamindari* system during the Mughal age were conducive to the growth of the hierarchical pattern of *zamindaries* and the ultimate evolution of an intermediary class with *taaluqdari* rights. The fact that a *zamindari* and *chaudharai* possessed heritable and proprietary traits helped the fragmentation of the *zamindari* jurisdictions and the shares in the joint family *zamindaries*. The absence of the law of primogeniture in the Muslim and the Hindu civil laws led to the division of the proprietary *zamindari* rights amongst the children in a fanily.[222] A *zamindari* might be held jointly by the members of a family but share of each co-partner was always clearly stipulated and the perquisites (*rasum*) were divided amongst the co-sharers in ratio to their respective shares in village. The share of every partner in the *zamindari* villages or a village was usually reckoned more in terms of assessed revenues[223] than in terms of measured agricultural lands. (*i.e. bighas* etc.). An apportionment of the assessed value of the villages might take place by dividing the entire *zamindari* property into either twenty shares (biswas) (on the analogy of twenty biswas in a bigha[224]) or sixteen shares (annas) derived from the fact that 16 annas made a rupee[225] or on the basis of some other local practice of arithmetical division.[226] Such a method of reckoning, based in principle on apportionment of the revenues of the *zamindari* villages, would in working *ipso facto* take into consideration both the quality and quantity of the lands based on detailed classification for the purposes of assessment. This system was valid in all cases – even when the *zamindari* consisted of a single village, with petty zamindars holding shares as also when the shares of a single zamindar were scattered in numerous villages.[227] An individual might alienate his personal share in a joint property village[228], but the sale of the entire village or a part of the common property could be effected only by all the co-sharers jointly and the sale document would bear the signatures of all the partners.[229] The Allahabad documents covering *subah* Awadh show that by the latter half of the 17th century, an individual's inherited *zamindari* property might range from a few villages to the 1/6th portion of a single village.[230]

Apart from the law of inheritance, the sale transactions further accelerated the process of fragmentation of *zamindari* rights. The same documents show that as small a portion as 1/6th or 1/3rd of the inherited share in a *zamindari* village (*i.e.*, 1/18th portion of the village) was sold out by the owner to an outsider.[231] Ordinarily, it was not possible for every petty shareholder with limited resources to make direct arrangement with the State for the payment of revenues as he could not afford to take on the *zamindari* obligations for the collection of the revenues in the entire area. So when a village was shared by many zamindars, the settlement might be made with the biggest of the zamindars whom the other co-sharers would appoint as their representative. Similarly, the petty zamindars of a village of a single village or several villages might undertake to pay through a superior zamindar.[232] Thus whether the petty *taaluqdars* paid revenues through a superior zamindar as in Bengal or the inferior zamindars paid through a superior zamindar named *taaluqdar* as in Awadh and some other provinces, the basic tendencies in the development of the agrarian structure in the latter half of the 17th century is the same throughout the Mughal empire. The fact that the *taaluqdars* are mentioned in the Code of Revenue instructions issued by Aurangzeb suggests that the class was more numerous and widespread than can be actually ascertained for the available contemporary regional records.[233]

Of course, in various regions of North India, both the superior zamindar and his dependent zamindars continued to be designated as zamindars.[234] It cannot be asserted that this became the universal practice in the whole of North India. In many regions, the petty co-sharers in the joint *zamindari* villages continued to pay revenues on an individual basis without the intermediary institution of *taaluqdari*.[235] However, the 18th and the 19th century sources reveal that in the major portions of North India, the *taaluqdari rights* were found in existence as an established fact[236] though the regional names of the *taaluqdari* rights might vary.[237]

The process of alienation of the *zamindari* villages and the evolution of the practice on the part of inferior zamindars of paying revenues through a superior zamindar (i.e. a *taaluqdar*) had an important impact on the land rights of the various intermediary classes. The 17th century documents pertaining to the *subahs* of Awadh and Bihar reveal that a rich and influential zamindar would purchase *zamindari* villages or a single village or fractional portions of various villages lying not only within one *pargana* but scattered over different *parganas* in a *subah*.[238] Consequently, some *zamindari* families expanded their territorial jursidictions and *zamindari* villages or fractional shares in various *zamindari* villages while others who sold out their *zamindari* shares in full or part gradually dwindled in economic and social importance. Similarly, the sale of the *chaudharai* rights on the part of a zamindar-cum-*chaudhari* for the clearance of the arrears of revenues equally resulted in the reshuffling of the *chaudharai* and the *zamindari* shares in the inherited *zamindari* villages.[239] A resourceful zamindar not only inherited his own shares in the ancestral *zamindari* and *chaudharai* villages but could also buy out the shares of the defaulters both from within his own joint-family *zamindari* villages[240] as well as from the outside zamindaries.[241] Presumably, these developments which are known to have taken place in Awadh and Bihar would be equally true for other territories of the Mughal Empire. Thus it was not only the royal power for the grant of a large *zamindari* but also the power of the purse which became an important factor in the expansion of the non -*sanadi zamindari* rights. Similarly, the growing practice of the dependent zamindars paying revenue through a representative zamindar led to the evolution of a new type of superior zamindars (entitled *taaluqdars* in some regions) who claimed large territorial jurisdictions (*taaluqas*) composed of both their personal *zamindaries* and those of the petty zamindars and paid revenues to the state for the entire territory. The emergence of this class of superior zamindars owed its origin to the local social and agrarian conditions and was based on mutual agreement between the parties concerned rather than on royal grant.[242] It equally found favour with the Mughal state policy which was mainly concerned with the realisation of the revenues of the *zamindari* villages with multiple shares. All the same, such zamindars with *taaluqdari* rights were clearly distinguished from the zamindar holding ancestral *zamindaries* simply through royal grant.[243] Lastly, the widespread sale transactions affecting the *zamindari* rights fundamentally altered the original caste basis of the old *zamindari* villages. The hereditary *zamindari* or even *muqaddami* rights over the villages or the village shares were freely transferred on an inter-communal or inter-caste basis.[244] Thus the economic factor led to the reshuffling of the old caste-or clan-based *zamindari* settlements in various villages in North India and greatly fostered the growth of composite settlements and villages. This process becomes marked in the later half of the 17th century though in the newly colonised settlements and villages in particular, the caste or clan basis remained an important feature of agrarian organisation throughout the Mughal age.[245]

Quite distinct from the evolution of the *taaluqdari* institution, the *zamindari* system was drifting towards a hierarchical pattern of rights in other ways as well. The Mughal state would appoint a zamindar through a royal *sanad* with jurisdiction over numerous villages which had proved recalcitrant.[246] Ordinarily, a high *mansabdar* exercising *faujdari* powers was entrusted with *zamindari* rights over the *taaluqa* villages in recalcitrant areas.[247] At times, the Mughal Emperor, when pleased with the meritorious services rendered by a local official or a zamindar, would reward him with *sadr zamindari* (big *zamindari*) covering numerous *parganas*.[248] Such a highly placed zamindar might act as *sadr* zamindar for the. entrusted *parganas* and as a simple zamindar for other *parganas* even on an interprovincial basis.[249] The creation of such big *zamindaries*, more or less parallel to the already existing *zamindaris* of hereditary chiefs (*zamindaran-i-umda*), is a significant example of the emperor's role in the evolution of the *zamindari* rights. The hierarchical pattern of the *zamindari* system was still more widespread in the territories belonging to the Chief-Zamindars (*zamindaran-i-umda*) where there were different categories of zamindars enjoying different types of perquisites (*rasum*).[250]

References

1. M. I. Berlin, fols 24a-24b. (draft, dated A.H. 1065/1654-55) *Dasturulaml,* Ms. Br. M. Add 6599, fol. 40b. R.A.J. vide f.n: 10.
2. R.A.J. '*Yaddasht-i-Dehat-i-Mazru*' (i.e. list of cultivated villages) of *Pargana* Dadakar (*sarkar* Alwar, *subah* Agra) of Aurangzeb's reign gives the names of the villages as well as those of the *muqaddams* and the primary zamindars who usually belong to the Meo tribe. A zamindar's *taaluqa* jurisdiction may cover a few villages. '*Yaddasht-i Muwazat-i Pargana Deosa sarkar* and *subah Akbarabad* (Agra)' gives list of the *taaluqa* villages of Raja Bishan Singh (Aurangzeb's reign) and the *raiyati* villages in the *pargana.* S.N. Ms. no. 858, C.R.O. Hydbd, fols. 28b-29b (draft of *Siha Tashkhish Jama* for *kharif* and *rabi* Crops, dated A.H. 1104/1692-93 A.D.) fols. 46a-49a (draft of *Jama Kharch wa Kharch Mal-aihat wa Sair-Jihat* dated 40th-41 R.Y., Aurangzeb/F.Y. 1104/1696-97 A.D.). Also, Mirat I, pp. 173-74; Also suppl., pp. 215-17, 228-29. Dr. Irfan Habib's distinction between the *taaluqa* and the *raiyati* villages is quite correct. (*The Agrarian System of Mughal India,* 1963. pp. 141-43) but his analysis of the relationship of the zamindars to the agrarian lands within the *taaluqa* villages cannot be accepted in view of the explanation offered later.
3. M.I. Berlin fols. 4b-5b; A.D. nos. 897 (1-2), dated 1684; no. 1218, dated 28.2.1687; no. 1223, dated 19.11.1688.
4. M.I. Berlin, fols. 5b-6b.
5. Jahangir's *Farman,* dated 13th R.Y./1613 A.D. confirming *zamindari* and *chaudhurai* rights on Hiranand s/o Madhusudan in the *tappas* of Barari, Kabarha Dewara, Arar and *tappa* Haveli, *pargana* Kahalgaon, *sarkar* Monghyr, *subah* Bihar. The *farman* also mentions that the family had been in the possession of the royal *farman* for the same rights since *kharif,* A.H. 975/1567-68 A.D. (vide I.H.R.C., Vol. XVIII, January, 1942, pp. 188-196. Original *farman* and tr. by M. L. Roy Chaudhuri). Also, see f. nos. I, 53-57.
6. A.D. nos. 897 (1-2), dated 1684; no. 1223, dated 19.11.1688; 1220, dated 31.3.1688.
7. A.D. no. 1218, dated 28.2.1687 states that in the village of Aharwara, *pargana* Fatehpur (*subah* Awadh) the *zamindari* of Sayyid Muhammad Arif, the assessment as well as the collection was made by the Sayyid Muhammad Qaim, the royal *mutsaddi.*
8. A copy of *mahzarnama* of Sunder Thakur of Darbhanga, dated A.H. 1062/1652 vide Qeyam Uddin Ahmad, 'Origin and Growth of Darbhanga Raj (1574-1666), Based on Some Contemporary and Unpublished Documents', I.H.R.C., Vol. XXXVI, Part II, pp. 92-94.
9. M.I. Berlin, fol. 24a; Also, Jahangir's *farman,* dated 13th R.Y./1613 A.D. vide f.n. 5.

10. *Ibid*. fols. 5b-6b, 24a-24b; Ms. Br. M. Add. 6599, fols. 40b, 42a-43a, 45b.

11. R.A.J. *Muwazna* documents of *pargana* Khizrabad (*sarkar* Sirhind, *subah* Delhi), dated A.H. 1069/1658-59 A.D.) ; M.I. Berlin fols. 24a-25b; Ms. Br. M. Add. 6599, fol. 40b. The same procedure was continued in the 18th century in *subab* Bihar. See documents relating to the *mauzas*, *tappahs* and *mahals* etc. of *pargana* Bhagalpur, *sarkar* Monghyr, dated F.Y. 1179-1180/1771-73. A.D., S.C.R.O. Patna. Also see introduction to my Paper on '*Raqba-Bandi* documents of Akbar's Reign', *I.H.R.C.*, 1961, pp. 55-57.

12. M. I. Berlin, fols. 4b-6b.

13. *Ibid*.

14. R.A.J. vide f.n. 98 (for *subah* Ajmer). Ms. or. Oct. 113, Berlin, fols. Is-4a (for *subab* Bihar); Elliot, C.A., 'Chronicles of Oonao', pp. 29-85. Based on numerous family documents, Elliot has given an excellent account of the various clannish settlements in the villages *tappas* and *parganas* of the district of Oonao (erstwhile *subah* Awadh) during the medieval period down to the end of the 17th century.

I5. *Ibid*.

16. For example in *subah* Gujrat, a *desai* who also belonged to the *zamindari* class paid land revenue on his own cultivated lands amounting to 3000 *Mahmudis* (vide Ms. Suppl. 482, fols. 170b-171a. B.N. Paris, a *parwana*, dated 9th *Muharram* A.H. 1003/24th September, 1594 A.D. Also see my paper on "The Position of *Desai* in the *pargana* Administration of *subab* Gujrat under the Mughals". *I.H.C.*; 1961, pp. 150-55; f.n. 13). Also see R.A.J. *Qalbabandi* documents of *pargana* Riwari, *subab* Delhi, dated A.H. 1067/1656-57 AD. Also, M.S. pp. 191-92 for *subah* Sindh.

17. M.S. p. 182.

18. *Ibid*. pp. 191-92.

19. See f. n. 14.

20. An original *Farman*, dated 23rd *Muharram* 4th R.Y (Bahadur Shah I) A.H. 1122/24th March, 1710 A.D. concerning the *muqaddami* rights and abolition of *jizya*, *begar* and other cesses in village Annasagar (*Pargana* and *Subab* Ajmer) mentions three clans of the resident cultivators in the village viz. *Baghbans*, *Gujars* and *Jats* besides the non-cultivating professional castes of the *Attars* (scent-manufacturers) and the *Baqals* (green-grocers). The cultivating clans are mentioned along with their hereditary tenants (*muzarian warasan*) which shows that those clans had settled in the village since long. The names of the *muqaddams* are mentioned but their clan or caste is not mentioned.

21. *Ibid*. This is in fact as much true of a zamindaŕ on a larger scale as of a *muqaddam* in a village though a *muqaddam* may also belong to a

zamindari family. For the heterogeneous tribes and castes of the *riaya* and tenants in *zamindari* villages, see *Cavendish Enquiries*. In village Hoth, *pargana* Ramsar, there were *Jats, Raiputs* and *Jogis* (fol. 154a); in village Sawaila, *pargana* Ramsar (fol. 374b) *Jats* claiming rights of settlement since 8 generations and *Rajput Rhumias*; village Thahari, *pargana* Ramsar (fol. 516b), *Jats, Gujars, Brahamans, Mahajans, Biraghis* and *Kalals*.

22. Elliot, C.A., *op. cit.*, pp. 45-47. Elliot quotes that from the time of Babur onwards, the Sengur Rajputs established their *zamindaris* in *pargana* Asoha (*sarkar* Lucknow *subah* Awadh) after having subjugated the *Lodh* zamindars and for eleven generations, the two tribes lived more or less peacefully. *Ain*, however, names the caste of the zamindars in this *pargana* as *Ahnin* (J. II. tr. pp. 189) which in any case shows the suppression of the *Lodhs*. Also see C.L. Tupper, *'Punjab Customary Law in Different Districts*, Calcutta 1881, Vol. II, Introduction, pp. 1-98.

23. *T. J.*, tr. Rodgers, I, pp. 100, II, pp. 28, 160-61, *R.A.J.* Shahjahan's *farman* regd. no. 39/64, dated 22nd *Shahban* 5th R.Y./14th March, 1632 A.D., M.S., pp. 10-11, 40-42; *The English Factories* (1655-60), pp. 65-67; Elliot, C.A. *Chronicles of Oonao*, pp. 53-54, 63-65.

24. *Waqai R.* (M. U. Aligh) pp. 4-5.

25. M. S., pp. 191-92.

26. The *Ain* in its statistical tables gives the castes of the zamindars for practically all the *parganas* in the provinces (*Ain*, Br. M. Add. 7652, fols. 177b, 274b) and the 17th century documents provide the *taaluqa* villages practically for every *pargana* (see f. n. 2).

27. *R.A.J.* vide f. nos. 2, 99.

28. See f.n. 46.

29. *Waqai. R.* pp. 4-5.

30. *Ibid.*

31. For helping the Mughal State in the conquest of Palamau and suppressing the recalcitrant zamindars of Morang (North Eastern border of *subah* Bihar), Aurangzeb rewarded Mahinath Thakur (1667-87) of Darbhanga with the *sadr zamindari* In *Sarkar* Tirhut (*subah* Bihar) and *zamindari, malkiyat, chaudhurai* and *muqaddami* rights in a few *parganas* in the *subahs* of Bihar and Bengal (vide a copy of Aurangzeb's *farman,* dated 14th, *Rabi* II 9th R.Y./1665 A.D., *I.H.R.C.*, 1961, pp. 94-98). Also see f. n. 248.

32. M.I. Berlin. fols. 24a-b, 26a-27b-74; Ms. Br. M. Add. 6599, fols. 40b, 42a, 43ab, 45a-53a.

33. *Ibid.*

34. *Ibid*; Also M. S. pp. 18-22, (*sarkar* Bhakkar, *subah* Multan), 174, 182, 191-92 (*sarkar* Sehwan, *subah* Sindh); *Mirat* I. p. 173 (*subah* Gujrat); Also see f. nos. 180-83.

35. Under Akbar and Jahangir, the assessment work was done by the *karori* and *bitikchi* (*Ain*, Br. M. Add, 7652, fols. 142a-144b; Ms. Hamilton, Berlin, fols. 120a-121b; A.N. Br. M. Add 26, 207, fols. 161b-162b; Also, *Tarikh-i Arif Qandhari*, Ms. Rampur, p. 178) or a specially deputed officer (vide B.G., B.N. Paris, fols. 61b, 284b). From the reign of Shahjahan onwards, the assessment work was done by the *Amin*. (Kh. S.N.A.I., p. 32; Ms. no. 74, Sulaman Collection, M.U. Aligarh, fols. 15b-16a; *R.A.J.* 'Maharaja's Letters', regd. nos. 835 and 840, dated 39th R.Y. A.H. 1106/1694-95, A.D. M.I., Berlin fols. 4b-4b).

36. *Ibid*.

37. *Ibid*.

38. *Ibid*.

39. *Ibid*.

40. A.D. no. 1218, dated 28.2.1687 states that in the village Aharwaro, *pargana* Fatehpur (*subah* Awadh) which was in the *zamindari* of Sayyid Muhammad Arif, the realisation was made by Sayyid Muhammad Qasim, the *mutsaddi* in F.Y. 1094/1687 A.D. As the document states that the assessment was also done by the same *mutsaddi*, the latter cannot be taken as the *gumashta* of the zamindar.

41. *Ibid*. It further states that Saiyed Muhammad Qasim, the *mutsaddi* over-realised the amount of Rs. 155/- from Madhuwan Das (the *riaya*) who subsequently realised it from Sayyid Muhammad Arif, the zamindar.

42. *A. N.* Br. M. Add 27, 247, fols. 331b-332 a.

43. *Ibid*; also M. S., pp. 82-87; '*Maktubat-i-Khan Jahan*', Br. M. Add. 16,859 fols. 48a, 52a-52b, 55b-56b, 62b; *Muraqqat-i Hasan*, Ms. 217 Rampur, p. 252; *R.A.J. Vakil* Reports, no. 369/239 dated 28th *Shaban* 34th R.Y. A.H. 1101/17th May, 1690 A.D.

44. For *Faujdar*, see *Ain*, Br. M. Add 7652, fols. 141a-142a; A.N. Br. M. Add 27, 247, fols. 331b-332a: S.N. Hydbd, fols. 52a-52b; *R.A.J.* category no. 4 regd. no. 1395, dated 14th *Safar* 37th R.Y. A.H. 1105/15th Oct, 1693 A.D. For *Thanadar*, See B.G. I tr. Borah, pp. 341, 352; II, pp. 403, 516-17; *R.A.J. Waqai pargana* Othal *sarkar* Ujjain (*subah* Malwa) regd. no. 688, dated 24th *Jamada* I 49th R.Y. A.H. 1117/13th September, 1705 A.D. 656, dated 19th *Rabi* II, 49th R.Y. A.H. 1117/30th July, 1705 A .D.

45. *Ibid*.

46. *Waqai. R.* pp. 256, 397-98. The retention of a *zamindari* was always subject to the payment of revenues and in case of recalcitrance, the Mughal state was competent to dismiss the recalcitrant zamindars

and to appoint new ones (vide Mughal *farman* dated 3rd *Shawwal* A.H. 1124/3rd Nov., 1712 A.D. in '*Majmua-i mutfarika*', Ms. Orient. fol. 306, Berlin).

47. According to an expert opinion of Sayyid Gulam Muhammad, a *zamindari* or *chaudhurai* or *taaluqdari* could not be auctioned during the Mughal age and that this practice was introduced only by the English Government in Bengal. (vide Ms. or. fol. 234, fols. 18a-b).

48. The *mahzarnama* of Sunder Thakur of Darbhanga vide *I.H.R.C.* 1961, pp. 92-94. See details of the sale of the *chaudhurai* shares on account of arrears of land in A.H. 1062/1652 A.D. in the above mentioned *mahzarnama*. The *zamindari* shares were also sold in the same manner.

49. *Ibid.*

50. See f. nos. 229-30.

51. Akbar's *Farman*, dated 38th *Ilahi* Year/A.H. 1001/1593 A.D. states that Gosain Vithal Rai of village Jaitpura (near Mathura *subah* Agra) purchased land from the zamindars (vide K.M. Jhaveri, *farman* no. IV, fol. 13) also, f. nos. 161, 165.

52. Ms. Suppl. 482, B.N. Paris, fols. 170b-171b; M.S., p. 182; A.D. nos. 897, 1206 and 1233 (Aurangzeb's reign); Ms. Br. M. Add 24, 039, fol. 36a; Ms. Or. Oct. 113J, Berlin.

53. M.S., pp. 191-92 comments for the zamindars of *sarkar* Sehwan (*subah* Sindh) that most of the *zamindari* lands of the *arbaban* (*chaudharis* etc.) and the *muqaddams* were cultivated by their men and that the zamindars of their own did not put in any physical labour for the development of their lands (*chaks*). Also A.D. nos. vide f. nos. 218, 238. See the case of Sayyid Muhammad Arif holding *zamindari* villages in *subah* Awadh.

54. See f.nos. l, 4 and 8.

55. M.S. p. 182, 191-92.

56. M.I. Berlin, fol. 6b; Kh. S. N.A.I. p. 33.

57. See f.n. 53.

58. *Ain's* statistical tables of the *parganas* in the account of the *subhas* vide f. a. 26.

59. A.D. nos. 789, dated 1684 A.D., 1225 (late Aurangzeb's reign, after Dec. 1689 A.D.); Baikus Ms. no. 954/4 Subbanullah Collection, M.U. Aligarh, fol. 61a. Every zamindar did not own a fortress. Throughout the medieval ages, the local tribes and the zamindars possessed fortresses at strategic places in a territory (M.S., pp. 6, 10, 59-60, 199-200). There was usually a fortress in a *qasba* or the headquarters of a *pargana* (*Ibid*). In its detailed statistical account of the *parganas* and *mahals* of the *subahs*, the *Ain* is particular to mention *pacca* (brick or

stone made) fortresses against the names of the *parganas* wherever situated.

60. M.I. Berlin, fols. 4b-5a, 6a-b clearly states that for the employment of soldiers (both footmen and horsemen), the *zamindars, tappadars* etc., had to pay salary in cash or kind to the soldiers from within their own remunerations. Also *R.A.J.* Category no. 4 regd. no. 149, dated 1693 A.D. ; Vakil Reports dated 29th *Rajab* 31st R.Y./1688 A.D.

61. *R.A.J. 'Yaddasht Haqiqat-i Arazi Muwazna Pargana Riwari'* (*subah* Delhi), uncatalogued sheet no. 7 (Aurangzeb's reign) ; Aurangzeb's *Farman* to Mahinath Thakur of Darbhanga, dated 14th *Rabi* II 9th R.Y. vide *I.H.R.C.*, 1961, pp. 89-98; M.I. Berlin, fol. 74b ; Ms. Oct. 113J, Berlin.

62. *R.A.J.* (*Ibid*) ; S.N. Hydbd, fols. 53a, 59a, S.C.R.O. Patna, *Behi* (Register) of Nawab Hushiarjang, Vol. I., no. 1823, of District Bihar, fols. 3a-b.

63. Akbar's *Farman* to Gopal Das of Darbhanga vide *I.H.R.C.* 1961, pp. 90-91; A.D. nos. 782 and 1214 (Aurangzeb's reign) ; Baikus, fol. 45a, 52a-b.

64. M.I. Berlin, fols. 24b, 26b, 45a, 69b, 74a ; Ms. Br. M. Add 6599, fols. 51b-53a ; R.D. vide ms. or Oct. 113J, fol. 5b; *Nigar Nama,* N.A.I. fol. 76b; Ms. no. 132/362 Abdus Salam Collection, M.U. Aligh, fols. 162a-b.

65. Ms. Br. M. Add 6599, fols. 28b, 42b, 47a; *Nigar Nama,* M.U. Aligh, fols. 162a-b ; Baikus, fols. 41b-42b; *Cavendish Enquiries, Pargana* Binai, p. 3.

66. Akbar's *Farman* issued to Gopal Thakur of Darbhanga vide *I.H.R.C.* 1961, pp. 90-92. A small copper *tankah* was equal to a *fulus* or a *dam* weighing nearly 315-27 grains and was reckoned at 1/40th, *i.e.*, 2.5% of a rupee. (vide Stanley Lane-Poole, *The Coins of the Moghul Emperors of Hindustan in the British Museum*, edited by Reginald Stuart Poole, London, 1892, pp. XCIII-XCIV). A large copper *tankah* weighing about 618-644 grains was equal to 2 *dams*. (See details, *Ibid;* S.H. Hodivala, *Historical Studies in Mughals Numismatics*, Calcutta, 1923, pp. 113-114 ; J.A.S.B., N.S. XXVII, pp. 80-96; Irfan Habib, 'The Currency System of the Mughal Empire (1556-1707)', *Medieval India Quarterly*, M.U. Aligh, Vol. IV. No. 1-2, pp. 8-12). Here in this context, it seems that a *tankah* stands for a small copper *tankah* equivalent to a *fulus* or a *dam* which is confirmed by the continuance of a similar practice in some of the territories of *subah* Awadh in the 18th century. (See details vide A.D. no. 299, f.n. 82). Taking the full value of the gross produce of the crops per *bigha* in terms of regional contemporary prices of the crops, the *zamindari* demand (*rasum*) of a copper *tankah*, small or even large, would form just a fraction of the gross produce.

67. Aurangzeb's *Farman,* dated 14th *Rabi* II, 9th R.Y./1665 A.D. issued to Mahinath Thakur of Darbhanga, *Ibid.*, pp. 94-96.

68. M.I. Berlin, fol. 74b and Ms. Br. M. Add 6599, fols. 42b, 46a-48b, 53a put 2.5% as the joint emoluments of the *chaudhari* and the *qanungo*. At

the same time, the details of the drafts show that 2% was claimed by the *chaudhari* and 5% by the *qanungo*. That a *qanungo* claimed only 1/4th share of that of the *chaudhari* is confirmed by Akbar's *Farman* to Gopal Das of Darbhanga (vide f.n. 66). The incidence of the *nankar*, of course, varied from region to region. F.K., M.U. Aligarh shows 2.7% as the joint customary charges of the *chaudhari* and *qanungo*. In contrast to this, an 18th century *dasturulaml* quoting the *sanad* appointments of *chaudharis* in some of the *parganas* of *Subah* Shahjahanbad (Delhi) puts 1% as the fixed *rasum* of the *chaudhari*. It does not state the exact incidence of *rasum* of a zamindar but mentions it as based on local practice (vide Baikus, fols. 41b-43a, 45a-b).

69. A *sanad* of the *subadar* granting the *rasum* of *chaudhurai* of 4½ per cent upon waste lands, dated 1020 F.Y./1613-14 A.D. vide M.L. Roy Chaudhuri, *I.H.R.C.*, Vol. XVIII, January 1942, pp. 191. This *sanad* was conferred on the same *zamindari* family of Bharokar Raj in *pargana* Kahalgaon, *sarkar* Monghyr, *subah* Bihar which had been granted the *zamindari* by Jahangir in the 13th R.Y. See f.n. 5.

70. 'A *Sanad* of a *Subadar* granting an *inam* (free gift) of a fishery', dated 1040 F.S. (1633 A.D.) *Ibid.*

71. *Cavendish Enquiries*, *pargana* Binai, pp. 2-3.

72. M.I. Berlin, fols. 24a-28b, Ms. Br. M. Add 6599, fols. 40b-47a, 49a-53a.

73. *R.A.J.* '*Yaddasht Haqiqat-i Arazi Muwazana Pargana Riwari*' (*subah* Delhi), uncatalogued Sheet no. 7 (Aurangzeb's reign) Aurangzeb's *Farman* to Mahinath Thakur of Darbhanga vide f.n. 66; M.I. Berlin, fols. 74b; Ms. Oct. 113, Berlin, Baikus fols. 45a-b. Also see details vide S.C.R.O. Patna, Register of Nawab Hushiar Jung, Vol. I., no. 1823, District Bihar dated 1165 *Fasli* Year/1757-58 A.D. fols. 3a-b.

74. See f. nos. 66 and 67.

75. *Cavendish Enquiries. Pargana* Binai, pp. 2-3.

76. Every zamindar did not exercise *chaudhurai* powers. Only an influential zamindar acted as *chaudhurai* on behalf of the *riaya* as well as the petty zamindars (vide M.I., Berlin fols 4b-6a ; also f.n. 72).

77. See f.n. 69; Baikus, fols. 45a-b, 52b.

78. See f.n. 69; Also a Mughal *Farman* issued to the *Naib* of *subah* Orissa, dated 3rd *Shawwal* A.H. 1124/3rd November 1712 A.D. vide Ms. Orient fol. 306, Berlin; Ms. Br. M. Add 6603. fols. 60b.

79. *Ibid.*

80. Baikus, fol. 35a ; Ms. Ber. M. Add 6603, fols. 61a-b.

81. Ms. or quart 216, Berlin; Ms. Br. M. Add 6603, fols. 60b, 66b.

82. This practice persisted in South-Western Punjab even after the British occupation in 1849. See details in the Settlement Reports of the district

of Muzaffargarh by Mr. O' Brien, Chapter VI Paras 17, 19 and district Multan by Mr. Maclagan vide James Douie, *Punjab Settlement Manual* 1930; pp. 77-83, Paras 167-173. Also the *Multan Gazetteer*, pp. 168-69, 171-73, *Dera Ghazi Khan Gazetteer*, Para 81. In the 18th century in some of the territories of *subah* Awadh (near Lucknow), a zamindar claimed Satarahi *i.e.* 10 seers of grain and a *fulus* (copper coin) per *bigha* of land (vide A.D. 299).

83. Ms. or quart 216, Berlin.

84. A.D. 1203, dated 19.4.1676.

85. M.I. Berlin, fol. 5b. As a matter of custom, a faithful zamindar was entitled to a *Saropa* (robe of honour) from the state after the assessment of either of the crops, Kharif or Rabi. R.A.J. '*Jama Kharch*' (Income and Expenditure statement) documents of *Pargana* Riwari, *Subah* Delhi, dated A.H. 1076/1665-66 A.D. mentions the *inams* in cash in lieu of *Saropa* (*Inam Saropa*) bestowed on the zamindars, *muquddams* of the villages as well as the *muzarian* (tenants). This custom continued in South Western Punjab even till after the middle of the 19th century. (vide the *Multan Gazetteer*' pp. 170-171 ; James Douie, *Punjab Settlement Manual*, p. 80).

86. Ms. Or. quart 216; Berlin Baikus, fols. 45a-b.

87. A.D. nos. 782, dated 1672; 1203, dated 19.4.1676; 1228, dated 26.3.1697.

88. *Waqai R.* p. 5; Ms. or. fol. 234, Berlin.

89. Ms. Or. fol. 234, Berlin, 'Commentaries on land revenue practices under the Mughals by Sayyid Gulam Muhammad'; Ms. Or. quart 216, Berlin ; Ms. Br. NI. Add 6603, fols. 58a-b, 61a-b, 66a-b.

90. *Ibid.*

91. *Ibid.*

92. *Ibid.*

93. *Ibid.* In a general manner, it was considered as subsistence allowance (*Bataur-i-Nankar*) and technically it was reckoned as *Haq-i-Zamindari* or *malikana.*

94. Ms. Or. Oct. 113,1, Berlin.

95. *Ibid.*

96. *Ibid.* Also f.n. 89.

97. See f. n. 75.

98. R.A. J. *Muwazna* documents of *Pargana* Amber (*subah* Ajmer), dated A.H. 1088/Samvat 1937/1777-78 A.D. to A.H. 1097/Samvat 1746/ 1685-86 A.D. Document of village Ram Singhpur *tappah* Lahowa, dated A.H. 1091/Samat 1740/1680 AD. Also see f. nos. 99, 102.

99. R. A. J. '*Yaddasht Haqiqat-i Arazi-i Mazruat Wa Uftada Pargana Riwari*', dated 1073 A.H./1662-63 AD. *i.e.* Measurement records of agrarian land under cultivation and fallow land under reclamation for Haveli Riwari (*subah* Delhi), fols. la-16b. *Nigar Nama*, Bod. Oxfd, fols. 98a-b; Ms. N.A.I. fols. 74b-75a.

100. *Nigar Nama*, Ms. Pers. e. I. Bod Oxfd. 79a-b ; Ms. N.A.I., fols. 62b, 110b-111a.

101. Cavendish Enquiries, *pargana* Ramsar, fols. 153a-b.

102. *Ibid*, fols. 153b.154a; *pargana* Binai, p. 3; Jonathan Duncan, dated 1794 A.D., Revenue Selections. I. P. 169. Also see f. nos. 98-99.

103. See f. n. 6

104. M. I., Berlin, fols. 5b-6b; Baikus, fols. 41b-43b, a-54b.

105. Akbar's *Farman*, dated A.H. 990/1582 A.D. vide Ms. Rampur, pp. 9, 722. *Makatabta-i Allami*, Ms. N.A.I., p. 105; Shahjaban's *Farman*, dated 5th R. Y./1633 A.D. vide Qazwini's *Padshah Nama*, Br. M. O.R. 173 fol. 258b; *Amal-i Salih*, Printed text, I, pp. 543-46 ; Letters of Rustam Khan to Sadaullah Khan Ms. R. A. J. Letter no. IV (Shahjahan's reign); M. S., pp. 172; Aurangzeb's *Farman*, dated A.H. 1077/1666 A.D. vide *Mirat* I. pp. 259-63 ; R. A. J. *Akhbaran* nos. 1495/2, dated *Jamada* I 23rd R.Y. (Aurangzeb)/May-June 1680 A D.; no. 1563, dated 14th *Rajab* 23rd R.Y. (")/10th August 1680 A. D. Maharaja's Letter no. 1066, dated 10th *Ramzan* 49th RY. (") A.H./1116/6th January 1705 A.D. *Riyazal Wadad*, Br. M. OR 1725, fols. 18a-b; *Ibriya* (Continuation), od. Oxfd., OR. 589, fols. 109b-111a. 127a-131b ; Khafi, II pp. 88-90.

106. *Mirat* I. p. 174. For *subah* Gujrat, Mirat complains about the levy of *Gras, Waodal* and *Khichri* by the Rajput and *Koli* zamindars on the ryots and notes that such a development took place only after the death of Aurangzeb. Also see details *Mirat*. Suppl. pp. 229-39.

107. See f. nos. 238, 244.

108. See my paper on 'Nature of Land Rights in Mughal India' *The Indian Economic and Social History Review*, Vol. I, No. 1 July-September 1963, pp. 1-2, f. nos. 1-3, pp. 16-17. The English administrators understood the ownership of *zamindari* to imply only property rights and essentially associated the hereditary ownership of the *zamindari* with the proprietary rights in the land therein. Tired of prolonged discussion over *zamindari* rights, Warren Hastings conceded the right of proprietorship and inheritance to the zamindars though he asserted the claim of the E. I. Co. over the revenues of the *zamindari* lands and the power of the Government to dispossess the zamindars "on any failure in the payment of their rents, not only *pro tempore*, but in perpetuity". (See G. W. Forest's *Selections from State Papers of the Governor Generals of India*, Vol. II, reproduced from the *Fifth Report*, Introduction, XXXVII). Phillip Francis, Sir John Shore and

Boughton Rous emphasized the proprietary rights of the zamindar in the soil of the *zamindari* lands. (*The Fifth Report*, Introduction XXXVII; Shore's Minute, dated 18th June, 1789, Vol. II, Appendix I, *Op. cit*, Para 8, p. 3; C. W. Boughton Rous, *Dissertation concerning the landed Property of Bengal*, London, 1791. Though all these administrators rightly repudiated James Grant's thesis of the proprietary claim of the sovereign over the *zamindari* estates (James Grant, "Historical and comparative Analysis," *Op. cit.*), none of them could appreciate the Mughal connotation of *zamindari malkiyat* which meant the hereditary proprietary rights of the zamindars over the revenue collection and entitlement to the perquisites rather than proprietary title to the soil of the *zamindari*. Sir John Shore, who was considered to be a great expert on the Mughal land revenue system in Bengal, seems to have reviewed the position in his minute, dated 21st Dec., 1789 and concluded, "The relation of a zamindar to Government and of a *ryot* to a zamindar is neither that of a proprietor nor a vassal but a compound of both. The former acts of authority unconnected with property rights. The latter has rights without real property and the property of the one and the rights of the other are in a measure held at discretion." (vide N.K. Sinha, *The Economic History of Bengal From Plassy to the Permanent Settlement*, Vol. II, Calcutta, 1962, pp. 1-2). Shore could not properly comprehend the nature of the *malkiyat* rights of the zamindars and the *ryots* even at this stage though it cannot be denied, that the situation in the latter half of 18th century in Bengal was fluid enough to warrant such comments. Firminger, in his Introduction, reviewed the viewpoints of the early English administrators in Bengal but even he could not appreciate the nature of the *malkiyat* (ownership) rights of the zamindars. He rightly thought that there were zamindars with varying jurisdictions owing responsibility for the collection and payment of the revenues to the Government and that the *zamindaris* were not their private estates (in the English sense of private proprietary estate). At the same time, he incorrectly believed that the zamindars were like the Government revenue farmers. A zamindar might assume the role of a revenue-farmer but under the Mughal system of Government, it was always discouraged. (M.S, pp. 19-22; *Mirat* I.p. 292; *Nigar Nama*, N.A.I. fol. 114b; Bod. Oxfd. fols. 154b-155a; Ms. Aligarh, fol. 253a; D.U. Bod. Odfd: fols 65a-b). In the early 19th cent. Elphinstone and Lord William Bentick were nearer the truth when they recognised the proprietary title of the varying classes of the *riayats* to the agrarian land. (See my Paper, *Ibid*, p. 19, f.n. 20). Regarding the Assigned Territory of Delhi, A. Seton expressed doubt if the zamindars possessed any proprietary title to land similar to that which prevailed in the Lower Provinces, *viz.*, a right which included that of disposal of his land, including even the power of selling it. (From A. Seton, Esquire, Resident at Delhi to C.T. Metcalfe, Esquire, Acting Superintendent of the Assigned

Territory, Delhi, dated 21st December, 1807, vide *Records of Delhi Residency and Agency* (1807-57), pp. 21-24). Later on, T. Fortescue, the Civil Commissioner of Delhi, gave a detailed picture of the proprietary rights of the *zamindari* families and the resident *ryots* as well as the nature of the title of the *paikashtkars* and partial cultivators on land in the *zamindari* colonised villages. (*Report of the Revenue System of the Delhi Territory*, 1820. *Ibid*, pp. 74-80). After the annexation of the Punjab (1849 A.D.), the early British revenue administrators could very well appreciate the concept of proprietary rights in historical perspective and in many a region (especially in the South-West portion of the Punjab *i.e.* the erstwhile Mughal *subahs* of Lahore and Multan) wherein they found the two-fold aspects of the *malkiyat* rights in the *zamindari* villages, those of the zamindars to revenue collection and perquisites (*haquq-i-zamindari*) and those of the *raiyats* to agrarian lands. (James Douie, *Punjab Settlement Manual*, pp. 60-61, 76-91 ; Also see f. nos. 82, 216).

109. R.A.J. *Akhbarat*, regd. no. 1460, dated 29th *Rabi* 1/23rd R.Y. (Aurangzeb)/19th April, 1680 A.D. issued a royal order that the State servants should not encamp on the low-lying or agrarian lands but should set up their camps only at high places especially towards the *Id Gah* (Annual Id Prayers Mosque). Such of them (i.e. the State servants) as had encamped on the agricultural soil (*Zamin-i Zarai*) should duly compensate the proprietors of the agricultural soil (*malikan-i zamin*) in accordance with the value of the (ruined) agricultural produce. Here the words *malikan-i zamin* denote the agriculturists rather than the zamindars. This is further confirmed by the fact that such an order for safeguarding the agricultural fields of the cultivators was in line with the standing orders of the Mughal Government since Akbar's reign. See, A.N. Br. M. 27, 247 fol. 303a; Lahori, *Badshahnama*, Printed text. I, Part II, p. 4 ; II, Part I, p. 317; Qazwini, *Padshahnama;* Ms. Rampur, p. 616 ; *Mirat* 1, pp. 251-52 ; Khafi Printed text. II. p. 492.

110. M.S., pp. 19-21, 191-92.

111. R.A.J. vide f.n. 165.

112. See my Paper on "Nature of Land Rights in Mughal India," *The Indian Economic and Social History Review*, Vol. I. No. 1 July-September, 1963, pp. 3-5.

113. The *Cavendish Enquiries* in the district of Ajmer reveal that the village practice and the tribal custom also played a determining factor for the exercise of the right of mortgage and sale. At times, within the same village, a cultivating tribe might exercise alienable rights while others might not, see fols. 4a-b, 7a-b, 149a, 153a-154a, 228a-b. Also, see C.L. Tupper, "Punjab Customary Law" *op.cit.*, Vol. II, Introduction, pp. 1-98.

114. A.D. nos. 332, dated 9th *Zulhijja* A.H. 1030/15th Oct., 1620 , 435, dated 15th *Rabi* I A.H. 1110/11th Oct., 1698 A.D.; 51, dated 17th *Shawwal*, A.H. 1113/6th March, 1701.

115. M. S. pp. 1748, 191-92.

116. *Ain*, Br. M. Add 7652, fol. 145a; Ms. Or. Oct. 113J. Berlin, fols. lb, 4a.

117. *Cavendish Enquiries, pargana* Ramsar, fols 149a, 151a-154a, 228a-229b, 374b, 516b. Also for Punjab, See Report of Sir Richard Temple, 1851, James Douie's *Punjab Settlement Manual*, pp. 54-56. Also see Douie's views on proprietary rights, pp. 59-68.

118. Copies of lease deeds, dated 4th *Shawwal* A.H. 1035/19th June 1626 A.D.; 7th *Zulqada* 13th RY. Muhammad Shah/3rd May 1731 A.D. vide family Archives of Sayyid Sarfaraz Ali, *Khadim* Dargha Sharif, Ajmer.

119. M.I., Berlin, fols. 5a-b; Baikus, fols. 45a-b.

120. See f.nos. 95-97 ; Also D.U. Bod. Oxfd. fol. 90a.

121. *Ibid*; Also M.H. vide *Mirat* I, p. 271.

122. *Cavendish Enquiries*, fols. 149a, 228a-29b.

123. *Ibid*, fols. 4a-b, 228-29b, 274b, 516b ; Also f.n. 110.

124. See f.nos. 138-39.

125. A.D. no. 329 (*sarkar* Lucknow, *subah* Awadh); *Cavendish Enquiries*, fols. 228a.29b (District Ajmer, Rajasthan).

126. *Cavendish Enquiries, Ibid*; *Diwan-i Pasand*, Ms. Br. M. O.R. 2011, fols. 7b-8a; Ms. Asafiya, Hydbd, fols. 5b-6b.

127. See f.n. 118.

128. *Cavendish Enquiries*, fols. 228a-b.

129. R.A.J. *Jama Kharch* (Income and Expenditure) *pargana* documents of *pargana* Rewari, dated A.H. 1076/1665-66; A.D. *Qalba* documents of *pargana* Rewari, dated AH. 1067-1073/1656-1663 AD. Documents of the income of the villages (*Amadani-i Fotah Muwazai*) of *pargana* Fateh Abad, *Rabi* Crop, *Jamada* II A.H. 1092/June, 1682, Kh. S. Ms. N.A.I., pp. 32-33, Ms. Aligarh, fol. 16a ; Baikus, fol. 66b.

130. *Ibid*; also R.D., Ms. Or. Oct. 113J, Berlin, fols. 2a-4a; *Nigar Nama*, Bod. Oxfd, fols. 127a-128b; *Ibid*, Ms. N.A.1., fols. 75a-b ; Baikus, fols. 67a.68a, 69a-69b.

131. *Ibid*.

132. *Ibid*.

133. *Cavendish Enquiries*, fols. 4a-b (Kharwa territory), fols 153a-b (village Hoth, *Pargana* Ramsar) fol. 374b (village Sowaila, *Pargana* Ramsar).

134. *Ibid.* fol. 374b.

135. Cavendish Archives of Sayyid Sarfaraz Ali, *Khadim* Dargha Sharif, Ajmer. A copy of receipt issued by Sayyid Inayat S/o Syed Mahmmud, *Khadim* Dargha and aimmadar of village Nandla dated 7th *Zulqada* 13th R.Y. Mohammad Shah/2 May, 1732 A.D. It states that the forefathers of the tenants ever since the time of Sayyid Mian Bahai S/o Syed Dan had been utilising the well water of the landlord and been paying an annual rent of Rs. 1/-. Syed Dan was contemporary of Shahjahan and his son, Mian Bahai, lived in the 2nd half of the 17th century. (vide *A Descriptive List of the Farmans, Manshurs and Nishans*, Bikaner, published 1962, p. 71; Also family geneology of Sayyid Sarfaraz Ali).

136. *Nigar Nama*, N.A.I. fols. 62b, 74b-75a, ll0b-111a.

137. *Ibid.* fols. 110b-111a; Ms. Aligh, fols. 243b-244b.

138. *Ibid.* fol. 74b-75a.

139. *Ibid.* Also f.n. 137.

140. *Ibid.*

141. *Cavendish Enquiries*, fol. 153a. (Village Hothah, *pargana* Ramsar, District Ajmer). However, in *Pargana* Masuda, the hereditary tenants possessed their own well but no rights of mortgage and sale of agrarian lands (*Ibid.* fols. 4a-4b).

142. See f.n. 135.

143. Family Archives of Sayyid Sarfaraz Ali, *Khadim* Dargha, Ajmer. A copy of acquittance deed, dated 9th RY. of Shahjahan executed by Bahman S/o Behari, tribe Baghban states that he has relinquished the tenancy of *madad-i maash* land of Syed Dan of his own. The land had been in occupation of the family of the tenants for a long period (*Qadimul ayam*).

144. See details vide my Paper on 'The Position of *Desai* in the *Pargana* adniinistration of *Subah* Gujrat under the Mughals', *op. cit.* pp. 152-155, f. nos. 20-21.

145. See Details vide my Paper on 'Nature of land-rights in Mughal India', *op.cit.* pp. 4-5.

146. *The Fifth Report*, W.K Firminger's Introduction pp. 1-11. Warren Hastings called them "The vagrant reiats."

147. *Cavendish Enquiries*, fols. 153a, 154a, 374b.

148. *Ibid.*

149. *Ibid.*

150. R.A.J. '*Yaddasht-i Haqiqat Qalba hi Muwazai Pargana Rewari*', dated A.H. 1067/V.S. 1716/1656-57 A.D., fol. 10b; also f. nos. 22a-22d.

151. R.A.J. *'Yaddasht Mal-o-Jihat wa Sair-O Jihat' rabi* and *kharif* Crops, *pargana* Sokhar, dated A.H. 1069/1658-59 A.D.; *pargana* Riwari (*subah* Delhi), dated A.H. 1072-1073/1661-63; *pargana* Kohari (*subah* Malwa), dated A.H. 1072/1661-62 S.N. Ms. no. 858, CRO Hydbd, fols. 27b-28a, 197a-197b, 200a-202a.

152. S.C.R.O. Patna, no. B-335, dated 22nd *Jamada* I. A.H. 1066/18th March, 1656 narrates a sale deed executed by Bhala Ram S/o Har Narain, Caste Brahaman, *malik* and *muqaddam* of village Bakauri, *pargana* Tirsath, *sarkar* Tirbut, *subah* Bihar transferring the *malkiyat* and *muqaddami* rights to Sayyid Ala. Also see Ms. Br. M. Add. 6603, fol. 81a (Yasin's Glossary) which mentions that "in revenue terminology, the *malik* of one village is known as *Muqaddam*". Also see *Diwan-i Pasand* (Ms. Br. M.O.R. 2011, fol. 7b; Ms. Asafiya, Hydbd, fol. 5b) which puts a few *muqaddams* as the *maliks* of a village (*mauza* or *Deh*).

153. *Ibid*. The above mentioned sale deed, dated 18th March, 1656 gives details of the total transfer of the *malkiyat* and *muqaddami* rights over the entire village comprising 609 bighas for Rs. 72/-10 annas. The nature of *malkiyat* and rights (*Haquq*) over both the agrarian and non-agrarian lands along with their boundaries are described in details. For nature of *zamindari malkiyat* rights, See Ms. Or. fol. 234, Berlin; Ms. Or. quart 216, Berlin.

154. See f. nos. 152-53.

155. See f. nos 227-31; 244 (for Awadh); 223 (Bihar); 197, 205 (Bengal) respectively.

156. *Ibid*. Also, see details of sale deed of village Bakauri, *subah* Bihar, dated 18th March 1656 vide f.n. 152.

157. A.D. no. 1191, dated 9.1.1672. A sale deed of village Anbhapur, *pargana* and *sarkar* Bahraich (*subah* Awadh) shows the sale of culturable and residential land, wells, gardens, trees along with all the '*dakhili* and *kharaji*' rights but excluding the area under Gopal's cultivation for Rs. 195/- executed by Ram Chand and five other named partners in favour of Sayyid Ahmad S/o Mir Sayyid Ziauddin.

158. A.D. no. 1199, dated 20.1.1676.

159. Irfan Habib, *op. cit.* pp. 143-44.

160. *Nigar Nama*, N.A.I. fols. 110b-111a; Ms. M.U. Aligh, fols. 243b-244b.

161. A.D. no. 317, dated 22nd *Safar* A.H. 994/2nd February, 1586. A sale deed of village Jarha, *pargana* Sandila (*subah* Awadh) executed by 12 persons (Narain and others holding the village on joint family basis in favour of Mian Ammam; no. 51, dated 17th *Shawwal* A.H. 1113/46th R.Y. (Aurangzeb)/6th March, 1701 shows the sale of a garden in *qasba* Malanwah by 11 persons comprising 4 families.

162. *Cavendish Enquiries*, fols. 7a-b. In 22 self-developed villages in *pargana* Kharwa (District Ajmer), the zamindars claimed proprietary rights over the agrarian lands though the cultivators belonging to the Mir tribe had been allowed to settle as tenants for over two centuries.

163. Ms. Or. Oct. 113 Berlin, fols .1a-4a. Baden Powell, on the testimony of Muslim lawyers, conceded that the rights of land as acquired by 'first clearing' on the part of "such overlord families (zamindars) especially when they settled on, or extended their possessions into, waste land which they themselves first cultivated, might combine in themselves both kinds of rights – as first clearance and as overlords". Though Baden-Powell rightly points out that this right was also based on inheritance, he has failed to recognise any other class of the zamindars as distinct from the 'ruling families, or of conquering clans'. For details of Baden-Powell's views, see 'Is the State the owner of all Land in India?" *A.Q.R.* July-Oct, 1894, pp. 5-6.

164. *Ibid.*

165. R.A.J. regd. no. 1721, case no. 9, dated 7th *Zul-hijja* A.H. 1074/1664 A.D. In a sale deed, the *muqaddami* families of village Bahrola *pargana* Shahjahanbad (*subah* Delhi) claim both *zamindari* and *biswadari* rights and sell out a plot of 84 *bighas* of agrarian land in favour of the Vakils of Mirza Raja Jal Singh for Rs. 840/-. The *biswadari* rights could be claimed by only families cultivating their own land or by the owners of those who had developed the villages themselves.

166. M.S. pp. 191-92.

167. See f.n. 169.

168. R.A.J., O.H. Records, *Kapat-dawara* Documents, Serial no. 7, no. 177 CPh; Shahjahan's *Farman* dated 26th *Jamada* II 1043 A.H./28th December, 1633, for purchasing land from Maharaja Jai Singh for the construction of Raj Mahal in Agra.

169. Only a few of the numerous available documents can be cited. R.A.J. category 4, reg no. 1721, case no. 9, dated 7th *Zulhijja* A.H. 1074/ 1664; A.D. No. 1192, dated 14.2.1669, no. 1215, dated 1.2.1681, no. 1222, dated 10.4.1688, no. 1224, dated 26.4.1689, no. 1227, dated 15.12.1695; S.C.R.O., Patna, no. B-335, dated 22nd *Jamada* I A.H. 1066/ l8th March, 1656 for giving of gifts; also see A.D. no. 1226, dated 28.8.1692, no. 1192, dated 14.2. 1669.

170. Ms. Or. Oct. 113 Berlin, fols. 1a-4a.

171. *Ibid.* Also Ms. Or. fol 234, fol. 9b. According to the above 18th century sources for the *subahs* of Bihar and Bengal, the Mughal policy of extension of agricultural areas through the clearance of the jungles and the reclamation of waste cultivable lands led to the creation of large *zamindaris* through royal *sanads* in Shah Jahan's reign. There is every reason to believe that this policy was pursued throughout the Mughal age though it may have gained in tempo under Shahjahan.

172. M.S., pp. 45-48; R.A.J. Shahjahan's *Farman* no. 39/64, dated 5th R.Y./ 1633 A.D.

173. Letters of Balkrishan Brahman, Br. M. Add. 16859, fols. 107a-109b (Late Shahjahan and early Aurangzeb's reign).

174. Such descendants were known as *Zamindaran Warisan*. Baikus, fols 50-b; Captain Hector Mackenzie, '*Settlement Report of Gujrat* (*Punjab*)', Paragraph 160 vide James Douie, *Punjab Settlement Manual*', pp. 57.

175. See f. nos. 191-202 under the *Taaluqdars*.

176. *Ibid*, also f. n. 234.

177. The petty zamindars as co-partners in the villages game to be known by various regional appellations, viz., co-parcerners, *pattidars*, *thokedars* or *behriwars*. *Vide Selections from the Duncan Records* by A. Shakespear, 1873, Vol. I, pp. 137-38, 143-45; 245-46 T. Fortescue, Civil Commission Dehlee, Report of the Revenue System of Delhi Territory, dated 28th April, 1820, vide *Records of Delhi Residency and Agency* (1807-57), pp. 74-76. Holt Mackenzie's Memorandums dated 1st July 1818 and 19th Oct. 1826, *Selections from the Revenue Records of the North-West Provinces*, 1818-20 and 1822-33, 92-206-7; 84-202 respectively. Also *Report of the United Provinces Zamindari Abolition Committee* Vol. I, 81-84, 90-96; S.C. Gupta, *Agrarian Relations and Early British Rule in India*, pp. 37-42, 52-55, 169-204, Moreland, *Agrarian System* pp. 160-68.

178. *Ibid*.

179. In the territory of Delhi, even a petty zamindar as a co-sharer in a *zamindari* village was not known as *pattidar* or *thokedar* etc. but continued to be entitled a zamindar. For details of revenue settlements in the *zamindari* villages, see Letters from C.T. Metcalfe, Esqr, First Assistant, Assigned Territory of Delhi, to A Seton, Esqr. Resident at Delhi, dated 2nd December, 1807 in '*Records of the Delhi Residency*, pp. 14-15; From A. Seton, Esqs, Resident at Delhi to C.T. Metcalfe, Acting Superintendent of the Assigned Territory, Delhi dated 21st December, 1807 (*Ibid*), pp. 21-24; T. Fortescue to Holt Mackenzie, dated 28th April, 1820 (vide f. n. 177) pp. 74-78, 85-98.

180. *Nigar Nama*, Bod. Oxfd. fols. 75b-76b; Ms. N.A.I., fols. 47b-48a. 61a-b, 70a; Also Original Letters addressed to Khan Sahib (*Suzeran de Bander Surat*), B.N. Paris, no Suppl. Persian 2052 (pertaining to *subah* Gujrat in Aurangzeb's reign).

181. Khs. S.N.A.I. pp. 62-65 ; Ms. M.U. Aligh, fols. 27b-29a; *Nigar Nama*, Bod. Oxfd, fols. 66ab-67a, 76b-77a, 84a-b ; Ms. N.A.I., fols. 54b-55a, 60b-61b, 64a-66a, *Waqai, R.*, pp. 5, 229, 359, 405; *Mufidul Insha*, Bod. Oxfd, fol. 61b.

182. '*Lettres de Jivan Rani employe de Abdullah bin IdRas*'. B.N. Paris, no Suppl. Persian 2052 (pertaining to *Subah* Gujrat in Aurangzeb's reign);

Mufidal Insha, Ms. 679 Bod. Oxfd, for 61b; S.D.A.R., pp. 15; *Waqi, R.* pp. 229, 404 Baikus, fols. 57b-58a ; Khafi, II, pp. 89, 377. *Mirat* I, pp. 21-22.

183. *Ibid*; Also A.D. no. 1185, dated 1685; 811 (1-2), dated 1701; Also R.A.J vide f. n. 2.

184. *Ain*, Ms. Br. M. Add. 7652. fols. 177b-192b; tr. J. II, pp. 146, 148. Here the *taaluqs* are stated to be subsitutes for *mahals* and are associated with named persons rather than with territories.

185. *Ibid.*

186. B.G.I. tr. Borah, pp. 18, 100, 123; II, pp. 517-18, 521-22 566, 568. Also Borah's introduction, I. pp. XIV-XVIII; T. R. Chaudhuri, *Bengal under Akbar and Jahangir*, pp. 1-5.

187. R.A.J. vide f. n. 2; Also f. n. 182.

188. Kh. S.N.A.I., p. 121 ; Ms. M.U. Aligarh, fol. 32a (see details of the revenues of *subah* Multan); *Maasir-i Alamgiri*, p. 206; Also *Mirat* I. pp. 21-22.

189. Of the numerous documents, see A.D. nos. 1192, dated 14.2.1669 1196, dated 28.11.1672, dated 22.11.1681; 1224, dated 26.4.1689.

190. AD. no. 897 (1-2), dated 1684. For only *taaluqa* of a named person see A.D. nos. 1185; 211 (1-2), dated 1801.

191. A.D. nos 1263, dated 23.5.1808 (for zamindar); no. 1264, dated 10.7.1810 (for *taaluqdar* and *tafriqdar*); Also see details in *Dasturul Amal of Nawab Saadat Ali Khan of Oudh* tr. Khan Bahadur S. Abu Muhammad, '*The Journal of the United Provinces Historical Society*'. Vol. IV, Oct. 1928, part I, pp. 28-67.

192. Ms. Or quart 258, Berlin, fols. 145b-146a.

193. Talish, Bod. Oxfd. fols. 155b-156a. For the territory of Arakan (*subab* Bengal), Talish places the Rajas, zamindars and *taaluqdars* in order of priority in respect of their territorial jurisdiction and status. It seems that this is equally true of the early 17th century Bengal after its complete subjugation by the Mughal State. (See f. n. 186).

194. Ms. Or. quart 258, Berlin, fols. 145b-146a, 306a.

195. *Ibid.*

196. *Ibid*. Also Ms. Or. fol. 234, Berlin.

197. *Ibid*; Also see a copy of sale deed written both in Persian and Bengali (fols. 125b-126a) by Chaudhari Kahori Bose of his shares in *taaluqa* villages in *pargana* Chahotipur, *sarkar* Salim Abad, *chakla* Hugli, dated 27th *Jamada* II 7th R.Y. (Shah Alam II)/29th August 1172 Bengali year/15th July, 1766 A.D. Also another copy of a sale deed written both in Persian and Bengali (fols. 128b-129b) by Chaudhari Nar

Narain of *tappa* Sahkana *pargana* Sultan Partab selling his shares in different *taaluqa* villages, dated 31st *Badhon* 1161 Bengali year/Sth September, 1754 A.D.

198. *Ibid.*

199. See f. nos. 208, 209.

200. See f. no. 194.

201. See f. nos. 208, 209.

202. See f. n. 194.

203. *Ibid;* also Ms. Or. fol. 234, Berlin.

204. *Ibid.*

205. Ms. Br. M. Add. 24,039, no. 36 Quotes a copy of a *Parwana* issued under the seal of Ibrat Khan, *Diwan,* dated 2nd *Shabban* 46th R.Y. (Aurangzeb) 2nd January, 1702 A.D. stating therein the purchase of the villages of Calcutta, Sutanuti and Gobindpur, *pargana* Amir-abad, *chakla* Hugli (*subah* Bengal) by the English East India Company. The *Parwana* mentions Manohar Datt etc., the zamindars as the vendors and the East India Company as the buyers to be considered as the *taaluqdar*. Similarly, a copy of the sale deed (*Ibid.* no. 39 mentions the E.I.C., the purchaser as the *taaluqdar*. Later on, the *Farman* of Emperor Farrukhsiyar, dated 4th *Safar*, 5th R.Y./18th January 1717 A.D. (vide a copy of the original *Farman* in Persian and translation in Surman's Diary preserved in I.O. Records, Home Series Vols. LXIX, pp. 130-31; Also a photostat copy of the letter published by S. Bhattacharya, '*The East India Company and the Economy of Bengal* from 1704 to 1740 London,' 1954, Appendix IV, p. 234) not only confirms the already acquired *taaluqdari* rights of the above mentioned villages but further authorises the E.I.C. to purchase the *taaluqdari* of thirty-eight new villages from the respective owners and the *Diwan-i Subah* is enjoined to permit the sale transaction. The Farman insists on designating the E.I. Co. as the *taaluqdar* with *taaluqdari* rights over the purchased villages. Also Moreland, '*Agrarian System*' pp. 189-23. Moreland has correctly insisted on designating the E.I. Co. as the *taaluqdar* though he has not been able to distinguish between the status of the *taaluqdar* in Bengal and other portions of North India. Dr. Irfan Habib's analysis of the above mentioned *Parwana* and identification of the zamindar and the *taaluqdar* as synonymous is not correct and his criticism of Moreland is not very much justified. (*The Agrarian System of Mughal India*, pp. 172-73, f. n. 18). However, as the E.I.Co. paid revenues of the purchased villages directly to the State, it assumed the role of the zamindar only in general usuage. It is quite clear from the above quoted documents that both officially and technically, till 1717 A.D., the E.I.Co. was the *taaluqdar* and that it was only after this year the E.I.Co. was officially recognised as the zamindar through a royal

Sanad. In 1757, Mir Jafar also granted lands to the E.I.Co. on the payment of the revenue "in the same manner as the other zamindars" (vide the Fifth Report, Firminger's Introduction, p. X.). It is only under the direct administration of the E.I.Co. that with effect from the 1194 Bengali Year/1788-89 A.D., that in the district of Dacca and the other territories of Bengal that the technical distinction between the zamindar, *chaudhari* and the *taaluqdar* was mitigated and each one of these revenue officials came to be designated as zamindar (vide Ms. Orient Quart. 258, Berlin, fol 275a).

206. Barwell, *Proceedings of the G.G. in Council, Revenue*, Vol. 41 vide N. K. Sinha, *op. cit.* pp. 9, 21, f.n. 17.

207. See f. n. 194 Also *Nigar Nama*, N.A.I. fols. 116b-l 17a; A copy of a Mughal *Farman*, dated 3rd *Shawwal* A.H. 1124/3rd November 1712 A.D. 4th clause vide Ms. Orient fol. 306, Berlin.

208. Nawab Muhammad Reza Khan, *Proceedings of the Revenue Board consisting of whole Council*—Vol. V, vide N. K. Sinha, *op.cit.*, pp. 7-9, 21, f.n. 15.

209. Nawab Muhammed Reza Khan, *Proceedings of G.G. in Council*, dated 11-25th July, 1789, Vol. 151 vide N. K. Sinha, *op cit.*, pp. 13, 22, f.n. 23.

210. Ms. Br. M. Add. 6603, fols. 54b-55a.

211. A.D. no, 897 (1-2), dated 1684 A.D.

212. Ms. Br. M. Add. 6603, fol. 24b-55a.

213. *Ibid.*

214. That is how Ms. '*Dasturulaml-i Khalsa Sharifa*' Edinburgh, no. 130. pp. 19 defines *taaluqadar* as a small *zamindar*.

215. See f. no. 210; In the last three decades of the 17th century, Sayyid Muhammad Arif, A *zamindar* and *taaluqadar* in *pargana* Hisampur, *sarkar* Bahraich (*subah* Awadh) purchased various shares of different *taaluqa* villages of which he claimed *malkiyat* rights. (See f.n. 238).

216. Such *malkiyat* rights of the twofold intermediary classes in hierarchical manner over those of the *riaya* persisted in the South-Western and North-Western Punjab (erstwhile Mughal *subah* Lahore) and Cis-Sutlaj tract (erstwhile *subah* Delhi) right till the mid-l9th century. For details of *malkiyat* rights, see James Douie, '*Punjab Settlement Manual*' pp. 67, 77-87.

217. *Ibid.*

218. For example, Sayyid Muhammad Arif's position after having purchased various *taaluqa* villages as known from the Allahabad documents may be cited as a case study. See f.n. 238.

219. *Kawaif-i Gorakhpur*, M. U. Aligarh, dated 1810 A.D. fols. 14a-b. The inferior *zamindars* of the villages in Gorakhpur (erstwhile Mughal

Subah Awadh) were known as *Birteeas*. They paid revenues at times directly to the states and at times through the *taaluqdars* entitled the Rajas. In the early 19th century, they claimed 10% of the total realisations (*Dehyak or Do Biswi*) and paid to the *taaluqdars* in the shape of fixed lump-sum amount (*chukti*). This naturally implied the sharing of the *malikana* rights between the *birteeas* and the *taaluqadars* and passing on the assessed revenues to the State. Also see *Selections from the Revenue Records of the N.W.P. (1822-33)* pp. 131, 135-38.

220. See f.n. 205.

221. Ms. Br. M. Add. 6603, fols. 54b-55a; Ms. Or. quayrt 258, Berlin, fols. 125b-126a, 128b-129b. See sale deeds vide f.n. 197. Also, see f.n. 205.

222. D.U. Ms. Walker 104, Bod. Oxfd. fols. 43a-44a; A.D. No. 319, dated 1579; no. 1185, dated 1658; no. 1200, dated 7.2.1676 (for Muslim families); no. 317, dated 2nd February 1586; no. 1196, dated 28.11.1672, no. 1216, dated 22.11.1611; no. 51, dated 6th March, 1701 (for Hindu families).

223. *Mahzarnama* of Sunder Thakur of Darbhanga, dated A.H. 1062/1652 A.D. vide *I.H.R.C.*, 1961, pp. 92-94. The Allahabad documents (vide f.n. 222) may be interpreted in this light.

224. R.A.J. A sale deed vide regd. no. 1721, case no. 9, dated 7th R.Y. (Aurangzeb)/A.H. 1074/1664 A.D.; Another sale deed vide M.K. Records, no. 99, 235 Ph, dated 1st *Ramzan* 7th R.Y. (Farrukh Sayer)/ 7th July, 1719.

225. See f.n. 223.

226. T. Fortescue, Esquire, Civil Commissioner, Delhi, to Holt Mackenzie, Esquire, Secretary to the Government in Territorial Department, dated Fort William, 28th April 1820. '*Report on the Revenue System of the Delhi Territory*, 1820. It divides villages into *Panas* and *Thalas* (Para 16, p. 74). The lands in a single village may be divided by *jhoondees* (*i.e.* lots), one *jhoondee* consisting of a fixed number of *bighas* (Para 101, p. 95), according to *biswa* involving the division of a village into 20 shares (Paras 102, p. 96); *Thekrees*. constituting anciently apportioned lands of the village into 31½ shares; *Ghurrees* (like 24 hours being equivalent to 60 *Ghurrees*) and each person contributing 1/60th part of the assessment for every *Ghurree* occupied in the irrigation of the lands from the Grand Canal or *Shah Nahar* (Para 104, p. 96).

227. See f. nos. 238,244.

228. A.D. no.1196, dated 28.11.1672; 1200, dated 7.2.1676; 1221, dated 19.5.1688.

229. AD. no. 317, dated 2nd February, 1586 (The sale deed is executed by twelve persons); no. 51, dated 6th March, 1701 (The sale deed is executed by 11 persons comprising 4 families).

230. A.D. no. 1200, dated 7.2.1696.

231. A.D. no. 1221, dated 19.5.1688; no. 1221, dated 26.4.1689.

232. A.D. no. 1220, dated 31.3.1688 records an acknowledgement receipt (*Qabuliat*) executed by Sheikh Ghulam Ahmad and others, the *zamindars* of villages Hajipur etc., *pargana* Sadrpur, *sarkar* Khairabad, *subah* Awadh, for the payment of assessed revenues of Rs. 1390/9 annas for the year (*kharif* and *rabi*) 1090 Fasli/1682-83 A.D. The documents contain a detailed account of the revenue of each village and the signature of Sheikh Ghulam Ahmad. Another *Qabuliat* vide no. 1223, dated 16.3.1688 on the same lines is also executed by the same persons for the payment the same amount. The documents show Sheikh Ghulam Ahmad and others as the zamindars. The fact that the assessed revenues are also shown as a consolidated sum to be paid by a group of zamindars of various villages under the signatures of one superior zamindar namely Sheikh Ghulam Abmad shows that apart from paying his own revenues as the zamindar, the latter also acted as the representative of the other zamindars grouped under him. A.D. no. 897 (1-2), dated 1684 A.D. records the assessment (*Tashkhish Jama*) of village Badura etc. *tappa* Chaurasi, *pargana* Hisampur, *sarkar* Babraich (*subah* Awadh) at Rs. 425/ and mentions Mir Muhammad Arif, the zamindar and *taaluqdar* of the aforesaid villages and makes him responsible for the depositing of the above-mentioned amount in the royal treasury. When all the three documents are read together, they clearly show that in case of nos. 1220 and 1223, Sheikh Ghulam Ahmad is both the zamindar and the *taaluqdar* even though the documents do not clearly say so. On the contrary, in case of no. 897 (1-2), though Mir Muhammad Arif is mentioned as the zamindar and *taaluqdar*, the jurisdiction of his *taaluqa* (like those of nos. 1220 and 1223), comprised both his personal *zamindari* and those of other dependent zamindars attached to him and for the purpose of assessment, all the villages are grouped under the village Badura etc.

233. *Nigar Nama*, Bod. Oxfd. fols. 99b-l00a; Ms. N.A.I. fol. 76a; Ms. M.U. Aligarh, fols. 160b-161a. The code of standing revenue instructions (*Dasturulaml* issued to the *diwan* (*Diwanian i.e.* Provincial *diwans* and the *diwans* of the *sarkars* etc.) comprise 15 clauses. The very first clause orders the *diwans* not to grant any private interview to the *amils, chaudharies, qanungos* and the *taaluqdars*. However, Ms. Or. Oct. 1133, Berlin and Ms. Orient Quart 259, Berlin fyls 56a-63b. consider these instructions as an integral part of the *Farman* issued to Rasik Das *Karori* in the 8th R.Y. and at the same time, the 1st clause refers only to the *amils* and the *chaudharies* and makes no reference to either the *qanungos* or the *taaluqdars*. As all the three copies of *Nigar Nama-i Munshi* quoted above do refer to the *qanungos* and the *taaluqdars* as well, this can be accepted as a reliable version.

234. M.I., Berlin, fols. 4b-6b. makes distintion between the simple zamindars and those with a higher status in the villages of a *pargana*.

It also suggests that the *diwan* and the State revenue officers should appoint reliable persons from within the zamindars as *chakladars* and *Sitadars* for the realisation of the land revenue. At the same time, on fols. 24a-b, it mentions that one of the influential zamindars, may be even the *chaudhari*, would act as guarantor for the appearance and the payment of the revenues on behalf of other zamindars. Also Br. M. Add 6599, fol. 40b; Also *Waqai. R.*, dated, 22nd R.Y. (Aurangzeb) pp. 89-90, 391-92. The text quotes Debi Das etc., the zamindar of *pargana* Binai (*sarkar* and *subah* Ajmer) had not paid three lacs dams and the revenues of Paibaqi territory for over a number of years. It is clear from the text that Debi Das owed revenues for his personal *zamindari* and the revenues of the other dependent zamindars attached to him.

235. T. Fortescue the Civil Commissioner of Delhi (*op .cit.* Para 62, p. 86) reported that in the *khalsa* lands, no person styled as *Rajah* or termed as *Taalluqdar* and *Putteedar* etc. were known.

236. Ms. Br. M. Add 6603, fols. 55b-55a, 58a; Ms. 230, *Dasturulaml-i Khalsa Sharifa*, pp. 10, 19; *Kawaif-i Gorakhpur* vide f.n. 219; *The Fifth Report*, Vol. I., pp. 91-92; *Revenue Selections* (1818-20), Holt Mackenzie's *Memorandum*, dated 1st July, 1819, pp. 9-193; *Revenue Selections* (1822-33), Lord William Bentick's minute, dated 26th September, 1832, pp. 390-96 ; Also S. C. Gupta, *Agrarian Relations and early British Rule in India*, pp. 65-69; 29-122, 169-180; 299-306. James Douie, '*Punjab Settlement Manual*, pp. 67, 84-87.

237. James Douie, *Punjab Settlement Manual*, pp. 67-68. In Cis-Sutlej tract, the superior *malik* (Proprietor or zamindar) was known as *biswadar* and the inferior zamindars attached to him were simply known as zamindars.

238. As a case study, it is known from the Allahabad Documents that in the *subah* of Awadh, Sayyid Muhammad Arif inherited *zamindari* property in the villages of *parganas* of Selak (*sarkar* Awadh) and Hisampur (*sarkar* Bahraich) apart from *madad-i maash* land in village Kantaur *pargana* Selak. (A.D. no. 1201, dated 20.4.1676; 1202, dated 19.5.1676; 1214, dated 4.5.1679). Sayyid Muhammad Arif also purchased various *zamindari* shares in the villages of the *pargana* Hisampur. See also deeds vide A.D. nos. 1205, dated 30.11.1677; 1216, dated 22.11.1681; 1219, dated 31.5.1687; 1221, dated 19.5.1688; 1222, dated 10.4.1688; 1221, dated 26.4.1689). A receipt no. 1218, dated 28.2.1687 shows that Muhammad Arif had also *zamindari* villages in *pargana* Fatehpur (*sarkar* Lucknow). Later on Sayyid Muhammad Husain also served as the Qazi and Mufti of *pargana* Hisampur (A.D. no. 1225, dated 15.11.1689). Also see the *Mahzarnama* of Sunder Thakur of Darbhanga (*subah* Bihar) vide f.n. 223.

239. See f.n. 223 for *Chaudhari* cum *zamindari* shares in the *pargana*, of *sarkar* Sirhut, *subah* Bihar.

240. *Ibid.*

241. See f.n. 238.

242. Though many a *taaluqdari* right and jurisdiction may have been established by the *chaudharis* and *qanungos* through the influence of the local officers or by fraud or force during the 18th century disturbed political conditions (vide Selections of Revenue Records 1822-33, Allahabad, 1872), p. 160; Lord William Bentick's Minute, dated 29th September, 1832, pp. 392-95; S. C. Gupta, *op.cit.* pp. 65-68, 300-303), in origin and character, the *taaluqdari* institution based on mutul convenience of the superior and the dependent zamindars was already known to the 17th century Mughal administration. The view-point of the 19th century English administrarors in India about the origin of the *taaluqdari* system (*Ibid*) is not absolutely correct. It is equally incorrect to say that the *taaluqdari* grants were made by the Mughal state.

243. See f. nos. 164-68, 171, 177-78.

244. For sale of the *zamindari* villages by the Hindu zamindars to the Muslims, see A.D. nos. 317, dated 2nd February, 1586; 1194, dated 9.1.1696, dated 28.11.1672; 1227, dated 15.12.1695; For sale of *muqaddami* rights, A.D. 1183, dated 14.3.1653. Also S.C.R.O., Patna, B-335, dated 2nd *Jamada* I. A. H. 1066/27th February, 1656 A.D. For sale of *zamindari* village by the Muslims to the Hindu zamindars, see AD, no. 1180, dated 21.1.1643; 1200, dated 7.2.1676 ; 1226, dated 28.8.1692 (*Hiba Nama*); for the sale of villages by the Muslims to other Muslim families, sc A.D. no. 1199, dated 1676; 893, dated 1679; for sale by Hindus to Hindus of other Caste, R.A.J. regd. no. 1721, case no. 9, dated 2nd *Zulhijja* A.H. 1074/26th June, 1664 A.D. (See detail. vide f.n. 224).

245. See f.n. 19.

246. *Nigar Nama*, N.A.I., fols. 116b-117.

247. R.A.J. vide f.n. 2, Also *Waqai R.* pp. 218-19; Also f.n. 246.

248. Aurangzeb's *Farman,* dated 14th *Rabi* II, 9th R.Y./14th October 1666 A.D.; Aurangzeb's letter to Lashkar Khan, the Governor of Bihar, dated 1st *Rajab* A.H. 1077/28th December, 1666 A.D. *I.H.R.C.*, 1961, pp. 94-97. Mahinath Thakur of Darbhanga (*subah* Bihar) helped the *faujdar* of Darbhanga in suppressing the recalcitrant zamindar of Morang (N.E. Sub-Himalayan border of *subah* Bihar). In lieu of his meritorious services, Aurangzeb granted Mahinath the *sadr zamindari* (including *zamindari, malkiyat* and settlement rights) of 103 *parganas* in the *sarkars* of Tirhut and Monghyr, (*subah* Bihar) and 7 *parganas* in the *sarkars* of Purnea and Tajpur (*subah* Bengal).

249. *Ibid.*

250. A Chief zamindar (*Zamindar-i Umda*) would usually divide his *watan jagir* and *tankhwah jagir* (when enrolled as *mansabdar*) amongst his own family members consisting of his sons, brothers, cousins and their dependents who were all known as zamindars. Even when certain *parganas* of a *zamindari* were not a part of either *watan jagir* or *tankhwah jagir* and formed a part of the *khalsa*, the zamindar's family members acted as the local zamindars for the realisation of the revenues and were entitled to *Rasum* thereupon. Apart from the members of the family of the Chief zamindars, the primary village zamindars, and the superior zamindars with *taaluqdari* rights wherever developed operated as much in these territories as in others. As a case study, the *zamindari* of Binai (*pargana* Binai, *sarkar* Ajmer, *subah* Ajmer) for which contemporary and later documents are available may be taken for examination. For details, see *History of Binai* (unpublished) and personal family Archives of the Raja, Binai; Cavendish Enquiries, *pargana* Binai ; Also for the 22nd R. Y. of Aurangzeb's reign, see *Waqai R.*, pp. 89-90, 391-92, 397-98.

Chapter 5

Evolution of the *Zamindari* and *Ta'aluqdari* System in Bengal (1576-1765 AD)

As Bengal was the first Indian Province to fall under the English occupation for administration, its *zamindari* aspects attracted the largest discussion at the hands of its early English administrators.[1] Though in the later-Mughal period of the 18th century, the *zamindari* system developed some new features so as to puzzle the English administrator-scholars about its indigenous character, in principle, the main traits of the *zamindari* system in Bengal during the late 16th, and more particularly in 17th century of the Mughal age, are the same as in the other provinces. During the Mughal age, the institution of *zamindari* covered a variety of individuals with hereditary landed interest as distinct from those of the *ryots*.[2] It covered a wide range of landed interests, from the chiefs of the princely territories to petty intermediaries. It comprised officials and non-officials of varying degress and importance, which was determined by their respective positions and ranks.

Though the system of *zamindari* was known to the Sultanate of Delhi and the independent Chieftainships of pre-Mughal Bengal, in some respects, it was adopted by the Mughals as such, while in others, it was sufficiently replenished with new features so as to incorporate it in the military and the revenue structure of the Mughal administration. Under the Mughals, it was evovled into a regular pattern of land revenue administration. The hitherto belief of the three-fold division of the lands into *khailsa* (crown), *jagirs* (assignments) and *zamindaries* (so-called princely states) has to be modified, as for the purposes of land administration, even the portions of *zamindari* territories were assignable to the Mughal state

---

Paper presented at *Bangladesh History Congress*, Third Session (May 12-14, 1973), Dacca.

officials or to the zamindars themselves in lieu of their services to the state. This is true of the Mughal administration from Akbar's reign down to the later Mughal times. The analysis is equally applicable to the *subah* of Bengal under the Mughals. For the *subah* of Bengal, the *Ain-i-Akbari* mentions the castes of various zamindars in a few *sarkars*. The association of the term *taaluq* with some of the *mahals* signifies the jurisdiction of the zamindars. Later on, for the early 17th century, "Mirza Nathan" *Baharistan ghaybi* freely associates the term with the princely chiefs as well as the other landed intermediaries.[3]

After the final overthrow of the Afghan power in Bengal in 1576 A.D.,[4] its territories were divided into *khalisa* and *jagir* recognising at the same time the de facto position of the zamindars within the pattern of the Mughal *jagir* system. Although, in Bengal as in other provinces, a uniform *subah* administration was introduced in 1586 A.D., the land revenue operations based on Mughal procedure of survey and measurement were comparatively less in vogue.[5] The *Ain-i-Akbari* does not record the measurement tables for any of the 487 *mahals* in 24 *sarkars* in Bengal[6] which shows that the *zamindaries* in all the *sarkars* were *ghair-amli*. In Akbar's reign, the zamindars in Bengal remained mostly turbulent[7] and various semi-independent up-start landlords sprang up and resisted the proper enforcement of the Mughal rule. Such an insecurity of the political situation casts doubt on the proper working of the *zamindari* system based on Mughal principles and reveals a cleavage between the theory and practice of the administrative polity. It was only in the last years of Akbar and early phase of Jahangir's regin that Raja Man Singh Kachhwa and Islam Khan took stringent and effective measures for the enforcement and consolidation of the Mughal authority.[9]

The real character of the working of the Mughal *zamindari* system in Bengal emerges only in Jahangir's reign and its picture can be clearly drawn from *Baharistan-i-Ghaybi* of Mirza Nathan. As a general rule, the Imperial policy was aimed at forcing them to submission rather than to extinguish them completely.[10] Under the terms of submission, two-fold principles were followed towards the zamindars in Bengal (and Orissa). Ordinarily, such zamindars who submitted either voluntarily or without fighting after getting an ultimatum were given back their *zamindaries* as *jagirs*.[11]Secondly, usually after the failure of armed resistance on the part of the zamindar, a major portion of the erstwhile *zamindari* was annexed to the Mughal territory and a portion was assigned to him as maintenance *jagir*. If a zamindar became rebellious, a major portion of his territories was assigned in *tankhwah-jagir* to the Mughal *mansabdars*.[12] In any case, whatever be the position of the zamindar as *jagirdar*, he had in either case to make obedience in person before the Governor and sometimes would be despatched to the Imperial Court for submission.[13] He had to offer a near relative in surveillance as guarantee for further loyalty.[14] All loyal zamindars had to render military service for the expansion of the Mughal Empire and some were even enlisted in regular Imperial service.[15] They had essentially to pay *peshkash*, though, some paid as a nominal gift while others as regular revenues for the *zamindari* areas other than the *watan* or maintenance *jagir*.[16]

After reduction to terms, the zamindars viz. Satrajit of Bhunsa, Bir Hamir of Birlehum, Shams Khan of Pachet were restored their *zamindaries* as maintenance *jagir*.[17] Musa Khan, the chief of the Bhuyans and his allies in Bhatti area were all given back full territories of their *zamindaries* as *jagir* wih full authority for internal administration.[18] They were all obliged to pay *peshkash* (stimulated revenues) and to join the Imperialists for repelling the other rebellious zamindars and for further expansion of the Mughal territory.[19] They had to present themselves at the Governor's Court.[20] Anwar Khan of Baiachung was assigned his whole territory in *jagir* after submission. He presented himself personally at Islam Khan's Court and joined the Imperialists.[21] But later on, after his rebellion, his territories were annexed and he was sent to the fort of Rohtas.[22]

As distinct from the above category, the zamindars of Jessor and Bakla, though confirmed in their entire *zamindaries* were assigned only a portion of their respective territories in personal *jagir*. The rest of the *zamindari* territories were either asssigned away to the Mughal *mansabdars* or incorporated in the *khalisa* land. Raja Pratapaditya (of Jessor) was confirmed by Islam Khan in all his possessions and was granted the revenues of the districts of Sripur and Bikrampur in lieu of his allowance.[23] Raja Ram Chander of Bakla was put under surveillance and assigned by Islam Khan as much of his territories as was necessary for the maintenance of his fleet while the rest of his *zamindari* territories were given to the *karories* and the *jagirdars*.[24] As he proved recalcitrant, his entire territory was attached to the *khalisa*. Later on during Qasim Khan's Governorship, he was reinstated in his territory with the above mentioned *jagir*.[25] The sons of Raja Pratapaditya of Jessore, also having proved turbulent, were forced to submission and were sent under surveillance to the Imperial Court. But with a view to improve relations with Jessore and the European (*Firingi*) pirates, they were sent back and reinstated in their territory with the aforementioned *jagir*.[26] The majority of the *Bhuyans* were placed in this class of zamindars and were assigned only a portion of their *zamindaries* as personal *jagir*.

Still distinct from the 2nd category, after submission of Bayizid Karrani, the *zamindari* of Sylhat was totally annexed to the Mughal State and was placed under the management of a Mughal administrator.[27] Though *Baharistan-i-ghaybi* mentions about the submission of the zamindars of Kachar, Tippera and Bhalwa, it does not say anything about the nature of their *jagirs*. The very fact that the Mughal *Thanas* were established therein,[28] suggests that either like Sylhat they were totally annexed or a major portion of their territories were put under direct administration leaving them only with small *Jagirs*.

As regards the land revenue administration, it is clear that such of the *zamindaries* which were entrusted in *jagir* in entirety were declared *ghair amli* and the zamindars were left with autonomy for revenue administration. But such *zamindaries,* whereof only small portions were assigned for personal *jagir* to their Chiefs, were declared *amli* subject to the Mughal procedure of assessment and collection of the revenues. In case of *zamindari* of Bakla, *Bharistan-i-Ghaibi* notes that apart from the personal *jagir* assigned to Raja Ram Chander, the rest of the territories was entrusted to the *karories* and the *jagirdars*[29] who, were under the Mughal rules, were bound to get their revenues assessed after a regular survey. Similarly, in Jessore, the Raja was given a small *jagir* and his territories were placed under direct Mughal administration. Khwaja Mohammad Tahir deputed to assess the revenues of Jessore prepared the *jama* (assessed revenue) documents bearing the signatures of the *chaudharies* and the *qanungos* and this was consequently enforced on the *ryots* and the *jagirdars* for revenue realisations.[30]Apart from this, the *zamindaries* totally annexed to the Mughal State were essentially declared *amli*. This is borne out by *Bharistan-i-Ghaybi's* detailed narration of the revenue operations enforced in Sylhat.[31]

In the *Ain-i-Akbari's* geographical account of the *subah* Bengal, the Chief of Kutch finds mention with a contingent of 1,000 cavalry and 1,000 infantry and having also under him the territory of Kamrup (Kampta)[32]. As these territories do not find any place in any of the *sarkars* of *subah* Bengal, it seems that under Akbar, they remained free from Mughal interference[33] and were brought under the Mughal control only in Jahangir's reign. After submission, Raja Parikshit Narayan was reinstated in his territory with a nominal *jagir* but for revenue administration, major portions of the Kamrup territory were brought under the pattern of Mughal administration.[35] Some *parganas* were reserved in the *khalisa,* while others were assigned in *tankhwah jagir* or assigned to the revenue farmers for the collection of the land revenue.[36] The territory of Kamrup was brought under the Mughal system of land revenue administration and *karories* were appointed for the collection of the revenues in its *parganas.*[37] Raja Lakshmi Narayan of Kamta had already submitted and having been placed under surveillance, his territory was placed under the Mughal administration.[38] Later on, along with cousin, Raja Parikshit, he was also reinstated as zamindar with some *jagir* by Ibrahim Khan, the Governor. He helped the Imperialists in the further expansion of the Mughal territory.[39]

The *zamindari* of Kuch Bihar continued to exist till 1661 A.D. As Raja Bhim Narain gave shelter to the Raja of Assam, the territory of Kuch Bihar was annexed to the Mughal State.[40]Shabuddin Talish bears testimony that the land revenue administration was brought in line with the other provinces. Besides this, all other petty *zamindaries* of Kuch Bihar, though they continued in existence were inevitably brought under the Mughal pattern of administration. The contemporary evidence of late Aurangzeb's reign reveals that usually their territories were assigned in *tankhwah jagir* to the Mughal State officials.[42]

The variation in treatment of the zamindars in the initial stages of conquest was inevitable in the face of the doubtful allegiance and oft-repeated recalcitrance on the part of certain zamindars. By Ibrahim Khan's time, the situation had comparatively settled down and the Mughal court decided to set free the Princes kept under surveillance and reinstated the chiefs of Jessore and Kuch.[44] But the restoration of the *zamindaries* never meant any recognition of the Chiefs as semi-independent with only nominal allegiance to the Mughal states.[45] Even their *jagir* grant never comprised the full territories of their respective *zamindaries* but only a part thereof, the rest still remaining with the Mughal officers for revenue administration. Moreover, the Chiefs also remained subject to the Mughal *zamindari* regulations of allegiances and military towards the Chiefs of Kuch Bihar, Kamrup and Assam Hills clearly suggests that the zamindars were left only a portion of *zamindari* territory in personal *jagir* and it could not have been otherwise in the already consolidated areas in Bengal. The final policy pursued towards the

Bengal zamindars was not exceptional but was exactly in line with the general policy adopted in the other Mughal Provinces.

After its consolidation in Bengal, simultaneous with pre-Mughal hereditary Chiefs and Bhuyans, the Mughal Government also created a new class of official zamindars who, like their counterparts in the other Mughal Provinces, were assigned *jagirs* in lieu of the discharge of police duties and collection of the revenues in their territories. Such *zamindaries* were essentially *amli* and the revenue realisations were always deposited as *peshkash* with the Mughal state. The zamindars, of course, exercised police, judicial and financial powers for the collection of the revenues. But except in a *ghair amli* territory, the herediatry chiefs were never vested with assessment powers. Their *amli* territories and the territories of the official zamindars were always assessed by the Mughal officials. With the gradual consolidation of the Mughal authority from Jahangir's reign onwards, it can be maintained on the basis of fresh contemporary evidence that by and large, *ghair amli* territories of the *zamindaries* were rendered *amli*.

More than *Bharistan Ghaybi* for Jahangir's time, *Murraqat-i Hasan* and *Fathiya Ibriya* of Shahabuddin of Talish completely bear it out for the reign of Aurangzeb.

Mir Abul Hasan Alamgir's compilation of the official correspondence of the Mughal officers entitled *Muraqat-i Hasan*[47] covers the working of the land revenue administration of the regions of the *Subah* of Bengal and Orissa for early years of Aurangzeb's reign. It gives a detailed view of the working of the *zamindari* system and significantly even brings out the position of the zamindars who paid fixed annual revenues *(peshkash muqarari)* assessed periodically by the Mughal state. Notwithstanding occasional re-calcitrance and evasion of the revenue payment on the part of the zamindars, the Mughal state rigidly enforced its revenue regulations. For early Aurangzeb's reign, Shahabuddin Talish also clearly mentions the revenue realisations of the *khalisa*, *jagir* and the *aima* lands based on measurement operations in practically the whole of Bengal excepting Chittagong which had been entered by the *qanungos* as *ghair amli* ever since the Mughal conquest and had always been assigned in *tankhawah jagir* for the *mansabdars*.

In principle, the *zamindari* system in Bengal worked on the same lines as in other Mughal Provinces. Mirza Mohammad Hadi's and Murshid Quli's revenue reforms marked the culmination of the process of integration in the realm of land revenue administration. Mirza Muhammad Hadi, an expert in the revenue and *faujdari* affairs, was appointed Diwan of Orissa and later was transferred by Aurangzeb as Diwan of *subah* Bengal.[49]Mirza Hadi extended the revenues of the *khalsa* by curtailing the proportion of the *jagir* territories in *subah* Bengal. Most of the *jagirs* of the Mughal *mansabdars* were diverted to the *subah* of Orissa. Mirza Hadi enforced revenue reforms for the preparation of assessment, based on survey and measurement and the state regulations in all categories of land inclusive of the *zamindari* territories. He confirmed the assignments of the zamindar as *tankhawh jagir*. He appointed revenue officers who assured the land revenue and other miscellaneous source of revenue (*Malwa Sair*) in respect of all the *paraganas, chaklas* and *sarkars* of *Subah* Bengal. It seems that before his appointment, the Mughal revenue regulations were not properly enforced which left greater autonomy to the *tankhawa jagirdars* and the zamindars. The zamindars were enjoined to be extremely regular and punctual in the realisation of the land revenues and to look after the interests of the *ryots*.

All these measures led to the increase of Mughal states revenues in Bengal. Murshid Quli Khanas the Diwan and the Governor of Subah Bengal (1700-1727) reinforced the revenue reforms and Mughal regulations and like Mirza Muhammad Hadi, tightened the machinery of the *zamindari* institution.[50] Under him a survey and measurement based on detailed classification of the agrarian land, was carried out for the fixation of his revenues. A detailed survey of the agricultural and fallow land of the villages in the *parganas* was conducted by the *shiqdars* and *amins*. Based on these operations, a fresh settlement of the revenues of the territories of the zamindars of *subah* was effected. The unauthorised allowances and expenditure of the zamindars were fixed. In line with the Mughal practice, the administration tried to establish contact with the *riyaya*. Needy *riyaya* were given *taqavi* loans and all efforts were diverted at the increase of agricultural productions and the revenues (*Malwa Sair*) in the *subah* of Bengal. The assertive *zamindari* of Virbhum and Bishanpur were forced to abide by financial regulations. The zamindar of Kutch Bihar, who had often been recalcitrant and aimed at independence, was equally obliged to make annual payment of the *peshkash* regularly. Murshid Quli Khan also recognised the administration of the *parganas, chaklas* and the *sarkars* in the *subah* of Bengal. The appointment of the state revenue officials like the *amils* in the territories of the zamindars was equally calculated to check the influence of the zamindars and confine them to the Mughal practice of financial regulations. The *chakla* of Midnapur, having been detached from *subah* Bihar, was incorporated in *subah* Bengal. In order to curb the recalcitrant nature on the part of zamindars, he rearranged Bengal, into official *zamindaries*, increasing their extent and diminishing their number. Thus he encouraged the formation of big *zamindaries*. Under him nearly half of the revenues of Bengal were paid by six large zamindars viz. Raj Shahi, Burdwan, Dinagepore, Nadia, Virbhum and Bishanpur who had under their jurisdictions the petty zamindars and the *taaluqdars*, the *chaudhari's*, the *mandals* (headmen) and the *riyaya* in the villages. Though the reduction in the number of official zamindars facilitated the collection of the revenues on the part of the *subah* administration, it definitely gave impetus to the growth of hierarchical pattern of the landed intermediaries within the newly formed big *zamindaries*. Murshid Quli Khan also withdrew the *sehbandi* deductions (i.e. charges for the maintenance of regular contingent forces) from within the revenues of *zamindaries*. It gave a blow to the military position of zamindars who were expected to confine their role as the revenue collectors with the help of their locally maintained militia. The appointment of the state officials like *amils* in the territories of the zamindars was equally calculated to check the influence of the zamindars and to confine them to the Mughal practice of financial regulations.[51]

In the administration of Bengal from the *subahadari* of Shujja-ud-doula to that of Mir Qasim, notwithstanding the varying personal attitute of harshness or leniency on the part of the *subahdar* for the realisation of the revenues from the zamindars and variation in the *rasum* (allowances forming percentage of *Jama*) fixed for the latter, on a structural plane, the *zamindari* pattern ran practically on the same lines as before.[52] However, the spirit of administration underwent a radical change.[53] The growth of the extensive practice of the *ijaradari* system, the under-farming and further under letting the revenues within the *zamindari* jurisdictions seriously undermined the working and spirit of the revenue administration of the Subah of Bengal.[54]

The *Taaluqdars*

The late 16th to the 18th centuries sources record the existence of a class of *taaluqdars* acting as intermediaries like the zamindars.[55] In the technical territorial sense, the term *taaluq* or *taaluqa* seems to have connoted only a *zamindari* or *taaluqdari* territory. In the *Ain-i-*

Akbari's detailed revenue tables of the *mahals* of *subah* Bengal,[56] some of the *mahals* are mentioned as *taaluqa* and are associated with named persons rather than with territories. Excepting Bengal and Orissa, the *Ain-i-Akbari* does not record the term *taaluqdar* for any other *subah* of the Mughal empire. Besides, it mentions the existence of the zamindars in Bengal as in the other *subahs* mentions their castes in the *mahal* tables. For the territory of Orissa (*subah* Bengal), apart from the castes, even the number of the local contingent forces maintained by the zamindars is given. The information is also available for some *taaluqdars* who are declared independent. It cannot be stated with certainty if the *Ain* identifies *taaluqdars* with the zamindars and *bhuyas* but it is clear that the *taaluqs* or the *mahals* of the *taaluqdars* were in the nature of *zamindari* territories. When the *Ain* specifically declares some *taaluqdars* in Orissa as independent, it perhaps means to distinguish them from such *taaluqdars* who may hold dependent *taaluqas* within the territorial jurisdication of the zamindars. Evidently, the term *taaluqdars* were known to Bengal under Akbar or even in the pre-Akbar era. In Bengal too, with the consolidation of the Mughal rule late in Akbar's reign and under Jahangir, the *taaluqdars* were brought within the Mughal pattern of the *zamindari* and revenue regulations. The term *taaluqa* in the territorial sense was associated as much with a zamindar as with a *taaluqudar.* At the same time, it is through half of the 17th and 18th centuries that even though a *taaluqdar* belonged to an intermediary class, technically he was always distinct from a proper zamindar. This fact raises doubts as to whether the two terms zamindar and *taaluqdar* were synonymous. For the *subah* of Bengal, the revenue literature of the 18th century not only insists on but even offers adequate explanation of the difference in the status of the two ranks.[57]

According to this evidence, a *taaluqdari* compared to a *zamindari,* had a lower territorial jurisdiction and status. This is in line with the 17th century tradition in Bengal and Orissa. For the territory of Arakan (*subah* Bengal) Shihabuddin Talish places the *Rajas,* zamindars and *taaluqdars* in order of priority in respect of territorial jurisdiction and status.[58]It seems that this is equally true of 16th, 17th century Bengal after its complete subjugation by the Mughal State. For early part of Aurangzeb's reign, Muraqat-i-Hasan refers to the realisations to be made by the revenue staff (*chaudharis* and *qanungos*) from the *taaluqdaries* in *subah* Orissa.[59] The *taaluqdars* are also mentioned in the code of revenue instructions issued by Aurangzeb.[60]This suggests that the *taaluqdari* class was more numerous and widespread than can be actually ascertained from the available contemporary regional records.

The act of *zamindari* lay in the payment of revenues *(malguzari)* to the state; a zamindar was always confirmed by a royal *sanad* and paid *peshkash* to the State.[61] On the other hand, a *taaluqdar* would assume the role of a zamindar and was deemed as such when he paid the revenues of his territory directly to the state[62] but, by and large, the petty *taaluqdars* paid the revenues of their *taaluqas* through a superior, zamindar-cum-*chaudhari* who acted as the representative.[63] Such a zamindar paid the revenues not only of his own *zamindari* but even of the petty *taaluqas* of the *taaluqdars* under his jurisdiction. His *zamindari* was reckoned to cover both his personal *zamindari* and the petty *taaluqas*. However, he possessed no rights of sale or mortgage of the *taaluqdaris* under his jurisdiction.[64] A zamindar in Bengal, unlike one in North India, could not alienate the title of *zamindari* but could sell only his rights over *panj-taaluqa* (i.e. rights over revenue collection) and *chaudharai* rights along with the relevant perquisites.[65] Ordinarily, the hereditary charitable grants, viz., *Debottars, Brahmottar, Mehtran* and grants to the medicants *(fakirs)*, were not affected when a zamindar sold *taaluqa* village and the holders of such grants retained their rights under the purchaser now entitled the *taaluqdar*.[66] Unless otherwise stipulated in his *taaluqdari* patta, a *taaluqdar* possessed alienable rights and could sell the *taaluqdari* title.[67] Except in the case of the *taaluqa* villages colonised and developed by the *taaluqdar* himself, a *taaluqdar* was not the owner of the soil or the agricultural lands of the *riaya* and his proprietary rights in a *taaluqa* were exactly of the same nature as the zamindar's rights over his *zamindari*. But unlike a zamindar or a *chaudhari*, he was not entitled to *nankar* ar *maafi jagir* from the state but possessed both customary rights of *rasum* as well as *malikana*.[68] He claimed *malikana* only when the *taaluqa* was declared *air-i-hasil*.[69]

By the close of the 17th and early 18th century, there were families with an ancient claim to the *taaluqa* but the majority of the *taaluqas* were established after they were purchased from the original zamindars or *taaluqdars*.[70] This may well be illustrated from the position of the English East India Company in the 18th Century. A *parwana* issued under the seal of Ibrat Khan, *diwan*, dated 2nd Shabban 46th R.Y.(Aurangzeb) 2nd January, 1702 A.D. mentions therein the purchase of the villages of Calcutta, Sutanuti and Gobindpur, *pargana* Amir-abad, *chakla* Hugli (*subah* Bengal) by the

English East India Company from the zamindars.[71] In lieu thereof, the English East India Company had to deposit Rupees one thousand one hundred and ninety five and annas six only (Rs. 1,195.6 as. only) as yearly *jama* (revenue) in the Mughal State treasury. The *parwana* mentions Manohar Datt etc., the zamindars as the vendors and the East India Company as the buyers to be considered as the *taaluqdars*. Similarly, a copy of the sale deed also mentions the East India Company, the purchaser as the *taaluqdar*. Later, as the *farman* of Emperor Farrukhsiyar dated 4th *Safar*, 5th R.Y./18th Januarary 1717 A.D., not only confirms the already acquired *taaluqdari* of the above mentioned villages but further authorises the East India Company to purchase the *taaluqdari* of thirty eight new villages from the respective owners and the *Diwan-i-Subah* is enjoined to permit the sale transaction.[72] As the East India Company had already acquired the *taaluqdari* rights after the purchase of the villages from the zamindars, the annual *jama* (revenue) of these villages viz. Calcutta, Sutanati and Govindpuri in the *pargana* of Amirbad amounting to Rupees one thousand one hundred and ninety five and annas six only (Rs. 1,195.6 as.) was confirmed for payments to the Mughal Government. The *taaluqdari* of the thirty-eight new villages adjoining the aforesaid towns was to be purchased from the respective owners with the permission of the *Diwan-i-Subah*. The annual *jama* (revenue) of the newly purchased villages amounting to Rupees eight thousand one hundred and twenty one and annas eight only (Rs. 8121.8 as.) was to be paid by the East India Company to the state treasury. The *farman* confirms the *taaluqdari* of the above mentioned villages with the East India Company on the condition of the payment of the annual *jama* of the above mentioned amount and further directs the revenue officials to accept the duly stamped attestation by the *Qazi-ul-Kazat* in respect of all the previous documents and the present *farman* relating to the purchase of the *taaluqdari* of the villages. It is significant to note the *farman* (1717 A.D.) insists on designating the East India Company as the *taaluqdar* with *taaluqdari* rights over the purchased villages. However, as the East India Company paid revenues of the purchased villages directly to the states, it assumed the role of the zamindar only in general usage. It is quite clear from the above quoted documents that both officially and technically till 1717 A.D., the East India Company was the *taaluqdar*. In 1757, Mir Jafar also granted lands to the East India Company on the payment of the revenue "in the same manner as the other Zamindars".[73] The English were placed in possession of the 24 *parganas* in July 1757[74] and as such, the Company assumed the role of the zamindars. In 1760, Mir Qasim ceded to the Company Burdwan, Midnapore and Chittagong for "all charges of the Company and of the army and provisions for the fields, etc." Here, the East India Company assumed the role of the chief zamindar as a provision in the treaty clearly stipulated that the company would "continue the zamindars and renters in their places". In 1763 when Mir Jafar was restored, another formal treaty confirmed Mir Qasim's grant for "defraying the expense of the troops of the Company." This was a reaffirmation of the position of the East India Company as the chief zamindar for Burdwan, Midnapore and Chittagong. In 1765, the East India Company was granted the *diwani* of the *subahs* of Bengal, Bihar and Orissa. However, the technical differentiation between the *zamindari* and *taaluqdari* positions continued. It is only under the direct administration of the East India Company that, with effect from the 1194 Bengali year/ 1788-89 A. D., in the district of Dacca and other territories of Bengal that, in general usage, the technical distinction between the zamindar, *chaudhari* and the *taaluqdar* was mitigated and each of them came to be designated as zamindar. [75]

The extensive sale transactions of the 17th and 18th centuries established a large class of petty *taaluqdars*.[76] A person who did not hold any *zamindari* from the state but purchased *zamindari* rights of a few villages or a village from the original zamindar was known as *taaluqdar*. Ordinarily, the sale or mortgage of the petty *zamindari* shares would take place without the prior sanction of the government but in the case of transactions involving large *zamindari* shares, formal sanction of the Government was generally solicited and always granted by the state. The purchaser of a *zamindari* property comprising *taaluqa* villages would hold the *zamindari* title only when confirmed with *zamindari* rights by the states for the direct payment of the revenues to the latter. The essential criterion of *zamindari* lay in the recognition by the state through an issue of a *zamindari sanad* and a *taaluqdar* of a few villages, unless confirmed by a royal *sanad* in the *zamindari* rights, could not be designated as a zamindar.[77] Whatever be the origin of the *taaluqa*, ancient or acquired through purchase, the dependent *taaluqdars* paid the revenues through the zamindar and both the parties viz. the *taaluqdars* and the zamindar enjoyed their respective perquisites (*rasum* and *haquq*) based on local practice. According to Muhammad Raza Khan, revenue consultant to the Governor-General in council (1789 A.D.), there were different categories of the zamindars and the *taaluqdars*. [78] A *zamindari* might be an ancient one covering territories colonised and developed by the zamindars or might have been purchased or granted as a gift by the state or created through the award of a royal *zamindari sanad*. A colonising zamindar could alienate tracts of waste culturable land to persons entitled *taaluqdars* who, after having developed the land, might exercise the *malkiyat* rights in it for sale or gift but would pay the revenues to the state only through the zamindar. A purchaser of *taaluqa* villages from a *taaluqdar* or a zamindar acquired similar *malkiyat* rights but would have to pay the revenues through the original zamindar. But if a zamindar granted a *taaluqdari patta* to any one in respect of villages and lands already under cultivation, the *taaluqdar* would enjoy such *malkiyat* rights only if these were specifically transferred to him according to the terms of the *patta*. A *taaluqdar* who paid direct revenues to the state was named *huzuri* whereas a *taaluqdar* who paid through a zamindar was described as *muskuri*.

In many other parts of North-India, wherever the *taaluqdari* system existed, the position of the *taaluqdar* was a zamindar who was engaged with the state for the payment of the revenues of his own *zamindari* villages as also of various other petty *zamindaries* under him. The revenues were assessed by the state and the *taaluqdar* was subject to all the rules and regulations binding a zamindar for the payment of revenues to the state. He assumed the role of a superior zamindar who was not only responsible for the payment of revenue for his own *zamindari* villages but also acted as a channel for the revenue payments of the inferior zamindars who did not deal directly with the Government. Similarly, in joint *zamindari* villages, one of the co-sharers who acted as representative for the collective payment of the revenues, was known as a *taaluqdar*. But when a zamindar and a *taaluqdar* had under them villages paying equal amounts of revenue, the former invariably enjoyed a better income and a higher status. It is, however, significant that where such a system of *taaluqdari* came into being, three parallel claims, by no means mutually incompatible, were established on the *taaluqa* villages and their dependent zamindars belonged to intermediary classes in hierarchical order whereas, a few categories of *riaya* were the owners of the agricultural land. Their families, of course, owned lands, especially in the self-colonised villages. However, the *taaluqdar* and his dependent zamindars shared their respective perquisites and the details of apportionment would depend upon customary local practice.

A *taaluqdar*, when mentioned as the *malik* of the *taaluqa* comprising his own *zamindari* and dependent *zamindari* villages, was entitled to only a share in the perquisites of the dependent *zamindari* villages. Like a zamindar, a *taaluqdar* might own his personal lands in his *taaluqa* but neither he nor his dependent zamindars could claim proprietary rights in the soil and the agricultural lands of the *riaya* under them.[80]

In Bengal, a zamindar always enjoyed a superior status to the *taaluqdars* who held dependent jurisdictions under the former. However, both the zamindars and the *taaluqdars,* like their counterparts in other parts of North India, belonged to the intermediary classes and enjoyed their respectives perquisites. Except for personal lands, they were not the owners of the soil and agricultural lands of the *riaya* under them. In this respect, they stood on the same relation to the *riaya* as *taaluqdars* and the zamindars of the other provinces of the Mughal Empire. However, a striking feature of the 17th and 18th century agrarian structure of North India is the emergence of the hierarchical pattern of the landed intermediaries. Whether the inferior zamindar named *taaluqdars* paid revenue through a superior zamindar in Bengal, the basic tendency in the development of the agrarian structure in the 17th-18th centuries is the same throughtout the Mughal empire.

References

1. For details, see Grover, B.R., "Nature of Land Rights in Mughal India." *The Economic and Social History Review*, Delhi, Vol. I., No. 1: July-September, 1963, pp. 1-2; 17-18; also Grover. B.R., "Some Rare Persian Manuscripts and Documents on India (16th-18th Centuries) in the German Libraries," *Max Mueller Bhavan Publications, Year Book*, New Delhi, 1964, pp. 59-72; Grover, B.R., "Nature of *Dehat-i-Taaluqa* (*zamindari* villages and the Evolution of the *Taaluqdari* System during the Mughal age." *The Economic and Social History Review*, Delhi, Vol. II., No. 3. July-1965, pp. 277-78.
2. Grover B.R., *Nature of Land-Rights in Mughal India*, pp. 10-15.
3. Mirza Nathan, *Baharistan-i-Ghaybi* entitled *Baharistan, Historie de Bengala dequirs*, 1040 AH/A.D. No. Suppl 252, Bibiliotheque Nationle, Paris (henceforth Baharistan Paris). tr. M.I. Borah, 2 Vols. Gauhati, 1936, (henceforth B.G. tr), fols. 53 a; 61 b; 152 a; 165 b; 284 a.
4. *Akbar Nama* of Abul Fazl, translated into English by H. Beveridge, 3 Vols., 1912 (henceforth A.N. tr. Bev.), pp. 248-49.
5. *Ain-i-Akbari* of Abul Fazl (Ms. British Museum. Add 7652 (henceforth *Ain*, Br. M.) fol. 175 b, translated into English Vol. II by Col. H.S. Jarrett and annotated by J.N. Sarkar, Calcutta, 1949, (henceforth *Ain*,

tr. J. II.), p. 134. Here Abul Fazl does not rule out the possibility of initial survey and measurement of lands but asserts that it is not repeatedly practiced.

6. *Ain.* Br. M. fols. 177b-192b, tr. J. pp. 142-157. However, the 18th Century sources insist on the detailed land revenue settlement effected in Bengal under Akbar. According to *Akbarual Tasdiq dar Kafiat Bangala* (Ms. O.R. Fol. 270 Berlin), Todar Mal carried out the Revenue Settlement in Bengal twice, firstly as Secretary to Muzaffar Khan for three years, i.e., from 25th year to 28th year of Akbar's reign and secondly in the 39th year when he was the Vakil. The same Ms. mentions categorically that Muzaffar Khan and Todar Mal, musaddies of Emperor Akbar, carried out measurement operations in the whole province of Bengal, fixed the *Tumar* and levied 'Jama' according to three methods of assessment and delivered the Taqsim papers to the Qanungo. Also James Grant, *Historical and Comparative View*, The fifth Report, (vide f. n. 49) Vol II., p. 291.

7. A.N. tr. Bev. vide f. no. 9. *Ain.* tr. J, II., p. 130 makes an implied statement that in East Bengal (Bhatti), the Mughal Government was content with its formal recognition. It comments, "The tract of country on the east called Bhatti, is reckoned a part of this province. It is ruled by Isa Afghan and the Khutba is read and the coin struck in the name of the present Majesty." According to *Ain,* the Bhatti region comprised the eastern portions of Dacca.

8. See f.n. 9; also R.N. Prasad, Raja Man Singh of Amber, Calcutta, 1966, pp. 90-105. The Bhuyans comprised a set of powerful Chiefs who rose to power after the fall of Dauds the last Karrani Sultan of Bengal in 1576 A.D. Mirza Nathan puts their number at twelve which is appoximate rather than exact of the numerous minor Zamindars who fought against Islum Khan under the leadership of Musa Khan, son of Isa Khan and his ally Usman. Nathan does not specifically mention which of these the Bhuyans were. For further discussion on Bhuyans, see Dr. Wise, Bara Bhuyans, J.A.S.B., 1824, pp. 197-214; Blochmann, J.A.S.B., 1873, 223; Beveridge, J.A.S.B., 1904, p. 57, B.G.tr. II; Notes, pp. 799-800; also Tapan Kumar Ray Chaudhuri, *Bengal under Akbar and Jahangir*, Calcutta, 1953 pp. 1-3, (henceforth T.R. Chaudhuri).

9. Raja Man Singh was Governor of Bengal from 1594 to 1604 A.D. A.N.tr., Bev. III., pp. 1001, 1040-41, 1151, 1155, 1174, 1213-14, 1231-40, 1256-57. Islam Khan was the Governor from 1608 A.D. to 1613 A.D. For details, see Baharistan, Paris, fols. 4b-61b. Also B.G. tr. I., pp. XIV-XVIII, T.R. Chaudhuri, pp. 1-5.

10. Baharistan, Paris, folio 53a, 61b, 152a.

11. *Ibid.*, fol. 53a, tr. B.G. tr., I., p. 18. Islam Khan sent Iftikhar Khan against Satrajit of Bhunsa with the instruction that if the latter submitted , he should be given the hope of his territory as *jagir*

otherwise his country should be left as a prey to the horse of the Imperial Karoris.

12. *Ibid.*, fol. 53a, 61b, 152a, 170a, 208a, 312b, 325b, B.G.tr., II, p. 518.

13. B.G.tr., II, pp. 566-67.

14. B.G.tr., I, p. 100.

15. Baharistan, Paris, fol. 53a, B.G. tr., I, p. 100; II, 517, 522, 568.

16. Baharistan, *op. cit.* f.n. 9 and 10, B.G.tr.,I, p. 123; II, pp. 521-22.

17. *Ibid.* fols. 53a; 165 b, B.G.I, tr., I, pp. 18-20, 327. For geographical situation of these territories, see Rennell's Map. no. 7; also B.G. tr., II., Notes, pp. 800-801.

18. B.G.tr., I, p. 100. After the surrender of Musa Khan and his allies, " the estate of each of them was given back to them as *jagir* for their maintenance." For geographical situation of Bhatti Chieftainships, See J.B.O.R.S., IV, p. 188; *Bengal Past and Present*, 1928, XXXV, 33 and XXXViii, p. 25; also B.G.tr. II, p. 796.

19. *Baharistan*, Paris, fols. 53a, 152a, B.G.tr.,I, pp. 19, 29, 319.

20. *Ibid.* fols. 53a, 165b, B.G.tr., I, p. 327. "When, of all the zamindars, Shams Khan, Zamindar of Birbbum, Bir Hamir, zamindar of Pachet, and Bahadur Khan, newphew of Salim Khan Hijliwal did not present themselves (at the Governor Court), Shaykh Kamal was depatched against Shams Khan and Bir Hamir."

21. B.G. tr., I, p. 105.

22. *Ibid.* p. 140.

23. *Baharistan*, Paris, fols. 61b, 300a, B.G.tr., I, p. 28. Jessore is included in the *Ain* as Mahal of Sarkar Khalifatabad. *Ain*, Br. M. vide f.n. 4, *Ain*, tr., J. II, p. 134. Baharistan mentions it as 'Jasar'.

24. B.G.tr., I, p. 132.

25. *Ibid.*, II, p. 521.

26. Baharistan, Paris, fols. 273 a, 299 b-300a. B.G.tr.,II, p. 521.

27. B.G.tr.,I, p. 208; Mukarram Khan was appointed as Sardar (Administrator) of the whole Sarkar of Sylhat (pp. 326-27). Later on, Mirza Nathan, the author of Baharistan, was himself appointed the Sarkar of Sylhat. (*Ibid.* II, p. 633). *Ain*, tr., J. II, p. 152, mentions Sylhat as a Sarkar division with 8 Mahals in *Subah* Bengal. For details, Geographical situation, Rennel's Map, 6; 13.G., tr., Notes, p. 819.

28. *Ibid.* II, p. 690.

29. *Ibid.* I, p. 132.

30. Baharistan, Paris, fol. 61 b, B.G. tr., I, pp. 156-57 "Khwaja Muhammad Tahir, who went to Jessore to assess its revenues, returned to Islam

Khan with the register of revenues of that country, which was prepared to the satisfaction of the *ryots* and to the advantage of the Imperial treasury.

31. B.G. tr., I, pp. 326-27; II, p. 633.

32. *Ain.* tr., J., p. 130. The *Ain* and the other Mughal historians sometimes use the terms Kamrup and Kamta as synonymous. Kamta originally comprised the western part of the Brahmputtra valley upto Karatoys and was included within the kingdom of Kamrup. Both Kamrup and Kamta collectively consititute the territory of Kuch Bihar. Bharistan puts Kamrup to the east of Manas river under Raja Parikshit Narayan and Kamta to the west of the river under Raja Lakshmi Narayan. For details, B.G. tr., Borah II, f.n. 15, pp. 806-7.

33. A.N. Bev. III, 349, 1067; Also *Ain* tr. J., II; also B.G. tr., II., Notes, pp. 826-29.

34. B.G. tr., I, pp. 252-53, 272, 410.

35. *Ibid.*, p. 272, 410; II, p. 521. Raja Parikshit was forced to make obedience to the corpse of the deceassed Governor Islam Khan (*Ibid.*, pp. 257, 264) and presented before the new Governor Qasim Khan (*Ibid.* pp. 292, 297, 409, 452). His territory was brought under direct Mughal administration by Qasim Khan (*Ibid.* pp. 409-10). But later on the next Governor Ibrahim Khan reinstated the Raja as a loyal zamindar on the condition of payment of Rs. 700,000 as *peshkash* to the Mughal State (*Ibid.*, II. p. 521).

36. *Ibid.*, I, pp. 272-73. After Raja Parikshit submitted, "Abdus Samad was appointed the Commandar of the army at Kuch and he ordered Mirza Hasan, the *Diwan* and *Bakshi,* to arrange for the collection of the revenues in the Parganas and other places. The aforesaid Mirza, due to his great experience, divided the Parganas of the Kuch territory into 20 well-defined circles, some being entrusted to the Imperial Karories and Jagirdars for realisation of revenues, some lands were given to Mustajirs", (Revenue Farmers, *Ibid.*, pp. 272-73). Later on the administration was entrusted to Shaykh Ibrahim Karori (*Ibid.*, p. 410) and still later given in *jagir* to Quliji Khan , the *sarkar* (administrator) of Kuch.

37. *Ibid.*, I, pp. 288-89. A revenue officer of a Diwan's rank was appointed in Kuch Bihar and Kamrup and he acted under the authority of the Diwan-i-Subah and the Governor of Bengal. After the dismissal of Mirza Hassan Mashaddi, the Diwan and Bakshi of Kuch, Mir Safi was appointed for the office. He introduced changes in the revenue assessment of all the Parganas of Jahangirabad but because of the excessive fixation of the assessment demand, he was also dismissed. Shaykh Ibrahim was appointed the Chief *Karori* for the whole country of Kamrup. He managed the revenue and settlement affairs and Imperial Thanas were set up for this purpose in Kamrup. (*Ibid.*, p. 403).

38. Baharistan, Paris, fol. 152a, B.G.tr., I, pp. 290 290, 352; II., 503. Of the two Rajas of Kuch Bihar, Lakshmi Narayan of Kamta division was the first to submit to the Mughal authority.

39. B.G.tr., II, p. 521.

40. *Ibid.*, pp. 589, 605, 612, 621.

41. Abul Fazl Mamuri, Ms. 2093, State Library Rampur (U.P.), pp. 449-450.

42. Ibriyah, Ms. Orient, Quart 266, Berlin, fol. 55a-55b. Rashid Khan was appointed as *faujdar* vide fol. 134b.

43. Even after submission, rebellion against the Mughal authority was quite frequent on the part of some Zamindars. For details, see B.G.tr., I, pp. 32, 105-6; 127, 131, 134, 136, 139; B.G.tr., II, 623-25, 639, 782.

44. Baharistan, Paris 299b-300a. *Ibid.*, II, p. 521.

45. Prof. T.R. Chaudhuri, pp. 18-20. concedes the fact that during the governorships of Islam Khan and Qasim Khan, 'the semi-Independent princelings were all reduced to the position of *jagirdars* or subordinate zamindars' and' 'some also became officers of the Mughal Empire' he considers the position anomalous. He further points out that Ibrahim Khan's policy of reconciliation ended this anomaly and that "a more or less uniform relationship was now established between the Mughal Government and the zamindars who became fullfledged vassals of the Empire. The restoration of territories was no longer nominal but real. "Prof. Chaudhri has not realised that differentiation in the treatment of the zamindars in the initial or final position of the Mughal conquest would by no means render the position anomalous. In fact, variation in relationship between the Mughal state and different categories of the zamindars due to various geographical, military and political factors was the very essence of the Mughal state policy. Moreover, the restoration of the erstwhile territories of the *zamindaries*, even when real, did not mean that the Mughal state had surrendered its rights over the revenues of these *zamindaries*.

46. *Ibid.*, pp. 20-23. But Prof. T.R. Chaudhury's assertion for autonomy for every category of *zamindari* is erroneous. In fact, the exercise of the administrative powers inherent in the *zamindari* insitution itself did not imply any autonomy, least of all in the sphere of land revenue administration. In this respect, further distinction has been made for every category of zamindar. Only such zamindars who paid *peshkash muqarari* i.e., fixed annual *peshkash* (Zamindaran-i-Peshkash Muqarari), may enjoy certain discretionary power in the land revenue administration. However, the *peshkash* was subject to periodical revision. Despite errors in some respects, Grant's "Historical and Comparative Analysis in Finances of Bengal," dated 27th April, 1786, (vide The *Fifth Report from the Select Committee of the House of Commons on the Affairs of the East India Company*, July 1812, 2 Vols., edited by W.K.Firminger, 1917 edition), Vol. II, p. 170. Moreland's criticism

(W.H.Moreland, *The Agrarian System of Muslim India*, Appendix G) of grant is not justified and his view that the zamindars paid a fixed lump sum unassessed amount of the State is based on his wrong reading of the *Ain-i-Akbari*. Even if Moreland's analysis of the *Ain* be accepted, it cannot be asserted that the nature of land revenue administration in the *zamindaries* of unsettled Bengal, as under Akbar, remained static throughtout the Mughal age. Moreland's difficulty arises from his rigid concept of *Ain's* statistics of revenue tables and also his belief to the effect, "As time went on, they disappeared because there was, in fact, no difference on the incidence of the various positions, and all alike came to be known as zamindars". The later view is not at all true for the 17th century and the 18th century till atleast the Diwani and Governorship of Murshid Quli Khan (1700-1727 A.D.) Murshid Quli Khan's revenue reforms make clear-cut traditional distinction between different categories of revenue officiates and the zamindars. In view of the available contemporary documentary evidence, it is equally doubtful that the technical distinction between the chiefs, revenue farmers and revenue officials disappeared so as to entitle them to be known as zamindars.

47. Mir Abul Hasan Alamgir, *Murraqat-i-Hasan, Insha-i-Farsi,* 217, State Library Rampur (U.P.), pp. 90-146, 248-329. The author himself was a Mughal State official attached with the Governor of *subah* Orissa and served as official correspondent. Later on, he compiled the letters which he had written on behalf of the *subah* administration. The letters comprise correspondence with Mughal state *mansabdars*, revenue officers, *Diwani-i-Subah* (Bengal and Orissa) and the Central Government. The correspondence throws light on the working of the *zamindari* and the revenue administration in the *subah* of Bengal and Orissa.

48. Shihabu-addin Talish, *Fathiya-i-Ibrya,* Bodleian Library, Oxford, OR 289, fols. 118a-119a, 164a. The MS is a continuation of the earlier text of the same work to 1666 A.D. It narrates the administrative and revenue reforms of Shaista Khan in Bengal. The late 17th Century *Dasturulamals* give a detail of the villages and the arazi (measured) land in Bengal. See Ms. Fraser. 86, Bodlein Library, Oxford, *Intkhab-i-Dasturulamal Padshaahi*, Ms. 224, Edinburgh Library (U.K.). Also, Fol. 270, Berlin (18th Cent.).

49. *Tarikh-i-Bangala,* Ms. 1038 Tarikh, Asifiya State Library, Hyderabad, (India), fols. 14a-15b. *Tarikh-i-Bangala,* Ms. or quart 248, 4B, Tubingen, (West Germany).

50. *Ibid.*

51. Prof. T.R. Chaudhuri (pp. 11, 42) thinks that Murshid Quli "merely put the Zamindars under a binding obligation to pay their revenues regularly. Even this sole mark of bondage had apparently been ignored in the preceding years, when Mughal authority is supposed to have been most firmly entrenched in Bengal" and that the zamindars

"were certainly the masters of the situation within their estates"... He concludes, "The zamindars, within their territories were free to rule as they liked: free to rule, and free to oppress." Prof. *chaudhuri* has not fully understood the working of the institution of *zamindari* in Bengal. Whereas the police, administrative and revenue powers were inherent in the institution of *zamindari*, the revenue powers were more of an obligation than a privilege and were always subject to the State regulations of Survey and assessment. Prof. Chaudhuri is inconsistent and shifty in his arguments. When face to face with *Bahristan-i-Ghaibi* and the original Mughal documents, he is inclined to believe that the zamindars were reduced to the status of *jagirdars* and tax-gatherers but while banking on the later family annals and Bengali literature (*Ibid.*, pp. 18, 22-3; Bibliography, p. 236), he believes in the complete authority and unrestrained revenue powers of the zamindars. Similarly, while analysing the Mughal *farman* of Shah Jahan's reign concerning a *zamindari* appointment, Prof. Bhaudhari recognises that in return for his privileges, the zamindar" was required to be punctilious in his remittances of revenue and to look after the welfare of the people." (*Ibid.*, p. 21.). On the other hand, without realising the implications of the conditional grant or confirmation of personal *jagir* of a zamindar, and without any substantial contemporary evidence, he jumps to the conclusion that the obligation of the revenue duties was a mark of bondage which was always ignored by the zamindar during the Mughal rule (*Ibid.*, p. 22).

52. For details of the revenues and administrative measures of Nawab Jaffar Khan and Nawab Shujjauddin Muhammad Khan, See *Haqiqat-i-Subah Bengala* (18th Cent.), Ms. Br. M. Add 6586, fols. 24b-27a, For 18th Cent. revenue history of Bengal, also see Ms. or fol. 27Q, Berlin, Ms. or quart 148, Berlin; also Sinha N.K., *The Economic History of Bengal*, Vol. II, Calcutta, 1962, pp. 1-47. (henceforth, Sinha, N.K.).

53. Ms. Orient . Oct. 105, Berlin, fols. 12a-13b.

54. Ms. or. quart 258, Berlin, fols. 310a-313a; Also Sinha, N.K., pp. 23-36.

55. For detailed discussion on the *taaluqdari* system in Bengal and the other Mughal provinces, see Grover, B.R., *Nature of Dehat-i-Taaluqa*. op. cit., f.n. 1, pp. 269-288.

56. *Ain*, Br. M. Add. 7652, fols. 177b-192b.

57. Ms. or. quart 258, Berlin, fols. 145b-146a.

58. *Fathiya-Ibriya*, op. cit., f.n. 48, fols. 1556-156.

59. *Muraqat-i-Hasan*, op. cit., f.n.47, pp. 317-18.

60. *Nigar Nama-i-Mushi*, Bod. Oxf., fols. 99b-100a., Ms. National Archives of India (N.A.I.), fol. 76a.

61. Ms. or. quart 258 Berlin, fols. 145b-146a.

62. *Ibid.*, fol. 306a.

63. *Ibid.*, fols. 145b-146a.

64. *Ibid.*, also, Ms. or. 234, Berlin.

65. *Ibid.*, fols. 125b-126a, 128b-129b. quotes copies of sale deeds both in Persian and Bengali, dated 15th July, 1966 A.D., and 5th September, 1754 A.D; Also see details, Grover B.R., *Nature of Dehat-i-Taaluqa*, op. cit. 1, f.n. 197, p. 283.

66. *Ibid.*

67. *Ibid.*, fols. 145b-146a; also Sinha, N.K., II, pp. 7-9, 13, 21-22, f.nos 15, 23.

68. *Ibid.*

69. *Ibid.*, also Ms. or fol. 134, Berlin.

70. *Ibid.*

71. Ms. Br. M.As. 24, 039. Document no. 36.

72. India Office Records (London), Home series, vols. LXIX, pp. 130-131; also a photostat copy, S. Bhattacharya, *The East India Company and the Economy of Bengal from 1704 to 1740*, London, 1954, Appendix IV, p. 234. Also, W.H. Moreland, *The Agrarian System*, pp. 189-23. Moreland has correctly insisted on designating the E.I.Co. as the *taaluqdar*. Prof. Irfan Habib's analysis of the *parwana* (op. cit. 71) and his identification of the zamindar and the *taaluqdar* as synonymous is not correct and his criticism of Moreland is not justified. (*The Agrarian System of Mughal India*, Bombay, 1963, pp. 172-73, f.n. 18). S. Bhattacharya's (pp. 24-25) reading of the above mentioned *farman*, dated 1717 A.D., while designating the E.I.Co as the zamindar is equally incorrect.

73. The *Fifth Report*, Firminger, Introduction, p. X.

74. For details of the acquisition of the E.I.Co in Bengal, see Sinha, N.K., pp. 24-26.

75. Ms. Orient Quart. 258, Berlin, fol. 275a.

76. For details, see Grover, B.R., *Nature of Dehat-i-Taaluqa*, op. cit., f.n. 1

77. See f.n. 61, *Nigar Nama-i-Munshi*, N.A.I. fols. 116a-117a, Ms. Orient fol. 306, Berlin, 4th clause of a Mughal Farman (copy), dated 3rd November, 1712 A.D.

78. *Proceedings of the Revenue Board consisting of the whole Council*, Vol. V, vide Sinha, N.K., pp. 7-9, 13, 22, f.nos. 15, 23.

79. For details, see Grover. B.R., *Nature of Dehat-i-Taaluqa*, op. cit., f.n. 1.

80. *Ibid.* Also for discussion on the nature of land-rights in Bengal and importance of the Persian Mss. and documents quoted in the above footnotes, see Grover, B.R., *Some Rare Persian Manuscripts and Documents on* India (16th-18th Centuries) in the German Libraries, op. cit., 1.

Chapter 6

The Evolution of the *Ta'aluqdari* System in Awadh During the 18th and early 19th Centuries (till 1814 AD)

A

The origin and growth of the *ta'aluqd'ari'* land tenure remained an extremely vexed problem for the British Indian revenue administrators after the occupation of North India in the late 18th and 19th centuries. The English administrators showed not only a keen academic interest in the origin of the institution of the *ta'aluqd'ari* under the native rule prior to the British occupation, some of them were also deeply interested to base their concepts of land settlements from region to region on historical basis. But practically all of them, inclusive of the early settlement officers, based their views either upon the family annals and traditions of the *ta'aluqd'ars* or rudimentary evidence derived from a few late 18th century and early 19th century original documents. Consequently, with a view to finding an historical justification for their land settlements, divergent views were expressed from time to time on the genesis of the *ta'aluqd'ari'* system.

Before the enforcement of the Permanent Settlement, Muhammed Reza Khan, the revenue consultant to the Governor General in Council (1789) and Sir John Shore, dilated on the existing position of the *ta'aluqd'ari* tenures in Bengal. Most of the *ta'aluqd'ari* tenures were described of recent origin and their landed interests were aligned with the lesser land-owning gentry and smaller zamindars. No attempt was made to trace the historical evolution as a socio-

---

Proceedings of *Colloquium on 'The Influence of Social Organization on Land Revenue in India'*, 1964, University of Wiscousin, U.S.A.

economic phenomenon.[1] Later on, when in the Ceded and Conquered Provinces great difference of opinion prevailed with regard to the comparative rights of the *ta'aluqd'ars* versus primary village zamindars in the large *ta'aluqd'aries* and the course to be pursued by the British Government for the settlement of the revenues with either of the parties, an attempt was made to trace the pre-British historical evolution and the rights of the *ta'aluqd'ars*. Holt Mackenzie thought that the origin of most of the *ta'aluqd'ari'* estates was of a questionable nature and that they were created by force or fraud in disturbed conditions prevailing before and immediately after the British annexation.[2] Only very few *ta'aluqd'ars* had hereditary grants or life grants fully authenticated, originally made or confirmed by the past native ruling power.[3] Mackenzie, however, refers to no evidence about the details of the hereditary grants and the period in which they had been made by the past rulers. No reflections are made on the genuineness of these grants either. Mackenzie also thought that some of the *ta'aluq'dari'* rights had been established by the big zamindars (*Rajas*)[4] or they may have secured possessions before the British conquest by their vigorous character, good management and indulgence to the undertenants.[5] *The Regulation VII, 1822 A.D.* recognised a class of estates *(ta'aluqa's)* in which there might be separate heritable and transferable propreitary rights viz. that of the superior, i.e. *ta'luqda'rs* and that of the inferior, i.e. the village proprietors (zamindars).[6] However, the Act required various further clarifications and the position of the two parties was again controverted on historical grounds. Lord William Bentinck attempted a vague historical approach and thought that like the *zamindari*, the *ta'aluqd'ari* tenures were adventitious and artificial and, generally speaking, were a creation of the Mughal Empire and that *ta'aluqd'ar* or zamindar was originally neither more nor less than a contractor with Government for its revenues.[7] Thus William Bentinck considered the *ta'aluqd'ar* class as a legacy from the Mughal Government but with regard to the period of its evolution, he considered that generally speaking the *ta'aluqd'ar* held the hereditary estates for second, third or the fourth generation at the maximum. He correctly compared the *ta'aluqda'rs* in the Ceded and Conquered Provinces to the big zamindars in Bengal but made no attempt at any detailed comparison, either in evolution or in the existing position. Later on, J. Thornton, secretary to the Government of North Western provinces (1844 A.D.), while considering the comparative rights of the *ta'aluqdars* and the village zamindars, stated that the *ta'aluqd'ars*, having been created by patent, were subservient to those of the village zamindars and *biswahdars* who would have been recognised by the British Government as absolute proprietors if there had been no *ta'aluqda'rs*[8]. Still more elaborate historical explanation was given by his contemporary, James Thomason, Lieut. Governor of the North Western Provinces (1843 A.D.), who belonged to the Bird School of thought. He contended[9] that before the formation of the *ta'aluq'a* or large estate comprising numerous villages (*mauzas*), these villages had originally separate proprietors (i.e. zamindars) who paid their revenue direct to the Government treasury. The native Government (prior to the British occupation) in former times made over by patent (grant), to a person called the *ta'aluqd'ar* its rights over these villages, holding him responsible for the whole revenue, and allowing him a certain percentage, with other privileges, compensating him for the risk and labour of collection. The wealth and influence acquired by the *ta'aluqdar* often made him independent and he was allowed to manage the estate as he pleased so long as he paid regularly the sum demanded from him. No provision existed for protecting the rights of the village proprietors (zamindars), though no one questioned the existence and inviolability of those rights.

Prior to the introduction of the British rule, the *ta'aluqd'ars* had often endeavoured to eject the village proprietors (zamindars), and had sometimes succeeded in their object. In his well-known *Directions for Settlement Officers and Collectors,* which appeared in three parts between 1844 and 1848, Thomason surmised a better and more systematic historical growth of the *ta'aluqd'ari* system.[10] He ascribed the *ta'aluqd'ari* tenures to grant by the native Governments or by voluntary act of the people (i.e. village zamindars) themselves whereby a *ta'aluqd'ar* became an intermediary between the primary village zamindars, exercising inferior proprietary rights and the state. For many of the villages under his jurisdiction bearing the responsibility of the revenue collection, a *ta'aluqda'r* may have been previously unconnected with the area. On the contrary, his jurisdiction should also comprise villages in which there were no inferior proprietary rights of the primary village zamindars. Such villages may have been the ancestral property of the *ta'aluqd'ar* himself or they may be the villages in which he had purchased the proprietary rights or in which he had succeeded in completely overbearing it , so as to have obliterated it over a period of time.

Though Thomason based his inferences and conclusions mostly on the early 19th century conditions prevalent immediate to the

British occupation, it appears that of all the British revenue administrators who had hitherto dwelt on the subject for the Ceded and Conquered Provinces, he possessed the greatest insight into the *ta'aluqd'ari* problem. Thomason did not run into any details of the background history of the *ta'aluq'dari* families and, as such, could provide only a general premise of the *ta'aluqd'ari* institution. He correctly pointed out that the *ta'aluqa* of a *ta'aluqd'ar* consisted of both hereditary *zamindari* villages (i.e. his personal estate) and such *zamindari* villages of the dependent zamindars with which he may have been unconnected before their incorporation into the *ta'aluqa*. But in his general analysis, he underestimated the extent of the personal ancestral *zamindari* villages of such *ta'aluqd'ars* who had also commanded the status of high dignitary zamindars since generations. So his picture was not very apt for a territory like Awadh in which not only ordinary zamindars but even the chief zamindars *(zamindaran-i-umda)* like the hereditary *Rajas* had also assumed the role of the *ta'aluqd'ars*.

After the annexation of Awadh by the British in 1856, the problem was once again highlighted for this territory in particular. While tracing the growth of the *ta'aluqd'ari* estates in Awadh, it was thought that the oppressive revenue policy pursued under the inefficient rule of the native *Nawabs* constituted an important step in enlarging the estates and the importance of the *ta'aluqd'ars*.[11]

The *Ijara* system was criticitzed as according to it revenues were farmed out to influential men and, in many cases, the zamindars and the *ta'aluqd'ars* themselves assumed the role of *mustajirs* (revenue farmers). Under this system, though the Awadh Government saved the cost of collection and was assured the payment of assessed amount, it was disadvantageous to the immediate holders of the soil. Even the *amani* 'trust system' of Nawab Sa'adat Ali Khan, though planned as a genuine reform, came under the severe attack of English writers who thought that this system had resulted in loss to the Government and increased oppression of and extortion from the holders of the soil. The exacting *nazims* or *chakladars,* the *amils* and the *amins* overassessed the holders of the soil and thereby suppressed the independent proprietors or "proprietary village communities". Unable to withstand the oppressive and inordinate demands of the *chakladars,* the village proprietors (i.e. primary zamindars) sought the protection of their more powerful neighbours and surrendered some of their rights to them. The *ta'aluqd'ari* estates were always increased by the *ta'aluqdar's* forcible encroachment on the lands of his weaker neighbours, the adoption of fraudulent means, sale deeds obtained by force, forced sales by the auction for arrears of revenue and bonafide sales by the primary zamindars and holders to meet the revenue demands of the state. It may be observed that in Awadh, the above mentioned factors accelerated the development of the large *ta'aluqd'ari* estates in the 19th century, especially after the death of Nawab Saadat Ali Khan. As explained later, such an assessment of Saadat Ali Khan's revenue policy is rather erroneous and it is doubtful if this was a vital factor for the growth of the *ta'aluqd'ari* system in Awadh. In fact, the institution of the *ta'aluqd'ari* had been known ever since the Mughal age and had developed fast from the second half of the 17th century onwards.

C.A. Elliot, author of the well-known book *Chronicles of Oonao*[12] challenged the theory of the upstart growth of the *ta'aluqd'ari* and tried to give an historical analysis to the evolution of the *ta'aluqd'ari* rights. He challenged the Thomason school of thought that the villages under the jurisdiction of a *ta'aluqd'ar* may have been absolutely unconnected with him prior to the stage they passed under his *ta'aluqa'* for the rights of collection at any stage of historical development. Elliot believed that the *ta'aluqa'* villages were the ancestral property of the Rajput and Mohammaden *ta'aluqd'ars* who may have either conquered or colonised them during the medieval ages from the 14th to the early 18th centuries and that increase in the territorial jurisdiction of the *ta'aluqd'ari* families from 17th to the 19th centuries could be better explained on account of the multiplication and growth of the new villages and further colonisation. The numerous *ta'aluqa* villages of a *ta'aluqd'ar* sprang out of a single parent village and were its subdivisions developed in the course of centuries and did not represent an amalgamation of the villages with separate primary proprietors. Elliot denied that the laws governing proprietorship in the early stages of civilization warranted the existence of primary village zamindars for separate villages. He held that Thomason had failed to understand the evolution and concept of a village *(mauza)* and the notions of proprietary rights governing the growth of villages. He further contended that the fixation of village limits, when done by the people, was contingent on the sub-division of proprietorship, and not the proprietorship contingent on the existence of separate villages. The fixation of boundary limits done by the Government was rather arbitrary. As such, it was not true to say that a *ta'aluqd'ar* had not *abinitio* exercised properietary rights over all the villages in his *ta'aluqa*. Elliot also believed that the *ta'aluqd'ari* tenures, based on proprietary rights of the undivided clannish settlement governed by the law of primogeniture, were older than the village communities themselves. In support of his theory, Elliot referred to Sir Henry Main's work on Ancient Law and the evolution of the Society in three main steps viz. the earliest clannish structure vesting the whole "Patria Potestas", authority and proprietorship in the head of the clan, the disintegration into Houses comprising aggregation of families vesting proprietorship either as communal in the viilage communities or in the sole possession of the eldest male of the family, and finally into distinct family groups which were perpetual. Property was governed by the law of heredity. The true *ta'aluqd'ar* belonged to the most primitive form of society where the clan was represented by their head, and all proprietorship vested in him. Such an analysis of the origins of the *ta'aluqd'ari* system based on pure theorisation of the concept of proprietary rights is untenable and in various respects, Elliot's criticism of Thornton is absolutely unjustified.

In fact, Elliot's Chronicles narrate the history of the *zamindari* families of the District of Oonao in Awadh. Many of these zamindars had been conquerors and colonisers and even held the status of *Rajas,* both under the Mughal and the Lucknow governments. By the 19th century, many a powerful zamindar holding the designation of *Rajas,* also acquired the status of the *ta'aluqd'ars.* Elliot failed to distinguish the dual institutional character of *zamindari* and *ta'aluqd'ari* embodied in the same person or family. Of course, he was quite correct on contending that a *ta'aluqd'ar* had a hereditary *zamindari* with which he was not historically unconnected. But his denial of the existence of a distinct class of the primary village zamindars is historically incorrect. The primary village zamindars may be descendants of the same clan and the founder family to which the Raja-*ta'aluqd'ar* himself belonged. They may as well belong to different clans and castes and their ancestors may have been either suppressed by the family of the ruling chief or may have commended themselves voluntarily to the latter because of varying socio-economic and political factors. Thus, Elliot did not realise the fact that the *ta'aluqa* of a *ta'aluqd'ar* comprised both the portions viz his personal hereditary *zamindari* and the *zamindaries* of his dependent petty zamindars, who at one stage in history, may have been completely unconnected with the *ta'aluqd'ar's* family. Elliot, who was otherwise a keen student of the local history of Awadh, wrongly attributed the traits of the *ta'aluqd'ars* with those of the chief zamindars *(zamindarn-i-umda)* holding the titles of the *rajas* during the medieval ages. He had the least concept of the relationship between the zamindar *rajas* and the Mughal State, from the middle of the 16th to the middle of the 18th centuries. He equally failed to appreciate the historical and socio-economic changes which took place in Awadh in the later half of the 18th and first half of the 19th centuries by which the erstwhile *Rajas* also acquired *ta'aluqd'ari* estates and came to be designated as the *ta'aluqd'ars.* Elliot was misled by the dual status of the *Rajas* cum *ta'aluqd'ars* in the 19th century which was rather a peculiar feature of the evolution of the *ta'aluqd'ari* system in Awadh and a few other territories of North India.

Mr. Wing Field, Chief Commissioner of Awadh (1864 A.D.) [13] also attacked the Thomason theory and fell in line with Elliot's concept of the evolution of the proprietary rights and thought of the *ta'aluqas* as the ancestral hereditary houses of the *ta'luqd'ars.* Wingfield maintained that this was generally applicable to all the Rajput *ta'aluqd'ars* who formed the larger portion of that class. He refuted Lord Canning's version of the growth of upstart class of the *ta'aluqd'ar* excepting few who represented the ancient families. Wing Field held that apart from the anicent Rajput families, the Mohomadan *ta'luqd'ars* were descendants of the grantees of land settled in Awadh since about the middle of the 16th century. Only three bankers or capitalists became the *ta'aluqd'ars* in Awadh and few (not above twenty) *nazims* and *chakladars* accquired the status of the *ta'aluqd'ars.* Though Wing Field concedes recent growth of the *ta'aluqd'ars* from the commercial and administrative classes, his concurrence with Elliot for holding the *ta'aluqd'ari* status synonymous with the anicent Rajput principalities or ancestral Muslim *zamindaries* since medieval age is rather misconceived. Like Elliot, he did not understand how the ancestral Rajput or Muslim Chief zamindars of Awadh assumed the role of the *ta'aluqd'ars* during the course of the 18th and 19th centuries.

Mr. Currie, Settlement Commissioner of Awadh,[14] also took exception to Thomason's theory that the *ta'aluqd'ar* was a middleman unconnected with the soil, whose connection with his estate originated in having been appointed by the Government to collect the revenues of such estate. Currie's criticism of Thomason's Despatch is rather partial for the latter in his, *Directions for Settlement Officers and Collectors* had clearly underlined the fact that apart from the above mentioned *zamindari* villages, a *ta'aluqd'ar* may have also hereditary ancestral villages in his *ta'aluqa.* It has already been pointed out that relying on his experience of the Ceded and Conquered Provinces, Thomason had essentially underestimated the extent of the ancestral hereditary villages which may comprise a significant portion of the *ta'aluqa* of a *ta'aluqd'ar*. Though Currie supported Elliot's version of the hereditary *zamindaries* of the *ta'aluqd'ars,* based on further experience, he elaborated on the genesis of the *ta'aluqd'ari* system and the composition of the *ta'aluqa* of a *ta'aluqd'ar*. He considered that the *ta'aluqa* of a hereditary Raja-*ta'aluqd'ar* consisted of three categories of villages: viz., ancestral villages inherited in direct line from the common progenitor of the clan; the villages of the kith and kin (cadet villages termed *'Bhaewadee'),* which having been from the parent estate were in some way or another incorporated in the *ta'aluqa;* and the villages of other castes and clans (gentile villages) which had been acquired at earlier or later periods of history by the *ta'aluqd'ar's* family. Apart from this, there may be *ta'aluqd'ars* who had no hereditary ancestral villages but had built up *ta'aluqas* through the purchase or auction of the villages of the other clans and castes. Currie's concept of the *'ta'aluqa* of a Raja-*ta'aluqd'ar* was quite correct but he could not appreciate the dual status of the chief zamindar (i.e. the *Raja*) and the *ta'aluqd'ar* as well as the manner in which this transformation had taken place in the course of history. Nor did Currie properly comprehend the concept of proprietary relations involved between the *ta'aluqd'ar* and his dependent petty zamindars.[15]

For tracing the genesis of the *ta'aluqd'ari* institutions, Baden Powell has relied only on the early Settlement Reports and Mr. Bannet's *Oudh Gazetteer*. Baden Powell's historical portion[16] is too sketchy and vague and he failed to realise the fact that the 18th century *Rajas* had various limitations upon them during the proper Mughal age, when they were treated as state servants and tax gatherers with entitlement to *jagirs* and *nankar* under the state regulations. Apart from this, the 19th century English records on Awadh divided the *ta'aluqd'ari* class into two categories of 'true' and 'false' *ta'aluqd'ars.* The *rajas* with hereditary claims continued over centuries were designated as true *ta'aluqd'ars* while others (not belonging to the Chieftains families) who developed *ta'aluqd'ari* rights recently were considered as upstart and 'false' *ta'aluqd'ars.* Baden Powell calls them 'pure' and 'impure' *ta'aluqd'ars* respectively. Such a distinction between the 'true and 'false' or 'pure' and 'impure' *ta'aluqd'ars* has absolutely no historical justification because as an institution, the *ta'aluqd'ari* system based on socio-economic factors could be traced to the 17th century whereas the transformation of the hereditary Chiefs into *ta'aluqd'ars* took place in the course of the 18th and the first half of the 19th centuries. The main plea, for regarding the hereditary Chiefs as the 'true' or 'pure' *ta'aluqd'ars* is that they had for centuries claimed hereditary estates exercising 'an *imperium* in *imperio*' on the spot whereas, the other categories of the *ta'aluqd'ars* were regarded as outsiders who had secured their position through talent or wealth. Such an explanation based on the family annals of the local Chieftains has no historical foundation so far as the Mughal age is concerned when they were governed by the *zamindari* regulations and the revenues of their *zamindari ta'aluqas* were regarded as the revenues of the Mughal state. Though varying categories of the families viz. the influential village zamindars and the *chaudharies*, guarantors, revenue-farmers, government officials and *rajas* developed *ta'aluqd'ari* rights and the phases of their historical development could be traced from the 17th to the first half of the 19th centuries, as an institution the *ta'aluqd'ar* standing between the dependent village zamindars and the state for the payment of the revenues enjoyed the same status.

Of the English writers who made reflections on the evolution of the *ta'aluqd'ari* system in Awadh, W.C. Bennet [17] possessed great knowledge and experience. He traced the genesis of the Raja-*ta'aluqd'ars* from the later half of the 18th century. However, Bennet's historical analysis remains partial as he did not take into account the economic factors leading to the growth of the middling group of *ta'aluqd'ars (ta'aluqd'aran-i mufassalan)* who can be traced back right to the 17th century. Notwithstanding the legal brilliance of Sykes[18] on the Compendium of the *ta'aluqd'ari* law, his historical understanding of the evolution of the *ta'aluqd'ari* stands in the same plane as Bennet. It is evident from the 18th century Awadh archives that both the primary zamindars and the *ta'aluqd'ars* were regarded as the tax-gatherers in lieu of *malikana* rights as well as pecuniary advantages of *nankar,* etc. Except for their personal family lands, they were not the proprietors of the lands of the *riaya.* But much confusion was caused by the English connotation of the association of the proprietary *(malkiyat)* rights over the villages with the rights of ownership of the agrarian lands therein. Similarly, the term *ta'aluqa* which during the Mughal age had been associated as much with the *zamindari* territorial jurisdictions of the primary zamindars as with those of the zamindars cum *ta'aluqd'ars* came to be applied only to the estates of the *ta'aluqd'ars.* The dependent *zamindari* villages were completely absorbed in the *ta'aluqa* estates of the *ta'aluqd'ars* whereas, the primary zamindars who were able to keep up their independent status for revenue settlement were regarded as simple owners of their *zamindari* villages than of a *ta'aluqa*. This change in the concept of a *ta'aluqa* was not understood by the English administrators and the settlement officers of the 19th century. In all these respects, they have relied mostly on the 19th century sources especially after 1814, and were not able to trace correctly the historical genesis of the *ta'aluqd'ari* system ever since the 17th and 18th centuries and at the same time were not able to distinguish between the land rights of the various classes in the *zamindari* and the *ta'aluqa* villages before the British took over the Awadh administration in 1856.

B

The main features of the *ta'aluqd'ari* system for the 17th century have already been analysed separately by the present author.[19] Except Bengal, in major portions of north India, especially Awadh, a *ta'aluqd'ar* was a zamindar who engaged with the state for the payment of the revenue of his own *zamindari* villages as also of various other petty *zamindaries* under him. The revenues were assessed by the state and the *ta'aluqd'ar* was subject to all the rules and regulations binding a zamindar for the payment of revenues to the State. He assumed the role of a superior zamindar who was not only responsible for the payment of revenue for his own *zamindari* villages but also acted as a channel for the revenue payments of the inferior zamindars who did not deal directly with the government. Similarly, in joint *zamindari* villages, one of the co-sharers who acted as representative for the collective payment of the revenues, was known as a *ta'aluqd'ar*. A *ta'aluqd'ar*, when mentioned as the *malik* of the *ta'aluqa* comprising his own *zamindari* and dependent *zamindari* villages, was entitled to only a share in the perquisites of the dependent zamindars and, as such, both the intermediaries claimed parallel rights of *malkiyat* over the *zamindari* village. However, in Bengal, a zamindar always enjoyed a superior status to the *ta'aluqd'ars* who held independent jurisdictions under the former.

In the course of the 18th century, the *ta'aluqd'ari* system in Awadh continued to develop on an extensive scale in line with the 17th century socio-economic forces which operated on a still larger scale. The official documents covering various *parganas* of *subah* Awadh narrate numerous mortgage and sale transactions of the *malkiyat* rights over the *zamindari* villages or their portions.[20] The sale transactions are mostly of the same pattern as for the 17th century. A distinct characteristic of 18th century sale transactions is that a zamindar purchasing the *zamindari* shares was also entitled to "profits from trees bearing fruits, canals, reservoirs and brooks, etc." This means that a zamindar's pecuniary rights *(haquq)* formed a fractional share not only of the land revenue *(mal-o-jihat)* but even of the cesses *(sair-o jihat)* and some important cesses imposed upon the fruit trees and the irrigation water utilised from the canals, reservoirs and brooks, ets., find special mention in the transaction. In case of mortgage of a *zamindari* share, the mortgagee could always get his share redeemed on the payment of the borrowed amount and its interest. The partition deeds of the *zamindari* villages based on the law of inheritance equally show the further fragmentation of the *zamindari* shares. Thus a wealthy and influential zamindar not only extended his personal *zamindari* estate through the purchase of various *zamindari* shares but even assumed the role of a *ta'aluqd'ar* by undertaking the responsibility of the payment of the assessed revenues of the dependent *zamindaries* included in his *ta'aluqa.* Such a situation was well exploited by the families of the *chaudharies* who continued to extend their *zamindari* and *ta'aluqd'ari* estates throughout the 18th century.

Apart from the above mentioned facts, two more factors, viz. political and economic contributed to the growth of the *ta'aluqd'ari* system in the 18th and first half of the 19th centuries before the final annexation of Awadh by the British in 1856. The political instability of the Mughal Empire towards the close of Aurangzeb's reign shook the foundation which governed the relationship of the Mughal states with the zamindars. The growing imbecility of the Mughal government towards the close of the 17th century and the gradual disintegration of the Mughal state resulting in the breakdown of the agrarian structure was a weighty consideration for many a petty zamindar to commend themselves to big zamindars who assumed the role of *ta'aluqd'ars.* The political weakness of the government was exploited as much by the influential *chaudhari* families of the zamindars as by the hereditary local *rajas* who were also known as the zamindars.[21] The transformation of the local chiefs (*rajas*) into the *ta'aluqd'ars* in the last decades of the 18th and the first half of the 19th centuries is a most remarkable feature of the agrarian structure of the territories of Awadh.[22] During the Mughal age, the local *rajas* were designated as the zamindars and such of those who possessed large *zamindaries* or held high *mansabs* in the Mughal government were designated *zamindaran-i-umda* i.e., the chief zamindars.[23] They were entitled to both *watan-jagirs* (patrimony) as well as *tankhwah-jagirs* (i.e. *jagirs* in lieu of salary) in accordance with the *mansab*. A few of the zamindars in Awadh had held *mansabs* and *tankhwah-jagirs* under the Mughal government whereas, others remained as the local *rajas* cum zamindars for the purpose of the collection of the State revenues and maintenance of law and order. They were also entitled to some *watan-jagirs* and *malikana* rights over their *zamindari* villages. Their *zamindaries* could be assigned in the *takhwah-jagirs* to the Mughal state officers entitled to *mansabs* and *jagirs*. Of course, if any of the local *Rajas* was a *masabdar* of the Mughal state, the revenues of his own *zamindari* territory could be assigned to him in proportion to his *mansab*. If the *Rajas* did not hold any *mansab*, they were regarded as official tax-gatherers and were awarded *watan-jagirs* or rent free grants of land in lieu of their service. The *masabdar*-zamindars had the right to alienate *jagir* portions to their brethren on condition of military service and could also make religious grants from their *watan-jagir* portions . Similarly, the local *Rajas* entitled only to *watan-jagirs* and *malikana* rights could also share the income from the sources with their family members and brethren who participated in the administration for the collection of the revenues. It is clear from the letters of Bhupat Rai, the author of *Insha-i Roshan Kulam*, that by the opening years of the 18th century, many of the zamindars were in state of recalcitrance against the Mughal State and were evading the payment of revenues.[24] All the same, they were known as zamindars rather than *ta'aluqd'ars*. During the first half of the 18th century, as a result of constant mutual welfare, the *zamindari* territories of the Chieftains (*rajas*) underwent considerable change in the traditional boundaries. The family annals consulted by Mr. W.C. Bennet still mention them as the zamindars. The earliest reference of a *ta'aluqd'ar* in place of a zamindar traced by Mr. Bennet based on documentary evidence dates as early as 1769 A.D. and relates to Diwan Baksh of *pargana* Morawan who owned only three personal villages and for the rest of the villages in his *ta'luqa* received one rupee for each harvest from the dependent zamindars.[25] As the *ta'aluqd'ar* was also by himself a zamindar, this accounts for the fact that major portions of the available documents deal with the *zamindari* aspects. However, a few of them clearly mention the dual role of the zamindar cum *taaluqdar*. In fact, even after the battle of Buxur (1764 A.D.), which gave stability to the personal position of the Nawabs of Awadh under the British protection, a state of war between the Lucknow government and the recalcitrant zamindars was a recurring feature and the agrarian society was never at peace.

The Chief zamindars (i.e. *rajas*) went on extending their network of extension of the *ta'aluqas* as *ta'aluqd'ars* either by showing favour to the dependent zamindars or coercion and foiled every attempt of the Lucknow government to make revenue settlement with such of the primary zamindars who commended themselves to them. At times, the extent of the *ta'aluqas* of the *Raja-ta'aluqd'ars* themselves underwent a change when they themselves failed to pay the stipulated revenues to the government and portions of their *ta'aluqas* were passed on to the guarantors who also became the *ta'aluqd'ars*. In case of recalcitrance and consequent suppression by the government, their *ta'aluqa* villages could be entrusted to other chieftains (*rajas*) who would undertake to make payment of the revenues to the States. As such, the territorial extent of the *ta'aluqas* of the *Raja-ta'aluqd'ars* remained in constant state of flux and was by no means co-terminus with the *zamindari* estates held either in the pre-Mughal era or the Mughal age. As the Central government was paralysed, the ties of family and clans were being widened and consolidated on territorial basis. Moreover, in midst of disturbed political condition, they offered protection to dependent zamindars against any tyranny from without. Apart from this, based on the same circumstances, many zamindars who were the descendants of the erstwhile ruling Rajas and ordinary zamindars found equal opportunity to develop their *ta'aluqas* as the *ta'aluqd'ars*.

During the course of the 18th century, another economic factor for the extension of the *ta'aluqd'ari* jurisdictions played a dominant role. During the Mughal age, ordinarily the assessment in the *ta'aluqas* of the primary zamindars and the *rajas* was done for every harvest and the revenues were based on actual assessment done by the States. Thus, the zamindars were entitled to their perquisities *(haquq)* according to the local practice and the revenue regulation. But with the disintegration of the Mughal Empire, this method of assessment broke down in the first half of the 18th century. The assessment of the revenues was done periodically to be paid as the fixed lump sum by the zamindars of the *ta'aluqas.*[26] The periodically fixed assessment could be enhanced only under the strong pressure of the central authority. When Saadat Ali Khan was appointed Governor of Awadh, he found that the revenues of the province had fallen into great disorder under his predecessor Raja Girdhar Bahadur. Though the assessment of the revenue of the parganas was revised during the Governorship of Saadat Ali Khan and Safdar Jung, it had to be enforced only after the suppression of the recalcitrant Chiefs. This tug of war between the Lucknow government and the Chiefs for the fixation of the revised revenues was a constant feature throughout the 18th century. The laxity and occasional ineffectiveness of the Awadh government resulting in the payment of revenues by the zamindar and *ta'aluqd'ars,* either on the obsolete or spurious rent-rolls, the exaction of *ta'aluqd'ari* rights from the dependent zamindars left a great margin of profit to the Chieftains to play the role of *ta'aluqd'ar* rather than simply living on the *malikana* rights of their own directly administered *zamindari* territories. During the chaotic period, in many cases they completely obliterated the *zamindari* rights of the petty zamindars while in other cases, wherever possible, they incorporated the petty *zamindari ta'aluqa* into their own *ta'aluqas* which came to be composed of their personal *zamindari* villages and those of the dependant zamindars. Though in Awadh practically all the Chieftains and *Rajas* acquired the new status of the *ta'aluqd'ars,* such a development did take place to some extent in the late 18th and 19th centuries even in the erstwhile Mughal *subahs* of Allahabad and Ajmer (Rajasthan). In the *sarkar* of Gorakhpur (*subah* Allahabad), the Chiefs who assumed the role of *ta'aluqd'ars* were designated as such whereas, in some parts of Rajasthan they came to be known as *Istmrardars.*[27] In Awadh, the process of the extension of the *ta'aluqd'ari* rights of the Chiefs continued in the 19th century till its annexation by British government.

In some parts of Awadh, the inferior zamindars of the villages were known as *Birteeas.*[28] They paid revenues, at times, directly to the states and, at times, through the *ta'aluqd'ars* entitled the *Rajas.* In the early 19th century, they claimed 10% of the total realizations *(dehyak* or *do biswi)* and paid to the *ta'aluqd'ars* in the shape of fixed lumpsum amount *(chukti).* This naturally implied the sharing of the *malikana* rights between the *birteeas* and the *ta'aluqd'ars* and passing on the assessed revenues to the State.

It is not intended here to give any details of the development of the *ta'aluqd'ari* system in the full first half of the 19th century except to comment that the ever growing weaker position of the Lucknow government after the rule of Saadat Ali Khan (1797-1814 A.D.) and the stronger military and financial position of the *Raja-ta'aluqd'ars* resulted in the absorption of the weaker petty *zamindaries* by the families of the *Raja-ta'aluqd'ars* by abuse of power, fraud, violence and collusion.[29] Some of the old primary zamindars were crushed and driven out of their possessions. Apart from the Chieftains, even some of the government officials, many of whom belonged to the *zamindari* families, bankers *(sarafs)* and guarantors, speculators, revenue-farmers and *chaudhari* families equally resorted to the similar tactics of purchasing the *zamindari* shares either through direct negotiations with the parties concerned or auction of the delinquent *zamindaries* for creating or extending their *ta'aluqas*.[30] However, many primary zamindars were powerful enough to withstand all sorts of pressures of rack-renting policy of the government with the cooperation of their *riaya* for the punctual clearance of revenues and the support of the neighbouring primary zamindars by forming common defence and tribal ties. In various regions of Awadh, they were able to keep up their entity for making direct settlement with the government and, as such, were recognised even by the British government after annexation in 1856. It may be well conceded that the practice of granting *ta'aluqd'ari* rights over a *ta'aluqa* by a grant or a *sanad* on the part of the Government originated only with the Lucknow government under the Nawabs and was unknown to the Mughal age. It seems to have sprung up owing to the extreme weakness on the part of the government in order to conciliate the often revolting chieftains and to recognise the *fait accompli* after they had acquired *ta'aluqd'ari* rights through various means.[31] In many cases, the inefficient local government officers preferred to make settlement with the *ta'aluqd'ars* than realising revenues from different primary village zamindars. The British government also continued the policy creating *ta'aluqd'ari* tenures by making fresh grants thinking that it was the continuation of the old prerogative inherited from the past native rulers.

C

During the 17th century[32] where *ta'aluqd'ari* system came into being, three parallel claims, by no means mutually incompatible, were established on the *ta'aluqa* villages and their dependent zamindars belonged to the intermediary classes in hierarchical order whereas a few categories of *riaya* were the owners of the agricultural land. Their families, of course, owned lands especially in the self-colonised villages. However, the *ta'aluqd'ar* and his dependent zamindars shared their respective perquisites and the detail of appointment would depend upon customary local practice. Like a zamindar, a *ta'aluqd'ar* might own his personal lands in his *ta'aluqa* but neither he nor his dependent zamindars could claim proprietary rights in the soil and the agricultural lands of the *riaya* under them. As such the *ta'aluqd'ars,* big or small, belonged to the intermediary classes and enjoyed their respective perquisites. Except for personal land, they were not the owners of the soil and the agricultural lands of the *riaya* under them. In this respect they stood in the same relation to the *riaya* as the other zamindars.

It is evident from the 18th century and early 19th century official documents that in line with the 17th century Mughal concept, the zamindars with dependent or co-sharing attached *zamindaries,* the *Raja-ta'aluqd'ars,* the ordinary *ta'luqd'ars (ta'aluqd'aran-i mufassalan)* and the *muqaddams* of the villages were all considered official tax-gatherers and were entitled to *nankar* and *inam* etc. in lieu of their *malikana* rights. The villages could also be farmed to the *mustajirs* (revenue-farmers) for a fixed period. A *mustajir* undertook to pay fixed annual lumpsum amount in instalments during the term of *ijara* (contract). He was responsible for the collection of revenue and was entitled to profit *(takhfif)* in the revenue collection and the annual instalments contracted under the terms of a *patta.* The *Dastur-ul-aml* (Code of revenue regulations) of Nawab Saadat Ali Khan (1798-1814 A.D.) reveals the developed stage of the *ta'aluqd'ari* system and clearly brings out the concept of land ownership.[33] A hierarchical pattern of *zamindari* and *ta'aluqd'ari* system existed in Awadh by the beginning of the 19th century. A *zamindari* of the villages may be held on individual or co-sharing basis. The periodical assessment (in this case triennial settlement) of revenues on the *zamindari* families and other *riaya* was done by the *amin,* appointed by the Lucknow Government. But in such circumstances where it would cause loss to the Government, annual assessment was to be made. The head of the co-sharing *zamindari* village, entitled *zamindari,* was engaged for the payment of revenues. The assessment of revenues was made after deduction of *nankari* on account of *malkiyat* (ownwership right) conceded by the Government. The balance amount was recorded as demand. At times, *nankar* was given to the zamindar by way of grace even when the settlement with that zamindar was rejected by the Government. Where the land (of villages) was shared by many zamindars or *ta'aluqd'ars,* the settlement was made with the biggest of the zamindars whom the other co-sharers appointed as their representatives. Apart from the petty-cosharers, the principal co-sharers were named *pattidars.* The zamindar and the *pattidars* may lease out a few villages to a *mustajir* (revenue-farmer) who may further sublet to a sub-lease holder. At the same time, a zamindar representing the co-sharing *zamindari* families may commend himself to a superior zamindar entitled *ta'aluqd'ar* who at times still further commended himself to a superior zamindar cum *ta'aluqd'ar* or a *Raja-ta'aluq'dar.* Invariably a zamindar would commend himself directly to a superior *ta'aluqd'ar*.

However, the perquisites *(rusum* and *haquq)* were shared by all the parties, viz. the *ta'aluqd'ars*, zamindars, *pattidars* and other petty-co-sharers, the lease holders (*mustajirs*), the sublease holders and the *katkandars* (underproptrietors) in accordance with an agreement settled amongst themselves. If a zamindar or a *ta'aluqd'ar* failed to pay the dues, provided the latter accepted it and the lower petty co-sharing proprietors undertook to pay the revenues to him. In such an arrangement, the original zamindar would be dispossessed of his title of landlordship but he would continue to possess his personal *zamindari* lands *(jot khas)* and act as an underproprietor to his erstwhile *pattidar* now entitled zamindar. The title of *zamindari* may be transferred to one or more *pattidars.* Similarly, if any *ta'aluqd'ar* or a zamindar was dispossessed of his lands on account of default in the revenue payment, the land could as well be handed over to a lease holder. The *Dasturulaml* goes to the extent of suggesting that in case of outstanding yearly balance left by an old zamindar, his *malikana* (ownership) rights should be dispensed with and a new zamindar as *malik* be appointed. If he failed to realise the arrears, the arrangement for the payment of revenues should be made with the *muqaddam* of the village or any reliable *muzariah* (occupancy tenant). If the latter or any revenue-farmer did not accept the engagement, the original *malik* (zamindar) may undertake to pay the arrears alongwith the revenues of the next year and failing that, the *mahal* (unit of villages for assessment and collection of revenues) may be given to any other person providing security for payment. But in case neither the zamindar nor the *muqaddam* nor any *muzariah* accepted the possession or ownership of land (here villages under assessment) or any new revenue-farmer failed to pay the amount due, the land (i.e. the villages) shall be converted into *tahsil kham* (wherein the responsibility of collection of revenues rested directly with the State officials), and shall be subject to all procedures for sequestered land.

In fact, the *riaya* and the various intermediary classes from the bottom to the top (viz. the sublease holders, lease holders, petty-co-sharers, *pattidars,* zamindars and *ta'aluqd'ars*) always arrived at a prior agreement with regard to the ultimate responsibility for the payment of the arrears and if, according to the prior agreement, the responsibility lay with the *riaya,* the latter were liable to make payment directly to the Government officers on the existing rates prevalent in the *pargana.* Notwithstanding the prevalence of the above mentioned *zamindari* and *ta'aluqd'ari* system, if a co-sharing *zamindari* family wanted to withdraw from a joint settlement, it was free to apply to the Government for the partition of his *zamindari* lands and could make separate settlement with the Government for the payment of the revenues. The *Dasturulaml* clarifies the concept of *malkiyat* (ownership) of the villages or *mahal* as essentially associated with the *malkiyat* or perquisites thereupon. In this context, the text of the *Dasturulaml* holds the *malkiyat* (ownership) of the villages and the land *(zamin)* as synonymous and interchangeable terms. It does not mean that the zamindar or a revenue-farmer as the *malik* of the villages or as *malik-i-zamin* was the absoulte owner of the agrarian land in the English or the Roman sense. Even when the text puts a zamindar or a revenue-farmer as *malik-i- zamin* (land owner), it implies his rights of the revenue collection and enjoyment of the attached perquisites. The *Dasturulaml* also states that the landlords *(maliks* or zamindars) and revenue-farmers with whom the settlement was made, may transfer their property *(malkiyat* for the revenue collection and enjoyment of the perquisites) according to the rules to any body, provided the title of the petty *ta'aluqd'ars (ta'aluqd'aran-i mufassal* i.e. intermediary zamindars between superior zamindar cum *ta'aluqd'ar* and the *riaya)* and cultivators was not affected thereby. The engaging landowner *(malik*-here a superior zamindar or *ta'aluqd'ar)* had to enter into a clear cut agreement with the primary zamindars (dependent zamindars) and cultivators for the exercise of such *malkiyat* rights and any over-realisation from the latter was to be deemed as extortion. In any sale transaction, a zamindar could transfer only the revenue paying villages and lands and the purchaser would undertake to pay the revenues and enjoy perquisites. Such lands, which were not developed and were not assessed for the revenues, could not be sold without the prior permission of the Lucknow Government.

All this makes it absolutely clear that by the beginning of the 19th century, the superior zamindars were dependent on the primary village zamindars and that they only shared the customary perquisites in lieu of the revenue collections done in their *ta'aluqas.* The superior zamindars or *Raja-ta'aluqd'ars* were the owners (in the absolute sense) of the land in their ancestral self-developed villages and over the other incorporated dependent *zamindaries* they only enjoyed *malkiyat* (ownership) rights simply for engagement, revenue collection and the enjoyment of the perquisites. Same is true of the primary zamindars who, as self cultivating *riaya,* owned self developed ancestral villages. Such *zamindari* families may own villages and lands on individual or co-sharing basis. Many of these families enjoyed *chaudharie* and *muqaddami* status. Their villages may be entirely self-cultivated or a few villages passed on entirely to *muzarihan* (also termed *riaya* as occupancy tenants) and still in others, the lands may be partly under self-cultivation and partly with the *muzarihan*. Even though the periodical or annual assessment on the villages was done by the State, the rights of the land-owning *riaya* and *muzarihan* for the extent of their holdings and the rates of assessment were regulated by the *patta* system. The engaging zamindar would give *patta* to the *riaya* and lease holders for the assessed demand who would in return give written acceptance *(qabuliyat)*. The *patta* would specify the area of land to be brought under cultivation, the kind of crops to be sown, the rate and amount of assessment and the limit of holding with a provision to revise the assessment in case of change of pattern in the crops. The *patta* clearly mentioned the revenue demand and a lumpsum amount of compounded legal cesses. The terms of the *patta* were governed by customary regulations. In case of any conflict between the zamindar and the *riaya* over the terms of the *patta*, arbitration was to be done by the Government revenue officers. Whenever a *zamindari* was sold on account of arrears of the revenues, the *pattas* would be renewed by the new zamindar. The *pattas* were granted only for the period of assessment. Some of the *riaya* may acquire long termed *pattas* but they were liable to alteration with the mutual understanding of the zamindar and the *riaya*.

Apart from the two clear-cut classes viz. the *zamindari* families and the *muzarihan* (occupancy tenants), the lands in some of the *zamindari* villages may as well be owned by the peasant proprietor *riaya* who were the descendants of the erstwhile *zamindari* or *muqaddami* families but did not enjoy such designations. The *pahi-kashtkars* may as well be employed by the *zamindari* families. Thus the concept of ownership of land in a *zamindari* village would be dependent upon the nature of the village as to whether it is owned by a single self-cultivating *zamindari* families on co-sharing basis or partly by the *zamindari* families and partly by the *muzarihan* (occupancy tenants) and *pahikashtkars* or entirely by the *muzarihan* and *pahikashtkars*. It seems that in concept, the position of the land rights of various classes of *riaya* (both *zamindari* and others) did not differ in any fundamental manner from the later half of the 17th century. Of course, during the course of a century, the process of multiplication of the co-sharing *zamindari* had worked on a grandiose scale both on account of the law of inheritance and alienation of the *zamindari* shares. At the same time, at the upper level, the *ta'aluqd'ari* system had developed accelerando because of the various factors already examined.

It is, however, significant to observe that during the 18th century, notwithstanding the breakdown of the Mughal Empire, chaotic intermissions or laxity of the Lucknow Government, the attack on the part of the powerful superior zamindars or *Raja-ta'aluqd'ars* was not on the land in possession with varying classes but on the *malkiyat* rights for the sharing and enjoyment of the perquisites of the *zamindari* families who ultimately came to be commended to them due to various reasons. This is how the situation stood at the turn of the 18th century. In the beginning of the 19th century, Saadat Ali Khan in his attempt to stabilise the Lucknow Government issued comprehensive revenue regulations which accepted the *fait accompli* of the institution of *ta'aluqd'ari* and at the same time permitted the settlements to be made with zamindars, as representative of co-sharing *zamindari* families, *muqaddams* and *mustajirs* revenue-farmers). The revenue of various territories could be realised directly by the State officials from the zamindars and *riaya* as *tehsil kham.* The land rights of all classes viz the *ta'aluqd'ars,* zamindars, *riaya* and *muzarihan* were clearly defined. There does not seem to be any justification in the fact that it was the revenue system of Saadat Ali Khan marked by overassessment and extortion of the revenues by the official revenue collection machinery which suppressed the zamindars, as the independent proprietors (or the "proprietary village communities") and forced them to commend themselves to the *ta'aluqd'ars.* But after the death of Saadat Ali Khan, even though the revenue regulations were promulgated from time to time, their enforcement remained a pious wish. The tyranny of the local revenue officials like *nazims* and *chakladars* to resort to coercion for subordinating the ordinary zamindars and even to devour their perquisites, the occasional volts on the part of the *ta'aluqd'ars* and subordination of the rights of the dependent *zamindari* families mitigating the line of demarcation between the commended *zamindari* villages and personal *zamindari* villages comprising the *ta'aluqa,* complete suppression of the *zamindari* families and *riaya* unwilling to join the *ta'aluqa* of the powerful *ta'aluqd'ar,* the fight of the *zamindari* families and the cultivators from the villages more or less destroyed the concept of the land rights upon which the agrarian structure of Awadh rested at the beginning of the 19th century.[34] The agrarian picture became sufficiently blurred and the *ta'aluqd'ars* found themselves in a powerful position. The concept of proprietary *(malkiyat)* relationship evolved between the *ta'aluqd'ar* and the dependent *zamindari* families for sharing the perquisites varied from one region to another for in some places the *malkiyat* rights of the dependent *zamindari* villages were completely destroyed and at other places they were fully or partially retained. The concept of the *ta'aluqa* itself underwent a change. The dependent *zamindari* villages were completely absorbed in the *ta'aluqa* estates of the *ta'aluqd'ars* whereas the primary zamindars, who were able to keep their independent status for revenue settlement, were regarded as simple owners of *zamindari* villages than of a *ta'aluqa.* Even at the lower village level, due to disturbed conditions and abnormal agrarian situation, in various villages the land rights of the peasant proprietor *riaya muzarihan* (occupancy tenants) were sufficiently shaken and the concept of their title to land underwent a change. At places, over-exaction by the State revenue officials or the *ta'aluqd'ars* from the zamindars and *riaya,* at another place continual conflict between the government and the *ta'aluqd'ars* or between the latter and the zamindars and the *riaya,* the occasional flight of the cultivators from their fields, the settlement of new cultivators by the zamindars for bringing the deserted lands under cultivation led to the less of value of the attachment to land on the part of the peasant proprietor *riaya* and the *muzarihan* (occupancy tenants).[35]

Apart from the *zamindari* families, self cultivating or otherwise, no distinction remained between the self-cultivating peasant-proprietor *riaya* and the *muzarihan.* At the same time, it was not worthwhile for the latter class to claim any occupancy rights either. The question whether the *muzarihan* as cultivating *riaya* possessed occupancy rights or were merely tenants-at-will remained simply an academic one. The original title of the *muzarihan* class to occupancy rights in land came to be shrouded in obscurity. Face to face with the dearth of agricultural labour and in their anxiety to cover the land for tillage, the *zamindari* families in their own interest never questioned the occupancy rights of the cultivating *riaya* to village though in case of desertion of land, they were obliged to settle either new *riaya* or to get the land cultivated by *pahikashtkars* on reduced State demand. After the annexation of Awadh (1856 A.D.) and more especially with the creation of the *ta'aluqd'ars* as the land-owners after the 1857 Revolt, a conscientious probe into the land rights of the primary village zamindars (termed as under proprietors) and the cultivating *riaya* was conducted by the settlement officers and senior administrators who expressed divergent views in their copious reports, memoranda and high level official correspondence.

References

1. For details, see Grover, B.R., 'The Evolution of the *Zamindari* and *Taaluqdari* System in Bengal (1576-1765 A.D.)', *Bangladesh History Congress,* Third Session (May 12-14, 1973), Dacca.
2. Holt Mackenzie's Memorandum, 1 July, 1819, *Selections from the Revenue Records of North-Western Provinces* (henceforth *Selections Revenue N.W.P.*), 1818-1820, Calcutta, 1866, paras 406-7, p. 91.
3. *Ibid.,* para 745, p. 149.
4. *Selections Revenue N.W.P.* 1822-33, Allahabad, 1872, para 419, p. 145.
5. *Ibid.*, para 421, pp. 146-47.
6. *Ibid.*, para 172, p. 42; Selection 10, Clause I.
7. Minute of Lord William Bentick, dated 26th September, 1832, *Ibid.*, pp. 385-418.
8. *Selection from the Records of the Government North-West Provinces* (hence forth *Selections Records N.W.P.)* Mr. Thomason's Despatches Vol.I, Allahabad, 1855; letter from J. Thornton, Secy. to Government, N.W.P. Agra, the 17th January 1844 to H.M. Elliot, secy to the Sudder Board of Revenue, N.W.P., paras 3-6, pp. 23-33.
9. *Ibid., Thomason's Despatches* Vol. I, letter from J. Thomason, Lt. Governor, N.W.P., Agra, the 31st January, 1844 to Lord Ellenborough, G.G. of India, paras 1-44.
10. J. Thomason, *Directions for the Settlement Officers,* 1844, Section 99; also see "Settlement of N.W.P.", *Calcutta Review,* December, 1849; *Selections of Papers Relating to the Directions for Revenus Officers Regarding the Settlement and Collection of Revenues, 1849. Parliamentary Papers,* No. 999, 1853.
11. See, for instance, Financial Commissioner to Chief Commissioner Oudh' 31 March 1856, UPSA Oudh Abstract Revenue Department Proceeding, 4th April, 1856.
12. C.A.Elliot, *The Chronicles of Oonao,* a District in Oudh, Allahabad, 1862, pp. 146-156.
13. *Papers Relating Under Proprietary Right and Rights of Cultivations in Oudh,* (henceforth *Papers under proprietary and cultivators- Oudh),* Calcutta, Vol. I, pp. 1-7; 38-40; Vol. III, Calcutta, 1867, pp. 114-30. Also Jagdish Raj, *The Mutiny and British Land Policy in North India 1856-68,* Bombay, 1965, pp. 30-40.
14. *Ibid.*, Vol. III., paras 1-12, pp. 56-60; paras 2-34, pp. 156-66.
15. For criticism of Wingfield's and Culture's views by their contemporary officials, See *Papers Under Proprietary and Cultivators Oudh,* Vol. III, Minute of H.S. Maine, dated 10th July, 1864, paras 2-24, pp. 118-123, C.U. Aitchison, Calcutta 13th April, 1864, Vol. III., pp. 98-104, Minutes

of the G.G. (John Lawrence), dated 20th June, 1864, Vol. III., paras 2-34, pp. 104-112.

16. Baden-Powell, B.H. *Land Systems of British India,* Oxford, 1892, Vol. II. Most of the present writers have accepted Baden-Powell's viewpoint, See Jagdish Raj vide reference No. 13, pp. 1-2.

17. W.C. Bennet, *Gazetteer of the Province of Oudh, Vol. I.,* 1877, Introduction, pp. xliii-liv, *The Chief Clans of Rai Barreli District,* Lucknow, 1870, pp. 27-70.

18. Sykes, J.G.W., *Compendium of Oudh Taluqdari Law,* Calcutta, 1886. Also see reproduction of the views of Sykes, C.B. Lal, *The Taluqdari Law of Oudh,* Allahabad, 1910, Introduction, Historical and Comparative, pp. 1-72.

19. For details, see Grover, B.R., "Nature of *Dehat-i-Taaliqa* (*zamindari* villages) and the Evolution of the *Taaluqdari* System during the Mughal Age." *The Indian Economic and Social History Review,* Vol. II, No.2, April 1965, pp. 166-177 and Vol. II, No. 3, July 1965, pp. 269-288.

20. Of the numerous documents, see No. 1238, dated 9.1.1717 (mortgage) relating the village Kaudi, *pargana* Hisampur, *sarkar* Bahraich; No. 1247, dated 27.7.1773 (mortgage) relating to village Rasuli, *pargana* Sirhar, *sarkar* Lucknow; No. 1256, dated 26.8.1795 relating to village Kaundu, *pargana* Hisampur (mortgage), No. 1261, dated 25.12.1801 (mortgage); No. 1264 dated 10.7.1810. This important document refers to the mortgage of a *taaluqa* Sayyid Ghulam Mahdi S/0 Sayyid Mahjuj, *taaluqqadar* Qara Mula Pargana Hasampur, states that he has given his *taluqqa* to Sayyid Safdar Husain, son of Sayyid Mahdi Hussain, *taluqqdar* and *tafriqdar* of the aforesaid *Ilaqa* on the condition that so long as the sum mentioned below is paid to him as *Wankar,* he would have no concern with the *taluqa.* The details of the amount to be paid are also given; National Archives of India, OR 144, (undated) mortgage by Bhikhi S/o Luchu mortgaging piece of *malkiyat* land in village Mirzapur to Kalai S/o Bhola of Qasba Bijnor with an asurance to give *malikana* and *muqaddami* rights to the latter. For Sale Deeds, see - NAI, OR 143, Original sale deed, dated 28th *Rabi* I, 47thR.Y. of Aurangzeb's reign (1703 A.D.) in respect of a portion of village Bharosa, *pargana* Lucknow, executed by Nidhi and others in favour of Shaikh Yasin for a consideration of Rs. 46/, NAI, OR 145, Original sale deed, dated 29th Moharram, AH 1120/AD 1708 in respect of land in village Bharosa, *pargana* Lucknow; Executed by Hadi and others in favour of Rs. 52¼; Allahabad, Document No. 43/147, dated 4th Shaban, 1157 A.H. (27th year of Muhammad Shah's reign). For Partition Deed, A.D. 1257, dated 15.8.1796, Partition deed of village Kaundli, *pargana* Hisampur, Sarkar Bahraich between the heirs of Zain Ali.

21. Elliott, C.A., op. cit., pp. 100-102; W.C. Benett, A Report on Ray Baraily District, Ref. No. 17, pp. 49-51; *Oudh Gazetteer* Vol. III., pp. 274-280, 535-36.

22. Benett, W.C., *Oudh Gazetteer,* Introduction vide ref. No. 17.
23. See, Grover, B.R., "Nature of Land Rights in Mughal India," *The Indian Economic and Social History Review,* Vol. No. 1, July-September, 1963, pp. 10-15.
24. Bhupat Rai, *Insha-i-Roshan Kalan,* Ms. India Office, 401 fols 6b-8a and 13a.
25. Benett, W.C., *Oudh Gazetteer,* Vol. III., vide reference No. 17. pp. 250-252.
26. Ms. Or. Oct. 113, I, Berlin.
27. *Cavendish Enquiries,* 1829, para 5 of his letter of July 10, 1829 addressed to Sir Edward Cola-Brooke, Resident on Rajputana and Delhi.
28. *Kawaif-i-Gorakhpur,* M.U. Aligarh, dated 1810, fols. 14a-b, also *Selections (1822-33),* pp. 131, 135-38.
29. Sleeman, W.H., *A Journey through the Kingdom of Oudh, 1849-50,* London, Bentley, 1858, Vol. II., pp. 25-245.
30. Butler, Donald, *Outlines of the Topography and Statistics of the Southern Districts of Oudh and of the Cantonment of Sultanpur-Oudh,* Calcutta, 1839, pp. 48-54.
31. Benett, W.C., *Oudh Gazetteer,* Vol. III., pp. 27-29; 36-37; 274-280; 534-536; Sleeman, W.H., *op.cit.,* Vol. I., pp. 336-337.
32. For details, see, Grover, B.R. 'Nature of *Dehat-i-Taaluqa..........', op. cit.*
33. Dasturulaml of Nawab Saadat Ali Khan of Oudh, dated 14th Shaqqal A.H. 1229/30th September 1813 A.D., tr. Khan Behadur S. Abu Muhammda, *The Journal of the United Provinces Historical Society,* Vol.IV, Oct., 1928, Part I, pp. 26-67.
34. Sleeman W.H. *op. cit.;* Butler, Donald, *op. cit.*
35. *Ibid.,* also for details see-*Papers Under Proprietary and Cultivators.* Oudh, Vol. I, pp. 1-178; Vol. III, pp. 21 to 163.

Chapter 7

The Impact of the *Zamindari* System

The institution of *zamindari,* with its manifold aspects, played an extremely important role in the Mughal land revenue administration and the agrarian set up of the country. Ethnographically, a chieftainship or a petty *zamindari* belonged either to a dominant ruling minority or majority of its own tribe or clan. Such settlements and territorial principalities were known to pre-Mughal India since ages.[1] Though otherwise for all *subahs, Ain* provides only for the *zamindari* castes in the Provincial *sarkar* and *pargana* tables. Fortunately, for the geographical description of *subah* Gujrat, it also gives ethnographical divisions of the territories associated essentially with the Chieftainships.[2] This is equally suggestive of the *zamindaries* in the other provinces. Founded on parochial socio-economic and political territorialism, fortified by the ethnographic historical traditions of the cult of leadership and sentimental allegience on the part of the people, the institution of *zamindari* found due recognition in the Mughal polity. Where hereditary Chieftaincies or petty *zamindaries* did not exist, a similar artificial atmosphere was created on a miniature scale through the institution of the official class of the zamindars. Even though subject to regular State control in respect of assessment and realisation of the land revenue, in due course of time, this official class equally tended to acquire landed and more or less hereditary interests in the *zamindari* territory. Thus, underneath the Supra local Pax-Mughalia Imperialism and uniform administrative polity lay the *zamindari* territories and village communities resting essentially on the clannish social structure and casteism.[3]

As a class, the chief zamindars with *mansabs* enjoyed more priviledged position than the *mansabdar* nobility. Such a zamindar held both hereditary *watan jagir* and transferable assignments as against his counterpart noble with the same *mansab* holding transferable *jagir* during the period of service.

At times, apart from the *watan* and the *tankhwah jagirs,* he also held unconditional *inam jagirs*. In practice, even the conferment of *mansab* and *tankhwah jagirs* acquired a hereditary practice. Even if not enrolled as a member of the Imperial service, apart from confirmation in the *watan jagir,* the zamindar acted as revenue collector in the other territory of his *zamindari,* and after the deduction of the collection charges, would pass on the revenues as *peshkash* either directly to the State or its assignees. An official zamindar held *jagir* in lieu of his jurisdiction and *mansab* which invariably tended to be hereditary and the *jagir* grant was gradually regarded as *watan jagir*.

Such a system of *zamindari,* based on semi-feudal structure, possessed two-fold potentialities running simultaneously in opposite directions. If a zamindar remained faithful, it extremely facilitated the task of the State and its assignees for the revenue collection but if the zamindar was recalcitrant, he was a constant source of trouble for the State revenue authorities. The original revenue records of the 17th century divide the zamindars into two categories, firstly those who were quite docile in the payment of *peshkash* (revenues) and secondly those named *'Zur Talab'* (requiring force) who would seldom pay the revenues unless coerced to do so through armed action.[4] As a precaution against the recalcitrance of the zamindars, the State provided various safeguards.

(a) Every chief zamindar was required to maintain his representative (*vakil*) either at the Central Court or at the Provincial Head Quarters as determined by his *zamindari* status. The *vakil* submitted the requests of his Chief to the Mughal Court and got constant directions from the Mughal State authorities. For any disputed matter and objectionable behaviour on the part of his zamindar, he had to execute a bond (*muchalka*) for the latter's future proper behaviour.[5]

(b) A zamindar with doubtful behaviour had to send a member of his family as a hostage at the Central or Provincial Head Quarters. Whenever called upon, he had to come for personal submission at the *Subahdar's* Court.[6]

(c) The *zamindari* territories were always attached to the *faujdari* circles. Regular *thanas* with local contingents were always established in many of the *zamindari* territories and the *thanedars* acted under the directions of the *faujdars.*[7]

(d) The revenues of the *'zur talb' zamindaries* were always on the *'tankhawah' jagir* of either the *faujdar* of a division[8] or a powerful *mansabdar*[9] or another powerful zamindar who commanded large military establishment to meet any armed opposition from the recalcitrant zamindar.[10]

(e) The provincial authorities had the special responsiblity for the maintenance of the proper control and realisation of the *peshkash* (revenues) from the zamindar. At times, a *Naib Subahadar* (Deputy Governor) was specially appointed for the above job.[11] Similarly, the Provincial Diwan entrusted especially with the same task gave particular instructions to all the revenue officials under him viz. the *Faujdars, Diwan-i Sarkars* and the *Shiqdars* to deal sternly with the situation.[12] At times, special *amins* were appointed for the assessment of the *zamindari* territories.[13] At the same time, special realisation officers named *'Tehsildar-i Peshkash'* or *'Darogha-i Tehsil-i Peshkash'* were appointed to realise the *peshkash* dues from the zamindars.[14] At times, this post was combined with that of the *faujdar* of the area.[15]

Abul Fazl characterised the behaviour and policy of the zamindars in India as based on opportunism.[16] Notwithstanding all the above analysed precautionary steps taken for the consolidation of the Mughal Empire, it has to be conceded that throughout the Mughal age, one or another of the chief zamindars was occasionally in revolt against the Mughal rule[17] and isloated cases of private warfares amongst the zamindars themselves are also on record.[18] In the initial stages after submission, a few of the zamindars were often recalcitrant unless fully suppressed into the *zamindari* pattern.[19] All the same, the *centripal* Imperial polity always successfully met the fissiparous tendencies in the late 16th and the 17th centuries compared to any past or future Government in Indo-Muslim history. More persisting and irritating was the problem of the realisation of *peshkash* (revenues) from the *'zur talb' zamindari* territories assigned to the State officials. The tussle between the recalcitrant (*zur talb*) zamindars and the State assignees over the realisation of the *peshkash* (revenues) from the former was a frequent feature of the Mughal administration.[20] Though the situation undoubtedly deteriorated in the second half of Aurangzeb's reign,[21] such a conflict did not lead to any dual demand on the peasantry by either of the combatants—the zamindars and the *jagirdars*.[22] The revenue literature of the 17th century is replete with such information that either the provincial and the local revenue machinery had to be often mobilised for helping the assignees in the realisation of the revenues from the zamindar[23] or the rights of the latter had to be safeguarded against the high-handedness of the *jagirdars* and the local administration.[24] Comparatively, much less trouble existed with the official zamindars who acted more as Mughal Government officials enjoined to help the local officials in the assessment and realisation of the land revenue.

Dr. Irfan Habib has recently advanced a theory that before Aurangzeb's reign, the excessive State demand and unrestrained exploitation of the peasantry led to local and isolated peasant uprisings. The zamindars as a class had their own grievances as within their own territories, they had been shelved of their revenues by the tyrannical policy of the *jagirdars*. The Mughal State had always shown hostility to them and though they had often indulged in sporadic revolts supported by the peasantry of their own *zamindaries*, they had always felt helpless to fight against the mighty arm of the Mughal Empire. As in Aurangzeb's reign, the starved peasantry took to arms of its own, the zamindars who were the natural leaders of the peasantry, organised them into large bands and armies resulting in open large scale popular peasants revolts which ultimately brought about the fall of the Mughal Empire.[25] Such an over simplified agrarian picture on Dr. Habib's part and his assignment of the zamindar's role in the agrarian polity is a gross misrepresentation and is completely misleading. As a matter of polity, the Mughal State never showed any hostility to the obedient zamindar class within the *zamindari* pattern, though of course, it always resented any fissiparous tendency or refractory attitude for the non-payment of the *peshkash* (revenues). Far from being hostile, by far, the majority of the chief zamindars too, as a class, worked for the integration and expansion of the Mughal Empire and formed the backbone of the Mughal nobility. The keynote to their allegience was based on self-interest for the higher *mansabs*, multiple official assignments and larger *jagir* grants.[26] Based on their personal affiliation with the Mughal princes and with written promises of higher *mansabs* and *jagirs* from them, they played significant role in the disputes to the succession to the Crown. With written *Nishans* for *jagirs* in their pockets, they fought in the opposite camps in the famous war of succession amongst the sons of Shahjahan.[27]

All the same, with his fissiparous tendency, a refractory zamindar was guided by purely personal factors based on political and economic considerations. Politically, he aimed at independence and economically, he wanted to be free from the *jagir* regulations of the *zamindari* system though undeniably, he could claim general approbation of his people based on the dynastic and clannish loyalty. Even such a phenomenon of recalcitrance had persisted throughout the Mughal age and Aurangzeb's attempts at Islamic polity gave a further edge to the cause of some of the Hindu zamindars.[28] On the other hand, the Mughal State always employed one set of zamindar to suppress the revolt of the recalcitrant zamindars.[29] There is no denying that the indigenous and traditional revenue demand in the *watan-jagir* and *ghair-amli* territories of the *zamindaries* was comparitively lighter than in the proper Mughal territories[30] where it was somewhat higher. But the Mughal *zamindari* system did not temper with it for the purposes of assessment of *peshkash* (revenues). Of course, the *amli* areas of the *zamindari* territories were brought in line with the Mughal policy. Though immediately after conquest, in the initial stages of taking over by the Mughal Revenue Department, some of the territories did show resentment against the enhanced assessment of '*jama*', the higher Mughal authorities were immediately constrained to adopt a conciliatory policy for the continuation of the indegenous State demand.[31]

After the consolidation of the Mughal rule, never an identical agrarian cause with the peasantry inspired a revolting zamindar. In his private warfare against another zamindar, he was rather mundane and aggressive against the peasantry of an attached *zamindari*.[32] Of course, on revenue grounds, some of the petty zamindars showed more grudge against the Mughal State than the chief zamindars . By far, the largest number of the petty *zamindaries* were reduced to *amli* territories under the Mughal system of assessment and their *peshkash* (revenues) were fixed by the *Amin*. A few of the zamindars were traditionally and habitually recalcitrant (*zur talb*) and would never pay the *peshkash* unless forced by the assigness of the State. Here, too, a strong passion for pocketing the realisation from the peasantry[33] rather than any identical agrarian cause or sympathy with the latter lay at the root of the recalcitrance. The original records offer quite a vivid picture about the position of the zamindars. At times, the higher authorities had to step in to safeguard the interest of the petty zamindars against the high handedness of the *jagirdars* and the *khalsa* administration. Still, on other occasions, the *jagirdars* petitioned to the Central or the Provincial authorities for help in the realisation of the *peshkash* from the recalcitrant zamindars. At some places, the zamindars themselves acted tyrannically towards their own peasantry and the Mughal State had to safeguard the interests of the latter.[34] At other places, the State authorities had to afford protection to the zamindars in their conflict with the overweening *muqaddams* of the villages.[35] Comparatively, the official class of the zamindars who enjoyed office and *jagir* remunerations during their good behaviour remained faithful to the Mughal State in the discharge of their revenue and administrative duties.

On the whole, it can be argued that right till the mid of Aurangzeb's reign, the Mughal State successfully crushed any recalcitrance on the part of a chief zamindar or refractory (*zur talb*) attitude of a petty zamindar in contravention of the *jagir* and the revenue regulations of the State. Aurangzeb brooked no opposition from any zamindar. Whereas his predecessors had as a matter of policy, of course with rare exceptions, contended themselves with the suppression of recalcitrant zamindars to the Mughal pattern of *zamindari* administration, Aurangzeb invariably took the extreme inexpedient imperialist step of outright annexation of the recalcitrant *zamindaries* to the *khalsa* administration of the Mughal State.[36] It is only when the religious factor crept in the local administration polity and the imposition of *jizya* upon the Hindu zamindars, *muqaddams* and the peasantry, and when the energies of the Mughal State were fully concentrated on the Deccan problems that the fissiparous tendencies of the zamindars in the North got sharper and the vitality of the Mughal administration suffered.[37] Even as such, though leaving an instable legacy, the Mughal Government successfully met the situation till the death of Aurangzeb.[38] After the intial stages of conquest and consolidation under Akbar, for nearly a century and a quarter, the Mughal Imperial polity and administrative unity successfully subdued the zamindars to its pattern of revenue administration. It mostly ended the constant feature of mutual wars amongst both the Chief and the petty zamindars and saved the peasantry from the dread of pillage. It gave comparative peace and security to the agrarian life in Northern India. However, once the Imperial hold was loosened after Aurangzeb's death, the assertion of local autonomy, mutual warfare and squabbles amongst the zamindars brought about the ruination for the peasantry.[39]

References

1. See Tod, James, '*Annals and Antiquities of Rajasthan*, i, Calcutta, 1916, pp. 32-106; Elliot, Charles, '*Chronicles of Oonao*', Allahabad, 1862, pp. 28-77, 85-92.

2. *Ain*, II, tr., Jarret, pp. 250-255. For example, the *sarkar* of Sorath has 60 *Mahals* and ports but, on tribal basis, is divided into 9 districts, each covering a varying number of *parganas* and each district is inhabited by a different ruling tribe (i) New Sorath *parganas* of Ghelot tribe. There is also a settlement of the Koli tribe. (ii) Old Sorath *parganas* of Chelot tribe. There is also a settlement of the Ahirs tribe called Babriyas. (iii) Lathi etc. of Gohel tribe. (iv) Mahwah etc. of Wala tribe. (v) Jagat (Dwarka) etc. of Badhel tribe. (vi) Barra (Barda) or Jaitwar tribe. (vii) Sordhhar etc. of Baghelah tribe. (viii) Jhanjhmer etc. of Waji tribe. (ix) *Parganas* of Timbel (Charan) tribe. For details, see *Ibid.*, narrative and foot notes. Similarly, Jhalwar, a pre-Mughal principality containing 1,200 villages with four divisions, inhabited mostly by the Jhala tribe of Rajputs, included in the *Ain* in the *pargana* of Ahmadabad. (*Ibid.*, pp. 248-49).

3. The ethnographic territorial division and the dominant role of the tribe at the basis of the social structure has continued till recent times. For the details of different parts of Northern India, See Risley H., *The People of India*, ed. 1908; Enthoven, R.E. *The Tribes and Castes of Bombay*, Vols. I & II; Ibbeston, *Panjab Castes*, Lahore, ed., 1916; Blunt, E.A.H., *Census of India*, 1911, Vol. XV, United Provinces of Agra and Oudh; Tallents, P., *Census of India*, 1921, Vol. VII, Bihar and Orissa; Enthoven, R.E., *Census of India*, 1881, Vol. II; *Census of India*, 1901, Vol. IX, Bombay; Hutton, J.H., *Census of India*, 1931 (Ghurye, G.S., *Caste and Class in India*, 1937. Also A.K. Nazmal, *Changing Society in India and Pakistan*, 1953, Dr. Tara Chand, *Caste and Tribes in the History of the Freedom Movement in India*, I, 1961, pp. 84-107; D.N. Majumdar, '*Races and Cultures of India*', ed. 1961, pp. 367-73, 389-396. For the present day, ethnic field studies, See '*Village India, Studies in the Little Community*', 1961, edited by Mckim Marriot with articles on 'Notes on an Approach to a Study of Personality Formation in Hindu Village in Gujrat,' by Gitel P. Steed, pp. 110-125; *Peasant Culture in India and Mexico, A Comparitive Analysis Based on Study of Rani Khera, a North India Village (District Delhi)* by Oscar Lewis, pp. 148-173; '*Little Communities in an Indigenous Civilisation*', by McKIM Marriot, based on study of the *North Indian Village Kishan Garhi* (Uttar Pradesh), pp. 175-196.

4. R.A.J. '*Yaddasht-i Haqiqat-i Zamindaran Mutilqa Subah Malwa*, category no. 3, Reg no 226, (Aurangzeb's reign) counts 16 zamindars of *Subah* Malwa paying *peshkash* out of which 8 are submissive in payment (regular) while 8 are *Zurtalb*. Similarly, the *Hidayat-al Qawaid*, an early 18th Cent. Ms., fol. 65a-b also qualifies the zamindars into those who were submissive and revenue paying and those who were *Zur-talb*.

5. R.A. Jaipur, vide numerous *Vakil Reports* and *Khatut-i Maharajangan;* Also, *Vir Vinod,* pp. 740, 747-48.

6. See R.A.J. Reg. no. 1714, category 4, dated 22 Rabi I, 1117 A.H./1705 A.D. Also, *Akbarnama,* III., pp. 604-6, tr., Beveridge, III., pp. 922-24. B.G. II., tr., Borah, pp. 328-29.

7. See Faujdar's jurisdiction and duties. Also see *Zamindars in Kangra and Jammu divisions.* Also R.A. Jaipur, Reg. no. 1622, category no 4, dated 1701 A.D.; *Akhbarat* no. 1438, dated 7th *Rabi* I, 23rd regnal yr. in respect of *faujdari* of Mewat and the *zamindari parganas.*

8. R.A.J. *Vakil Report.* Reg. no. 336/189, 30th *Rajab* 1100 A.H.; Also, *Mirat -i-Ahmadi, Supplement,* pp. 205-6.

9. R.A.J. Regd. nos. 226, 229, 300, category no. 3 (Aurangzeb's reign).

10. See Ref. no. 8; also Reg. no. 389, 29th *Rabi* I, 49th regnal year, 1117 A.H./1705 A.D.

11. R.A.J. Reg. no. 1714, category 4, dated 22 *Rabi* I, 49th regnal yr. 1117 A.H./1705 A.D. quotes a letter from Maharaja Sowae Jai Singh addressed to the zamindars of *subah* Ujjain that he had been appointed as the *Naib Subahdar* to realise *peshkash* from them. It directs the zamindars to send their *vakils* to him. Amongst the various representations of the *jagirdars* to the Naib Subahdar for help in the realisation of *peshkash,* See R.A.J. Reg 389, dated 29th *Rabi* I, 49th yr., 1117 A.H./1705 A.D.

12. B.G. tr., Borah I. pp. 123, 139, 272-73, 410. Also, see R.A.J. Reg. no. 1622, dated 1701 A.D.; Case no 338, catagory 2, dated 1689 A.D.; also, see *Functions of the Diwan-i Sarkar,* the *faujdar* and the *shiqdar.*

13. R.A.J. reg. nos. 229-30 quote memorandums (*yaddasht*) of the *peshkash* to be realised by the *Amin* Mir Hamid from the various zamindars in numerous *parganas* in *subah* Malwa; Also, *Muraqqat-i Hasan,* no. 217, Farsi, Rampur, pp. 328-30.

14. This office existed right from Akbar's reign to that of Aurangzeb. For Aurangzeb's reign, see R.A.J. *Akhbarat,* no 1331, 23rd of *Rabi* II, 10th regnal yr.; reg no 1616, 13th of *Shawal,* 23rd regnal yr. (for Multan); Reg. no. 1321, 12th *Rabi* II, 10th regnal yr. for Turhat; 4th *Safar,* 10th regnal yr; Reg. no. 755, catagory no. 3.

15. *Ibid. Akhbarat,* 26th *Rabi,* 44th regnal yr. (for Multan).

16. While describing the suppression of the revolt of Sultan Sikander Sur, who had found refuge with Raja Bakht Mal of Maukot (Nurpur) in 1557 A.D., Abul Fazl comments on the general behaviour of the zamindars, "It is the practice of most zamindars in Hindustan, not to adhere to one another, but to look about on every side and ally themselves with whatever side they see is winning, or is most capable of continuing the struggle. Thus at this point, he (Bakht Mal) came in

and joined the Imperial Camp.... Now it is not considered a laudable practice to injure those who have submitted of their own accord, even if it has occurred under compulsion of necessity." (vide *Akbarnama*, II, p. 63; *M.U.* II., p. 157).

17. For example, in Akbar's reign, the zamindars of the Panjab Hills in the Kangra and Jammu ranges rebelled thrice on a large scale. In the 23rd yr. (1579 A.D.), Todar Mal suppressed the revolt. (vide A.N.II. tr., Bev. p. 358). In the 35th yr., Zain Khan Koka suppressed nearly thirteen hill Chiefs between the rivers Chinab and Sutlej. "In the thirty-fifth year of Akbar, Zain Khan received an order to punish the northern zamindars. From near Pathan (Pathankot), he advanced and did not turn the face till he reached the Sutlej. All the dwellers in the territories became submissive, Raja Bihi Chand of Nagarkot, Raja Paras Ram of Mount Abu, Raja Basu of Mau, Raja Anrudh of Jaswan Kamluri (Kahluri-Bilaspur), Raja Jagdish Chand, Dahwal (Dadwal) Raja Sansar Chand of Panna, Rai Partap of Mankot, Rai Bhaso Buzrung of Jasrota, Rai Balbhaddar of Lakanpur, Daulat of Kot-Bharta, Rai Krishan Balauria (Basholi); Rai Raodeh, Dhamerwal, although they had 10, 000 horsemen and more than one lakh of footmen, submitted and presented themselves at Court with valuable presents." (vide *M.U.* II., p. 160), also *Ain*, tr. I., p. 344. In the 41st yr. (1594-5 A.D.), there was another rebellion among the hill chiefs led by the Raja of Jasotra. (vide details in *A.N.* tr., Elliot, VI., pp. 125-129; *M.U.* II., pp. 167-170). In Jahangir's reign, Raja Suraj Mal of NurPur rebelled and ravaged most of the *parganas* at the foot of the hills, which were in the *jagir* of Itimad-ud-daula. (*M.U.* II, p. 178). In 1623 A.D., on Prince Khurram's revolt against Jahangir, Raja Jagat Singh of Nurpur sided with the Prince but was later on pardoned through the good offices of Nur Jahan Begum. (*Tuzk-i-Jahangiri,* tr. II., p. 289). In Shahjahan's reign, the same Raja and his son Raja Rajrup rebelled in 1638 A.D. and were suppressed by Sayyid Khan Jahan Bara, Sayyid Khan Bahadur Zafar Jung and Asalat Khan. (*B.G.* II., pp. 237-38). From the Jammu group, Raja Gur Singh of Kashtwar rebelled in 1619 A.D. and was suppressed by Dilawar Khan, the Governor of Kashmir. (*Tuzk-i-Jahangiri,* tr. II., pp. 135-38). In the 8th yr. of Shahjahan's reign, the *faujdar* of the Panjab Hills suppressed the revolt of the zamindar of Srinagar (in Tihri Gharwal and not the capital of Kashmir) with the help of other zamindars in his jurisdiction and realised the *peshkash.* (*Amil Sahil,* II., pp. 136-39). Similarly, other examples could be cited from the chronicles for every reign.

18. In Rajasthan and Gujrat, for the details of the campaigns of the Mewar Chiefs, Raja Jagat Singh and Raja Raj Singh against Dungarpur, Banswara, and Sirohi, See *Vir Vinod,* pp. 319, 434-36, 1061; Original Letters of Asad Khan, the Central Minister to Rana Amar Singh, dated 19th December 1700 A.D., *Ibid.*, p. 746; Asad Khan's letter, dated 23rd April 1702 A.D. vide *Ibid.*, p. 747; Kishan Rai's (Vakil's) letter to

Mahrana., *Ibid.*, pp. 735-36; Rana Bhim Singh's exploits against Idar, vide *Mirat, I,* p. 294, *Tod. I,* p. 304; For Bengal, *B.G. tr. Borah II,* Raja Satrajit of Bhunsa conspired with Kansa Narayan to molest Dungor Dev, pp. 669, 674-75. For mutual conflicts between the Bengal zamindars, see *B.G.* II, pp. 665, 669, 674-75.

19. For example, in Bengal and Assam under Jahangir, *Baharistan* records various revolts on the part of the Rajas even after submission to the Mughal State. For revolts, see *B.G. tr. I & II,* Anwar Khan, pp. 105-6; Bahadur Ghazi, zamindar of Chawra, p. 106; Bahadur Khan of Hijli p. 631; Raja Baldev, p. 409; Chandr Bhan, pp. 139, 782; Hasta Raja alias Kandana, p. 571; Pitambar, zamindar of Chilajuwar, pp. 123, 821; Raja Ray, zamindar of Shahzadapur, pp. 32, 106; Shumaruyed Kayeth, p. 623; Raja Satrajit of Bhunsa, pp. 623-25, 639; similarly for the Panjab Hills Chiefs, see ref. no. 14.

20. Though the archival and the other documentary evidence in hand relates mostly to Aurangzeb's reign, it is evident in the context that the problem was a chronic one ever since Akbar's age. *Akbar Nama* mentions the recalcitrance of the zamindars without clear distinction between the chief zamindars and petty princely zamindars. For example, it refers to the revolt on the part of nearly 13 zamindars from Kangra to Jammu in the sub-Himalayan range.

    Akbar Nama, in the 27th yr. reforms (Br. M. Add. O.R. 27, 247, f. 332a) also refers in a general manner the problem of the insurgents (here in the context zamindars) as an obstacle to the revenue realisation and narrates measures to be adopted by the *faujdars,* the *karories* and the *jagirdars*. In Bengal and Orissa under Jahangir, Baharistan (tr. Borah) clearly refers to the assignment of the *jagir* in the *zamindari* territories of Shitab Khan who declined it unless permitted to go personally for punishing the recalcitrant zamindars. As he could not be spared, the territories were assigned to Saiyad Shajaat Khan (vide *Ibid.*, II, pp. 776-77). Moreover, helped by the geographical and strategical traditional of '*zur talb*', for example, in Gujrat, (vide *Mirat* Suppl., pp. 205-6), the zamindars of the *parganas* of Utleshwar and Chermandvi (*sarkar* Broach) would pay to the *jagirdars* only when forced to pay. Similarly, the Cheru Chiefs of Palaman (a hilly region in the Southern limit of Bihar) were always *zur talb* (also see, Sarkar's Aurangzeb, III, pp. 35-45).

    All the same, though the recalcitrance of the zamindars for nonpayment of the *peshkash* was known frequently in certain regions to the Mughal administration, it was not so widespread as after the mid of Aurangzeb's reign. It is evident from the earlier original documents that the Government control over the zamindars was rather rigid. *R.A.J. Akhbarat,* 3rd regnal yr. Raja Inder Singh, the zamindar of Balur (Rajasthan) reported about the full remittance of the past assessed *peshkash* and assured for the future payment;

Akhbarat reg. no. 1372, 27th *Zulqada,* 10th regnal yr., gives details about the regular *peshkash* payments made by the zamindars of Jamda, Dev Kada and Jawar Kada (Malwa); *Akhbarat* reg. no. 1291, 10th regnal yr, 11th Rabi I/1660 A.D., narrates that Haji Khan Baloch and Ismail Khan Hoot, the zamindars of *subah* Multan declined to pay the *peshkash* of Rs. 4,20,000 on the plea of natural calamity in their territories. Tahir Khan, the *subahdar* of Multan, on enquiry did not accept the excuse, sent the *Vakils* (his own and the zamindars') to the Central Court and later on arrested the zamindars. *Akhbarat,* reg. no. 1356, 2nd *Zulqada,* 10th regnal yr., orders the removal of the *mansab* and office of the zamindars (in Kashmir) on account of conflict with the royal servants.

21. Most of the available documents for such a phenomena pertain to the reign of Aurangzeb and more especially to his last two decades. See, *R.A.J. Regd.* no. 1110, 24th *Rabi Julawal,* 49th regnal yr., 1117 A.H./ 1705 A.D., Regd. no. 65, category 3; Regd. no. 829, 22nd Rajb 49th regnal yr., 1117 A.H./1705 A.D.; For Rajasthan, Reg. no. 416, catagory no. 2, 33rd regnal yr., 1100 A.H./1689 A.D., Regd. no. 964, dated 41st regnal yr., 1697 A.D.; Case no. 363, catagory 2, dated 22nd of *Rajab,* 37th regnal yr., 1105 A.H. For Oudh, see *Insha-i Roshan Kalan,* I.O. 4011, letters of Ra' dandaz Khan, the *faujdar* of Beswara (1702 A.D.), refer to various expeditions against the zamindars for the exaction of *peshkash.* For Mathura (Subah Agra), see *R.A.J., Vakil Reports,* Reg. no. 336/189 32nd regnal yr., 30th *Rajab* 1100 AH./1689 A.D.; Reg. no. 159/192, 32nd regnal yr., 1100 AH/8th June 1689 A.D. For Multan, *Akhbarat,* dated 21st of *Ramazan,* 44th regnal yr. (Aurangzeb).

22. Dr. S. Nurul Hasan is wrong in his surmise that "the peasant had to bear the dual burden of the zamindar and the *jagirdar,* and thus suffered more". Vide Presidential address, Section ii, *Medieval Indian History, I.H.C.* Delhi Session, Dec. 1961, pp. 13-14.

23. *A.N.* III, pp. 36-37; *B.G.* II. tr. Bohra, pp. 776-77; *Vir Vinod,* p. 740, a copy of an original representation of the *Vakil* of the Rana of Mewar to the Central Minister, Asad Khan (Aurangzeb's reign) regarding the assignment of the Parganas of Badnor and Mandalgarh etc. to Karn Singh and Jhajjar Singh; Of the numerous original documents of Aurangzeb's reign, *R.A.J. (Regd. no. 338,* catagory no. 2, dated 6th *Ramzan* 1103 A.H/1689 A.D. Sipahdar Khan sends a special Shiqdar to *Pargana* Sahar for helping Hari Singh in the realisation of the revenues from the zamindars). Reg. no. 416, catagory 2, 33rd regnal yr., narrates a request from Noor Mohammad for help against some of the refractory zamindars in *pargana* Pahasu. Also see, Reg. no. 829 Misc. Pers. Letters, dated 22nd *Rajab,* 49th regnal yr., regarding realisation from Rawat Pal, the zamindar of Gangher; also Reg. no. 389, dated 29th Rabi I, 49th regnal yr., 1117 A.H./1705 A.D.; Reg. no. 338. Also Reg. no. 685, Misc. Pers. letters, dated 12th *Jumadi* I, 1117 A.H./1705 A.D.; Also, see *Araiz-i Rustam Khan,* N.A.I. reference 17, *Ibid.*

24. *Mirat* I., p. 173. Akbar's *Farman,* dated 999 A.H./1590 A.D. directs the Diwan of *subah* Gujrat to make proper arrangement against any excessive demands from the zamindars and to essentially afford the latter Banth (one-fourth of their lands). That the interests of the zamindars were watched till the end of Aurangzeb's reign is clear from original documents. *Makhzanul Ihetsab,* Berlin, fols. 4b-6a gives clear cut instructions to the *amin* for taking the zamindars of the areas into confidence and to show them full consideration at the time of assessment. Also, the letters of Nawish Khan, Ms. J.N. Sarkar, fols. 8a-9b narrate the hard condition of the *ryots* and the zamindars in his *jagir* lands of Mandesor (*subah* Malwa) which were earlier in the *jagir* of Iftkhar Khan and also suggest measures for their amelioration. Reg. no. 1830, catagory 4, dated 2nd *Shaban* 1117 A.H/1705 A.D., quotes a letter from Maharaja (zamindar of Amber) to Azim Quli Khan informing that Rs. 1000/- were assessed as *peshkash* on the zamindar of Khilzipur and not to exact any more amount from the latter.

25. Dr. Irfan M. Habib, 'The Agrarian Causes of the Fall of the Mughal Empire' in *Enquiry,* Nos. 2 & 3, pp. 81-98 and pp. 68-80, respectively.

26. R.A.J., The *Akhbarat* and the *Vakil* reports give detailed information for Aurangzeb's reign and for earlier period, contemporary chronicles are full of such information.

27. For intrigues and politics on Shah Jahan's accession, See B.P. Saksena, *History of Shah Jahan of Dihli,* Allahabad, 1932. Tod, II, pp. 36-37; 145, 287, 297, (f. n. 2); Sarkar, *Aurangzeb.* For Prince Akbar's revolt against Aurangzeb, See *Tod,* I, pp. 308-13; *Ibid.,* II, pp. 48-9. *Vir Vinod,* 646-66. War of succession amongst the sons of Aurangzeb, *Tod. II.,* pp. 391-92.

28. For detailed criticism of Aurangzeb's policy and the antagonism of the Hindu chief zamindars, See *Orme's Fragments,* p. 165; Tod, I, pp. 297-300; 309, 315-16, 320; Aurangzeb realised the limitations of his religion's polity for application in the agrarian set up. *Vakil report,* reg. no. 423/541, dated 27th *Rabi,* I, 37th regnal yr. 1105/A.H., 16th November, 1693 A.D., informs the Maharaja (Bishen Singh of Amber) that in Rajasthan, the policy of the Emperor was to appoint Hindu Rajputs rather than Muslims as the (Official) zamindars and that the Maharaja should make recommendations for appointment accordingly.

29. See, Shah Jahan's *Farman,* dated 1047 A.H/ for the suppression of the Gujars in Pargana Devli Sanjari *Amil Salih,* II, pp. 136-39, see ref. no. 14. (R.A.J. *Original Farman,* Serial no. 48/85), Aurangzeb's *Farman* to the Raja of Dharbanga.(*Original Farman Dharbanga Darbar*), R.A.J., 'Letter to the Maharaja, Reg. no. 1110, dated 24th *Rabi,* I, 1117 A.H/ 1705 A.D. records a *Hasbulhukam* from Multafit Khan desiring the Maharaja (Sewai Mirza Raja Jai Singh) to recover two instalments

outstanding against Mohan and Paras Ram, the zamindars of Rajkhada. (*subah* Malwa).

30. Bernier (p. 205) noted that in the territories of the *rajas*, the peasants found, "less oppression and a greater degree of comfort."

31. At times, immediately after conquest, the *riaya,* inclusive of the peasantry based on their tribal or traditional association still owed allegience to their zamindars and would not readily accept the royal authority. (*B.G.* tr. Bohra I, pp. 230-31). On the same basis, the *riaya* in Khuntaghat (Bengal) fought for their defeated *rajas*. (*Ibid.* p. 293). At times, enhancement of the assessment immediately after the Mughal occupation led to discontentment. In Kamrup, the discontentment caused by the enhancement of the revenues by the Revenue-Farmer (*mustajirs*) led to the dismissal of Mir Safi, the Diwan. (*Ibid.,* pp. 288-89). Similarly, on demand from Sanatam, the zamindar, the oppressive Karori was replaced. (*Ibid.,* pp. 369-71). Similarly, after the annexation of Kuch Bihar in 1661 A.D., Mohammad Salih as against the settled policy of *Khan-i Khanam* resorted to assessment and collection of the revenues with harshness resulting in the revolt of the *riaya* and the recall of Raja Bhim Sen, the deposed zamindar. Thereupon, *Khan-i Khanam* ordered Mohamad Salih to leave, reconquered the territory, appointed Diwan and various *Karories* at different places and pacified the *riaya*. (vide. *Mammuri,* 5th Regnal yr. of Aurangzeb, pp. 449-50; *Alamgir Nama,* pp. 781-2).

32. In mutual private warfare, the pillage of the peasantry of the other territories was a common practice on the part of the zamindars.

33. R.A.J. Reg. no. 416, category 2, dated 33rd regnal yr. 1100 A.H. Apart from withholding the *peshkash* of his own territory, a zamindar at times would illegally realise the revenues of the adjacent Khalsa territories. R.A.J. Reg. no. 360, dated 3rd *Jamadi,* I, 35th regnal yr. 1103 A.H./1691 A.D., quotes an original *Parwana* from Jamlatulmulk, the Central Minister to Mir Mohammad Ali, Diwan of Akbarabad stating that he received an attested report from the *Amin-i Paibaqi* of *Chakla* Islamabad (*subah* Agra) to the effect that Tal Hamid, the zamindar of the *Qasba* (Qurya) Paranli had forcibly realised Rs. 20, 000 from the *Khalsa pargana*. The zamindar was arrested by Raja Kishan Singh and the aforesaid Diwan was directed to realise the amount from the zamindar.

34. *Maktubat-i Khan Jahan,* fol. 52a-b; Durr-al Ulm, fols. 51a-b; For 17th Century Bengal, B.G. tr., II, p. 665; also see Bengali Literature Mukundaram's *Chandimangala*, p. 7, *Vikrampurer Itihasa,* pp. 128-29; *Medinipurer Itihasa,* pp. 501-2 vide Ray Chaudhuri, Tapen Kumar, *Bengal under Akbar and Jahangir,* Calcutta, 1953, pp. 32-34, 173.

35. R.A.J. Reg no. 510, dated Rabi I, 1117 A.H./1705 A.D., quotes a *Parwana* Ahmad Khan to Jagat Singh, the zamindar of *pargana* Kauhi, informing

that it did not behove him to have run away from his territory. It directs him to settle in his *Watan* peacefully and that *peshkash* would be charged from him as usual. It also promises that all his property destroyed or captured by the *muqaddams* would be restorted to him on giving a sufficient proof thereof.

36. Abul Fazl categorically states (vide *A.N.* II., p. 63) that despite recalcitrance on the part of any disloyal zamindar, it was not considered a laudable practice to harm those who had made submission, whether voluntarily or through armed compulsion. As a punishment, some portions of the *zamindari* were either attached to the *khalsa* or assigned to a State official. In extreme cases of sedition, a recalcitrant zamindar would be sent to a tower or even beheaded and his *zamindari* was passed on to any of his kinsmen. (After his defeat, Raja Bakht Mal of Nurpur was executed in 1557 A.D. and replaced by his brother, Raja Takht Mal,. vide *A.N.* II., p. 63; In Bengal under Jahangir, Anwar Khan, after revolt, was blinded by the Governor Islam Khan and sent to the fort of Rohtas, vide *B.G.* tr., I, p. 140; Raja Satrajit of Bhunsa, after many revolts, was warned under Jahangir, vide *B.G.* tr., II, p. 781, but later on, executed in 1636 A.D. in Shah Jahan's reign, vide *B.N.* Lahori, II, pp. 79-80). Of course, under Akbar, the annexation of Kashmir was an exception as Akbar felt too tempted to spare Kashmir. Also, Mohibul Hasan, *Kashmir under the Sultans*, Calcutta, 1959. Similarly, Jahangir annexed Kangra and a few *zamindaries* in Bengal. Shah Jahan annexed Baglana and Bundala. Aurangzeb made annexations on a large scale, Kutch Bihar, 1661 A.D., Palamau 1661 A.D., Navanagar, 1663 A.D.

37. At the close of the 17th century, Bernier (p. 462) noted that "Usually, there is some rebellion of the *Rajahs* and zamindars going on in the Mogul kingdom." Also see Tod. *I*, pp. 315-22. By the end of Aurangzeb's reign, a few of the smaller and the official class of the zamindars also showed delinquency and disobedience. R.A.J. *'Misc. Pers. Letters'*, Reg. no. 685, dated 12th *Jamadi* I, 1117 A.H./1705 A.D., in a *Dastak* (official note) from the Maharaja assures Bahalya for all help in recovering Rs. 550/- from Kesri Singh, zamindar of *pargana* Sanwar or else to bring the zamindar to the Court. Another *Dastak*, reg. no. 539, *Misc. Pers. Letters*, dated 6th Rabi I, 1117 A.H./1705 A.D., addressed to Bodh Raj, informs that Balkishan and his companions, the *Gumashtas* (agents) of Prithvi Singh, zamindar of Taulai wanted to take village Mahori on lease forcibly. It directs him to check the aforesaid agents from this action to bring them to the court if they show further persistence. Such documents of delinquency on the part of the zamindars are increasingly available for the period following Aurangzeb's death. (vide 'Letters to the Maharaja'. 7th Rabi I, 1123, A.H./1711 A.D.; Reg. no. 1242, catagory 4, 1128 A.H./1716 A.D.).

38. Despite some local revolts, the Mughal Government asserted considerable control over the zamindars in Northern India. But in Deccan, due to the chaotic condition wrought by the Marhattas, the zamindars equally participated with the latter and the Mughal officials in the triangular game of the oppressive exactions from the peasantry. In the earlier stages, they sided with the Mughals against the Marhatta intruders but later on, finding that they were unable to defend themselves, joined hands with the latter against the Mughal rule. (Bhim Sen, *Nuskha-i Dilkusha*, 44th regnal yr., S. 1707. fols. 138b-140a). Dr. Irfan Habib concedes these facts (*Enquiry*, 3, pp. 75-76) but at the same time, draws contradictory conclusion by identifying the cause of the zamindars with the peasantry. He also regards the Marhatta insurrection as a Peasant's revolt.

39. For example, for *subah* Gujrat, *Mirat* (I. pp. 174-75) comments that the chief zamindars (*Zamindaran-i Umda*) were assigned (for the *Nazim*) only till the reign of Aurangzeb. Thereafter, they would come forward for service only by the military expedition of the *Nazim*; whether they would pay *peshkash* or not would depend on the personality of the *Nazim* and the circumstances. Regarding the behaviour of the petty Rajput, Koli and Muslim zamindars for the pillage of the villages, exaction of the cesses named *Gras* and *Waodal* in the *Banth* area and *Kichri* in the *Talpad* area from the *ryots* and devastation of the peasantry, See details in *Mirat* I, p. 174; Supply, p. 229.

Chapter 8

The Extension of the Irrigation System and the Administration of the Canal Works in the Punjab During the Mughal Age: 1556-1707 AD

I

The Mughal Government was keenly interested in the extension of irrigation facilities to the cultivators for the development of agricultural economy. Moreland, followed by few other scholars, thought that in Mughal India, there was no development of the irrigation and canal system worth the name. Such a summary and inaccurate view is uncharitable to the Mughal agricultural policy. Of course, the indigenous well-irrigation and the canal system under the Mughals are no match to the highly developed modern irrigation and network of canal works undertaken in the second half of the 19th century and 20th century in the Punjab. But that should not belittle the Mughal contribution, especially keeping in view the nature and the extent of needs of the artificial means of irrigation to the then land under cultivation and the agricultural population.

II

Our contemporary sources of information for the development of the irrigation facilities during the Mughal Age are more detailed for Punjab than for any other region of North India. Our main sources are : *Tuzk-i-Baburi; Tabaqat-i-Baburi* or *Tarikh-i Baburi* by Sheikh Zainuddin Khwafi; *Ain-i Akbari*; the chronicles of which Badauni's *Muntakhabu-t-Tawarikh,* the chronicles of the reign of Shah Jahan and Sujan Rai Bhandari's *Khulasatu-t-Tawarikh* (Aurangzeb's reign) deserve special notice; the accounts of the foreign travellers; *Insha* literature, especially the letters of Balkrishan Brahman written in the last years of Shah Jahan and early years of Aurangzeb (vide

Summary of the Paper presented at the 1st session of Punjab History Conference, Patiala.

British Museum Add. 16859); *Ruqat-i-Alamgiri* (Aurangzeb's letters); *Nigar Nama-i Munshi* by Malik Zada, 1684 A.D.; *Mahzar-i Shah Jahani* by Yusuf Mirak, 1634 A.D. (a recently discovered manuscript, published in Karachi, Pakistan); A pictorial roll of the Karnal-Delhi Canal drawn during the reign of Shah Jahan, Central Record Office, Hyderabad (India); *Akhbarat-i Darbar-i Maula,* Rajasthan Archives, Bikaner, dated 23rd R.Y. Aurangzeb relating to the Sialkot Canal, original documents (Aurangzeb's reign) relating to Batala and Lahore canals.

III

A. Wells: As in the past, the operation of the well – both the Persian wheeled and the Charsa system continued to occupy the most favoured position as a means of artificial irrigation throughout the Mughal Age. The Persian wheeled well was more efficient, cheaper and easier to operate than the charsa system and was widely prevalent in Punjab. Both lined and unlined (*basta* and *kham*) wells are known to have existed. It was an established practice on the part of the Mughal administration to help the cultivating families in the repair of the old wells and the construction of the new ones. Though the well digging was an individual responsibility of the cultivator, the Mughal government always financed the project with an advance of the *taqavi* loans. The well-digging operations were conducted by a class of diggers as well as on joint community basis. By and large, the *riaya* viz. the *zamindari* families and the simple peasant proprietor *riaya* always possessed their own wells. The *muzarian* (the occupancy tenants also constituting *riaya*) may or may not possess their own wells. Where the *muzarian* did not own their wells, they had to pay fixed annual rent to the owners for the utilisation of the wells situated on their lands. The *madad-i maash* (revenue free subsistence grants) assignees who developed their lands also owned their own wells and had a right to rent out the wells or well water to the *muzarian*. The extent to which a well was needed for artificial irrigation for the *Rabi* or both *Rabi* and the *Kharif* crops depended mostly upon the extent of the rainfall and the availability of their artificial means of irigation varying from one region to another of the Punjab territories.

B. **Embankment Reservoirs, Ponds and Lakes:** In certain regions in Punjab, the wells by themselves could not mature large areas without supplementing from the river floods (*sailab*) in autumn or irrigation from inundation, canals or embankments were erected. In the hilly or sub-mountain tracts, embarkments were erected. This practice has continued to the present day. In the plains, where conveniently available, the water was stored in the reservoirs, ponds and lakes for irrigation and spread out to the fields through water ditches.

C. **Inundation and Perennial Water Channels:** Both inundation and water channels were excavated from the rivers and their various tributaries for the irrigation of the villages and *parganas* near which the rivers or the streams (*nalas*) passed. Even though during the Mughal Age, the regularly constructed main canals were fewer in number and were confined to some regions of the Punjab, the irrigation from the inundation water-canals and channels drawn from the main rivers or rivulets was the most prominent feature of the agrarian life. Some of the rivers afforded an unfailing source of supply requiring no deep digging while many water sheds between the rivers and streams and the low lying regions offered a convenient irrigation for the *kharif* crop. Indigenous engineering methods helped the construction of inundation channels and more or less perennial canals utilising the river water whenever its level was high enough to permit its regular flow in the channels. In the case of inundation channels, there were usually no *bundhs* (weirs) at their heads and in many cases, no means of controlling the water entering them so that constant flow of water was normally assured during the summer months for the *kharif* crop.

Generally speaking, the *Ain-i-Akbari*, the chronicles and the regional contemporary historians always took such irrigation practices as a normal feature of the agrarian society and completely ignored description about them. But Sujan Rai Bhandari, the author of *Khulasatu-t-Tawarikh*, who otherwise mostly followed the pattern of *Ain-i-Akbari* proves an exception for his own native Shah of Lahore. Possessed with adequate and accurate data, he not only gives a detailed description of the courses of the main rivers of the Punjab but even of the small rivers which served as their tributaries. His description of the territories of the Doabs is very comprehensive. He mentions not only the main cities and *qasbas* by which these rivers passed but in some cases even mentions the limits of the villages of the numerous named *parganas* covered by the Punjab rivers. His description also gives the impression that *parganas* profited by irrigation. The village in the water sheds of the Doabs were irrigated not only by the indigenous canals but from the beds of the main rivers, their tributaries and the various *nalas*. This accounts for the major settlement of the villages and the *parganas* near the river courses and the water sheds of their tributaries which is true for the whole of India during the medieval age. Where such canals were purely seasonal, the well irrigation worked hand in hand with the canals. The archaeological physical remains of the *nalas* and the channels in the 19th century also clearly point towards such practices. *Mahazar-i Shah Jahani* gives a clear insight into the 17th century irrigation facilities in the territory of Bhakkar (*subah* Multan). It mentions that all the eight *parganas* of south Bhakkar were well-irrigated by the canals and water channels drawn from the main river Indus and its tributaries. The general impression given by *Mahazar-i Shah Jahani* shows that there was neither any dearth of agricultural land nor of perennial irrigation canals and channels. It is equally known from other sources that such perennial and inundation canals were widely prevalent in the whole *subah* of Multan.

IV

The Perennial Canals: The North West portions are the only regions in North India which have little and uncertain rainfall. By and large, all these regions were covered by the network of perennial canals or canals which would flow for the major portion of the year. This explains the fact that the major enterprises of the main canal works during the Mughal Age were concentrated on these regions whereas no documentary evidence is available for any such canal works in the Eastern or the Central portions of India which had always secure rainfall. In the latter regions, the indigenous canal works and the well-irrigation served the irrigation needs of the land under cultivation. In contrast to these, certain regions of the *subahs* of Delhi, Lahore and Multan (these regions formed a part of united pre-1947 Punjab under the British Rule) had always confronted the peasants with drought and famine in case of failure of rains. The Mughal Government repaired and constructed regular perennial canals in many of such regions. Though the chronicles attach importance to the construction of a few canals (like the East Punjab, i.e. West Jamuna and the Lahore, i.e. Upper Bari), scattered regional contemporary sources point towards the existence of many a perennial small canals in either parched areas or at places where even constant water was available from the streams and the *nalas*. Old canals were cleared, remodeled and extended; new canals were constructed both by the Mughal state and the Mughal *jagirdars* for stepping up the agricultural and horticultural production. In the 17th century, for want of constant labour and attention, many of these canals ceased to flow and remained in disuse until they were reopened by the British government.

(i) The East Punjab Canal (West Jamuna Canal), opened during the Tughlaq period, had fallen into destitute. During Akbar's reign, Shahabuddin Ahmad Khan, the Governor of *Subah* Delhi, got it repaired and flowing and this came to be known as *Nahir-i- Shahab*. This was further remodelled and repaired from Khizrabad to Safedon (30 krohs) in the reign of Shah Jahan. This formed the basis of West Jamuna Canal under the British Government.

(ii) The Delhi Canal, entitled *Nahr-i Bihisht* (The Paradise Canal) covering 30 krohs from the village of Safedon to Red Fort at Shah Jahanabad (Delhi), was in fact an extension of the East Punjab Canal as the very water of the latter canal from its terminus village Safedon was conveyed in the Delhi branch. This was also known as Karnal Canal. A recent discovery of the pictorial roll of the canal drawn in Shah Jahan's region and other contemporary sources shows that the canal was constructed not merely with a view to convey water to the fountains of the Imperial Palace (Red Fort) and to adorn the streets of Delhi, but it irrigated numerous *parganas* and villages all along its route of 30 Krohs (78 miles) and rendered the lands fertile with increased agricultural and horticultural production.

(iii) The Lahore Canal or the Ravi Canal (Upper Bari Doab Canal), originally planned by Ali Mardan Khan, a Mughal noble of Shah Jahan, was later on executed by Mullah Ala' ul-Mul Tuni, an expert engineer in the 16th R.Y. of Shah Jahan. The canal covered 37 krohs and continued to flow regularly till the 19th century when during Ranjit Singh's rule, it was extended upto Amritsar. After the annexation of the Punjab by the British, Sir Henry Lawrence, the Governor of the Punjab, converted it into a great hydraulic irrigation canal-an Upper Bari Doab Canal with headquarters at Madhopur.

(iv) From Shahpur to Shalimar in Lahore (Ravi Canal)

(v) Shahpur to *pargana* Pathankot (Ravi Canal)

(vi) Shahpur to *pargana* Batala (Ravi Canal)

(vii) Shahpur to *pargana* Biar Pati Haibatpur (Ravi Canal)

(viii) From Tavi to Ibrahimabad near Sodhara.

(ix) Sialkot Canal: a branch of river Aik with source in the mountains of Jammu.

(x) Nahr-i Chautung- The dry belt of Hissar in the South-West of *subah* Delhi (at present in the Province of the Punjab) has always remained purely on the mercy of the undependable monsoons and exposed to occasional drought. Apart from the operation of the East Punjab canal, which covered some portions in this region, a proposal made in the last years of Shah Jahan's reign for opening another canal in this region entitled *Nahr-i Chautung* is also on record. It emanated from Sadhaura hills (with 6 natural sources about 80 krohs from Hissar. For irrigation, the plan covered nearly 200, 000 villages and *qasbas*. According to the detailed report, the canal would irrigate the different *parganas* of Mustafabad, Indri, Karnal, Thanesar, Pandri, Fatehpur, Kaithal in *chakla* Sirhind (*subah* Delhi) and the *parganas* of Khandas Jind, Hansi, and Hissar in *chakla* Hissar (*subah* Delhi). The dry depressions, having existed till recent times, confirm the execution of the plan during the Mughal age.

V

Administration of Canal-Irrigation: Under the Mughals, the administration of the canal irrigation formed an integral part of the revenue and executive administration of the local government.

A. ***Darogha-i Ab-i Nahr* (Canal *Darogha*); The *Faujdar*; The *jagirdar*:** *Ab-i Nahr's* office was invariably combined with the *Faujdar* of the locality. Even where the offices remained separate, the overall charge of the administration of the irrigation works lay with the *faujdar*. In such localities where the *faujdari* powers were vested with the *jagirdar*, the latter was responsible for the management of the irrigation within his territorial jurisdiction.

B. **Mir-i Ab; Mehmar:** The *Mir-i Ab* was an expert irrigation engineer and had his own staff of masons (*mehmaran*) working under him. He was responsible for the digging of the new water-channels, to construct *bunds* (weirs) in consultation with the Diwan of the division and, above all, to see that equitable water was distributed to the cultive.

C. **The Zamindar:** The local zamindars who possessed expert knowledge of the geography of the locality helped government irrigation staff.

D. There were no private canals during the Mughal age. Even when some of the Mughal nobles got a few canals repaired or excavated at their own initative for the irrigation of their gardens or assigned *jagir* lands, they could not claim these canals as their private property.

E. In fact, the real basis of irrigation administration was co-operation between the government and the cultivators. The headworks of the canal, the main lines and branches, the distributaries were all constructed and maintained by the state administration but the water courses and the field channels were constructed and invariably maintained by the *riaya* (i.e. the primary zamindars, simple *riaya* and *muzarian*). In regions close to the main rivers or streams, the construction of the canals, the water courses and the bunds were the joint responsibility of the state and the *riaya*. Although, in this respect, the *riaya* met a part of the maintenance charges on collective basis for the Mughal age, there is no contemporary evidence to show that a water rate was levied in the canal irrigated areas.

Chapter 9

Extension and Administration of the Irrigation System under Shahjahan and Aurangzeb

The indigenous methods of irrigation had been known to Northern India since ages and subsisted under Akbar for the purpose of assessment. Regularly irrigated lands through wells, ponds and lakes, seas and perennial canals were reckoned at the *Polaj* rate. The Mughal Government was very much alive to the problem of extension of the irrigation facilities to the cultivators for the development of agrarian economy. Moreland, followed by a few other scholars, thought that in Mughal India, there was no development of the irrigation and canal system worth the name.[1] Such a summary and inaccurate view is uncharitable for the Mughal agrarian policy. Of course, the indigenous well-irrigation and the canal system under the Mughals is no match to the highly developed modern irrigation and network of canal works undertaken in the second half of 19th century and 20th century during British Rule in India. With the opening of the modern canal system and tube wells, the Indian agricultural economy under the British undeniably entered a new phase and made unprecedented progress in agricultural production. But that should not belittle the Mughal contribution, especially keeping in view the nature and the extent of needs of the artificial means of irrigation to the then agrarian population and the handicaps in the engineering techniques or the development of the irrigation system.

The operation of the well – both the Persian wheeled and the *Charsa* system – continued to occupy the most favoured position as a means of artificial irrigation throughout the Mughal age.[2] The Persian-wheeled well was more efficient, cheaper and easier to operate than the *Charsa* system though the former was known mostly to the N.W. regions (*subah* Sindh, Multan and Lahore) excepting

South-East and the latter was better known in other parts of North India.[3] Towards the close of the 17th Century, Sujan Rai mentions the prevalance of the well operation in the *subahs* of Lahore[4] and Delhi.[5] Aurangzeb noted the well-irrigation in the *subah* of Multan.[6] But other sources bear testimony to its wide-spread operation in the whole of North India.[7] In fact throughout the Mughal age, it was an established practice on the part of Mughal administration to help the cultivators in the repair of the old wells and the construction of the new ones.[8] Both lined and unlined wells (*basta* and *kham*) were known to have existed [9] and both needed periodical repairs for maintenance. Though the well digging was an individual responsibility of the cultivator, the Mughal Government always financed the project with an advance of the *taqawi* loans. The well-digging operations were conducted by a class of diggers.[10] as well as on joint community basis. By and large, the peasant proprieters, the zamindars and the *madad-i-maash* assignees always possessed their own wells but where some of the tenants did not own wells, they had to pay fixed annual rent to the landlord for the utilization of the well situated on their lands.[11] The extent to which a well was needed for artificial irrigation for the *rabi* or both the *kharif* and *rabi* depended mostly upon the extent of the rain fall and the availability of other artificial means of irrigation varying from one region of North India to another. The eastern or the central portion of North India with heavy or secure rain fall needed artificial irrigation more for the *rabi* crops and for the extension of the *kharif* crops, but in the Western or North West portions with comparatively less rainfall, the well irrigation was essential for the subsistence of both the *rabi* and the *kharif* crops.[12] The well irrigation has persisted throughout these centuries in North India[13] in co-existence with the modern tube wells.

It is, however, quite evident that in many a portion of North India especially in the North Western Provinces, the wells by themselves could not mature large areas without supplementing from the river floods (*sailab*) in autumn or irrigation from inundation canals or embarkments. In the hilly tracts or submountaneous regions where the water rushes down in torrents after a burst of rain, it has been restrained in embarkments from time immemorial and spread over the fields as required.[14] This practice has continued to the present day. Water is taken out of some river and carried in water channels to the fields for the growth of rice in the terraced embarkments of the hills and the submontane areas. In the plains, wherever conveniently available, the water was stored in the reservoirs, ponds and lakes for irrigation and spread out to the fields through water-ditches.[15] In respect of such an irrigation source prevalent in all the territories of the Mughal Empire, Tavernier's testimony falls exactly in line with Zainuddin Khwaja's statement made on the eve of the Mughal Empire.[16] Apart from it, depending on the rivers, both inundation channels and perrenial water channels were excavated from the rivers and their various tributaries for the irrigation of the villages and *parganas* near which the rivers or the streams (*nalas*) passed. Even though during the Mughal period, the regularly constructed main canals were fewer in number and confined to the North-West region, the inundation water-canals and channels drawn from the main rivers or rivulets was the most prominent feature of the agrarian life. Some of the North Indian rivers afford an unfailing source of water supply requiring no deep digging while many water sheds between the rivers and streams and the low lying regions offer vast fertile lands for a convenient irrigation for the *kharif*. Indigenous engineering methods helped the construction of a long series of inundation canals and more or less perennial canals even on the rivers with high banks utilising water whenever its level was high enough to permit its regular flow in the channels. In case of inundation canals, there were usually no *bunds* (weirs) at their heads and, in many cases, no means of controlling the water entering them, so that a consant flow of water was normally assured during the summer months (May-September) when water is plentiful owing to the melting of the snows in the Himalayas and the monsoon rainfall. Of course, such an irrigation source was subject to serious short-comings – little water during the years of scanty rainfall or even damage to the crops in case of high floods in any region. But despite these handicaps, such canals irrigated millions of acres of land and, as a constant feature of the agrarian society, continued right till the 19th Century.

Generally speaking, the *Ain*, the chronicles and regional contemporary historians always took such irrigation practices as normal feature of the agrarian society and completely ignored any description about them. But Sujan Rai, the native of the Punjab, who otherwise mostly follows the pattern of *Ain-i Akbari*, proves an exception for his own native *subah*. Possessed with adequate and accurate data, he not only gives a detailed description of the course of the main rivers of the Punjab but even of the small rivers which serve as their tributaries.[17] His description of the territories of the Doabs is very comprehensive. He mentions not only the main cities and *qasbas* by which these rivers passed but, in some cases, even mentions the limits of the villages of the numerous named *parganas* covered by the rivers.[18] He, of course, does not specifically mention that these *parganas* profited by irrigation but that is essentially what he means. The villages in the water-sheds of the Doabs were irrigated by the indigenous canals from the beds of the main rivers, their tributaries and the various *nalas*. This accounts for the major settlement of the villages and the *parganas* near the river courses and the water-sheds of their tributaries, which is true in fact for the whole of India during the medieval age.[19] Where such canals were purely seasonal, the well-irrigation and the inundation canal irrigation worked hand in hand with each other.[20] The archaeological physical remains of the *nalas* and the channels in the 19th Century also clearly point towards such indigenous irrigation practices.[21] While most of such canals were seasonal, in some regions, the rivers and the *nalas* provided more or less perennial water channels.

Mahazar-i Shahjahani affords a clear insight into the 17th Century irigation facilities in the territories of Bhakkar (South Multan) and Sehwan (South Sindh). It mentions that all the eight parganas of South Bhakkar were well irrigated by the canals and water channels drawn from the main river Indus and its tributaries. When the latter were well maintained by the Jagirdari administration, it always led to the development of new villages, growth in the millets (*jowar*) and rice (*shali*) in the *kharif* crops and wheat, barley, gram in the *rabi* crop. The revenues of the villages and *parganas* would also increase by 3 to 4 times. It always led to the agricultural prosperity of the *parganas*.[22] Similarly, for *pargana* Naraun (South Sehwan), it states that the said *pargana* was irrigated by four canals.[23] *Pargana* Baghban had traditional irrigation channels drawn from the stream (*nala*) Marwi and, when fully looked after, would lead to four-fold agricultural prosperity.[24] The village of Nar Pargana Haveli Sehwan was well irrigated by a perennial lake [25]. The general impression given by the *Mahzan-i-Shahjahani* shows that in the villages and the *parganas* of the *sarkars* Bhakkar (*subah* Multan) and Sehwan (*subah* Thatta), there was neither any dearth of agrarian land nor of perennial irrigation canals and channels[26] though, at times, there was the lack of proper maintenance of the irrigation channels on the part of the inefficient *jagir* administration against which representation was made to Shahjahani Court.[27] Though *Mahzar-i Shahjahani* deals with the problems of irrigation administration of the above mentioned regions, such perennial and inundation canals were widely prevalent in the *subahs* of Multan[28] and Thatta.[29]

Notwithstanding such irrigation facilities, some regions in the North West portions of India, i.e. certain regions in the *subahs* of Delhi, Ajmer, Lahore, with either little or uncertain monsoons, have always confronted the peasant with drought and famine in case of failure of rains. It goes to the credit of the Mughal government to have repaired and constructed regular perennial canals in many of such regions. Though the chronicles of Shahjahan's reign mostly attach importance to the construction of the West Jamuna and the Lahore (upper Bari) canals, scattered regional contemporary sources point towards the existence of many a perennial small canals in either parched areas or at places where even constant water was available from the streams and the *nalas*. As many of these canals needed periodical removal of silt, they had become choked and useless. Under the Mughals, strenuous efforts were made to restore them and to extend their scope. Old channels were cleared, remodelled and extended, new canals were constructed both by the Mughal state and the Jagirdars for stepping up both the agricultural and horticultural production. The 17th century sources reveal that the perennial canals in these regions were regularly maintained. It was mostly due to the administrative anarchy in the 18th century, that for want of constant labour and attention, many of these canals ceased to flow and remained in disuse until reopened by the British government.

The East Punjab Canal (West Jamuna Canal), which had already been repaired under Akbar, was remodelled and repaired from Khizrabad to Safedon (30 *Krohs*) i. e., 78 miles in length in the reign of Shahjahan.[30] Thereafter, it not only kept flowing for irrigation throughout the Mughal age but even its new branch was opened upto Delhi. The Delhi canal, entitled, *Nahr-i Bihisht* (The Paradise canal) also covered 30 *Krohs* (78 miles) from the village of Safedon to the Red Fort at Shahjahanabad (Delhi).[31] The Delhi canal was, in fact, an extension of the East Punjab Canal as the very water of the latter canal from its terminus village Safedon was conveyed in the Delhi branch. A recent discovery of the pictorial roll of the Canal drawn in Shahjahan's reign and other contemporary sources show that the canal was constructed not merely with a view to convey water to the fountains of the Imperial Palace (Red Fort) and to adorn the streets of Delhi, but it irrigated numerous *parganas* and villages all along its route of 30 Krohs (78 miles) and rendered the lands fertile with increased agricultural and horticultural production. Thus, the west Jamuna and its Delhi branch were an important inheritance to the prosperity and, after being remodelled and realigned on modern hydraulic engineering methods under the British administration, formed the basis of the present West Jamuna Canal.[32]

The Lahore Canal (Upper Bari Doab) was another great engineering and agrarian achievement of Shah Jahan's reign.[33] On the suggestion of Ali Mardan Khan, a Mughal noble at the Royal Court sanctioned Rs. one lac for the opening of the Ravi Canal (upper Bari Doab Canal) from the village Rajpur situated near Nurpur (*sarkar* Bari Doab *subah* Lahore) where the river entered the plains.[34] According to the first plan, the canal was to cover 48½ *Krohs* (125.8 miles) from the village Rajpur to Lahore, the capital of the *subah*.[35] But the plan could not be carried through on account of the faulty operations and inexperience of the engineers [36] even though they spent another amount of Rupees one thousand from a further grant of Rs. one lac.[37] Ultimately, Mullah Alaul Mulk Tuni, an expert engineer, completely revised the alignment plan of the canal cutting short by 11½ *Krohs* and covering in all only 37 *Krohs* (862 miles) in its course. He utilised the same course for the first five *Krohs* (13 miles) and for rest of 32 *Krohs* (83.2 miles) upto Lahore, a new course with fresh digging operation and realignment was executed.[38] The main purpose of the canal was to increase a *band* on the Karnal stream by Asalat Khan [39] where Shahjahan made a personal visit. He does not say anything about the irrigation facilities provided by the stream.[40] It is rather significant that the contemporary chronicles reflecting the taste of the ruling classes attached great importance to the construction of the monuments, the branches on the streams and the canals connected with the layout of the Mughal gardens. They mostly took the irrigation utility of the canals for agrarian purposes for granted. Thus, with the discovery of more archival regional evidences, it is possible to trace a few other small canals regularly managed by the Mughal state for irrigation purposes.

The dry belt of Hissar in the South-West of *subah* Delhi (at present in the province of the Punjab) always remained purely at the mercy of the undependable monsoons and exposed to occasional drought. Apart from the operation of the East Punjab Canal (West Jamuna Canal), which covered some portions in this region, a proposal made in the last years of Shahjahan's reign for the opening of another canal in this region entitled '*Nahr-i Chautang*' is also on record.[41] According to this plan, the sources of the Canal lay in the hills of Sadhaura (with 6 natural sources) 80 *Krohs* (208 miles) from Hissar (to the west of Jamuna) and was to be re-excavated after having been in disuse for nearly a century. The source had already plentiful water during the rainy season but was to be converted into more or less a perennial one, flowing for most of the months in the year. For irrigation, the plan covered nearly two hundred thousand villages and *qasbas*. According to the detailed report, the canal would irrigate the different *parganas* of Mustafabad, Indri, Karnal, Thaneser, Pandri, Fatehpur, Kaithal in *chakla* Sirhind (*subah* Delhi) and the *parganas* of Khandas Jind, Hansi, and Hissar in *chakla* Hissar (*subah* Delhi). The plan is submitted as a representation of the *ryots* of the *chakla* Hissar which, with semi-desert condition, always experienced extreme drought and seeks the royal favour for the appointment of expert engineers for a detailed enquiry regarding the digging operations and the regular flow of the water, the dimensions and the length of the canal, its total cost of construction and the number of months in a year it would serve for irrigation. As before, reaching the territory of Hissar, the canal would irrigate the above mentioned *parganas* of *sarkar* Sirhind which were mostly under the administration of the *jagirdars*, the representation seeks the royal favour for the issue of a *Farman* to Bhakkar Khan, the *faujdar* of *chakla* Sirhind for co-operation in this matter and for appointment of an experienced royal engineer for the execution of the plan. The representation also suggests co-operation on the part of the zamindars and the *ryots* of *chakla* Sirhind for the opening of the canal at the source as well as the construction of two or three *bands* in the jurisdiction of Sirhind with the help of experienced engineers and zamindars. It also offers equitable distribution of the cost of construction and maintenance of the canal between the *ryots* of the two *chaklas*. The proposal emphasises the irrigation facilities and the agricultural prosperity as a result of the implementation of the scheme. Though the evidence in hand does not state if the scheme met with final royal approval, there is every reason to believe that the plan of the canal was executed. This may be conceded not only on the plea that the plan fell within the Mughal state policy for the extension of irrigation and agricultral facilities, but the fact of the Chautang canal having once flowed regularly is confirmed by the dry depression in route of the canal exsisting till the recent times.[42]

In fact, though our contemporary knowledge about the canal works in the above mentioned North West regions is quite adequate, both irrigation canals and channels were practically known to all the provinces in North India, but as yet, there is no contemporary evidence to show that any new canals were constructed in other provinces during the Mughal age. For Kashmir, Bernier's eloquent testimony about the existence of canals and water-channels excavated from the rivers and rivulets[43] falls in line with Mirza Haider's comment nearly a century and half earlier.[44] There is every reason to believe that the Alaghani canal in the *Doab* (between the rivers Ganga and Jamuna) in the gangetic plains, inherited since the times of Firoz Tughlak, must have continued to flow throughout the Mughal age. For *Subah* Bengal, Bernier noted a network of lined irrigation channels flowing across thickly populated towns and villages and irrigating 'extensive fields of rice, sugar, corn, three or four sorts of vegetables, mustard, sesame for oil and small mulberry trees.[45] In the delta region, Bernier found innumerable islands extremely fertile, full of orchards abounding with fruit tress and a thousand water-channels running through them.[46]

Administration of Canal-Irrigation

Under the Mughals, the administration of the canal irrigation formed an integral part of the revenue and executive administration of the local government.

A main perennial canal was put under the charge of a *Darogha-i Ab-i Nahr* (Canal *Darogha*) but his office was invariably combined with the *faujdar* of the locality.[47]Even where the officers remained with separate officials, the *faujdar* had an overall charge of the proper administration of the irrigation works.[48]In such localities where the *faujdari* powers were vested with the *jagirdar*, the latter was responsible for the management of the irrigation within his territorial jurisdiction.[49]The *faujdar* would look after the irrigation facilities in his division with the help of the *Mir-i- Ab* (Superintendent of Canals), irrigation engineers and masons as well as the local zamindars and the *ryots* of the locality. The *Mir-i-Ab* was, in fact, a canal chief engineer and possessed full technical knowledge of the canal irrigation works. He was appointed by the Central Government as its *mutsaddi* for the management of the technical details of the canal works in his jurisdiction.[50] In the representation requests, the royal appointment of *Mir-i- Ab* was for the proposed *Nahr-i Chautang* to work out the details of the breadth, depth and the length of the water course of the canal as he was an expert irrigation engineer and had on his staff masons (*Mehmaran*) working under him[51]. He was responsible for the digging of the new water-channels, clearing the old channels and to keep the water flowing, to construct bunds in consultation with the Diwan of the division and above all to see that equitable water was distributed to the cultivators.[52]

There were no private canals during the Mughal age. Even when some of the Mughal nobles got a few canals repaired or excavated at their own initiative for the irrigation of their gardens or assigned *jagir* lands,[53] they were not entitled to any private cess on the cultivators of the villages and the *parganas* benefiting from the irrigation-water. The construction and the maintenance of the regular canals was mostly a state enterprise for the agricultural benefits of the locality, though the canal royal engineer (*Mir-i Ab*) and other canal engineers (*Mehwaran*) who were responsible for the layout, alignment and management of the *bunds* of a canal, could seek the co-operation of such of the local zamindars who possessed expert knowledge of the geography of the locality.[54] The representation for the construction of the Chautaung canal in the *chaklas* of Sirhind and Hissar is an interesting example of the initiative of the cultivators and the zamindars for opening a canal and also shows the voluntary offer of the *ryots* and the zamindars of *chakla* Hissar for contributing towards the cost of construction of the canal.[55] It is doubtful if the Mughal state charged any regular irrigation water cess.[56] But the agriculturalists had to share the burden of the maintenance of the canals and water channels. The headworks of the canal, the main lines and branches, the distributaries were all constructed and maintained by the State administration but the water courses and the field channels were constructed and invariably maintained by the *ryots* and the zamindars of the locality.[57] In fact, the real basis of irrigation administration was co-operation between the government and the cultivator. In regions close to the main rivers or streams, the construction of the canals and the water courses and the bunds was the joint responsibility of the State and the cultivators. The local administration of the *faujdar* or the *jagirdar* had to provide irrigation facilities but at places the zamindars and the affluent ryots, partly financed by the State, would themselves undertake digging operation of the canals from the river and the water channels from the canals to their fields.[58] Ordinarily, the State owned the responsibility of the erection of bunds on the streams but, at times, it offered advance to the cultivators of the needy regions for this purpose.[59] The *faujdar*, or the *jagirdars* and *Mir-i Ab* were, of course, responsible for the equitable distribution of the irrigation water. Thus, it can be said in conclusion that apart from the innundation irrigation canals, which were fully exploited all over Northern India, the perennial canals were known to the *Doab* region and the North Western *subahs* of the Mughal Empire. Considering the fact that India was par excellence an agricultural country, the account of the perennial canals undertaken by the Mughal state apparently looks very meagre in comparison with the 19th and 20th centuries achievement under the British Administration. At present, our knowledge about the small scale perennial and inundation canal in other subahs of the Mughal Empire is extremely scanty for want of any contemporary regional evidence. Many of the old canal beds have fast tended to disappear owing to the new weirs and the courses of the modern canals. But for any verdict on the canal irrigation works of the Mughal State, it is essential to bear in mind the population of the contemporary agricultural population, the extent of the land under plough, and its irrigation needs. The North West portions are the only regions in North India which have small and uncertain rainfall. By and large, all these regions were covered by the network of perennial canals or canals which would flow for the major portion of the year. This explains the fact that the major enterprises of the main canal works during the Mughal age were concentrated on these regions whereas no documentary evidence is available for any such works in the eastern or the central portions of India which had always secure rainfall. Besides, in the latter regions, the indigenous canal works and water courses drawn from the streams served the needed purpose of the land under cultivation. Moreover, the well irrigation served as an important source of irrigation throughout North India. Nonetheless, there is ample contemporary evidence to show that practically all the villages in South India had enough of irrigation facilities whatever were the irrigation methods resorted to in accordance with the geographical situation of a region (the Indian peasant traditionally relied mostly on the well irrigation for the yield on a well-irrigated land is higher than on canal watered lands).[60] In such of the regions where the well irrigation widely supplemented the vastly canal irrigated (perennial or inundation) areas or vice versa, both the *kharif* and the *rabi* crops were perfectly assured. Consequently, with fertile lands, their agricultural production was comparatively very high. Thus the *subahs* of Bengal, [61] Bihar,[62] Oudh, [63] Agra, [64] Malwa,[65] Delhi, [66] Lahore,[67] Multan[68] and Sindh[69] are highly spoken of by the contemporary sources for their agricultural fertility and the excellence of the crops, especially the '*Jins-i-Kamil*', (High grade and cash crops). It is only in the 18th and 19th centuries that an Indian peasant started feeling the dearth of the irrigation facilities. The lack of proper governance and administration during the chaotic periods of the 18th century led to the neglect of maintenance of many canals and water courses resulting in silted beds and consequent dryness.[70] To this was added the economic factor of the rise of population in the 19th century and the pressure on the land. This situation was met by the British administration with an initial attempt to clear up the old canals and channels and then by opening a network of new modern hydraulic canals all over North India.

References

1. Moreland W.H., *Punjab Administration Report 1921-22 (Land of Five Rivers),* p. 301; Thorburn SS. '*The Punjab in Peace and War,*' (Blackwood 1904), pp. 262-63. The latter two hold the view that the Punjab rivers had traversed the plain of the Punjab unutilised for thousands of years and on arrival in the Punjab, the British found little economic advance on the state in which Alexander had found it a few thousand years earlier. Also, Treveskis H.K., *The Punjab of Today,* pp. 241-43. As explained further, in view of the documenary evidence for the Canal irrigation work in N.W. regions of India, such statements evidently look exaggerated.
2. B.R. Grover, 'Classification of Agrarian Land under Akbar'. *I.H.C.* 23rd Session Aligarh, 1960, pp. 198-209.
3. Such well-irrigation practices have continued in these regions even to the present times.
4. For the *subah* of Lahore, Sujan Rai Bhandari *Khulasatu-t-Tawrikh,* Printed Persian Text (edited by Maulvi Zafar Hussain), Moradabad, 1918, pp. 78-79, comments, "Cultivation depends upon well-irrigation; old mechanics make water-wheels which require 360 large and small pieces of wood and more than 100 small pots. So skillful is their mechanism that a pair of oxen can turn such a wheel at every revolution of which many hundred maunds of water come out of the well in the pots and benefit cultivation. The autumn crops and the cheapness of grains depends upon rain." Also Manucci, II. p. 186.
5. Sujan Rai, p. 39.
6. *Ruqat-i- Alamgiri,* (ed.) 1930. p. 29.
7. Fryer, John, *A New Account of East India and Persia being Nine Years' Travels, 1672-81.* (ed.) W. Crooke, 3 Vols., London. 1912. II, p. 94, puts it as a general feature of Indian agrarian life. For *Subah* Ajmer, Tod, *Annals and Antiquities of Rajasthan,* II, pp. 481, 511, *Cavendish Enquiries,* fols. 151a-152a; 374b; 516b. Also, Pelsaert, Franscisco, 'Remonstrantie'.C. 1626, (tr. Moreland, p. 48) noted that for the Rabi crops, large number of wells had to be dug. For *subah* of Bengal and Bihar, See ms. Or. Oct. 113J, Berlin, fols. 1a-4a.

8. R.D. Ms. Or. Oct. 113J, Berlin, fol. 3b; *Nigam Nama,* Bod. Oxfd. fol. 128a, directs that the old wells fallen out of use should be repaired and the new wells be dug at different places for the extension of agriculture and '*jins-i-kamil*'.

9. Ordinarily, the contemporary records do not make much distinction between the *kham* (unlined) and *basta* or *pukhta* (lined) wells. It appears from Sujan Rai's description of wells in *subah* Lahore (vide f.n. 4) that the wells were constructed scientifically and were enduring. The family archives of a *madad-i maash* assignee in village Nandla (*pargana* and *subah* Ajmer) mention the existence of both lined-well *(Chah-i Basta)* vide copy of a *Patta* (agreement deed) between Khub Allah *(madad-i maash* assignee) and *baghban* (the tenant), dated 4th *Shawwal* A.H. 1035 and unlined well *(Chah-i Kham)* vide a rent deed between Nathan *(madad-i maash* assignee) and his tenants, dated 7th *Zulqada* 3rd R.Y. of Mohammad Shah's reign. The existence of lined and unlined wells depended essentially on the nature of the soil and the financial resources of the landowner.

10. Badauni, II, p. 243; *Akbar Nama* of Ilah-dad Faizi Sirhindi Ms. Br. M. fols. 58b-59b.

11. An original copy of a duly attested agreement between Nathan S/o Saiyyad Innayat, a *madad-i maash* assignee in village Nandla (*pargana* and *subah* Ajmer) and his tenants, dated 7th *Zulqada* 3rd R.Y., Mohammad Shahi states that for long time since the agreement between Saiyyadan (the assignee in Shahjahan's reign and the forefather of the present assignee) and his tenants, the latter and their descandants had always paid Rs. 1/- as rent for utilising the water from an unlined well (*Chah-i Kham*) situated on the land given on terms of a *patta* to them. The agreement confirms the previous practice to be mutually followed in future by the respective parties. It is evident that such a practice of renting out well irrigated water prevailed amongst all categories of landowners (zamindars and *muqarari riaya*) who sublet their lands to the tenants in case the latter did not construct their own wells.

12. The rich crops of *subah* Lahore (vide *Ain,* Br. M, Add. 7652, fol. 260bl, Sujan Rai, pp. 78-79) and *subah* Multan (vide f. n. 6) are chiefly ascribed to well-irrigation.

13. The early British records and the District Gazetteers point out long established practice of well irrigation in all of North India.

14. For example, for old embarkments in district Gurgaon (erstwhile Mughal *subah* Delhi), see, Trevaskis, H.K. *'The Punjab of Today'*, I, pp. 232-34; for Kangra (*subah* Lahore), *Indian Agriculture*, p. 12. In village Heentah (Mewar in Rajasthan) Tod noted water maintained by strong embankment of masonry to which no less than 4000 *bighas* were attached for irrigation (Tod. II, p. 483).

15. *Zainud-din Khwaf* and *Babur Nama, Ain* and *Tarikh-i Rashidi* vide f.nos. under 'Agrarian Classification.' For the irrigation lakes and ponds in *subah* Ajmer, the original *Farman* concering *muqaddami* rights in village Anna Sagar, *haveli, pargana* and *subah* Ajmer, dated 16th *Shawwal* A. H. 1121, mentions that the *riaya* and the tenants (*muzarian*) of the said village had for long lived for irrigation on the water of the tank known as Anna Sagar after which even the village was named. Though the document puts it as *Talab*, i.e. tank, it is in fact a field even to the present day. The *Ain* mentions that the lake of Udaipur was about 16 *krohs* in circumference and by its means wheat crops were grown. (*Ain*, Br. M. Add. 7652, fols. 245a-b tr., J.II., p. 278) Also, Tod I, p. 583, which puts its circumference at 12 miles-Rana Raj Singh of Mewar also constructed the Raj Samudra lake in 1676 A.D. to give relief to the famine stricken people of Mewar (Ms. Raj Vilas, Canto 8th, fols 102a-111b vide G.N. Sharma, *Mewar and the Mughal Emperors*, Agra, 1951, pp. 161-62, 195). Original *Chaknamah* of *madad-i maash* assignment in village Nandla (*pargana* Ajmer), dated A.H. 1138, tracing the boundaries of the agrarian fields irrigated by pond-water ever since the original assignment of the village by Jahangir in A.H. 1029; also *Cavendish Enquiries*, fols. 374b, 516b.
16. Taverniers, I., p. 40; also Fryer, II, p. 45.
17. The *British Settlement Reports* and the accounts of the Canal works are full of such instances of long established practice in the region. As by the 19th century, many of such canals had fallen into disuse, in many regions even the British administrators received the old practice. See *Punjab Administration Report 1921-22* (Land of Five Rivers), pp. 300, 329, 387; Sir James Douie, '*Land Administration Manual*' (Lahore, Civil and Military Gazette Press, 1908), p. 786; Trevaskis, H.K., '*The Punjab of Today*,' I., pp. 233-34, 247-48. For Bihar , for example, the District Gazetteer of Bhagalpur, B.R. Grover, *op. cit.*
18. Sujan Rai, pp. 67-68.
19. For example, for river Degh, it comments, "The river Degh issues from this place (i.e. Purmandal in Jammu hills). After leaving it and passing by the boundaries of villages of the *parganas* of Zafarwal, Haminagar, Pasrur, and Aminabad, it reaches the foot of the bridge of Shah Daula, which is on the highway. Flowing by the Parganas of Daulatabad, Mihrabad, Manish, Faridabad and others, it unites with the Ravi. This *pargana* is called Degh-Ravi." (*Ibid.*, p. 74).
20. For example., for Baglana in Deccan, Mohammad Sadiq Khan noted a network of canal-work in every town and village cut from the river for the agricultural benefits (T.S., Ms. Br. M. O.R. 174 fols. 60b-61a). For *subah* Malwa, Tod noted that as late as the close of the 18th century and the beginning of the 19th century, due to the Maratha intrusions and political instability in Mewar (Rajasthan), emigration took place

(1784 to 1818 A.D.) and the districts to which the emigrants fled were those Mundisore, Kachrode, Oneil, and others, situated on the feeders of the Chumbal (river), in its course through Malwa:" where they also dug wells for irrigation. (Tod II, p. 508).

21. For illustration, see f.n. 6 and Tod (*Ibid.*).
22. For Punjab, see H.K. Trevaskis, '*The Punjab Today*', II., pp. 247-48; for Beas-Sutlej region in the Punjab, see Rennel's Map, for Sindh, Lambrick, 'Early Canal Administration in Sind' vide *Journal of Sind Hist. Soc.*, III(1937), part I., p. 16.
23. Ms. pp. 17-19.
24. *Ibid*. p. 65.
25. *Ibid*. pp. 203-4.
26. *Ibid*. p. 211.
27. *Ibid*. p. 212.
28. *Ruqat-i Alamgir*, ed. 1930. p. 29. Nigar Nama, Bod, Oxfd. fols. 157a-b, Ms. N.A.I. fol. 116b; Ms. Aligarh, 257a-b.
29. For the Canals Begari Wah in Upper Sind and Naulakhi in the Naushahro Division, see Lambrick vide *Journal of Sind Historical Society*, III., 1937, Part I., p. 17. For a canal in Delta region constructed in early 16th century by the Jam Government irrigating the *parganas* of Sankora, the territory under the hills and around Thatta city, See *Tarikh-i Tahiri*; Also Irfan Habib, '*The Agrarian System*', p. 35.
30. Mohammad Warris, Ms. Rampur, pp. 57-58; *Amal-i Salih* III, p. 29, ed. Lahore, pp. 28-29.
31. *Ibid*. Also, Mulakhas, Ms. Patna, fol. 370b; Sujan Rai, pp. 29-30, 36-37. The Canal was completed in the 20th R.Y. of Shahjahan. Mohammad Sadiq (Ms. Rampur, pp. 164-65, 13th R.Y.) suggests that Ali Marden Khan proposed the construction of both the Delhi and the Lahore Canals for the increase of production. Apart from Mohammad Sadiq, no other contemporary chronicle associates the Delhi Canal with Ali Mardan Khan. In fact, Mohammad Sadiq's description is not very clear. He states that by this year (13th R.Y.), there were no canals for the cities of Lahore and Delhi. Thereupon, Ali Mardan Khan proposed that with the help of the expert Iranian engineers, the Canal be dug from the river Jamuna (which could be only Delhi Canal) for the prosperity of the city, horticulture and agriculture. Thereupon, a sum of one lac of rupees was sanctioned (in fact was done in the case of Lahore Canal) and that the proposed course of the Canal was 49 *krohs* (which also stands for the Lahore canal, *Ibid*). It is evident that either the Ms. is defective or the author having stated about the proposed Delhi Canal jumped on to the description of the Lahore Canal. This accounts for the later tradition of associating even the Delhi Canal

with Ali Mardan Khan (vide *Chahar Gulshan,* tr. Sarkar, p. 124; Trevaskis, H.K., '*The Punjab of Today,* I, p. 244).

32. C.R.O. Hydbd. A coloured pictorial roll of the Delhi Canal drawn during the reign of Shahjahan. It names all the *qasbas* and the *parganas* which it irrigated all through its course. Sujan Rai, pp. 36-37 particularly mentions the irrigation benefit it brought to many *parganas* (on its route and the gardens near the capital of Shahjahanbad. Also, f.n. 28.

33. *Punjab Administration Report*, pp. 304-5; H.K. Trevaskis, *The Punjab of Today*, II, pp. 244-46.

34. *Amal-i Salih* II, p. 312; ed. Lahore, II, pp. 238-39; Lahori, (Calcutta ed. 1868), II, pp. 168-69, 233-41, 311, 315; Sujan Rai, p. 77.

35. *Amal-i Salih* (*Ibid.*) writing in the 30th R.Y. of Shahjahan's reign comments that the canal, which was completed in the 16th R.Y., had been constantly irrigating the gardens since then.

36. Trevaskis, H.K., '*The Punjab of Today*', II, p. 246.

37. Sujan Rai, p. 74, Sujan Ṛai mentions that Ali Mardan Khan laid out a garden in the newly founded city Ibrahimbad and spent six lacs of rupees on its buildings, garden and a canal. The Mughal Government assigned to Ali Mardan Khan 2,000 villages in rent free grant for the maintenance of the garden and the city.

38. *Ibid.* p. 77. Shahpur is situated 32.23 N. 75. 44E (*Atlas*, sheet 29), north of Pathankot. The present main Bari Doab issues from Madhupur 7 m. N.W. of Pathankot. Also, Muhammad Akbar, '*The Punjab under the Mughals*, Appendix, p. 306.

39. R.A.J. *Akhbarat,* regd. no. 1487/2, dated 29th Rabi II, 23rd R.Y. Aurangzeb.

40. *Lahori, II*, p. 112.

41. Balkrishan Brahman, Br. M. Ad. 16859 fols. 107a-109b.

42. Trevaskis, H.K., *The Punjab of Today,* I., p. 244. Dr. Irfan Habib (*The Agrarian System*, p. 33), however thinks that no action was taken on the above proposals for the construction of Chautung Canal. He is mistaken in associating the Chauting stream with the Hissar Canal (*Shihab-Nahr*) which both before or after the repairs and realignment under Shahjahan carried entire water from the river Jamuna only (vide Warris, pp. 57-58). The reference in the report to the Chautung strean having flown about a hundred years ago is not directed towards *Shihab-Nahr* but to its own separate existence.

43. Bernier, p. 397.

44. *Tarikh-i Rashidi*, tr. Elias and Ross, p. 425.

45. Bernier, p. 442.

46. *Ibid.*

47. R.A.J. Akhbarat, regd. no. 1487/2, dated 29th Rabi II, 23rd R.Y. (Aurangzeb's) reign appoints Nizamud Din, the *faujdar* of the locality as the *Darogha* of the Sialkot Canal (*subah* Lahore).

48. Also, the representation of the construction of *Nahr-i Chautung* urges the Mughal state to issue a *Farman* to the *faujdar* of *chakla* Sirhind for co-operation in the construction of the canal in his jurisdiction (see f. n. 38).

49. Ms. pp. 17-19, 203-4.

50. Balkrishan Brahman, fols. 108a, 109a, vide f. n. 42. The representation for the proposed *Nahr-i Chautung* makes a request for the royal appointment of Mir-i Ale for working out the details of the layout of the Canal.

51. *Ibid*. Literally speaking, a *Mahmar* would mean simply a mason but for the canal works contemporary sources, use the term *Mahmar* in the general sense of technical canal engineers.

52. *Nigar Nama*, Ms. Bod. Oxfd. fols. 157a-b, Ms. NA.I. fol. 116b, Ms. Aligarh, fols. 257a-b.

53. The West Jamuna Canal under Akbar was repaired by Shahbud Din Ahmed Khan and Mullah Nuruddin Mohammad Tar Khan. For Ali Mardan Khan's Canal in Shahjahan's reign, see f.n. 35-39.

54. Balkrishan Brahman, Br. M. Add. 16859, fol. 108b.

55. *Ibid*.

56. Firuz Tughlak, while abolishing various other cesses, had charged water tax (*Haqi Shirb*) over and above the normal land revenue from those lands that were irrigated by the canals and watersubways. This cess was unanimously declared legal by his jurists. (Afif, pp. 129-30); Also, Tripathi, *Some Aspects*, p. 287. For the Mughal age, there is no contemporary evidence to show that a water-rate was levied in the canal irrigated areas. Of course, as explained above, apart from the main canals, the water channels and water ditches to the fields were maintained by the *ryots*, zamindars and the local state officials collectively.

57. Balkrishan Brahman, Br. M. fols. 108b-109a.2.

58. M.S. pp. 17-18 quotes this practice for *sarkar* Bhakar *subah* Sindh. It also states (vide f. n. 2 p. 17 of the text) that in *pargana* Chanduka, one of the zamindars named Abra dug out a big canal (*Ju-i Kalan*) from the main river and brought water to the agricultural fields. It led to the settlement of various new villages and the agricultural prosperity of the old ones. It equally led to the prosperity of the *pargana* Darbela of the same *sarkar*.

59. *Ruqat-i Alamgir*, p. 134. Under Shah Jahan, the Mughal government proposed to offer Rs. 40, 000-50, 000 to the cultivators in Khandesh and Panighat on Berar (Deccan) for the erection of bunds.

60. Trevaskis, H.K., *The Punjab of Today*, I, p. 239.

61. *Ain*, Br. M. Add. 7652 fol. 175b; Manrique, II, p. 56; Bernier, pp. 437-38, 442; Sujan Rai, p. 47.

62. *Ain* (*Ibid.*), fols. 193b-194a; Pelsaert; pp. 6-9.

63. *Ain* (*Ibid.*), fols. 204a-b; Pelsaert (*Ibid.*), Sujan Rai, p. 44.

64. *Ain* (*Ibid.*), fols. 199a-b; Pelsaert (*Ibid.*), Sujan Rai, pp. 42-43.

65. *Ain* (*Ibid.*), fols. 208a-b; Jerome Xavier, p. 121; De Laet, noted, "The whole country between Agra and Lahore is well-watered and for the most fertile part of India. It abounds in all kinds of produce, especially sugar"; Manrique, II, p. 153.

66. *Ain* (*Ibid.*), fol. 249a; Sujan Rai, pp. 36-37, 39. Manrique II., p. 180 comments about Delhi, 'Its wealth is due to the fertility of corn, rice and various kinds of vegetables', Bernier, p. 283, Manucci, II., p. 422.

67. *Ain* (*Ibid.*), fol. 260b-261a, Sujan Rai, pp. 78-79. Ruqat-i Alamgir, pp. 169-70. For some0000000 of the *parganas* like Gujarat and Sialkot etc., Aurangzeb compared each of such *pargana* upto a *subah* by itself (a simili in respect of revenues). In Aurangzeb's time, the *pargana* of Sialkot when included in the *khalsa* had revenues of 7 lac and 50 thousand rupees, (vide Ahkam, pp. 505-6). The *pargana* of Sialkot was also irrigated by a Canal Sujan Rai, p. 74 comments that when Ali Mardan Khan opened a canal from the river Ravi (flowing both in Jammu and Sialkot) for his gardens at Sodhra, due to the enroute irrigation facilities afforded by the canal, of the villages was detached from *Pargana* Sialkot and created a full-fledged *pargana* which became renowed for its agricultural prosperity. Similarly, Sujan Rai, p. 67 compares the revenues of his own native *pargana* of Batala to the mythical forty treasures of Qarun (the King of Egypt). The *pargana* of Batala was created in Akbar's reign (*Ibid.*) and was also irrigated by a canal excavated from the river Ravi; Also Thevenot, p. 85. Manrique, II., *Journey from Lahore to Multan* (1640-41 A.D.) p. 221; Manucci, II., p. 424.

68. *Ain* (*Ibid.*), fol. 266b. puts the climate of *Subah* Multan simliar to that of Lahore but with less rainfall, Sujan Rai, p. 61. Aurangzeb attributed the agricultural prosperity of *subah* Multan both due to innundation-canals and well-irrigation. For details of the *parganas* of *sarkar* Bhakhar, see M.S. pp. 5-22; For irrigation-canals and channels in *pargana* Takkar, *sarkar* Bhakkar, M.S. pp. 17-18; Manrique II, *Journey from Multan to Qandhar* (1642-43 A.D.) pp. 255-56, Manucci II, p. 427.

69. *Ain* (*Ibid.*), fol. 272a. Sujan Rai, p. 63, pays a special tribute to the Baloch territory (*Waliat-i Baloch*) for high state of culture and abundant agricultural production in both the crops (*kharif* and *rabi*); Manrique, p. 238.

Chapter 10
Classification of Agrarian Land Under Akbar

The classification of land as developed under Akbar was not only a continuation of the Sur regime[1] but with longer period at hand for agrarian experimentation, was evolved on broader lines. It embodied as much the indigenous and the Sur notions as the traditional Timuride ones[2]. The importance of the judicious assessment rates based on different kinds of land is clearly underlined in the *Ain*[3] and other chronicles. This system continued throughout the Mughal age and further modification in the State demand in the reigns of Shah Jahan and Aurangzeb was within the same classification order[4].

The description of the *Ain* is not so much in accordance with the categorisation of the nature of the soil such as clay, loam and sand since soils differ naturally from one another in respect of their minerological and chemical composition and in respect of the mechanical arrangement of their component parts. The *Ain,* in its chapter on land and its classification and proportionate dues of sovereignty,[5] emphasises the classification of the cultivable land rather than the classification of the soil. It is based on the simple principle of continued or intermittant cultivation, capability of the land for crops, the rate of assessment and state demand to be fixed for each class of land. Thus the land is divided into four classes, viz *Polaj, Parauti, Chachar* and *Banjar*[6]. *Polaj* land is annually cultivated for each crop in succession and is never allowed to lie fallow. It requires less of labour for ploughing. *Parauti* land is left out of cultivation for some time that it may recover its strength for recultivation. It needs comparatively more of ploughing labour. *Chachar* land lies fallow for three to four years and requires much labour for ploughing and recultivation. *Banjar* land remains

---

Papers presented at *Indian History Congress,* 23rd Session, Aligarh, 1960

uncultivated for five or more years. It needs tremendous labour for recultivation. Some of the land is rendered permanently barren and grows only bushes and thorns as if on a desert or hilly tract. For the purposes of assessment, the *Polaj* and *Parauti* lands are further divided according to the fertility of the soil into good, middling and bad where upon the medium produce and the state demand is fixed[8].

Apart from the above broad division, which is rather insuffcient, a detailed classification of land based on adventitous qualities can be done under two main categories, i.e. unirrigated and irrigated. The former comprises the *Barani* and the *Sailabi* whereas the latter includes the *Abi*, *Chahi* and *Nahri* lands.

Unirrigated

(a) ***Barani*** - dependent on rainfall[9]. Much of the agriculture in India depends on rainfall and its uneven distribution in different subahs.[10] *Ain* has given the topographical and climatic conditions of every *subah*[11]. In the *barani* land, the *kharif* crop is always assured after Monsoons, whereas, the fate of Rabi crop depends on the scanty and capricious winter rainfall[12]. For example, in the *subah* of Ajmer, 'the soil is sandy, and water obtainable only at great length, hence the crops are dependent on rain. The spring harvest is inconsiderable. *Jowari, lahdarah* and *moth* are the most abundant crops. A seventh or an eighth of the produce is paid as revenue, and very little in money[13].' Similarly, in the *subah* of Gujrat, 'soil is sandy, dependent on rains, and the spring harvest is small. Consequently, the staple crops are only *jowari* and *bajra* whereas wheat and foodgrains are imported from Malwa and Ajmer, and rice from the Deccan.' The *chachar* and the *banjar* lands described in *Ain* are mostly *barani* and the State demand is fixed accordingly[15].

(b) ***Sailabi*** - It is flooded or kept permanently moist by rivers and is rendered cultivable and fertile due to inundation caused by the rivers. *Ain* mentions specially of such land in the *subahs* of Delhi and Oudh. Regarding Delhi, 'the chief rivers are the Ganga and Jumna, and both take their rise in this *subah*. There are besides numerous other streams, amongst them the Ghaghar. Much of the land is subject to inundation and in some places there are three harvests[16]. As to Oudh , 'Agriculture is in a flourishing state, especially the rice of the kinds called Sukhdas, Madhkar, and Jhanwan which for whiteness, delicacy, fragrance and wholesomeness are scarcely to be matched. They sow their rice three months earlier in other parts of Hindustan. When the drought begins, the Sai and the Gogra rise high in flood and before the beginning of the rains, the land is inundated, and as the waters rise, the stalks of rice shoot up and proportionate lengthen: the crop, however, is destroyed if the floods are in full force before the rice is in ears[17].' In *sarkar* Bhakkar, *subah* Multan, 'the river Sin (Indus) inclines every few years alternately to its southern and northern banks and the village cultivation follows its course."[18] Of course, such crops stand in equal danger of being destroyed by excessive river floods. *Ain* puts most of such land dependent only on inundation as the *chachar* one and the State demand is fixed accordingly.[19]

Irrigated

Though the *kharif* crop thrives mostly on the rainfall,[20] at places invariably supplemented by artificial means of irrigation, so easily accessible during and after the rainy season, the *rabi* crop lives partly on the scanty capricious rainfall in some portions but mostly on the artificial means of irrigation developed throughout India.[21] Zainud-din Khawaf states that in practically all the villages in India, regularly settled permanent arrangements exist for the purpose of agriculture.[22] The fruit plants need regular watering for the first two years but thereafter depend only on rainfall.[23] But the vegetables and the '*Jins-i-Kamil*',[24] especially the *Rabi* crop, subsist on irrigation.[25]

(i) Though Babur regrets the absence of 'running waters'[26] and attributes it to the dependence of the crops mainly on the rainfall and some other artificial means of irrigation,[27] the presence of rivulets channelled out from the rivers for the purposes of irrigation for many of the towns in India is amply borne out by the historian Zainud-din Khawaf.[28] *Ain* mentions various Mahals and villages located on the streambanks, e.g. Mahal Hapur (*sarkar* Delhi, *subah* Delhi) on the Kali Nadi between two streams,[29] and in *mahal* Jamalpur (*sarkar* Hisar Firozah, *subah* Delhi) 'Ghaggar flows through several villages here.'[30] Such villages must have been irrigated by water course drawn from the mainstream.[31] Both *Tarikh-i-Rashidi*[32] and *Ain*[33] make special performances to *Abi* land in Kashmir with such means of irrigation.

(ii) As regards lakes, tanks and ponds for irrigation, Babur makes various references to this practice in the extremely limited portions of India toured by him.[34] Zainud-din Khawaf mentions large permanent *jalhas*, i.e. lakes and ponds, which in some villages extend from one to three *krohs* and serve source of irrigation and cultivation of the vegetables and fruits for the surrounding villages and *qasbas* inhabited for generations.[35] For irrigation, the *rabi* crop rests upon such permanant lakes and tanks stored with water during the rainy season.[36] *Ain* makes incidental references to the existence of reservoirs at some places. At *mahal* Mandauthi (*sarkar* Delhi, *subah* Delhi), 'the autumn harvest (is) abundant: near the town (is) a tank, which is never dry throughout the year,'[37] 'At Unah (*subah* Gujrat) there are two reservoirs, one of which is called Jumna, the other Ganga. The water bubbles up and forms a stream.'[38] Such methods of irrigation through water courses from the streams and ponds inherited from ancient times continued to operate throughout the Mughal age and find description in the early British records.[39]

(iii) Where running channelled water is not available, Babur notes that water supply for some crops is rendered through human labour on the part of men and women by carrying water by repeated efforts in pitchers drawn from tanks.[40]

B. ***Chahi*** - watered from wells. The irrigation of the land with the well water – the most indigenous and still an extremely efficient instrument of irrigation – has been known to many of the provinces in India since ancient times.[41] Babur notes the prevalence of both the (Persian) wheeled-well in Lahore and Dibalpur and the indigenous *charsa* system of well-operation in Agra, Chandwar and Biana.[42] The *charsa* system could work both on the well and the river bank.[43] Babur and Zainud-din Khawaf describe the well irrigation and the way both the systems of wells operate with much curiosity and interest.[44] Though *Ain* makes a special reference to the *subah* of Lahore with irrigation chiefly from wells,[45] the *chahi* land was known to practically all subahs in northern India[46] and was assessed separately as against the *barani* and *abi* lands.[47] The easiness of approach to the well water-table and irrigation would depend mostly on the nearness to the rivers and sufficient rainfall. For the *kharif* crop, in areas with secure rainfall, occasional well irrigation merely supplements the rains for covering large portions for cultivation resulting in better yields. At some places, wells are operated only for production of '*jins-i-kamil*'. Where the rainfall is scanty, the land under well-irrigation is essentially dependent upon the river floods or inundation canals and water courses for permanent moisture. The *rabi* crop is entirely dependent upon the artificial means of irrigation, mostly on the wells – a fact recorded both by Babur and Zainud-din Khawaf.[48] Thus wells exist both in the *barani* and *abi* lands wherein the well-irrigation assures regular cultivation, especially of the high grade crops and good produce both for the *kharif* and the *rabi* crops. With continuous cultivation in the *barani* and *abi* region, the *chahi* land could be put as *Polaj* with its normal rate of assessment.[49]

C. ***Nahri*** - irrigated from canals. Though some small-scale pioneering work had been accomplished by Ghyasuddin Tughlak,[50] in reality Firoz Tughlak was the first Muslim Sultan who realised the importance of the canals for the purposes of irrigation.[51] The two canals, Rajiva and Alaghkhani, opened by him in the East Punjab and Doab,[52] were permanent inheritance to agrarian development. They helped tremendously in the increase of the produce of the crops, especially the '*jins-i-kamli*, [53] avoided the recurrence of famines and increased the revenues of the State.[54] As with the lapse of time, the East Punjab Canal had fallen into decay, Shaihabu-din Ahmad Khan, the Governor of *subah* Delhi and later on *Diwan-i-Khalsa* in the 13th year of Akbar's reign, got it repaired and flowing to increase the agriculture of his own *jagir* land irrigated by the Canal, which came to be named as *Nahir-i-Shahab*.[55] The canal system was later on extended on the reign of Shah Jahan.[56] The *nahari* land was not only rendered fertile but was assured of continuous cultivation for both the *kharif* and the *rabi* crops. It could be reckoned as the *polaj* land for the rate of assessment.[57] Apart from the land revenue fixed in accordance with the classification of land, the State demanded extra charges as the water rate for the irrigation through the canals based on proper measurement of the canal-water consumed by the peasant-holdings.[58]

Though the *Ain's* main chapter on the classification of land does not take cognisance of the categorisation of the nature of the soil, it can be safely presumed that it is only a general and broad division. In its chapter on '*rawai rozi*' (currency of the means of subsistence), *Ain* explicity states, "And because the conditions of the royal state and prerogative vary in different countries, and soils are diverse in character, and some producing abundantly with little labour and others the reverse, and as inequalities exist also through the remoteness or vicinty of water and cultivated tracts, the administration of each state must take these circumstances into consideration and fix its demand accordingly."[59] The above factors responsible for the diversity in the nature of the soil exist as much within different regions and their tracts in a state as characterising one state from another. In *Ain's* chapter on instructions to the *Amal-Guzar*, the latter is enjoined to make assessment on each class of land carefully based on keen personal observation of its nature and only after scrutiny having familiarised himself with the quality of the soil.[60] The fields of agriculture vary considerably in different places with regard to the nature of their soils and certain soils are adapted to certain crops.[61] He should deal differently, therefore, with each agriculturist and take his case into consideration.[62] Thus, both the factors, the nature of the soil and the intermittancy of cultivation influenced by means of artificial-irrigation, if any, would accumulatively determine the nature and value of the agricultural land which is the real basis of assessment. *Ain*, of course, makes some reference to the nature of the soil in the description of the Provinces. Ajmer and Gujrat are stated to be with sandy soils.[63] Kashmir has three kinds of land, *abi*, i.e. watered through channels, *lalmi* i.e. *barani*-dependent on rainfall, *chalkhai*, i.e. stony, rough and bushy.[64] Moreover, the natural qualities of the soil and also the fact that the above mentioned methods of irrigation did create local conditions for the nature of the soil shows that the latter must have been taken into consideration locally at the time of assessment. Though the main division of the agrarian land in its classification, as explained hitherto, are the same throughout Northern India in the Mughal age, in their detailed subdivisions and the local terminology applied to them, the practice varied from region to region even wihin one province. This is confirmed by the later provincial and local records illustrating the indigenous methods with traditional notions of the classification of land.[65] The *Ain's* description is partial as well in the sense that it emphasises the gradual conversion of every class of land to *polaj*, for an assessment under the normal *polaj* state demand, even though the villages and *parganas* in every province are always marked by more or less permanent local categorisation of the soil and classfication of land for the purpose of assessment.

References

1. *Tawarikh-e-Daulat-Sher Shahi by* Hasan Ali Khan. Translated by Dr. R.P. Tripathi in *Medieval India Quarterly*, Vol. I, July 1950, No. I, p. 62. Hasan states that the land was divided into several classes and the rate of assessment determined on that basis. He, however, has not explained the way in which the land was classified.

2. *Mulfuzat-i-Timuri* : Ms. Or. Fol. 287 Berlin fols. 76b-77a. Timur mentions two classes of cultivable land, irrigated and Barani. The former is irrigated through lakes and water courses and the latter is dependent on rainfall.

3. *Ain,* Br. M. Add. 7652, fols. 148b-151b; Blochmann. Vol I, pp. 297-303. Jarrett Tr. II, pp. 68-75.

4. For Shah Jahan's reign, see *'Maktubat-i-Khan-Jahan-i-Muzaffar Khan-wa-Gwaliar Nama'*, Br. M. Add Rieu III 837, Add 16,859 fols. 107a-109b; for early Aurangzeb's reign of the various uncatalogued *Pargana* documents in Rajasthan Archives, Jaipur, confirm it. For example, *'Yaddasht-i-Haqiqat-i-Arazi-muzruaat wa Uftada muwazih pargana Riwari* (*sarkar* Riwari, *subah* Delhi) *Fasl-i-Kharif,* dated A.M. 1073 fols. Ia to 16b; *'Bal-wa-Jhat-i-Pargana Riwari Kharif wa Rabi'*, dated A.H. 1073, fols. Is to 9b. Such documents are in series with those of the last years of Shah Jahan's reign. For the *subah* of Shahjahanabad , *'Khulastau-t-twarikh'* Sujan Rai Bhandari, Printed Pers. Text (edited by Maulvi Zafar Hussain, Assistant Superintendent, Archeological Department Government of India), p. 39 mentions three main classes of cultivable land, *barani* (Dependent on rainfall), *sailabi* (flooded), and *chahi* (well-irrigated).

5. *Ain,* fol. 149b, Blochmann, p. 297, Jarrentt II., p. 68.

6. *Ibid.*, fol. 148b, *Ibid.*

7. *Ibid.*; also *Diwan-i-Pasand,* Ms. 537, Insha, Asafia Library, Hyderabad, fol. 5a.

8. *Ibid.*, fol. 149a; *Ibid.*, Such land which is cultivated for both the *kharif* and *rabi* crops in succession is also termed as *Dofasli.* " The term does not imply that the land yields every year two crops or cane, which occupies the ground for ten or eleven months and may be considered equal to two ordinary crops; it merely indicates that it often bears two crops in a single agricultural year (*Khari-Rabi*)." In contrast to this, " *Ekfasli* was used to describe land tilled according to the familiar rotation under which a spring crop in one agricultural year is followed immediately by an autumn crop, and the land then lies fallow for a twelve-month." (Douie; *Punjab Settlement Manual*, p. 127). As distinct from *Dofasli* being under *Polaj*, *Ekfasli* would be put in the next category and the rates of assessment for either of them would be different.

   Todar Mal's Instructions to the state land revenue official issued in the 27th year of Akbar's reign emphasise that at the time of measurement and inspection of the standing crops, a special note be taken of the *Eakfasli* and *Dofasli* lands in the villages under survey. After having recorded their areas, assessment would be done accordingly at their respective schedule rates (A.N. Br. M. Add. OR 27, fol. 3322). This reference to the *Ekfasli* and *Dofasli* lands cannot be traced in other versions of *Akbar Nama* texts, Br. M. Add. 26, 207 fol. 161B, Mr. Or. Quart 1822, Berlin fol. 2592 and the printed Pers. Text Bib. Indica. All these texts refer only to the agricultural condition of the land for the purposes of survey and assessment. Beveridge's translation III., (p. 563) also follows the later version.

9. *Ibid.*, Blochmann II., p. 562, Jarrett II., p. 352; also *Tuzuk-i-Baburi,* tr. Beveridge, III., footnote I, p. 488, have used to term '*Lalmi*' but the revenue literature of the 17th century puts it as '*Barani*'.

10. Both Babur and his courtier Zain-ud-din Khawaf bear it out for their times in *Tuzuki-Baburi,* Beveridge, III, p. 486 and *Tarikh-i-Baburi* Ms. Rampur, p. 149 respectively.

11. *Ain,* fols. 174a-296a, Blochmann II, p. 386-599, Jarrett II, pp. 129-417.

12. *Tuzk-i-Baburi*, Beveridge, tr. III, p. 486, *Tarikh-i-Baburi,* p. 149.

13. *Ain,* fols. 242b-234a. Jarrett II, p. 273.

14. *Ibid.* fol. 232a, Jarrett II, p. 246.

15. *Ibid.* fols. 151a-151b, Jarrett II, pp. 73-74.

16. *Ibid.* fol. 249a, Jarrett II, p. 283.

17. *Ibid.* fol. 204a, Jarrett II, p. 181.

18. *Ibid.* fol. 266b-267a, Jarrett II, p. 331.

19. *Ibid.* 151b, Jarrett II, p. 73.

20. Shaikh Zain, *Tarikh-i-Baburi,* p. 152.

21. *Ibid.* p. 153; Such is the position even today. This is very well explained in the '*Report of the Indian Taxation Enquiry Committee,*' 1925-25, Vol. I, p. 99. "The rainfall (in India) varies from 461 inches to about one-hundredth part of that figure. The results are seen at the one extreme in areas in which a crop can hardly be grown without irrigation. Between these two extremes every variety of case is to be found; Swamp land that will grow rice unfailingly without the aid of irrigation at all, rice land where the rainfall requires to be supplemented occasionally, land that will grow wheat without irrigation in a normal year, but requires supplementary irrigation in occassional years, and land which will yield a good crop with regular irrigation and nothing without. These considerations affect the value of the water which, in some cases, can convert an arid desert into a smiling plain while in others, it is really needed only in years of scarcity".

22. *Ibid.* p. 155.

23. *Ibid.* p. 153.

24. '*Jins-i-kamil*' means superior crops like sugar-cane, betel, vetches, tobacco, opium, cotton, indigo, kaiser, and fruits like grapes, bananas, pomergranate and melons, etc. (An 18th cent. dictionary Br. M. Add. 6603 fol. 57a; *Tawarikh-i Shahjahan* by Mohammad Sadiq, Br. M. OR 174, fol. 186a, Rajasthan Archives, uncatalogued *pargana* documents, and also *Ain,* Jarrett II, footnote p. 47).

25. Shaikh Zain, *T. Baburi,* pp. 79, 153.

26. *Babur Nama,* Beveridge, III, p. 487.

27. *Ibid.*

28. Shaikh Zain, *T. Barburi*, p. 149.

29. *Ain*, Jarrett II, 293.

30. *Ibid.* p. 299.

31. Though *Ain* makes only implied reference to such an irrigation, the early British settlement reports are full of such instances of long established practice in the regions. For example, the District Gazetter of Bhagalpur (*Bengal District Gazetters*), pp. 78-92 in a Note on Irrigation remarks, "Artificial irrigation, which is indispensable over a large area of South Bhagalpur, is generally effected by leading off from a natural stream or from a head of water collected in a bandh of tan. The channels are called *Danrhs* and their smaller branches are called *Singhas*." The *Danrhs* are classified into three classes, (a) those commencing from a river (shallow broad stream), (b) those commencing from a *Kharra* or *Jore* (deep channel with high bank); and (c) those commencing from a head of water protected by a bandh or from a tank. The methods of lifting water into the three kinds of *Danrhs* are different although the way in which it is utilised for actual irrigation is the same. All channels commence from the rivers Chandan and Chir, their tributaries and branches. The nature of such an irrigation-canals is described in a report of the Superintending Engineer, dated May, 1864:- "At its greatest width, the Chandan is about 1,500 feet from bank to bank. From the long-continued practice of embanking, its bed is actually higher than the lands on either side, and more especially than that on the eastern bank. Being a hill stream, it is liable to sudden and violent inundation, but except when in flood, the channel is a dry bed of gritty sand, bounded on either side with artificial embankment pierced through innumerable cuts for irrigation purposes." *Bunds* are also erected in the bed of the river to raise the level of the water so as to enable it to pass on the *Danrhs* (channels). During floods, water would naturally flow into the *Danrhs* without any artificial training devices. But when there is no flood or when there is not sufficient water in the river, devices are adopted to put the water in the *Dhanrh* either through a small canal dug in the bed of the river known as *Jonghar* or by digging pits in the bed of the river and by lifting the water by means of buckets, swing baskets, or spoons worked on lever. This kind of water is commonly called "*Jharana*".

32. *Tarikh-i-Rashidi*, translated by Elias and Ross. p. 425.

33. *Ain*, Jarrett II, p. 352, 'Abi signifies in the N.W.P., land watered from ponds, tanks, and water courses, in contradiction to that watered from wells, and being liable to fail in hot season, is assessed at lower rate.'

34. *Babur Nama*, Beveridge, III, pp. 487, 547, 611-12.

35. Shaikh Zain, *T. Baburi* p. 79.

36. *Babur Nama,* Beveridge III, p. 487.

37. *Ain,* Jarrett II, p. 293.

38. *Ibid.* p. 253.

39. The Provinces of Bihar, Bengal and the Punjab afford good examples. For the present district Bhagalpur which formed part of both *subahs* Bihar and Bengal in Mughal Period, see *Bengal District Gazetters, Bhagalpur* by J. Bryne I.C.S. pp. 78-92; for the Punjab, see *The Punjab of Today* by H.K. Trevaskis, I.C.S. pp. 230-234; for India in Gerneral, see *Indian Agriculture* by Albert Howard and Gabrielle L.C. Howard, pp. II-12; also '*Village Uplift in India*' by Branye I.C.S. p. 50.

40. *Babur Nama,* tr. Beveridge, III, p. 487. Shaikh Zain in *T. Baburi* p. 152 remarks that the water was carried in Mashkas, i.e., leather bags.

41. Baden Powell, *The Indian Village Community,* 94 note; H.K. Trevaskis, '*The Punjab of Today*', pp. 234-241, Dr. Tripathi in '*Some Aspects of Muslim Administration,*' p. 286 remarks, " It is well known that in Hindu India wells, tanks and canals were dug by the Princes on a large scale."

42. *Babur Nama,* tr. Beveridge, III, pp. 486-87.

43. Shaikh Zain, *T. Baburi,* p. 153.

44. *Babur Nama,* tr. Beveridge, III, pp. 486-87; *T. Baburi,* p. 153.

45. *Ain,* fol 260b; Jarrett, II, p. 3316. Also, for *Subah* of Lahore, *Khulasatut-twarikh'* of Sujan Rai Bhandari, Printed Pers. Text p. 67 adds, "Cultivation depends upon well-irrigation; old mechanics make water wheels which require 360 large and small pieces of wood and more than 100 small pots. So skilful is their mechanism that a pair of Oxen can turn such a wheel at every revolution of which many hundred maunds of water came out of the well in the pots and benefit cultivation. The autumn crops and the cheapness of grains depends upon rain."

46. *Babur Nama,* Beveridge, III, pp. 486-88; 532-33, Shaikh Zain, *T. Baburi,* p. 153. Aurangzeb's *Farman* to Rasik Das Karori, Ms. Or. Oct. 113j. Berlin, fol. 3b (also quoted in *Nigar Nama Munshi,* Bodlein, Oxford Ms. Pers. e. I. fol 128a) mentions two kinds of land, *Chahi* and *Barani.* It also directs that the old wells fallen out of use should be repaired and that new wells be dug at different places for the extension of agricultural and '*Jins-i-Kamil*'. The early British records and the District Gazetteers point out the long established practice of well irrigation in all the portions of Northern India. For example, see *District Gazetteer of Bhagalpur* (*Bengal District Gazetters*), p. 78.

47. Rajasthan Archives, (formerly known as *Daftar-i-Diwani wa Hazuri), Jaipur, (uncatalougued Pargana Documents) 'Mal-i-Jihat wa Sair-i-Jihat'* of village Fatehpur. *Pargana* Riwari (*sarkar* Riwari, *subah* Delhi), fols. 1-9b.

48. See reference 42 and 43; also see *"Economics of Wells"*, H.K. Trevaskis, *"The Punjab Today,"* pp. 238-241.

49. *Ain*, fols. 149b-150b; Jarret, II, pp. 69-71; also R.A. Jaipur, reference 47.

50. *Tarikh-i-Firoz Shahi*, Ziya'u-din, Barani Bib. Ind. Pers. Text, p. 442.

51. *Ibid.* p. 442. Dr. Tripathi correctly points out that this was a revival of the ancient Hindu practice of digging of canals by prince on a large scale. *(Some Aspects of Muslim Admininstration,* p. 286). The official view of *Punjab Admininstration Report 1921-22* (p. 302) and that of Trevaskis *(The Punjab of Today,* Vol. I, p. 244) that the main object of the work was to convey water to the Emperor's hunting lodge at Hissar than to irrigate the intermediate country' and that it was 'a linked series of drainages rather than of a canal, as the word is understood today' is not justified in view of an evidence from *Ain* (Jarrett. Vol. II, p. 285) which states 'Hisar (Hissar) was founded by Sultan Firoz who brought the waters of the Jamna to it by means of a cutting. A holy devotee predicted his accession to the throne and, at his request, the canal was made'. Apart from this, *Ain's* implied reference to the canal's use for agararian benefits, both Zia (pp. 569-70) and Afif (p. 295) point out the agricultural development following the digging of the canal. That the canal served Firoz Shah's hunting purposes is equally undeniable.

52. Zia, pp. 567-71. Afif. *Tarikh-i-Firoz Shah's* Bib. Ind. Pers. text, p. 127. *Tarikh-i-Mubarak Shahi,* Yahya bin Ahmad bin Abdulla, (a) f. 43rd. Ferishta, I, 146-47. Thomas' Chronicles, pp. 294-95; Tripathi, pp. 286-88 Articles of J.A.S.B. 1833, 1840, 1846, quoted by Dr. Tripathi in *Some Aspects of Muslim Administration.*

53. *Ibid.*, pp. 569-70; *Ibid.*, p. 295; Tripathi p. 287.

54. Afiif, pp. 295-96; Tripathi, pp. 287-88.

55. *Padshah Nama,* Mohammad Waris, Ms. 38 *(Tarikh-i-Farsi)* Rampur. pp. 57-58. Perhaps the same canal is mentioned by Badauni in Munkhibul Tawarikh, III, Printed Pers. text. p. 198, having been re-excavated by Mullah Nuruddin Mohammad Tarkhan in his *jagir, Pargana* of Safadun, *sarkar* Sarhind. (*subah* Delhi). This canal emanated from river Jamna and extended for fifty *krohs* towards Karnal and beyond it. It benefited the agricultural lands of the people tremendously and came to be named as Shakhuni Canal after Prince Salim who was called 'Shakhu Baba' by Akbar.

56. *'Maktubat-i-Khan Jahan wa Gwaliar Nama,* Br. M. Rieu, III, 837, Add 16,859 fols. 107a-109b, gives a detailed report on *'Nahr-i-Chitung'* i.e., Canal irrigating the different *Parganas* of Mustafabad, Indri, Karnal, Thaneser, Pandri, Fatehpur, Kaithal in *chakla* Sirhind and the *pargana* of Khand, Jind, Hansi, Hissar, in *chakla* Sirhind (Sirhind *subah* Delhi). For the repairs done on the Delhi canal, see *Padshah Nama,* Mohammad

Warris, Ms. 38 *(Tarikh-i-Farsi),* Rampur, pp. 57-58. For the Lahore Canal of Ali Marden, see *Padshah Nama* by Lahori Ms. No. 565, Khuda Baksh Liberary Patna., fol. 207b; *Tawarikh-i-Shahjahani,* Mohammad Sadiq, Ms. N: 2093, Farsi, Rampur, pp. 164-165; *Lubul Tawarikh-i- Hind* by Rai Bindra Ban, Ms. 954/15 F. Subban Allah Collection, M.U. Aligarh, fols 49b by Aurangzeb's. Sujan Rai Bhandari in *'Khulasatu-t-twarikh,'* Printed Pers. text, p. 74. mentions the existence of five canal's in the *Subah* of Lahore. One canal taken was river Ravi extended to Ibrahimbad, a newly founded town near Sodhra by Ali Mardan Khan in Shah Jahan's reign. Four canals emnated from river Ravi near Shahpur (a dependency of Nurpur) "Near Shahpur have been taken out of this river (Ravi), a royal canal which goes to the garden of Shalamar in Lahore, a second canal which goes to the *pargana* of Pathankot, a third canal which goes to the *pargana* of Batala, and a fourth canal which goes to the *pargana* of Biar Patti Haibatpur. These canals do good to the crops of the *mahals.*" Shahpur is situated 32,23 N. 75.44E. (*Atlas,* sheet 29), north of Pathankot. The present name Bari Doab issues from Madhupur, um. N.W. of Pathankot. Ali Mardan Khan's canal commenced a little below this point (*Imperial Gazetteer,* II., 153) Also, see *'The Punjab under the Mughals'* by Muhammad Akbar, Appendix, Translation of the description of the Punjab in *'Khulasatu-t-twarikh,'* p. 306.

Apart from this, every region in every subah had developed its own indigenous canal system drawn from the streams flowing in the territory. This is sufficiently borne by early British records noting such long established canal work in vouge in the area. See reference 31.

57. *Ibid.* 149-150b, Jarrett, II. pp. 69-71.

58. *'Muktubat-i-Khan Jahan',* Br. M. Add. 16859, fols. 107a-109b clearly mentions the canal water changes assessed on different holdings in the canal irrigated areas of the *chaklas* of Hissar and Sirhind (*Subah* Delhi) under the supervision of an officer called *'Mir-i-Ab'* (the Superintendent of Canal-water).

59. *Ain,* fol. 147b.,Jarrett, II, pp. 58-59.

60. *Ibid.* fol. 142a. Jarrett, II, p. 46.

61. *Ibid.*

62. *Ibid.*

63. *Ain,* fols. 242b-243a, 232a, Jarrett, II, pp. 273 and 246 respectively.

64. *Ibid.,* fol. 274a, Jarrett II, p. 352. As started above text, for Sarkar Kashmir (*Subah* Kabul), *Ain* mentions three kinds of land, *'Abi'*, *'Lalmi'* and *'Jalkhayai'*. For *'abi'*, see reference No. 9; for *'Lalmi'*, see reference 33. *'Jalkhayai* is a "parched land that has absorbed its moisture". (Jarrett, II., p. 352) Blochmann's text bears the wording of *'Chalkhai'*, which he has interpreted as 'stony, rough and bushy.' I would prefer the

wording as '*Jalkhayai*' to '*Chalkhai*', as the latter, if interpreted as 'stony land,' would not grow even flowers which find description in the context. All this is equally confirmed by the Turki Text of Mirza Muhammad Haidar's *Tarikh-i-Rashidi,* quoted in footnote I., p. 425, by Elias and Ross. The passage of the main text translated by the latter puts four kinds of land and runs as "In this region, all the land is divided into four kinds. The cultivation is (1) irrigation (*abi*); (2) on land not needing artificial irrigation; (3) gardens; and (4) level ground, where the river banks abound in violets and many coloured flowers. On (leave) ground, on account of the excessive moisture, the crops do not thrive, and for this reason the soil is not laboured, which constitutes one of the charms'. Not relying on the authenticity of this passage, Elias and Ross themselves comment in their footnote remarks, "The whole of this passage, regarding the land, is obscure and the translation uncertain. The Turki Ms. is clearer but mentions only three categories of land: "One kind is land where agriculture is done with river water; another where it is done with rain water; another is the level ground, where the river banks abound in violets and many coloured flowers. This land is too damp to cultivate'."

65. Ms. Or. Oct. 113j, Berlin fol 4a, an 18th century Ms. while explaining the colonising reforms of Shah Jahan's reign in *subah* Bihar gives detailed classification of land viz. *Bahi, Kahelfi Kanhel,* Jungle, well-irrigated and tank-irrigated. Also, the '*Records of the Delhi Residency and Agency*' (1807-1857), printed by the Punjab government, 1911. A.D., pp. 327-332, for many of the *parganas,* Pulwull, Rewari, Bohrah, Sonah, Shahjahanpur, Noh, Hutheen, Horul, which formed a part of the *sarkars* of Delhi and Rewari (*subah* Delhi) of the Mughal Empire (*Ain.,* Jarrett, II, pp. 291-301) give description of the detailer local categorisation of land, the crops grown on them and the consequent assessment made on them.

I. (1) The *Barani land* is divided into (i) *Duhur,* i.e., low land over flows by rivulets and often under water for 1 or 2 months. This land yields rice, *barance,* wheat and barley and is a rich stiff loam, assessed at Rs. 1-12 Ans. to Rs. 2/6 per *beegha; Dhur,* 2nd kind, called also *Chicknawat* i.e. land not over flown by rivulets, but surrounded with small fields banks to retain the water, yields cotton, *mukee, jowar, churree,* grain, barley and gram mixed. This is also a hard soil till wet. Assured at Rs. 1/4 as. to Rs. 1-6 as. each *beegah.*

(2) *Nurmotah,* also called *mudah,* is a soft but not sandy soil, yielding cotton, *jowar, kukkee, churree,* barely and gram mixed. Assessed at Rs. 1/- to 1-2 as. per *beegah.*

(3) *Bhoor.* 1st kind, i.e., a sandy soil yielding in general only a *Khurreef* crop. It is best adapted for *bajrah,* note, *jowar.* The crops are bad unless it rains about December, and it is therefore dangerous to rate it as rubee (rabi) land. Assessed at II annas to 14 annas per *beegah. Bhoor,*

2nd kind i.e., a white Sandy soil, yielding only *bajrah* and *mote*, provided it be allowed to lie fallow every third or fourth year. Assessed at 5 to 8 annas per *beegha*.

II. The *Chahee* (well-irrigated) is thus divided (a) *Chahee Dhur*, 2nd kind (there is no *Chahee Dhur* 1st kind here) and *nurmotah*-yields principally wheat, *surson*. Assessed at Rs. 3-6 as. to Rs. 3-12 as. per *beegha*. (b) *Chahee Bhoor*, 1st kind only (there is no *chahee bhoor* of 2nd kind),yields barley. Assessed at Rs. 3/- to Rs. 3/6. Both descriptions of *chahee* land yields tobacco, carrois, and other garden stuffs, but these products depend more on the peculiar properties of the water than on the soil and such details are to be found on the record of this office. Some wells yield from 200 to 400 maunds of corn, others are famed for red pepper (sic.). Some *chahee* land produces from 150 to 350 maunds of onions per *beegha*.

III. *Khadir*, i.e., low and over flown by the Jamuna, to be found only in *pargana* Palwal. It may be sub-divided as follows:- *Khadir*-(1st kind)-A rich black soil yielding *baranee* wheat or barely, and when not over-flown, *mukee* (maiz), *jowar* and cotton inferior to the *bangur*. Assessed at Rs. 1-8 as. per *beegha*. *Khadir* (2nd kind)- A light sandy and yielding *musoor*, barely and peas mixed or peas, *kungnee* and *mukkee* of inferior quality. Assessed at 12 Annas for each *beegah*. *Khadir* is again sub-divided into *chahee* (irrigated) and *baranee* (not irrigated). *Khadir* (low land) *chahee* is not equal to *bangur* (upland) *chahee* land. This is in general to be attributed to the inferior properties of its well water.

The two grand classifications of land are *bangur* (upland) and *khadir* (low land) subject to annual over flowing by rivers or rivulets. They are sub-divided as above explained. The *bangur* villages are in general the happiest and most afflient, the *khadir* crops are most uncertain.

IV. *Nahri:* The *Duhur, nurmotah* and *bhoor*, irrigated by canal-water could pay nearly the same as *chahee* (well-irrigated) land.

The first kind (*duhur*) and (*nurmotah*) will yield sugar-cane, rice and indigo, and part of the land two crops, viz. 1st *kunguee*, early *bahrah, jowar* or *churee*; the 2nd may also yield, if well manured, an inferior crop of sugar cane and two crops, viz. *kungnee samaih* (three monthly), early *bajra, jowar*, and the *rabi* crops as usual.

Similarly, the early British Settlement reports and the District Gazetteers give names of the local indigenous classifications of the land. For example, the *District Gazetteer of Bhagalpur*, pp. 71-72 mentions three main classes of soil clays, loams and sandy. The first clay soil has four indigenous divisions, viz. (a) *Kharar* or *Kaiari*, a blockist in colour stickly when wet and difficult to plough when dry. It is best suited for the growth of winter rice. When the rice crop is reaped, peas of various sorts, *Khesari dal*, gram and linseed are sown, broadcast in the mud before it dries up and luxurious crops are frequently raised in this day. (b) *Khewal*-This is also blackish colour, but is more friable when dry than *Kharar*. It is suitable for almost all crops except maiz, *Khurthi*, etc. If it lies very low and goes under water when the Ganges is in flood, the land is called *Char*. Such soils grow only rabi crops. (c) *Gorimati*-This soil is reddish yellow hue, and produces all kinds of crops if irrigated. (d) *Harin Chikai* and *pasooti* are whitish in colour and are suitable for winter paddy.

(2) Loamy soils are known as *Doras*. If low lying, winter rice is grown on them generally; if high, various *bhadoi* and *rabi* crops do well on them. This sort of soil is found around old village sites where it receives cow-dung anf all sorts of household refuse. It is generally called *Din* or *Goora*, and it is sown with potatoes, vegetables, tobacco, chillies etc. In low situations, loamy soils are called Tari, and all crops except maize, *kurthi*, etc. will do well on them.

(3) *Balmut* is sandy loam that will grow anything. *Dhus* is the name given to Sandy loam in the Gangetic diara. As it is submerged when the river is in flood, it is used for rabi crops only. These crops thrive in it exceedingly.

Soil that is almost pure sand is called simply *Balu*. When a thin layer of silt deposited on the top of the sand, it is called *Patpar*. In this state, it grows mustard well, but as the layer of slit gets deeper, it becomes also fit the barely, oats etc. *Diara* lands covered with sand are called *balu burd*. Water-melons do very well in such lands. Excellent crops can be raised from such land but there is no stability nor certainty about diara cultivation.

(4) Soils over which there is a Sabine of florescence due to the presence of the alkaline salt, etc. are infertile.

The above cited documents are intended to show the detailed local classification of the land with different rates of assessment rather than the actual rates which were based on quite different methods of assessment in the Mughal age. But such a classification of land falls exactly in line in the general statement made in the *Ain* in its instructions to the '*Amal Guzar*.' See the text with reference 60-62.

Chapter 11

Agrarian Set-up During the Mughal Age*

It would perhaps be a truism to say that there is a close connection between the Agrarian administration and the Agrarian set-up of a given society. The connection is very obvious. An administrative system cannot operate in vacuum, and it, in its turn, modifies the agrarian set-up, the agrarian class relations so to speak. Even the Britishers, who were supposed to have "planted" their own system of agrarian administration and agrarian relations, in fact, did so with the existing 'givens', not entirely in vacuum. If they created a class of Zamindars having proprietary rights in land, there already was a growing tendency towards a conversion of proprietary rights in the surplus of the produce into proprietary rights in land, especially in Bengal – the cradle of the Permanent Settlement.

Perhaps one can have a better understanding of the impact of Mughal Administration on agrarian relations by taking a cursory look at the setup which was bequeathed to the Mughals and within which they operated. It seems that in the pre-Mughal India, despite some urban development, the distinction between town and country was far less marked. With rare exceptions, the ruling class extracted their share of the surplus in kind and used it directly for their own consumption, and that of their retainers, sometimes making over their claims on their revenues in popular areas to their men for the latter's maintenance. Elaborate machinery of exchange for the distribution of the surplus was not necessary under these circumstances. This is pretty close to the Marxist model of subsistence based agrarian economy, supporting an autocratic power; only it was not classless. There is nothing to suggest that class divisions in agrarian society as well as property rights in land

* This article found in the papers of Professor Grover appears to be a review article.

originated with Babur's victory at Panipat. Yet, as the intermediary zamindar ceases to derive his claims on revenue from political and military jurisdiction and becomes a *malguzar,* ostensibly a revenue official living in the village, he becomes more closely integrated with the structure of rural society. The initial period, till the time of Iltutmish, was that of direct plunder, by a small section of the Turkish ruling class with the help of the now subdued local Rajas, Ranas and Rajputs,[1] often integrated into the (political framework) mass of peasantry. Certain changes were brought about in the period of the Delhi Sultans – their purpose and extent was to some degree, a function of the composition and needs of the ruling classes.[2]

The land revenue history of the Mughals really starts with Akbar, who built on and improved upon what Sher Shah had endeavoured to achieve during the five short years of his reign. A certain amount of 'routinization of authority', so to speak, had taken place by the time of Sher Shah, which he carried further. The transition can well be summed up in the distance and difference in the two concepts: the corps of 40 being referred by Iltutmish as *'Arakin-i-daulat-Wa-sutun-i-Sultan'* and Sher Shah's *'Raiyat-chu-bikh-ast-Sultan-Shajar'* (The *riyaya* are the roots and the Sultan the tree) manifested in the institution of *Patta* and *Qabuliat.*[3]

Before we come to grips with the Administrative System of the Mughals in its agrarian aspect, a word about the nature of the Mughal State would not be out of place, especially in as much as it impinged on the agrarian setup. The Mughal State was an Agrarian State – it had agriculture as its base; it extracted a major part of the Agrarian surplus and it was also the major determinant to the incentives to production.[4]

Bernier's attempt of looking at Mughal India through his tainted 'feudal' eyes led him to the erroneous conclusion of the State being the proprietor of land (he was much surprised not to have found any Dukes, Marquises, etc. in India). Habib had characterized the Mughal State as Feudal. This is a tricky exercise, for apart from there being certain objection to it on both empirical and purely 'a priori' grounds, this characterization has certain important implications as far as the agrarian administration and the agrarian relations of the Mughal Empire are concerned. And Habib does carry this exercise to its logical end. Thus the agrarian policy of the Mughals, according to him, consisted mainly in two things – total appropriation of the surplus from the existing regions under control, and continuous drive for maintaining a huge army and for indulging in feudal-conspicuous consumption. All this meant tightening of the pressure on the peasantry. The contradiction between the resources and expenses of the Empire gets sharpened. An agrarian crisis engulfs the Mughal Empire, peasant uprisings led by the local rural lordlings take place, which finally sounded the death-knell of the feudal Mughal Empire.

In brief, in Prof. Habib's scheme, the Mughal state was a Feudal State; the agrarian setup a feudal setup; and the Agrarian policy a Feudal one which finally became a victim to its own internal contradictions.

Without going into details, for our purposes, we would describe the Mughal society as characterized by the Asiatic mode of production with some modifications marked by an absence of private property in land in the bourgeois sense of the term, though not completely a self-sufficient village community but of a pre-class type stratified community with a hierarchy of rights based on a system of differentiated hierarchical claims to the agrarian surplus.

A word of caution about the tremendous store house of information – the *Ain-i-Akbari.* That a contemporary work need not be taken as the gospel truth is a well accepted fact. Thus the instruction to the *Amalguzar* in the *Ain,* that "he should not entrust the appraisement to the headman of the village lest it give rise to remissness, and undue authority be conferred on high-handed oppressors, but should deal with each husbandman, present his demand separately and civilly receive his dues" is not borne out by facts. Firstly, this statement refers to the state of affairs in the Khalisa lands which formed not too substantial a part of the land revenue; and secondly, Noman Ahmad Siddiqi, on the evidence of *Diwan-passand* and *Dastur-ul-Amal-i-Mahdi-Alikhan,* has shown not only the existence of a class of intermediary zamindars even in the *Riyati* villages (in relation at least to Gujrat)[5] but also that it was only when a zamindar declined, for some reason, to enter upon an engagement for the assessed land revenue that collections were made direct from the peasants on the basis of *Jamabandi* (rent-roll). That the *Zabt* schedules did not apply to the territories of the 'tertiary zamindars' and this included large tracts of territories ruled by the erstwhile Hindu ruling houses[6] and also the Banth lands of the Kolis, Rajputs, etc. in Gujrat[7] is well known, but what is more, Siddiqi's study of the *Allahabad Documents,* no. 329 reveals that 'the land-revenue paid by the peasants was a matter of bargain between them and the Zamindars and that the land-revenues were not *assessed* (emphasis added) by government officers as was the usual practice.'[8] The situation in the 'Village Community' was really one of an undifferentiated mass of peasantry. There existed a variety of landed rights based on the system of an hierarchial claim to the surplus of the produce, starting from the *Maliks* to *Riyaya Khud Kashata, Pahikashta, Muqarari Riyaya, Muzarian* and *Asminas* and coming down to the 'servile classes' castes – the *Chamars* or *begaris, dhanuks, thoris* or *balahars* at the lowest run of the ladder. The general policy of the Mughals was to let the traditional structure work, though under imperial central control. The rights of the various intermediaries at the *Pargana* level were left undisturbed, and even guaranteed by an Imperial *Sanad.*

The Mughals firmly consolidated the tendency already at work under the Sultans: namely, to claim from the peasant the bulk of his surplus produce. Such a claim was then possible to enforce particularly because of the growth of commerce, and the extension of cultivation for the market. Habib has put forward the thesis that the expropriation was total, i.e. one half of the produce, and that it was the express policy of the State rather than an illegal expropriation over and above the legally constituted limit. Apart from the fact that it might be physically impossible to survive if ½ of the produce is taken away, this thesis does not square up with certain other things as well as the existence of stratification, in the countrywide extension of cultivation, and the rapid switch over to 'non-food-crop', especially tobacco. Moreover, Habib takes this total appropriation to be characteristic of entire Mughal India – there was no difference between the *jagir* and the *Khalsa* lands in this respect; by adding the *Abwabs* to the *Jama,* the peasantry had to pay 50% of the gross produce.[9] However, it would be reasonable to presume that the incidence of the revenue demand was not the same all over. There seem to have been two categories of *ryots:* the one in the *Khalisa,* enjoyed a considerable degree of independence limited by a heavy revenue demand and obligation to cultivate which was at the same time a right, and another, in the *jagir* lands, semi-servile in practice, frequently constrained to abandon cultivation. At times (especially in the 18th century) owing to financial pressure on the administration, this line of demarcation is wiped off. The key to the actual incidence of the land revenue demand had to be sought not only in the social and economic set up but the manner in which administrative and political power was distributed and deployed.[10]

Norman Ahmad Siddiqi has further refined our understanding of the magnitude of the land revenue demand and its incidence by a detailed breakup of its components and by showing that the magnitude was directly linked to the system of assessment. His breakup of the total demand is as follows:

In *Zabt* areas:

Mal	1/3rd of the produce.
Jihat taxes	calculated at the rate of 5% of the *Jama.*
Sair-jihat	calculated at the rate of 5% of the aggregate amount shown as *Mal-o-jihat*
Total	an increase of 20% on the *Mal*=40% of the Produce

For *bhaoli* and *kankut,* the records do not show the land revenue demand separately under the heads of *mal, jihat* and *sair-jihat.* They only mention that the produce was equally divided between the government and the *ryots.* But even here, there doesn't seem to have been any hard and fast rule. The various administrative manuals insist that in crop-sharing the minimum land-revenue demand should be fixed at one-fourth or even less, whereas the maximum could go up to one-half. Certain conclusions can be drawn in this respect:

1. The land revenue demand varied according to the social and agrarian conditions not only in different areas but within a village also and ranged between ¼ and ½;
2. One half constituted the maximum and not the minimum of the demand;
3. As a general principle, the agrarian conditions prevailing in a particular area were to be taken into consideration to fix the revenue demand in accordance with the paying capacity of the peasant.[11]

But the most important factor that determined the actual burden of land revenue demand was the particular method of assessment which was generally practiced for the late 17th and early 18th centuries. By and large, an entire village or group of villages was assessed on the basis of previous records and the persons who were engaged for land revenue were the zamindars and taluqdars. The available evidence suggests that in reaching a settlement, the assessing officers and the zamindars engaged in a bid to outbid each other, and at times, the relative capacity of the contending parties to bargain decided the issues. It is well known that since the days of Akbar, the widely accepted methods of assessment were *nasq, zabt, kankut* and *bhaoli.* Many of these continued to operate in different regions of Northern India, but the extent of the area in which they were used underwent some change. The *nasq* in the form of group assessment had become the general practice in accessing the land revenue in the reign of Aurangzeb and continued to be so in the first half of the 18th century. This change was in a large measure due to changed political and administrative conditions during the period and to the emergence of certain tendencies in revenue administration under Aurangzeb. The decay of the *Jagirdari* system, accompanied by the widespread practice of *ijara,* created a situation which was too complicated for the successful operation of the older system of assessment.

This arrangement (*nasq*) implied that the unit of assessment was not the holding of individual peasant but the village, the *tappa* or the *pargana.* The distribution of the assessed *jama* under such an arrangement was left in the hands of the big zamindars or the taluqdars engaged for the collection of land revenue. It provided the big zamindars or farmers to raise the revenue demand against the small zamindars who shifted the burden on to the peasants. The available evidence does not indicate any increase in the magnitude of land-revenue demand sanctioned by the land revenue Ministry. It varied between ¼ and ½ of the produce as it had been in the 17th century. However, the administrative practices of the period such as *nasq* in the form of group assessment and revenue-farming coupled with the weakening of the administrative machinery at various levels tended to increase the total burden on the peasant, especially in the *riyayti mahals.*[12] Thus, we see how the *riyayati* lands, which were initially relatively better off because they were not subject to the whims and rapacity of temporary Jagirdars, finally came under the purview of the process of the disintegration of 'small intermediary zamindars'—local notables having local interests by a class of *Taluqdars* and revenue—farmers—who ruined both the zamindars and the peasants alike[13] and led to rack-renting and absentee landlordism in its wake.

Some importance has also got to be attached to the system of *naqdi*—commutation and payment of land revenue in cash. This was not a new thesis introduced by the Mughals for the first time in India. Allaudin had experimented with it much before. The cash nexus, it is true, considerably reduced the fluctuations in terms of money, since, generally speaking, princes should move in an inverse direction to the output,[14] but introduced other complications of its own. Though payment in cash had not entirely replaced payment in kind, it nevertheless meant that the cultivator had now to convert at least a sixth of his produce in cash (according to Moreland, it was one third). This introduced an element of the penetration of money which could work to the detriment of the cultivators. The cultivator may have to sell a part of his produce to the local *Baniya* in advance, or might lose at the time of selling by a glut in the market. In some places, special kind of kinds or even gold was demanded of the peasants which further added to his burden.[15]

The administrative arrangement under the assignment system was geared mainly to cope with two problems. The first was that of imperial control. The assignee was entitled to assess and collect the revenue, but in both these matters he was required to conform to imperial regulations. Although certain orders and rules were framed specifically for the *Khalisa,* most of these were set in general terms, applying by implication to both the *Khalisa* and the *jagirs*. Abul-Fazl's statements show that even in the early years of Akbar's reign, the Jagirdars were obliged to collect the revenue due to them in accordance with the annual cash rates sanctioned by the court. Todar Mal added his regulations of the 27th year by an article requiring all collections, whether by the Jagirdars or the officials of the *Khalisa,* to be in strict accordance with authorised rates: everything extorted in excess of these was to be recovered with such fines as were imposed. When in the late years of Shah Jahan, a reform was introduced in the revenue system of the Deccan, the change-over to crop sharing was enforced not only in the *Khalisa,* but also in the assignments of the Jagirdars.

Secondly, there would be the problem faced by the *jagirdar* who had to manage a new assignment after every short interval. Neither he nor his staff (*gumastas*) could have hoped to be familiar with the details of the revenue-paying capacity and the local customs of each of the new *jagirs*.

To meet these two ends, the administrative structure consisted of three distinct elements. First, there were the officials and agents of the assignee, whether the assignee was the *Khalisa* or a *jagirdar*. Then there were the permanent local officials, owing their position partly to birth and partly to imperial authority, but unaffected by the transfer of the *jagirdars*. Finally, there were the full-fledged officials of the imperial administration who could be used both to help and to control the assignee.

Thus the almost universal phenomena of the 'intermediary zamindars' scattered in every nook and corner of the Mughal Empire – they were to be found both in the *Khalisa* as well as *jagir* lands, in *dehati-taluqa* as well as in *riyati* villages (at least in Gujarat, see Siddiqi). Their various perquisites – *nankar/rusum-i-zamindari, malik* and *haquq-i-zamindari* amounted in all to about 1/10 of the land revenue demand.

Under all methods of revenue assessment, there was some scope for relief in the case of bad harvests. In crop-sharing and *Kankut,* this was automatic in that the State's share would rise or fall with the amount of yield obtained in the concerned area. A commutation of the demand at market prices meant that the authorities would also shoulder part of the risk from price fluctuations. In the *Zabt* and the form of *Nasq* associated with it, there had to be a deliberate provision of the reduction of *Nabud* from the assessed area, but revenue could be adjusted to drastic changes in the price-levels only through special actions of the court. Once the final assessment had been made, the duty of the revenue-collector or the *'amils'* was to collect it in full, leaving no balance behind. Nevertheless, in practice, it could hardly have been always possible to collect the entire amount; and the balance was generally carried forward to be collected along with the demand for the next year. In conditions of famine, remissions had sometimes to be granted on a large scale. There was a system of *taqavi* loans also, which were supplemented by loans from the village money lender. This fact suggests a penetration of capital into primary production to a degree never suspected before and traces the control of the late 19th century. It further indicates that the primary production was not concerned with exchange merely as a form of activity to secure the wherewithal for the payment of revenue; the process of production itself had become partly dependent on exchange operations. In order to continue his agricultural production, the peasant mortgaged or 'pre-sold' the whole or a part of his agricultural produce and the cash he got in return was used to replenish his stock, buy seed-grains, or maintain himself and his family until the harvest season.[16]

Apart from relief measures of this kind, which were meant to help the peasants to tide over situations of exceptional distress, it must have been obvious that the steps taken in aid of the development of agriculture could offer an effective means of increasing the revenue. The Mughal conception of development is frequently stated in documents and consisted simply of the objectives: the extension of the area under cultivation and increase in the cash crops (*jins-i-kamil*). The first objective derived its importance from the existence of large areas of land lying untilled, and the second held its attraction because the land under cash crops was taxed at the higher rates and an increase in their cultivation would naturally have enhanced the revenue. The collection of such statistical information as the administration possessed was, at least in part, motivated by the desire to discover the possibilities of extending and improving the cropping and to judge how far any progress had taken place. The *Karori* experiment under Akbar, which involved area-measurement on an extensive scale, is interpreted by the contemporary authorities as chiefly an effort to bring the uncultivated land under the plough.[17]

Both for reclamation of *banjar* land and the cultivation of virgin land as well as a switch over to cash crops, a sliding scale of revenue was applied as an incentive. The zamindars bringing wasteland into cultivation acquired *malikana* rights over those lands. The phenomenon of *pahikashta* can also be understood in this context. In North India, the *pahikashta* was always assessed on reduced rates as compared to *Khudkshta*. Thus financially, a *pahikashta* was in an advantageous position and this served as a bait for the physical exertion involved on the part of the family, for having either two different types of holdings in separate villages or a single village other than his own. Here is an example of State policy leading to a situation where there is little correlation between the level of land right on the one hand, and the agriculturist's income on the other.[18]

Can we, in the light of the above, talk about the changes brought by the Mughal Agrarian Policy in the realm of agrarian relations? Firstly, Mughal Policy accentuated existed class differentiations. There is evidence that the village headmen eventually started claiming that area from which they were collecting revenue as their property. However, this growing tendency towards acquisition of property rights in land was not aided by and abetted by working of land revenue policy of the Mughals, but by its not functioning. In Bengal, there was a continuous weakness of the Central authority, the local notables were in effective control not only politically, but also economically. The relative weakness of the peasantry and the relative strength of the zamindars gave the latter the position of virtual proprietorship.

There is some evidence that towards the end of the period, the zamindars were *defacto* exercising the right to eject tenants as an act of faith for the Mughals to depress the position of the other classes in relation to these two, who were more often than not one person. That the rights of the *riyaya* were guaranteed is clear from the numerous references to officials and zamindars. Even the rights of the *muzarian* were guaranteed vis-a-vis their overlords, occupancy rights of the 'tenants' were also recognised. Thus an encroachment on the rights of the weaker sections of the *riyaya* was not a function of the Agrarian Policy of the Mughals as such, but on the contrary, was a result of its dysfunctioning.[19] The crisis of the *jagirdari* system, the emergence of *Ijaradars,* the change of *zabt* to *nasq* seem to have been responsible for the misery of the latter peasant. The new class of *Ijaradars* hailing from the cities affected the position of the intermediary zamindar also. The rise of the new class of intermediaries who had been from above, created conditions which led to a keen competition to engage for land-revenue demand exceeding the normal *jama* figure for revenue settlement. The hereditary zamindars were thus faced with an extremely difficult situation. In case a zamindar engaged in an exorbitant land revenue demand, he could save little for himself unless he transferred the burden on to the peasants and indulged in callous rack-renting. But, the latter course could ruin the peasants and the village would be deserted.[20] To withdraw from the contest meant an immediate loss of livelihood. Thus the overall effect of the widespread practice of revenue farming was the ruin of a large number of ancient hereditary zamindars, who, outbidden by the *Ijaradars,* were compelled to sell their zamindari rights. The wealthier neighbouring zamindars and bankers from the cities availed themselves of the opportunities and these sale of zamindaris considerably affected the socio-economic complexion of rural India. The effect on the peasantry was even worse. And what is more, it meant a more intensive exploitation of certain lower sections of the peasants who gave up cultivation, seeking refuge, sometimes in the territories of *zamindar-i-zor-talb,* thus providing the canon-fodder to Habib's Peasant Revolts.[21]

Quite distinct from the evolution of the *Taluqadari* institution, the zamindari system was drifting towards a hierarchical pattern of rights in other ways as well.[22] The Mughal State would appoint a zamindar through a royal *sanad* with jurisdiction over a number of villages which had proved recalcitrant. At times, the Emperor, when pleased, would reward him with a *Sadar-Zamindar.* The creation of such Big-Zamindaris, more or less, parallel to the already existing hereditary chiefs, (*zamindaran-i-umda*) is a significant example of the role of the Emperor in the evolution of the zamindari rights. The hierarchical pattern of zamindari rights was still more widespread in the territories belonging the Chief Zamindars, where there were different categories of zamindars enjoying different types of *asums.* Thus, the relationship between the agrarian policy and agrarian relations, is not a simple one, it is one of interaction, of Mughal causation.

The institution of *madad-i-maash* grants was actuated by the motive of creating pockets of local influence. Economically, it created a class spread all over the country, which like the zamindars, depends for its livelihood on the surplus farm land. Generally, *madad-i-maash* grants enjoyed immunity from taxation, and this was equivalent to the *Nankar* lands. In the first half of 18th century, however, it appears that certain types of *madad-i-maash* land had acquired more or less the same character as the zamindari lands, and were subject to revenue assessment. Accompanying this, sale of *madad-i-maash,* rights were also taking place. Thus, a class of Muslims seems to have come to acquire zamindari rights through the institution of *madad-i-maash* lands, which initially had a purely non-economic function.[23]

References

1. Habib, in his 'Land Property in Pre-British India', *'Enquiry'* Winter 1965, suggests that the term Rajput as a name for caste which appears suddenly in Persian authorities in the 16th Century indicates an evolution parallel to the term zamindar and probably was result of the similar process of higher elements being pressed into the lower ranks of rural aristocracy, p. 55.

2. However, changes within it were limited because the appropriation of the surplus was as near total as was practicable.

   First during the 13th century, there was a simple division of the empire among tribute – receiving governors. Then in the 14th century, there took place an enlargement of the revenue demand, and so of the incomes of the *Iqtas*. Finally, from the middle of the 14th to the early 16th century there was a reversion to the simpler form of *Iqta*-organization, but with the difference that the assignees directly appropriated the bulk of the peasant's surplus for themselves. These changes seem to be linked with the changes in the composition of the ruling class. Habib, *op. cit.*, p. 50ff.

3. Though the situation – *Patta* and *Qabuliat* notwithstanding – was to a great extent, in Moreland's words, 'antecedant to the process of disentangling of the concept of private property from political

allegiance', one can not agree fully with Dietmar Rothrmund (Government, Landlord and Tenant, 1875-1900, *IESHR*, Vol. 6 no. 4) that the change from status to contract, and 'the commutation of rents, which was hitherto paid in kind (Allaudin? Akbar-*Naqdi*?) into rents payable in cash contributed more than anything else to the great changes in the relation of landlord and tenants in India in the 19th century; Moreover, Rothermund's description of the surplus as rent for the Pre-British period is equally inappropriate. Rent, in its Ricardian sense – and Rothermuned's, does talk a lot about Ricardo and the price affecting the rent and not vice versa – is a surplus which accrues owing to certain inherent and intrinsic qualities of land. In the bouergeois sense of the term, one can not speak of rent in this period. In the official version of Abul-Fazl, the land revenue is the share accruing to Sovereignty out of rent.

4. Habib has shown, Landed Property etc., that less than 450 men disposed off over 3/5 of the revenue of the empire. But the importance of the State comes up if we consider, as Habib also does, the fact that the expenditure on maintaining the troops for the State amounted to about 4/5 of the pay-bill.
5. Noman Ahmad Siddiqi: *Land Revenue Administration under the Mughals (1700-1750)*, p. 147, citing Mirat, Vol. I, pp. 21, 22, 173; Mirat, Supp. pp. 228-229. Irfan Habib does not seem to lay much store on this piece of evidence from the *Mirat* (supplement) in his Landed Property etc. loc. cit. p. 69, f. n. 230. He just states that this is a contrary view (to his – 'it seems that in most regions there were villages, termed *riyayti*, or peasant held, which were not subject in any way to a zamindar.)
6. *Mirat-i-Ahmadi* :– *A Persian History of Gujarat*. Translated from the Persian original of Ali Muhammad Khan by M.F. Lokhandwala, Oriental institute, Baroda, 1965, p. 194.
7. Siddiqi, *op. cit., p. 11; of. Dastu-ul-Amal-i-Mahdi Khan, f. 8b.* The collecting officers instructed not to make collections direct from the peasants unless it was unavoidable.
8. *Ibid*, p. 15. The collecting officers instructed not to make collections direct form the peasants unless it was unavoidable.
9. Habib, *Agrarian System*, pp. 61-81.
10. Tapan Raychaudhry, Agrarian System of Mughals, *Enquiry* Spring, 1965, p. 112.
11. Some of the principles which governed the magnitude of the land-revenue demand are clearly brought out in passages contained in the *Maasirul-Umara*. Thus three different rates of land revenue demand were prescribed for *batai*, Murshid Quli Khan. One half of the produce was taken for areas under natural irrigation. For cash crops like sugar-cane and grapes, the rates varied from 1/9 to ¼. Whereas most of the

production land was assessed at the rate of ½ of the produce, those which needed some capital and considerable labour were assessed at lower rates. The condition of the peasants also served as a determining factor in fixing the land revenue demand. Siddiqi, loc. cit., p. 46.

12. *Ibid.*, pp. 142-143.

13. *Ibid.*, p. 98.

14. Raychaudhry, loc. cit., p. 117.

15. *Ain-i-Akbari* specifically comments against such a practice.

16. Raychaudhry, *op. cit.*, p. 117.

17. Habib, *op. cit.*, p. 251.

18. Ravinder Kumar, *'State and Society in Maharastra in the 19th century'* points out that in the early 19th century, there was very little co-relation between the level of land holdings on the one hand and the agriculturists income on the other. Raychaudhry, loc. cit., p. 97, postulated a similar possibility for Mughal India also.

19. Siddiqi, loc. cit., pp. 98-99.

20. *Ibid.*, postulates that it was the effects of the Ijaradari system rather than the simple rapacity of the Jagirdars that might be responsible for mass desertations in the late 17th and early 18th century.

21. *Ibid.*, pp. 98-99.

22. B.R. Grover, 'Nature of Dehat-i-taluqa', *IESHER*, Vol. 2, 1965.

23. Siddiqi, *op. cit.*, p. 141.

Chapter 12

Agrarian Problems of the 18th Century Eastern India - A Reappraisal

During the later half of the 18th century, the eastern portions of north India were the first to fall under the English occupation for administration. Its agrarian aspects confronted the English administrators with the blindman's buff. From the assumption of the *Diwani* rights (1765) to the enforcement of the permanent settlement (1793), huge controversial revenue literature comprising the official memorenda, minutes, official reports and private correspondence highlighted the agrarian problems of the 18th century. Much less known hitherto, equally important and analytical revenue literature and commentaries on agrarian aspects in Persian were prepared by the expert Indian *munshis* and revenue officials to provide background material for discussion and controversy amongst the English authorities.[1] Some Indian revenue experts also wrote independent commentaries in Persian on the working of the land revenue system during the 18th century.[2]

Looking from the historiographical aspect, most of the works on agrarian problems undertaken by the English administrators, administrator-scholars and historians (English, Indian and others), right from the closing years of the 18th century down to the recent times, have relied largely on the above mentioned English records. It is not possible to analyse the pre-*Diwani* agrarian structure of the 18th century eastern India without the coordinated exploitation of the regional records, both in local and Persian language at varying levels (viz. *tappa, chakla, sarkar* and *subah*) and the English source material. Only a couple of Indian scholars have appreciated this aspect and have analysed some problems of the 18th century agrarian society in Bengal and Bihar.[3] As the administrator- scholars and the historians have basically relied on the above mentioned English records, the writings of one or another administrator, it will serve no purpose to treat them chronologically by offering comments on their inaccuracies when the very root of their source material is defective and inadequate in its analysis. Even when they have done their best to tread clearly over the zig-zag labyrinth of the agrarian problems, they have been equally caught in it. It will very much facilitate the task if the basically correct assumptions and limitations of the English administrators as well as the basic features of the agrarian structure of the pre-*Diwani* 18th century eastern India are borne in mind.

Philip Francis, James Grant and John Shore took an historical approach in understanding the pre-British agrarian structure in Bengal, Bihar and Orissa. Francis[4] advocated the adoption of the Mughal model of the English administration in Bengal. He considered that during the Mughal age, the land revenue was a moderately fixed tribute paid by the zamindar who was the ancient proprietor of the soil with rights of alienation. He thought that the Mughal administration did not interfere in the territories of the zamindars who comtinued with legal possessions of their lands on the condition of payment to the State of a moderate permanent '*Jumma* or quit rent'. Francis also contended that with regard to assessment practice, valuation of the *hast-wa-bud* was unknown to the Mughal practice. Francis had the least idea about the concept of the Mughal agrarian system. Nor did he realise the nature of the *zamindari* rights of the varying categories of the zamindars and their relationship with the Mughal State.

James Grant[5] wrote detailed reports on the revenues of Northern-Circars and the finances of Bengal. Grant asserted that the same principles of land ownership operated in India as in other Asiatic countries where the sovereign claimed the land ownership. In this context, the zamindars of Bengal did not have any right, in form or fact, nor the smallest pretensions to any territorial property beyond their *saverum* (perquisites) amounting scarcely to one-twentieth part of the local civil jurisdiction committed to their management by the sovereign proprietary government. He maintained that the *zamindari* rights were based on royal *sanads* and the zamindars during the Mughal period acted as mere agents of the State. They were official tax gatherers to realise the stipulated 'rent' (i.e. revenue) from the peasantry. They, of course, enjoyed certain privileges of having hereditary titles, developing of waste land, granting of *pattas*, *moffusil serinjamy* disbursements, distribution of *abwab* (cesses), paying his rents to the authorities. He also maintained that the incidence of revenue demand had increased partly due to relative inflation during the past two centuries and also the fact that the rise of the Marathas had led to a vigorous rise in the trade, commerce and prosperity in Bengal. The revenues of Bengal (*Jamma Toomary*) were not permanently fixed upon the zamindars but were repeatedly enlarged and corrected at various periods by actual survey and particular local administration in the course of period since Akbar's reign. It is worthwhile to make an observation that on the question of land ownership, Grant suffered from an erroneous generalized European concept that in all Asiatic countires the agricultural land belonged to the State. His assumption that the entire *zamindari* class of his days owed its title to the royal *sanads* issued during the 18th century during the governership of Murshid Quli Khan may be correct, but he did not realise that the *zamindari* titles were regarded as hereditary and were invariably renewed from one administration to another. As such, the old *zamindari* titles were naturally conferred under Murshid Quli Khan. His emphasis and the role of the *zamindari* as the official tax gatherers may be correct but he did not understand the varying characteristics of the land rights of the landed intermediaries and the *riyaya*. His assumption of the increase in the incidence of State demand due to the above mentioned facotrs, howsoever plausible, requires further probing. It would be improper to assume that the State charged one half of the gross produce at a flat rate. However, Grant's analysis that periodical assessments were made after actual survey and local investigation is basically correct for realisation of revenues as perpetually fixed *peshkash* was an extremely rare concession granted to the zamidars in the *ghair-amli* territories of eastern India based on geographical factors and political expediency. As such, criticism of Grant on the part of the later historians of the 19th and 20th centuries is rather unjustified.

John Shore,[6] equipped with much more background of translated Persian historical source material, attempted an inquisitional historical analysis of the land revenue administration in Bengal since the Mughal period. He made a comparative study of land revenue problems in the 16th-17th centuries and the 18th century, especially since the governorship of Jafar Khan (Murshid Quli Khan) as two distinct phases. He contented that the main consideration for comparison of the two periods were the population, the cultivation of the country, the relative value of the money specie, commerce, the taxes (land revenue imposed) and the extra demands (*sayer*) levied annually. He maintained that during the first phase, the incidence of State demand and cesses being moderate were based upon regular principles of revenue administration which took into account the state of cultivation and the above mentioned factors. Though the increase in the revenues in the first phase could be explained on account of annexation of new territories, expansion of trade and commerce and agricultural development, the second phase since Jafar Khan's period was marked by the imposition of heavy incidence of cesses (*abwab*) and the exactions of increased revenues from the *zamindari* and the *riyaya* class due to harsh treatment. This had led to the improvement both of the zamindars and the *riyaya*. Except for matters of detail, these observations by Shore are being confirmed by regional source material of the 18th century. Shore's understanding of the State demand as a share in the gross produce based upon sliding scale taking into account regional agrarian factors may be well appreciated. However, Shore had his limitations in understanding the various intricate and technical aspects of the Mughal agrarian system. He failed to understand the land rights of the zamindars. He thought that his main achievement lay in the fact of getting the recognition of the proprietorship of the zamindars. He asserted the proprietary rights of the zamindars in the soil of the *zamindari* lands. Though well guided by his revenue consultant Sayyid Gulam Hussain on the comparative land rights of the zamindars and the *riyaya,* Shore could not appreciate the Mughal connotation of *zamindari malkiyat* (ownership) which meant hereditary proprietary rights of the zamindar over the revenue collection and entitlement to perquisites rather than proprietary title to the soil of the *zamindari* villages. Shore could not easily shake off the impact of the English concept of the proprietary rights and found the situation a little confused. He wanted to keep his mind open for a further probe in the land rights of the *riyaya* before converging the relationship of the zamindar and the *riyaya* into that of a landlord and tenant in the pure and simple English sense on a permanent basis. Taking the *malkiyat* rights of the zamindars into consideration and with an instinctive insight into the virtual ownership of the land rights in certain categories of the *riyaya,* he found the situation by no means compatiable. This was Shore's main failing as under the Mughal administration the comparative land rights of the *riyaya* were neither vague nor inconsistent in lacking definition and precision. The Persian revenue literature used by the Indian *Munshis* and revenue experts underlining the land rights of the zamindars, landed intermediaries and stratification of the *riyaya* is rather clear about the pre-British position but unfortunately was beyond the comprehension of either Shore or his other contemporaries.

The institution of landed intermediaries comprising the zamindars and *taaluqadars* during the 18th century is a continued inherited feature of the agrarian structure from the 17th century Mughal era.[7] The institution of *zamindari* covers a variety of individuals with hereditary landed interest as distinct from those of the *riyaya.* It covers a wide range of landed interests from the chiefs of the princely territories to petty intermediaries. Under the Mughals, it evolved into a regular pattern of agrarian administration. The assumption of the divison of the lands into *khalisa* (crown), *jagirs* (assigments) and *zamindaries* has been rightly modified as for the purposes of land revenue administration even the portions of *zamindari* territories were assignable to the Mughal state officials or to the zamindars themselves in lieu of their services to the State. Different categories of the zamindars had come into being during the Mughal age. Ordinarily, such of the zamindars who submitted either voluntarily or without fighting after getting an ultimatum were given back their *zamindaries* as *jagirs.* Apart from this, in respect of the zamindar who failed in armed resistance against the Mughal state, a major portion of the erstwhile *zamindari* was annexed to the Mughal territory and some portion was assigned to him as maintenance *jagir.* If a zamindar became rebellious, on reduction a major portion of his territories was assigned in *tankhwah jagir* to the Mughal *mansabdars.* In any case, all the loyal zamindars had to render military service to the Mughal state and some may be even enlisted in the regular Imperial service. They had essentially to pay *peshkash,* though some paid fixed amount as stipulated in the treaty while others as regular revenues for the *zamindari* areas other than the *watan* or maintenance *jagir.* In some cases, the zamindars may be confirmed but were assigned only a portion of their respective territories in personal *jagir.* The rest of the territories were either assigned to the Mughal *mansabdars* or incorporated in the *khalisa* land. As an extreme case, a *zamindari* may be totally annexed to the State and would be placed under the management of an administrator. Ordinarily, such *zamindaries,* which were entrusted in *jagir* in entirety, were declared *ghair-amli* and the zamindars were left with autonomy in revenue administration. But such *zamindaries,* whereof only small portions were assigned for personal *jagir,* were declared *amli* subject to the Mughal procedure of assessment and collection of the revenues. The variation in treatment of the zamindars is an essential feature of the Mughal administration. But the restoration of the *zamindaries* never meant any recongnition of the chiefs as semi-independent with only nominal allegiance to the

Mughal state. Still more, the Mughal state also created a new class of zamindars who were assigned *jagirs* in lieu of the discharge of police duties and collection of the revenues in their territories. Such *zamindaries* were essentially *amli* and the revenue realisations were always deposited as *peshkash* with the Mughal state. The zamindars, of course, exercised police, judicial and financial powers for the collection of revenues. They were also competent to make religious grants but in the *amli* areas, such grants were subject to confirmation by the Mughal administration. Except in a *ghair-amli* territory, the hereditary chiefs were never vested with assessment powers. Their *amli* territories and the territories of the official zamindars were always assessed by the Mughal officials. Even though in the course of the 17th and 18th centuries most of the *ghair-amli* territories of the zamindaries were rendered *amli,* the process was by no means complete and there were *ghair-amli* territories in Chittagong (Bengal) and certain regions of Bihar and Orissa. In Orissa, towards the closing years of the 17th and early 18th century, many a zamindar paid fixed annual revenue (*peshkash muqarari*) assessed periodically by the Mughal state. In fact, there has been implied tussle between the zamindars for greater autonomy and payment of revenues as fixed *peshkash* on the one hand and enforcement of restrictions as well as fixation of revenues (*peshkash*) after periodical assessment by the Mughal state on the other. In the beginning of the 18th century, Murshid Quli Khan, as *Diwan* and the Governor of *subah* Bengal (1700-1727), reinforced Mughal regulations for revenue reforms and tightened the machinery of the *zamindari* institution. His revenue reforms marked the combination of the process of integration in the agrarian administration. He increased the revenues of the *khalisa* of subah Bengal by transferring most of the *jagirs* of the Mughal *mansabdars* to *subah* Orissa. After a detailed survey and measurement based on classification of the agrarian land, a fresh settlement of the revenues of the *subahs* of Bengal, Bihar and Orissa was effected. *Nankar* and maintenance allowance of the zamindars were fixed in line with the Mughal practice. The administration tried to establish contact with the *riyaya.* The *chakla* of Midnapur having been detached from subah Bihar was incorporated in subah Bengal. In order to curb the recalcitrant nature on the part of the zamindars, he rearranged the territorial jurisdictions of the zamindars increasing their extent and diminishing their number. Thus he encouraged the foundation of big *zamindaries.* Though the reduction in the number of official zamindars facilitated the collection of revenues on the part of the state, it definitely gave impetus to the growth of hierarchical pattern of the landed intermediaries within the newly formed big *zamindaries.* From the *subahdari* of Shujja-ud-doula to that of Mir Qasim, notwithstanding the varying personal attitude of harshness or leniency on the part of the administration for the realisation of revenues from the zamindars and variation in the *rasum* (allowances forming percentage of *jama*) fixed for the latter on a structural plane, the *zamindari* pattern ran practically on the same lines as before. However, the growth of extensive practice of farming (*ijaradari*) system, the under-farming and further under-letting the revenues within the *zamindari* jurisdictions seriously undermined the working and the spirit of the agrarian administration.

Unlike other parts of north India, in eastern India below the zamindar stood the *taaluqadari* class as landed intermediary. The act of *zamindari* lay in the payment of revenues (*malguzari*) to the State: a zamindar was always confirmed by a royal *sanad* and paid *peshkash* to the State. On the other hand, a *taaluqadar* would assume the role of a zamindar and was deemed as such when he paid the revenues of his territory directly to the State but, by and large, the petty *taaluqdars* paid the revenues of their *taaluqas* through the superior zamindar cum *chaudhari* who acted as a representative. Such a zamindar paid revenues not only of his own *zamindari* but even of the petty *taaluqas* of the *taaluqdars* under his jurisdiction and his *zamindari* was reckoned to cover both his personal *zamindari* and the petty *taaluqas*. A zamindar in Bengal, unlike other portions of north India, could not alienate the title of *zamindari* but could sell only his rights over *panjtaaluqa* (i.e. rights over revenue collection) and *chaudharie* rights alongwith the relevant perquisites. He possessed no rights of sale or mortgage of the *taaluqadaries* under his jurisdiction. On the other hand, unless otherwise stipulated in his *taaluqadari patta,* a *taaluqadar* possessed alienable rights and could sell the *taaluqadari* title. Except in case of the *taaluqa* villages colonised and developed by the zamindars and the *taaluqadars,* they were not the owners of the soil of the agricultural lands of the *riyaya.* A *taaluqadar* possessed both customary rights of *rasum* as well as *malikana* but he could claim the latter only when the *taaluqa* was declared *sir-i-hasil.* The extensive sale transactions during the 18th century established a large class of petty *taaluqadars.* A person who did not hold any *zamindari* from the State but purchased the *zamindari* rights of a few villages or a village from the original zamindar was known as *taaluqadar.* An essential criterion of *zamindari* lay in the recognition by the State through an issue of a *zamindari sanad* and a *taaluqadar* of a few villages, unless confirmed by a royal *sanad* in the *zamindari* rights, could not be designated as a zamindar. The acceleration of the process of hierarchical pattern of the landed intermediaries in the eastern regions of north India is a marked feature of the agrarian structure. It is, however, significant that in such an agrarian structure, parallel claims of the zamindars, *chaudharis* and *taaluqadars,* by no means incompatiable, were established over the *taaluqa* villages. Expect for the self-developed lands, they could not claim the ownership of the agricultural land of the *riyaya.*

It may be well appreciated that during the Mughal age, the terms *riyaya* and *raiyat* were synonimous and covered all the cultivating families paying land revenue to the State. Thus the *riyaya* covered the primary *zamindari* families of varying categories; the free peasant cultivators named varyingly in different portions of India; *muzarain* (occupancy as well as short-tenure cultivators) and the *paikashtkars* (non-occupancy and non-resident cultivators). The revenue-free grantees (*madad-i-maash* and *aima*), even though cultivating families, were not termed *riyaya* or *raiyat.*[8] The primary zamindars owned ancestral self colonized villages and paid revenues thereupon. They possessed self-cultivated (*Khudkashta*) lands and also rented out their lands to *muzarian* and to *paikashtkars*. This may not be true of the zamindars who acted merely as landed intermediaries. In the latter *zamindaries,* apart from land under self-cultivation of the zamindars, there were *khudkasht* and depending upon the nature of the composition of the villages, there may as well be *muzarian* and *paikashtkars*. The *muqaddams* (*mandals* etc. in Bengal), even though in lineage belonged to the *zamindari* families, always constituted the principal *khudkasht riyaya* of the villages. The *khudkasht* was a free peasant who himself organised cultivation and resided in the village of his cultivation. It seems that his holding was not only hereditary but he also possessed free rights in land for the purposes of transfer, mortgage and sale. As such, primary *zamindari* families of the self-developed villages, the *muqaddami* families, free peasants who descended from original colonizers of the village though not vested with any *chaudhrie* or *muqaddami* rights – all consituted the *khudkashta riyaya* class. The *paikasht riyaya* was initially an outsider who undertook the cultivation in the village. A *paikasht* may opt for permanent stay and, in due course of time, may enjoy occupancy rights. He may also retain only temporary cultivation in a village for a particular period. It seems that the *muqarri riyaya* was subject to assessment even though land was not brought under cultivation but ordinarily he may be put in the category of the free peasant proprietor. As in other portions of north India, in eastern India as well, the different categories of the *riyaya* had varying nature of rights and privileges in the village society and were as well governed by different rates for the purpose of assessment on their holdings.

Boughton Rouse[9] was a staunch advocate of the proprietary rights of the zamindars. He considered that even though intially *zamindari* may have been for life time only, later on it became landed inheritance. Even when *zamindari* may be considered as an office, it also gave the zamindar the possession of land with features of property such as mortgage, alienation, bequest, or adoption. A person could be divested of his *zamindari* only on grounds of delinquency, rebellion and failure to make the payment of revenues. In case of reclamation of waste lands, a new occupant may acquire proprietary right independent of his official right. A zamindar was entitled to certain cesses (*abwab*). He argued that the Indian society had 'its best, if not its only cement' in the zamindar class as the zamindars were essentially intermediaries between the State and the peasants and looked after the interests of the latter against the inquisitorial officers of revenue or revenue-farmers. A *taaluqadar* has practically the same rights as the zamindar. A *taaluqadar* could under-let the land in the same way as the zamindar. He also maintained that the *ryots* held their rights based on customs. Boughton Rouse did not understand the genesis of the *zamindari* and *taaluqadari* system. He could not make distinction between the title of the *zamindari* class as a landed intermediary over the settled villages constituting varying categories of agriculturists and the self developed proprietary villages of primary zamindars and *mandals* (*muqaddams,* headmen) who equally constituted the principal *riyaya* for payment of revenues to the State. Nor could he appreciate the rights of the other *riyaya,* especially that of *khudkasht.* However, his description about the rights and position of the various categories of the *ryots,* as he found in the later part of the 18th century, is very informative.

Harington[10] attacked the views of James Grant and maintained that the *zamindari* was not a mere office as its hereditary character was recognised by the government and that the issue of *sanad* by the State was a mere formality. Notwithstanding the fact that the State strove to treat the zamindar as an officer, the right of alienation of the *zamindari* rendered it a kind of property. Even though Harington has given details of the rights and privileges of the zamindars as landed intermediaries in the last three decades of the 18th century quite correctly, he could not visualise that the office of the *zamindari* had carried with it hereditary rights for the management of the lands and that the two could not be separated from each other. However, Harington very correctly remarked that the terms 'property of land' and 'actual property of the soil' could not be interpreted as land holder possessing the full rights of an English landlord or freeholder in fee simple, with equal liberty to dispose of all the land forming parts of his estate to his advantage or to oust his tenants, whether for life or for a term of years, on the termination of the respective leaseholder. The rights of the English landlord were not applicable to a landlord in Bengal as he did not possess an unlimited power over the *khudkasht* and other *ryots* in the *zamindari*. Harington considered the *taaluqadari* as a dependency of the *zamindari* and regretted that some of the *taaluqadars* had been reduced to the position of little more than *khudkasht ryots* in later times. Harington also considered that the assessment rates paid by the *ryots* were essentially customary in character and he spelled out the incidence of assessment rates in respect of each class of the *ryots* which was, of course, applicable during the second half of the 18th century.

During the last three decades of the 18th century, the main issue involved in controversy hinged on the concept of land proprietorship on the part of the zamindars versus the State whereas, the position of the land rights of the varying classes of the *ryots*, even though examined, were treated in a very casual and an unsympathetic manner. It was only in the course of the 19th century when the British revenue administrators gathered more experience about the nature of land rights of the agricultural classes in the ceded and conquered provinces that the judiciousness of the Permanent Settlement of Bengal was challenged and a keen academic interest was taken to review the position of the land rights of the agricultural classes prevalent in India before the inception of the British rule. It was believed, that with the exception of the variation in the incidence of the State demand on the land produce, most of the characteristics of the ancient Hindu society continued to dominate through the medieval ages. William Jones had brought out the main characteristics of the Hindu civilization as a product of the Hindu people and the concept of the continuation of the Hindu agrarian system throughout the medieval age reflected this approach in the study of India's civilization. The committee of the House of Commons, which enquired into East IndiaAffairs in 1810, drew a general picture of the pre-British India revenue practices.[11] It emphasized the role of the 'village community' as a 'corporation', or 'township' and that the inhabitants of India continued to live under 'this simple form of municipal government' or 'a small republic' throughtout the ages till the 19th century. Having dealt with variation in the incidence of the State demand on the land produce from the ancient to the Mughal rule, the Committee thought that the system of giving *pattas* to the *ryots* by the zamindars and the subrenting of lands by the latter to the revenue-farmers, the impoverishment and indebtedness to the money lenders were the resultant abuses of 'the Muslim rule'. Many of these surmises were incorrect but they definitely affected the later writers like James Mill, Elphinstone and Henry Maine. James Mill[12] made a cultural attack on the Indian civilization which in economic terms was equally responsible for the arrest and stagnation of the Indian economy in pre-British India. In economic aspect, James Mill belonged to the English utilitarian school of thought. In general thought, he was influenced by the English philosophical radicals. The English utilitarians and Evangelicals did not find anything commendable in the Indian societies. With its past unmittigated suffering, India's future depended on the British empire. In his economic views, James Mill had been sufficiently influenced by the ideas of Ricardo. James Mill attacked the Permanent Settlement which recognised zamindars as the landlords and which in the ordinary course of progress of a society increased their wealth at the cost of the State and the *ryots*. Like James Grant, Mill also thought that like all Asiatic countries under 'despotic' governments, the ownership of land in India lay with the king. However, Mill believed that during the ancient and medieval periods, the *ryots* developed perpetual, hereditable and even transferable rights in land which were not incompatible with the concept of land ownership on the part of the sovereign. The latter claimed the right to as much of the produce as he pleased. The cultivators were left with a mere compensation for the labour and the cost of cultivation and the benefit of land went to the State. Mill also confirmed his belief in the concept of the 'village community' as a 'corporation'. It may be observed that in view of the 18th century source material in hand, James's concept of State land ownership, the nature of land rights of the zamindars and other *riyaya,* the arbitrary incidence of State demand on the land produce, and the condition of the agriculturists consequent on his theoretical economic concept cannot be accepted either for the Mughal age in particular or for 18th century eastern India.

W.W. Hunter[13] also subscribed to the continuation of the ancient Hindu customs to the day of his writing though he attributed a regular survey, measurement and assessment of land on certain principles formulated by the Mughal state. Hunter had a superiority complex for the British revenue system and considered that during the Mughal age and even through the 18th century in pre-British era, the incidence of State share in the land produce was about three times the amount which the British charged. This is a questionable hypothesis. In a specialised study of Orissa,[14] Hunter pointed towards the absence of landlordism (*zamindari*) and the 'village community' system. Here in Orissa, 'a village lacked a corporate factor and was merely a collection of families'. This is a correct assumption which casts doubt if the concept of 'village community' had existed in Orissa during the 18th century.

Montstuart Elphilstone[15] being basically a revenue administrator, his approach to the study of agrarian system of pre-British India, unlike James Mill's, was not influenced by purely theoretical economic concepts. In outlook, both Hunter and Elphilstone had much in common with each other. Elphilstone has not given any comprehensive description of the pre-British agrarian structure as he claimed to have only 'a slight view' of the internal 'Mahomedan Empire in India'. For his sources, Elphilstone banked mostly on the enquiries made by the early 19th century British revenue administrators whose memoranda were embodied in the Reports of Select Committees of House of Commons (1812 and 1831-32) and other detailed regional enquiries of English revenue experts on the pre-British 19th century revenue practices in the Ceded and Conquered Provinces. He was equally influenced by the concept of 'village community' having persisted from ancient times till 19th century. He also believed that the 'municipal institutions of villages' with some local jurisdiction acted as a deterrent against the imposition of the theory of the 'Mahomedan Law' upon the Indian life. He surmised that the general state of the country must, no doubt, have been flourishing. He held that the nature of proprietary rights in land may vary from one village to another and that in the *zamindari* villages, the zamindars possessed hereditary transferable proprietary rights. The right to transfer was conditioned by law of pre-emption. The *ryot* class (also known as *khudkasht*) constituting the cultivators were the *assamies* of the land holders. They were the tenants of the land holder and had hereditary occupancy rights. They did not possess the right to sell, give away or mortgage their rights. In the non-*zamindari* villages, (not applicable to eastern India), the ownership of land was vested with the State rather than with the permanent *ryots*. Elphilstone's judgement of the *zamindari* villages is quite erroneous as in a *zamindari* village unless self-developed, a zamindar as landed intermediary did not have an exclusive right of land ownership and the *khudkasht* cultivators equally possessed rights of ownership in their lands. In line with Hunter, Elphilstone agrees that the true concept of 'village community' depended upon the land tenure and that the 'municipal concept of village governess' did not exist in the *zamindari* villages as autonomous character was not uniformally applicable to all the villages.

The concept of the Indian 'village community found a fresh re-orientation at the hands of Henry Maine, the great jurist and the sociologist.[16] Basing a study on 'Comparative Method' for analysing the European and the Indian societies, he formulated a regular theory about the Indian 'village communities'. He looked upon the Indian facts through the spectacles of European theories about German Mark relating to the ancient agricultural customs and forms of property in land advocated by Von Maurer and the Russian Mir involving the ancient customs of redivision of the lands. He found the Indian 'village community' as an organised self-acting group of families exercising a common proprietorship over a definite tract of land.' The village possessed "double aspect of a group of families united by the assumption of common kinship, and of a company of persons exercising joint ownership over land." Custom in India being sacred and perpetual accounted for the continunance of the archaic institution of the 'village community' as a living institution right till the 19th century. The 'village community' was so organised as to be complete in itself. It was the source of a land law which defined the relations of one another of the various sections of the group and of the group itself to the Government, to other 'village communities', and to certain persons who claimed rights over it. Maine's communal concept of the 'village community' was opposed to the regional evidence and the first principles of society in north India, especially the eastern portions with entrenched position of the zamindars and other landed intermediaries during the course of the 18th century. In fact, Maine confused the 19th century communal *zamindari* estates, *pattidari* and *bhaichari* land tenures with the communal concept of the 'village communities' - features which were not at all applicable to Bengal and other regions of eastern India during the 18th century. To assert that the 'archaic institutions' of the 'village communities' as understood by Maine lay underneath the structure of the village society in India despite any change in the course of centuries is sheer historical anachronism.

The agrarian structure of the village society of eastern India during the 18th century could, of course, be explained on different lines.

In his Tagore Law Lectures (1874-75) on the *Law Relating to the Land Tenures of Lower Bengal,* Arthur Philips covered at length the historical aspect of the land revenue practices since 16th century, divergent views of the authorities involved in controversy on the problem of land rights before the enforcement of the Permanent Settlement and its effects in the course of the 19th century.[17] His approach for tracing the historical development of the agarian practices based on the theoretical aspects of 'Hindu' and 'Mohamedan' concepts is erroneous. Arthur believes that under the Mughal agrarian system, the assessment on the *ryots* was done directly by the State and the zamindars were ignored. That under the Mughal land revenue system, assessment on the holdings and produce of land of all the classes of the *riyaya* was done by the State is true of the *amli* territories but the fact that it did not operate in the *ghair-amli* areas may be equally borne in mind. Moreover, except for the *raiyati* villages (not traceable in Bengal and Orissa) the institution of *zamindari* was not ignored either in the *amli* or in the *ghair-amli* areas. Having traced the origin of the *zamindari* institution based on variation factors, Arthur believed that the zamindars acquired a hereditary character in the course of 18th century, which was more of userpation. The zamindar also encroached upon the rights of the State and the cultivators and ultimately came to pay the State a fixed sum which was very loosely estimated and to appropriate the surplus, whether equivalent to the allowances or more. As the State fell in confusion, the zamindar grew more powerful and he even attempted to exact from the *ryots* for his own benefit. Many of the revenue officers acquired the tenancy to become zamindars. The confirmation of the *zamindari* by the State through the issue of *sanad* became very rare. He considered the zamindar as hereditary proprietor in a restricted sense. As regards *taalqaudars,* Arthur traced one class of *taaluqadars* from the ancient *rajahs* who differed little from the zamindar except that the former did not represent the State to the same extent. Arthur also distinguishes between the independent (*hazuri*) and dependent (*mazkuri*) *taaluqadars*. Though *taaluqadari* institution was hereditary, its confirmation was needed only in case of sale or exchange. He also thought that during the 18th century the *taaluqadari* class rose on the temporary fall of the zamindars; and to have contracted for, and generally acted as zamindars of the large official *zamindaries* created by Murshid Quli Khan. Since after Murshid Quli Khan's period, the old *zamindaries* were restored, the new *taaluqadars* and zamindars continued to build their power on the decline of the Mughal Empire. The zamindars resumed their former powers whereas the *taaluqadars,* when powerful, tended to become independent of the zamindars; and when they were weak, they became dependent *taaluqadars.* All this explanation of the evolution of the zamindars and *taaluqadari* institution during the course of the 18th century is not supported by any contemporary evidence and the entire hypothesis of Arthur is questionable.

Arthur was unable to trace the feature 'village communities' in Bengal during the 18th century on the lines spelled out by Henry Maine. However, he did believe that they may have existed in eastern India during the past but became extinct due to the suppression of the chiefs unto zamindars during the early Sultanate period. This is also just a surmise, which is not borne by historical evidence.

As regards the stratification of the agricultural classes in the village society, Arthur has well analysed the land rights of the *khudkasht, muqarari* and *paikasht ryots* based on the late 18th and early 19th century sources. By and large, he accepted the position as already outlined by Boughton Rouse and Harington. However, he thought that even though the *ryots* paid customary rights, varying with each class, the *khudkasht ryots* had acquired alienable rights in the land in the course of the 18th century whereas, the *muqarari ryots* did not possess such rights.

Baden Powell's excellent account of land systems of British India is primarily a work on the revenue settlements effected during the British rule and is based on the Settlement Report.[18] As such, for eastern India, he makes only brief general statements drawn from the *Settlement Reports* and the observations made by English revenue officers in their official Minutes and Memoranda.

In another series of Tagore Law Lectures (1895) on the *Land-Law of Bengal,* S.C. Mitra dealt with the agrarian problems of late 18th century and 19th century Bengal, mostly from the legal viewpoint.[19] On the concept of property and English theory of rent, he commented that the adoption of the theory of existence in the sovereign of proprietary right in land and its transfer to the zamindars, and the strict measures adopted by the government for the realization of its own dues acted most prejudicially on the actual cultivators. The English administrators and the judge, being unable to find out any distinct rules for the protection of the interest of the poor tenantry, attempted to introduce in India the theory of rent with which they were familiar. Whereas in England customary rent had been superseded by competition rent, in India there were still customary rates to be realized from the cultivators. The acceptance of the theory of rent in India by the judges undermined the customary practices. This seems to be a correct judgement. Even though Mitra tried to spell out the rights and privileges of the varying classes of the *ryots* in the village society, his analysis was circumscribed by the English view point of the late 18th century and judicial decisions. Mitra also examined the question of the 'village community' in relation to rights in land. He rightly commented that in Bengal, the village land was not the common property of the villagers as a body. Nor was there any communal idea of a common joint ownership of land current amongst the members of the village community. There was no kinship amongst all the families in a village who frequently belonged to different *gotras* and castes. The only tie that bound the members of the village society was a social one. Of course, one community had lands and landmarks distinct from those of another, but each family had rights in the land in its occupation well recognised and distinct from another. He noted that by 1892-93, of the permanently settled estates in Bengal and Bihar, there was not a single settlement with village community as such, not even a settlement with a village headmen as representing a village corporation. Mitra's analysis of the agrarian structure of the pre-British era is very vaguely and inaccurately attempted. However, it is a valuable contribution covering the genesis of the land tenures since the late 18th century based on the 18th century English records, judicial cases and case-laws of the 19th century.

W.H. Moreland, in his work on *Agrarian System of Moslem India,* has covered 18th century eastern India very briefly and based on the late 18th century English records, has made only some general observations.[20] Moreland's conclusion that the zamindars in Bengal paid a fixed lumpsum assessed amount to the State is based on his wrong reading of the *Ain-i-Akbari* . Even if Moreland's analysis of the *Ain's* accepted, it cannot be asserted that the nature of agrarian administration in the *zamindaries* of unsettled Bengal and Orissa, as under Akbar, remained static throughout the ages till the assumption of the *Diwani* rights by the East India Company in 1765. Moreland's difficulty arises from his rigid concept of the *Ain's* statistics of revenue tables and also his belief to the effect that with the passage of time, the distinction between chiefs, farmers and officials disappeared, because there was in fact no difference in the incidence of the various positions, and all alike came to be known as zamindars. This view is not at all true either for the 17th century or for 18th century till at least the Governorship of Murshid Quli Khan and Mir Jafar. As already explained, Murshid Quli Khan's revenue reforms made a clearcut traditional distinction between different categories of revenue officials and the zamindars. In view of the available contemparary evidence, it is equally doubtful that the technical distinction between the chiefs, revenue farmers and revenue officials disappeared so as to entitle them to be known as the zamindars. This can be asserted with much more vehemence for the territories of Bihar.

J. N. Sarkar and K. K. Dutta, covering the 18th century portions in the history of Bengal, have attempted mostly political narration based on contemporary Persian chronicles and English records.[21] However, Sarkar has tried to underline the revenue reforms of Murshid Quli Khan and their impact on the economy of Bengal. Sarkar subscribes to the view that prior to Murshid Quli Khan's period, 'the state used to get its dues from the land in the lump, from the old landed proprietors of Bengal, called zamindars'. He thinks that 'the direct collection of land-rent from the actual cultivators by State officials, which prevailed in upper India under Todar Mal's *zabti* system, was impossible in Bengal'. Hence Murshid Quli Khan, in accordance with his '*malzamni* system,' collected the revenues through the revenue farmers (*ijaradars*) who crushed many of the old *zamindaries* and themselves came to be called zamindars. From the time of Murshid Quli to the permanent settlement of Cornwallis, hereditary landed families of historical origins (except a few small fry) were extinguished and their places were taken by new men of the official and capitalist classes. The land revenue system taken over by the English was, in its main features, the creation of Murshid Quli Khan and it was continued in a more refined but more rigid form under Cornwallis' permanent settlement. According to Sarkar, it was the landed aristocracy created in Bengal under Murshid Quli Khan whose position was confirmed and made hereditary by Cornwallis. The land revenue of Murshid Quli Khan amounted to heartless squeezing of the peasantry as the pressure applied at the top passed through the intermediate grades finally on the actual cultivators, who were left with the bare means of subsistence. It has already been examined that the enforcement of the principle of periodical assessment, regardless of long gap, left little scope for most of the zamindars in the *amli* territories to claim payment of *peshkash* as perpetually fixed amount. No doubt *zabt* as method of assessment was never enforced in Bengal during the Mughal age but *zabt* was only one of the methods by which direct assessment could be done by the State in the *amli* territories. In fact, this has no relationship with the nature of *peshkash,* fixed or periodically changeable, which could be assessed in accordance with any method of assessment operative in the region. It has already been noted that Murshid Quli Khan's revenue reforms tried to enforce the Mughal pattern of administration according to which reshuffling or the creation of new *zamindaries* was an essential feature for the realization of revenues. Sarkar has not at all appreciated the spirit of the nature of these reforms and the new concept of proprietary right later on introduced by Cornwallis. Sarkar's study of the agrarian structure is extremely superficial as he has not at all made any analysis of the land rights of the *riyaya* at the village level.

S. Bhattacharya, in his work on *The East India Company,* has mostly covered the commercial aspects.[22] His chapter on general economic conditions based on English records is too general to have covered the agrarian structure and the economic condition of the peasantry in detail. While tracing the institution of *zamindari* during the course of 18th century, Bhattacharya has not appreciated the technical distinction between the zamindar and *taaluqdar*. Bhattcharya considers the East India Company as zamindar *ab-initio* though the Farman of Emperor Farrukhsiyar (18th January, 1717) not only confirms the already acquired *taaluqdari* villages but further authorises the East India Company to purchase the *taaluqdari* of thirty-eight new villages from the respective owners and the *Diwan-i-Subah* is enjoined to permit the sale transaction. It was only in 1757 that Mir Jafar also granted lands to the East India Company on the payment of the revenue 'in the same manner as the other zamindars'. The English were placed in possession of 24 parganas in July 1757 and, as such, the Company assumed the role of the zamindar. Bhattacharya's reading of the above mentioned *Farman* (1717) and designating the East India Company for the period of his study as the zamindar is basically incorrect.

N.K. Sinha, in his work on *The Economic History of Bengal,* has covered the evolution of the land revenue system during the course of the 18th century.[23] It is based on copious collection of the English records of the post-*Diwani* period. Notwithstanding the fact that Sinha utilized the enquiries conducted by the British administrators on the nature of land rights, the study is essentially on traditional lines recording considerable number of statements from multifarious sources without attempting to make any critical analysis of the evolution and basis of the agrarian structure in Bengal. At times the indiscriminate use of the English land terminology to the pre-*Diwani* agrarian situation and adoption of Persian revenue terminology without spelling out their connotation against the Mughal revenue practices causes confusion in the analysis of the issue involved. The nature of the *zamindari, taaluqdari,* 'superior *raiyat*' and 'lower *raiyat*' and life of rural Bengal has been explained on the lines already spelled out by John Shore, Boughton Rouse and Harrington. More stress has been laid on the narration of the main feature of the Permanent Settlement though its immediate impact on the rural life of Bengal has been briefly attempted with an insight into the new economic forces set forth at the level of the village society.

Ranajit Guha, in *A Rule of Property For Bengal,* has traced the idea of the Permanent Settlement from 1770 to 1793.[24] Guha has emphasised the impact of the theoretical British social and economic thoughts of the revenue administration in the formulations of the agrarian policy in the newly acquired colony in eastern India. Even though the protagonists of the 'assessment for ever' policy belonged to different schools of thought, Alexander Dow, the mercantilist; Henry Pattulla and Philip Francis, the physiocrats; Thomas Law, the free trader; and Cornwallis, a free trader to a lesser degree, their main target was the farming system with periodical assessment which was responsible for the subversion of the property. They advocated the principle of property and recognition of the proprietary rights of the zamindars than to vest the ownership of land with the State. Thus the question of Permanent Settlement as against the periodical assessment was linked with the proprietary rights on the part of the zamindars. Though the idea of the Permanent Settlement lingered for nearly a little over two decades, the gordian knot was cut by Cornwallis who had been influenced more by Thomas Law's ideas and experimentation on *'muqarari'* system than by Philip Francis. Even though Guha has marshalled the huge depository of the contemporary English literature on socio-economic thought and East India Company records in an admirable manner, it is difficult to agree with him for the weightage he has put on the theoretical aspect for the formulation of the economic policy in India. The local socio-economic conditions as well as economic and political factors for the enforcement of the Permanent Settlement have been rather eclipsed. A coordinated approach with comparative evaluation of the conceptual impact, the local customary regulations underlining the agrarian practices as well as the imperial interests for the exploitation and the colonial revenues in a rounded manner would have definitely yielded better perspective for Guha. Apart from this, in matters of detail, Guha has committed a number of errors. Only a couple of instances may suffice. Guha has accepted Francis's understanding of the Indian pre-British policy at its face value. As already analysed, Francis's ideas about the concept of Indian property, the position of the landed intermediaries and agrarian system of the Mughal age were basically incorrect. A critical analysis of Thomas Law's enforcement of the *muqarari* system in few *parganas* of Bihar would show that perpetual settlement of the village may be made either with the zamindar or a lessee. In the later case, a perpetual lessee would pay *malikana* to the zamindar. Law just surmised that the rights of one party would ultimately be purchased by the other party thus converging both the *muqarari* and *zamindari* rights in the same person. On the contrary, Cornwallis made Permanent Settlement with the existing hereditary zamindars and independent *taaluqdars*. Needless to say, an analytical and rounded account of the English policy comprising socio-economic and political factors prior to the Permanent Settlement against the pre-*Diwani* agrarian system of the 18th century has yet to be attempted.

Abdul Karim, in his scholarly work on *Murshid Quli Khan and His Times*, has utilized the Persian chronicles as well as English records, both contemporary and later.[25] He has analysed the administrative features of the *subah* administration and has equally stressed the importance of the land revenue reforms of Murshid Quli Khan. Following the line of thought of James Grant, Karim thinks that during the Mughal age, the fixed lumpsum amount paid by the Bengal zamindars was revised by Shah Shuja (17th century) and that further revision of the revenues based on detailed survey, measurement and classification of land was undertaken by Murshid Quli Khan. Of course, exception based on geographical factors and expediency, was made in respect of some *zamindaries*. Abdul Karim's criticism of the views of J.N. Sarkar is justified though neither of them have followed the significance of the *'mal zamni'* procedure. Karim inaccurately considers the collection of revenues by the zamindars and *amlis* as the direct and indirect methods of collection of revenues. In fact, in case of *zamindaries* of the *amli* territories, the assessment was done by the State officials and the collection of the revenues was by *amils* in collaboration with the zamindars. Karim has not attempted any description about the agrarian structure at the local level. Nor has he attempted any analysis of the land rights of the landed intermediaries and the *riyaya* in the rural society of Bengal.

Mazharul Huq, in his work on *the East India Company's Land Policy and Commerce in Bengal 1698-1784,* has relied on purely English records and the observations made by the English administrators at the close of the 18th century.[26] Huq's main contribution lies in the fact that he has linked up the commercial interests of the East India Company with its land policy. He has minutely traced the changes which primarily affected the peasants and the artisans whom he thinks to be the one and the same people. He has attempted an integrated account of the land policy and management of the East India Company in Bengal from the very beginning of its territorial acquisition. He has traced the effects of the farming system which adversely affected the position of the *raiyats* and the artisans long before the introduction of the Permanent Settlement (1793). Under the farming system of the East India Company, a new class of the *banians* and the *gomashtas* of the Company, which exploited the *ryots* and the artisans emerged as a vital social class in the economic life of Bengal. A coordination of the English as well as the available Persian sources would have given Huq a better perspective of the role of the Company as the zamindar of Calcutta (1698-1757) and other *zamindari* territories of the Company. The main thesis of Huq about the baneful effects of the periodical farming system and the emergence of the *banian* class as a social factor is correct though the extent to which the petty rural landed classed assumed the functions of the revenue farming has been undermined. The relationship of the latter with the *banian* class and the *sarafs* for the assumption of the farming rights is equally significant in the agrarian life of Bengal. However, in matters of detail, one may not agree with Huq on a number of issues. For the Chittagong area, he has not been able to appreciate the difference between the *jagir* and the *zamindari* system prevalent during the Mughal age wherein the zamindars themselves were bestowed with conditional *jagirs* from within their own *zamindari* territories for the maintenance of the local militia and law and order in the region. Similarly, based on the English sources, he has not understood the institution of *Qanungo* in the agrarian administration for the pre-*Diwani* period.

R.N. Sinha's *Bihar Tenantry (1783-1833)* has relied on the published English sources and secondary works.[27] Even though he has made a casual reference to a *farman* of Aurangzeb in respect of the functions of the *sadr qanungos* of Bihar, the description about 18th century agrarian position is merely narrative rather than analytical. He has examined the comparative land rights of various categories of the *ryots* on the basis of the viewpoints of the English revenue administrators, especially Harington and Buchanan. There has been no analytical approach for tracing the effects of the Permanent Settlement on the agrarian life of Bihar in the light of vast documentary source material available at the State Archives, Patna, which could have changed his perspective.

A.M. Serajuddin's *The Revenue Administration of the East India Company in Chittagong (1761-1785)*, based on the contemporary English sources and district records, has made a valuable contribution on the early British revenue administration in Chittagong.[28] Serajuddin has well analysed the features of the small *zamindaries* in Chittagong. He has rightly pointed out that the small *zamindaries* of Chittagong stood in great contrast to the usually prevalent big *zamindaries* of Bengal which inevitably demands change in the generalization about the position of the zamindars in Bengal. A number of zamindars paid less than Rs. 10/- and about 9/10th of the zamindars of Chittagong paid less than Rs. 500/- a year in land revenue. There the zamindars paid revenues directly to the State. Serajuddin thinks that these zamindars were as good as peasant proprietors. This is a correct assumption as further analysis of the factual data provided by him would clearly show that even though fragmentation of the *zamindaries* may have occurred during the course of time, by and large, these were self-colonized villages over which the *zamindari* families equally exercised the *khudkasht* rights involving ownership of land. Chittagong equally represents the example of the big zamindars who alienated their rights to the *taaluqdars* for the reclamation of land on the one hand whereas the primary zamindars colonized the villages as *khudkasht* families.

Narahari Kaviraj's *A Peasant Uprising in Bengal, 1783,* based on contemporary English source material, has dealt with the events, nature and significance of the revolt.[29] To what extent it was a *zamindari* revolt on the traditional lines or a genuine peasant uprising depends on the landed interests of the zamindars, village headmen and *raiyayas.* That the interests of the latter three parties involved were well integrated so as to revolt against farming system is an issue which demands further probe.

Professor S. Nurul Hasan, in *Thoughts on Agrarian Relations in Mughal India,* has brilliantly attempted the organisation of agrarian economy and the interests of the landed classes vis-a-vis the State during the Mughal age.[30] Referring to the well-known controversy over the land rights in the last decades of the 18th century, he has suggested that the concept of property, as defined by Blackstone in the pre-Adam Smith period, was very similar to the concept of property that was in existence here. So in that sense the property is not an exclusive property. 'In medieval India, the zamindars had absolute rights in terms of property. But he had simultaneously the obligation to ensure that the cultivation was continued, and that good quality crops (*Jins-i-kamil*) were sown. This system of overlapping and over-riding rights undergoes a change in the capitalist system, where taxation acquires a meaning totally different from the pre-capitalist relationship'. Thus the Mughal system was feudal and pre-capitalist in character. Professor Hasan has also challenged the old hypothesis of a *static* medieval society and has suggested that a nature of change may be determined. He has equally posed a number of issues regarding the nature and concept of the village community, monetary economy and the land system in India in the pre-British period. Referring to the question of proprietorship of the soil and the sharp differences of opinion amongst the British administrators and the contradictory information supplied by the Indians during the late 18th century, Professor Hasan has suggested further investigations based on the available records of the revenue administration of Bengal, Bihar and Orissa in India.

Professor Satish Chandra has well analysed the land rights and position of the zamindars (including *muqaddams* and *chaudharies* etc.), *khudkashta riyaya, riyaya-paikasht, muzarian* and artisans and professional classes (*balutedars, alutedars* and *chakaran* etc.) in the village society.[31] Based on the writings of Warren Hastings, Harrington and Hunter, he has concluded that during the 18th century eastern India, there was a substantial migratory population which consisted largely of the *pahikashtkars,* but to some extent of the landless and the low caste elements in the villages. This migratory section was a major factor in the extension of cultivation and in the settlement of new villages. These internal migrations equally tended to break up the old single caste/clan villages and enabled the ruling classes to presurrize the *khudkashta* cultivators to pay more and to make them more submissive. According to Satish Chandra, the syndrome of conflict between the zamindars, *khudkasht* and *pahikashtkars* is an important element in the growth of the village society which needs to be worked out more fully.

Rajat and Ratna Ray have emphasised the elements of continuity with agrarian society from the pre to the Post Permanent Settlement Period in Bengal and consider that the agrarian society of the late 18th century and thereafter was not fundamentally different from Pre-British India.[32] The Permanent Settlement did not transform the zamindars overnight to the English-style landlords owning 'estates' and enjoying actual control of land and labour. The zamindars had formerly enjoyed a right to a share in the produce of the soil, and the Permanent Settlement confirmed this as a propeirtory right in the land rent, which could be sold, mortgaged or bequeathed. But the land continued in the possession of the peasant families from generation to generation. They also assert that the Permanent Settlement did not create mainly urban capitalists associated with the East India Company as auction purchasers of the *zamindari* and *taaluqdari* rights after 1793 were smaller local *taaluqdars* and zamindars in their own right or were employed in the collection of the revenues of the *zamindaries.* The Permanent Settlement led to small properties, vertically and laterally divided through sub-feudation and sub-division which laid the basis for the independence and consolidation of the smaller local gentry formerly subservient to the big zamindars. Ratna Ray illustrates this aspect of land transfer and social change under the Permanent Settlement in the case-studies of Burdwan and Bishnupur. Ray's historical description in respect of these two *zamindaries* since the Mughal age is vaguley attempted. Ray has pointed out the loose structure of the 'Raj' of these *zamindaries* without realising that the internal structure of such *zamindaries* in Bengal essentially involved landed intermediaries and service tenures which were responsible for maintenance of peace as well as realization of the revenues. The establishment of the *patnidars* in hierarchical manner down to the village level created a new proprietory class not only of rent but also of the land in the same manner as the zamindars were considered the proprietory owners. The Permanent Settlement had definitely combined the proprietary rent receiving right with ownership of land. The village headmen and *khudkasht* lost their ownership rights. For purposes of assessment, they were no longer governed by customary practice. Prior to the Permanent Settlement, the revenue farmers held *ijara* only on periodical basis but afterwards the *patnidars* held perpetual heritable lease. The fact that at the village level, the village *mandal* himself invariably purchased the *patni* shares meant that the *ryots* were left completely at his mercy for the purposes of the distribution of the assessed revenues. This was a complete denial of the pre-British practice, which in the course of the 19th century adversely affected the position of the *ryots*. Under the new concept of land relations, the worst hit class was that of the *paikashtkars* which has no protection at least until the Act of 1859.

References

1. Some of the important manuscripts of the *staatsbibliothek* Berlin (East) are, *Nuskha Hai Bar Kaifiat -i-Suba Bihar; Nuskha Majmuaat; Sawalat-i-Malik-i Zamin Ki ast az Mister John Shore; Dar Bab-i-Nuskha Sarusa Hukm; Tawarikh-i-Badshahān-i Hind az ibtada-i-Shah Timur baghayat-i-Shah 'Ālam; Majumuaa-i Mutafariqqa; Akhbar-ul-Sadiq dar Kaifiat Bengala Darj Ast;* Grover, B.R., cf. no. 2; also Hasan Mahmud, S, : *Yasin's Glossary of Revenue Terms* -an annotated English translation (unpublished dissertation), A.M.U., Aligarh, 1970. This work was compiled at the instance of James Grant.

2. Grover, B.R., 'Some Rare Persian Manuscripts and Documents on India (16th-18th centuries) in the German Libraries'. *Max Mueller Bhavan Publications*, 1964 Year Book, New Delhi, pp. 59-73.

3. Grover, B.R., 'Evolution of Zamindari and Taaluqdari System in Bengal (1576-1765 A.D.), *Bangladesh Itihas Parishad, Proceedings of Third History Congress,* Dacca, 1973 (henceforth " Evolution of *zamindari* & c."); also Nurul Hasan, S, "Three Studies of Zamindari System", *Medieval India - A Miscellany,* I, Aligarh Muslim University, 1969, pp. 233-239.

4. Philip Francis, *Minutes of the Governor General in Council,* etc. pp. 30-31; Firminger's *Introduction to The Fifth Report from the Select Committee of the House of Commons on the Affairs of the East India Company,* July 1812 (1917) (henceforth *The Fifth Report*).

5. *The Fifth Report,* pp. 170-198; 205-212; Firminger's Introduction pp. XIV-XX.

6. *The Fifth Report,* 1. op. cit. *Introduction,* pp. XXVIII-XXIV; compare it with Sir John's Minute, dated 18th June, 1789, vide the *Fifth Report,* II, Appendix-I; also J. Shore, " Minute of April 1788" in J.H. Harington, *An Elementary Analysis of the Laws and Regulations,* Calcutta, 1814-15, II, pp. 233-34.

7. Grover, B.R., " Evolution of Zamindari & c."; Hasan Mahmud, S., cf. no.1.

8. Grover, B.R., 'Nature of *Dehat-i-Taaluqa* (*zamindari* Villages) and the Evolution of the *Taaluqdari* System during the Mughal Age, *The Economic and Social History Review,* Delhi, Vol. II, No. 3, July, 1965, pp. 166-77, 259-88. Nurul Hasan, S: *Thoughts on Agrarian Relations in Mughal India,* New Delhi, 1973 (henceforth *Thoughts on Agrarian Relations &*

c.); Satish Chandra, "Some Aspects of Indian Village Society in Northern India During the 18th Century, The position and Role of the *Khud-kāsht* and *Pāhī-kāsht*", *The Indian Historical Review*, March 1974, Vol. I, no. I, pp. 51-64; Hasan Mahmud, S., cf. no.1.

9. Rouse, Charles William Boughton, *Dissertation Concerning the Landed Property of Bengal*, London, 1791.
10. Harington, J.H., *An Elementary Analysis of the Laws and Regulations*, Calcutta, II, 1814-15.
11. *East India (Parliamentary Papers)*, 1810, *House of Commons*, Vol. V, p. 13, Paper 363, *East India Company, Second Report of Select Committee*, with Appendix.
12. James Mill, *History of India*, I, chap.V, p. 247, Vol. IV, chap. III, pp. 1-23. Eric Stokes,. *The English Utilitarians and India* (Oxford University Press, 1959), pp. 1-139.
13. W.W. Hunter, *A Brief History of the Indian People*, 2nd Ed., London, 1833, pp. 125-26.
14. W.W. Hunter, *Orissa*, Vol.II, p. 206.
15. Mountstuart Elphinstone, *The History of India*, 2 Vols., London, 1841, 9th edition, London, 1916, with Notes and Addition by E.B. Cowell, chap.II, pp. 66-87; 472-77.
16. H.S. Maine, *Village Communities in the East and West*, London, 1895, pp. 103-239.
17. Arthur Philips, *The Law Relating to the Land Tenures of Lower Bengal*, Calcutta, 1876.
18. Badan-Powell, B.H., *Land Systems of British India*, 3 Vols., Oxford, 1892.
19. S.C. Mitra, *The Land-Law of Bengal*, Calcutta, 1898.
20. W.H. Moreland, *The Agrarian System of Moslem India*, Cambridge, 1929.
21. J.N. Sarkar (ed.) , *The History of Bengal-Muslim Period, 1200-1757*, Dacca, 1948.
22. S. Bhattacharya, *The East India Company and the Economy of Bengal from 1704 to 1740*, London, 1954.
23. N.K. Sinha, *The Economic History of Bengal from Plassey to Permanent Settlement*, Vol.II, Calcutta, 1962.
24. Ranajit Guha, *A Rule of Property for Bengal: An Essay on the Idea of Permanent Settlement*, Paris, 1963.
25. Abdul Karim, *Murshid Quli Khan and His Times*, Dacca, 1963.
26. Mazharul Huq, *The East India Company's Land Policy and Commerce in Bengal 1698-1784*, Dacca, 1964.
27. R.N. Sinha, *Bihar Tenantry (1783-1833)*, Bombay, 1968.

28. A.M. Serajuddin, *The Revenue Administration of East India Company in Chittagong, 1761-1785*, Chittagong, 1971.
29. Narahari Kaviraj, *The Peasant Uprising in Bengal, 1783, The First Peasant Uprising against the Rule of East India Company*, New Delhi, 1972.
30. Nurul Hasan, S, *Thoughts on Agrarian Relations & c.*
31. Satish Chandra, "Indian Economy before the Industrial Revolution in Britain: The Village Society", (memeograph) paper presented at seminar on Colonization of Indian Economy, Aligarh Muslim University, 1972; also cf. no. 8.
32. Rajat and Ratna Ray, "The Dynamics of Continuity in Rural Bengal Under the British Imperium: A Study of Quasi-stable Equilibrium on Underdeveloped Societies in a Changing World", *The Indian Economic and Social History Review*, X, II, June 1973, pp. 103-128. Also Ratna Ray, " Land Transfer and Social Change Under The Permanent Settlement: A Study of Two Localities". *The Indian Economic and Social History Review*, XI, 1, March 1974.

28. A.M. Serajuddin, *The Revenue Administration of East India Company in Chittagong 1761-1785*, Chittagong, 1971.

29. Narahari Kaviraj, *The Peasant Uprising in Bengal, 1783, The First Peasant Uprising against the Rule of East India Company*, New Delhi, 1972.

30. Nurul Hasan, S. *Thoughts on Agrarian Relations* etc.

31. Satish Chandra, "Indian Economy before the Industrial Revolution in Britain: The Village Society" (mimeograph) paper presented at seminar on Colonisation of Indian Economy, Aligarh Muslim University, 1973 also cf. no. 5.

32. Ratan and Ratna Ray, "The Dynamics of Continuity in Rural Bengal under the British Imperium: A Study of Quasi-stable Equilibrium on Underdeveloped Societies in a Changing World", *The Indian Economic and Social History Review*, X, ii, June 1973, pp. 103-128. Also Ratna Ray, Land Transfer and Social Change Under The Permanent Settlement: A Study of Two Localities", *The Indian Economic and Social History Review*, XI, 1, March 1974.

Chapter 13
'Raqba-Bandi' Documents of Akbar's Reign

In the course of my research tour, I discovered some original *Raqba-bandi* (*i.e.* measurement and area statement) documents of the year 1001 Fasli, *i.e.* 1593 A.D. of Akbar's reign, preserved in the Secretariat Records Office, Patna. They comprise 76 folios and the first sheet bears the title "Raffba-bandi Todar Mali 1001 Fasli wa Tappah-bandi" in a bold *Nastaliq* hand. They all pertain to the detailed *Raqba-bandi* official records of the various *mauzas* (villages) and *tappahs* (Fiscal divisions) of *pargana* Bhagalpur, Sarkar Monghyr, Subah Bihar.[1] They were originally found by the district authorities piled in the old records of the District Record Office, Bhagalpur. Realising the antiquity and the genuineness of the documents, the district authorities transferred them to the Record office, Central Secretariat, Patna (Bihar). They are the earliest of such archives in the field of land revenue literature of the Mughal age and as such are followed by similar pattern of *pargana Raqba-bandi* documents for the reign of Aurangzeb, preserved in the *Daftar-i-Diwani Wa Hazuri,* now known as Rajasthan Archives. At Patna Secretariat, to these documents of Akbar's reign are also attached the original '*Fahrist-i-Dehat-i-Tappajat*' *i.e.,* the documents comprising the list of the villages and *tappahs* of the same *Pargana* for the *Fasli* year 1179 (1771 A.D.). There is a difference in the nature of the two documents to the extent, that whereas those of Akbar's reign pertain to the detailed *arazi* (measurement figures) of the named *tappahs* and *mauzas*, the later ones dated 1771 A.D. contain detailed list of *tappahs* with *dehats* and *mauzas* associated with a number of named *Choudhris.* Notwithstanding this difference, both the documents enumerate the same *tappahs* along with their respective *mauzas* even though with a gap of 178 years of record. This rather confirms the authenticity as well as the fact that the documents of

---

Indian Historical Records Commission, Chandigarh, 1961

Akbar's reign are complete in every sense. Moreover, such importance of these documents was realised by the British Collectors, who signed these sheets to ward off any confusion and spurious transcription. The above mentioned sheets of year 1001 *Fasli* (1593 A.D.) associated with Todar Mal, bear the initials of the collector afm, whereas the order for the sheets of the year 1179 Fasli (1771 A.D.) is noted in the hand of the Collector C.S. Skinner, dated April 29th, 1862 A.D., which runs, "To prevent any further confusion in future Mr. Dy. Collector Renny will sign each sheet of this first *Dehat* of Bhagalpoor of 1179 F.S."

As to the descriptive details of the documents of Akbar's reign, fol. Ia, under the title of the '*Haqiqat-i-Raqba-bandi*' (Area statement) of *pargana* Bhagalpur, *sarkar* Monghyr, *subah* Bihar, dated year 1001 *Fasli,* mentions the total number of *tappahs, mauzas* both original and additional, *mahal,*[2] total area both under the habitation boundaries of the *dehats* and the cultivable lands. Then from fol.2a to 76a, follow '*Haqiqat-Raqba-bandi*' for each of the mentioned *tappah,* giving its details of the total number of *mauzas*, both original and additional, areas of each of the mentioned *mauzas*, both for *dehat* under the habitation and cultivable land. Such details are mentioned for the following 29 *tappahs* in succession.[3] Jaha Nagar, fols. 2a-12b; Qasimpur, fols. 12b-17a; Kuraib, fols. 17a-18a; Fatehpur, fols. 18b-20a; Bhagalpur, fols. 20b; Rasulpur, fols. 20b-23b; Alwar Abad, fols. 24a-26a; Akbar Nagar, fols. 26b-28b; Rararqpur, fols. 29a-30a; Sikandpur, fols. 30b-32b; Wahilkeh, 33a-39b; Azimpur, fols. 39b-40b; Azim Nagar, fols. 41a-41b; Shahpur, fols. 42a-42b; Nur Anadas, fols. 44a-45b; Khanaha Manur, fols. 46a-48b; Chandina, fols. 49a-51b; Chanderi, fols. 51a-52b; Sujah Nagar, fols. 53a-56b; Bayadons, fols. 57a-60b; Amin Abad, fols. 61a-64a; Mohammad Nagar, fols. 64b-66a; Shah Abad, fols. 67a-70a; Chayator, fols. 70a-73a; Azim Abad, fol. 74a; Mandar, fol. 74b; Barkub, fol. 75a; Satda, fol. 75b; Minhari, fol. 76a.

The title of the documents associating the '*Raqba-bandi*' and '*Tappah-bandi*' for the year 1001 *Fasli, i.e.* 1573 A.D. with Todar Mal clearly shows that they are in exactly the same pattern and methodology of documentation as devised and enforced by the latter in his settlement operations carried out in Bihar after its incorporation with the Mughal Empire in 1574 A.D.[4] Todar Mal, as the Diwan of *subah,* had introduced land revenue system in Bihar similar to that already accomplished by him earlier in other provinces.[5]

The Importance Of the Documents

These documents are extremely important in so far as they bring out the main traits of the documentation of the Pargana 'Records-of-Rights' based on the survey of land and also illustrate some new aspects of the local organisation for the land administration in Akbar's reign.

(A) Survey of land and 'Record-of-Rights'

The importance of the '*Raqba-bandi*' documents embodying the measurement data can be well realised in the historical background and genesis of the Survey and measurement process in Akbar's reign.

A correct and systematic survey of land is a prerequisite for the accurate assessment and proper fixation of the State demand. Sher Shah had realised its importance and had resorted to the measurement of land as a matter of general policy. In this respect, Todar Mal carried Sher Shah's legacy to its logical conclusion. The problem of the fixation of the proper '*Jama*' and the latter's need to base it upon '*Hal-i-Hasil*' ultimately depended on a proper survey of the land.[6] Consequently, in the 19th year of the Ilahi era, all lands were declared '*Khalsa*'[7] and a comprehensive topographical and cadastral survey of the lands was undertaken.[8] Baudaoni gives a vivid picture of the operations. "In this year, for the betterment of the agriculture of the country and for augmenting the conditions of the *raiyats*, a device was promulgated. An area of the *parganas* (comprising all categories of land), whether dry or under water, countries inclusive of the cities, mountains, rivers, deserts, jungles, reservoirs, wells was to be recorded after measurement with the "*jarib*".[9] Though Baudaoni's statement describes only topographical survey operations, the original '*Raqba-bandi*' documents of Akbar's reign, the Jaipur Archives and the various *Dasturul amls* of the 17th century give comprehensive details of the Cadastral Survey of the '*arazi*' lands essentially devised in the reign of Akbar. [10] The introduction of the iron-ringed bamboo *Jarib* replacing the hempen-rope *jarib*,[11] the *Gaz-i-Ilahi* modifying the size of the previous *Gaz*,[12] and finally the standardisation of the size of the bigha, 60 *Gaz* each in linear dimensions,[13] made the bigha as the unit of measurement for the purpose of assessment. The statement of the measurement thus carried out on terms of bighas was recorded in the village and the *pargana* documents named '*Haqiqat-i-Raqba-bandi*'. The latter showed the total area, both the uncultivable as within the *deh* (village) boundries and cultivable for the respective *mauzas*, *tappahs* and finally for the entire *pargana*. All this is clear from the original *Raqba-bandi* documents of the reign of Akbar.

(B) The above virgin documents for the first time afford contemporary archival evidence with regard to the Survey and fiscal administration of the *mauza* and *qasba* as the units of local administration under Akbar, known hitherto only from *Ain* and later *Dasturul amls*. They equally bring out the importance and the place of the *tappah* as a fiscal unit in the local administration of the *Pargana*-a fact completely unknown to the historians on the Mughal administration so far.[14]

(i) The *mauza* was the smallest unit for multipurpose revenue operations, measurement, assessment and administration with '*Maqaddam*' as the headman. Every village consisted of two portions,, the area under '*abadi*' (Habitation) known as *deh* or *dehat*, and the surrounding cultivable and uncultivable areas, which along with the *abadi* (habitation) consitituted the entire village.[15] The boundary of every village was clearly demarcated through *chaknamahs*.[16] A full village record of the measured, both cultivable and uncultivable areas, was maintained in a document named "*Taqsim*".[17] At the time of every harvest, a record of the fields under cultivation, named '*Nuskha-i-Zabt*' or '*Khasra*' was prepared.[18] The assessment of the entire village was recorded in '*Jamabandi*'.[19]

(ii) The next territorial division was the *qasba*, which though at times comprising of only one large village, would usually consist of few *mauzas* within its circle, its number varying with every *qasba*.[20] The largest of the *mauzas* would give its name to the *qasba* and even to the *tappah*.

(iii) Above the *mauza* and the *qasba* was *tappah*, which was composed of numerous villages within its jurisdiction.[21] This is clear from the foregoing '*Raqba-bandi*' documents of Akbar's reign, which, as already stated, show twenty-nine *tappahs* in the *pargana* of Bhagalpur, *sarkar* Monghyr, *subah* Bihar. Every *Tappah* therein shows the total number of villages (original and additional) in its jurisdiction along with the total area, both cultivable and uncultivable. The *tappah* was a purely fiscal unit. It can be traced in some parts of India even in the pre-Mughal[22] era, and seems to have been made a uniform feature of the revenue administration throughout the dominions under Akbar.[23] As such, it remained a regular part of the hierarchical set up of the *pargana* land administration throughout the Mughal age [24] and even later. At the *pargana* headquarters, all land administration documents pertaining to Survey, assessments and revenue were prepared *tappah*wise. This is borne out by the above *Raqba-bandi* documents of Akbar's reign and various other land administration documents for the reign of Shahjahan and Aurangzeb.[25] Usually, the headquaters of the *tappah* were located at a bigger *dehat* or *quasba*[26] after which the *tappah* was named. The entire circle was managed by an official named *Tappaidar*.[27] The latter had to help the revenue staff for the collection of the land revenue. He had to extend cooperation at the time of '*Sehbandi*' *i.e.* detailing persons for the collection in cash or kind.[28] Any cultivator or tenant in arrears for instalment or unwilling for payment had to be produced before him for necessary action. Along with the *muqaddam*, he had to attest the forwarding note of despatch of instalments to the Treasury. [29]For all this, he was responsible to the *choudhry* of his *tappah* and to the *pargana Karori* and *Shiqdar*.[30]

References

1. At present, Bhagalpur is a district of the Province of Bihar as outcome of many changes. By 1765 A.D., when the East India Company was invested with the *Diwani*, Bhagalpur was a district with a huge tract in the east of *Sarkar* Monghyr, *subah* Bihar, lying altogeher to the South of Ganges except the *pargana* of Chai. Thereafter, it was transferred to the Province of Bengal and various changes brought in its jurisdiction in 1832, 1855-56, 1864, and 1874 A.D. have greatly restricted its area in the Southern portion and extended that in the north (*Bengal District Gazetteers*, Bhagalpur by Bryne, I.C.S. Calcutta, 1911, pp. 1-2, 28-30).
2. The *mahal* as distinct from a *pargana* was purely a fiscal unit. It was invariably, though by no means, essentially, co jurisdiction in territory with the *pargaña*. The above document of Akbar's reign puts only one *mahal* as against the *pargana of* Bhagalpur and, as such, both coincided in territorial limits.
3. *Ain*, Jarrett Vol. II, p. 167, simply mentions Bhagalpur as one of the third *mahals* in *sarkar* Monghyr, *subah* Bihar and does not give any further lower divisions. Though *Bhagalpur District Gazetteer* (pp.1-2) makes a casual reference to two of the *tappahs* being transferred to the newly formed district of Bhagalpur in the year 1855 A.D., it does not supply us with any list of the *tappahs* either in the old or in the new district.
4. *Akbar Nama*, tr. Beveridge, Vol. III, p. 122, *Tabqat-i-Akbari*, Pers. Text, Calcutta, 1931 edition, Vol. II, p. 284.

5. An Urdu Ms. (Bihar, Bengal and Orissa men Todar Mal ki Karguzarain) Khuda Bhaksh Library, Patna, quoted by B.P. Ambashtaya in *I.H.C. Journal*, 1958, pp. 306-307. According to the introduction of this Ms, it is a part of the earlier original Persian Ms. written at the order of Raja Todar Mal by his Mir Munshi, namely Safdar Ali in 1581. The Urdu version was translated from original in 1874 A.D., which quotes that after Behar was conquered, the Emperor appointed Munim Khan as its Governor, Todar Mal as *diwan*, Ram Dass Kachchwaha as *Niab Diwan*,. *I.H.C. Journal*, 1958, p. 309.

6. *'Iqbal Nama'* Ms. Mintoli 215 Berlin fol. 276a; Ms. Rampur p. 463. *'Jama'* denotes the state demand and the land revenue assessed whereas, *'Hal-i-Hasil'* stands for the actual land revenue assessed and demanded after making all deductions of the collection charges of the officials.

7. A.N. Br. M.Add. O.R. 27, fols. 270b-271a; *Tarikh-i Arif Qandhari*, Ms. 415, Rampur, p. 178.

8. *Muntakhab-ut-Tawarikh*, Baudaoni, Ms. Elliot, 248, Bodleian Library, Oxford, fol. 257b; T.A.Q., *Ibid.*

9. M.T. *Ibid.*, fol. 257b.

10. Rajasthan Archives, Jaipur, Uncatalogued *Pargana* Records. Amongst various *Dasturul amls, Khullas-ut Sayaq*, National Archives, New Delhi; *Farahauq-i-Kardani*, Ms. Orient Quart, 243, Berlin; also M.U. Aligarh; *Sayaq Nama* No. 858, *Daftar-i-Diwani*, Hydrabad, and *Makhazan-ul-khetsab*, Ms. Orient, fol. 217, Berlin, are the most outstanding.

11. *Ain*, Br. M. Add. 7652, fol. 148a; Blochman, Vol. II., p. 296. The theoretical size of the *jarib* remained the same at sixty *Gaz* but with the elimination of the element of contraction of *Gaz* to the ratio of four in every sixty *Gaz*, it increased the size of the *bigha* to 13%.

12. *Ibid.* The *Gaz-i-Ilahi* introduced in the 31st of the Ilahi era which replaced the Sikandari *Gaz* of 32 digits consisted of 41 digits. Moreland's (*Agrarian System*, p. 89) estimate of the increase in the bigha of the Ilahi *Gaz* over the Sikandari by 20% calculated in terms of 41 *angushta* (finger-breadths) is rather too arbitrary. Calculated on *Ain's* own statistics, the total increase of the *bigha* as against the Sikandari (hempen-roped *bigha*) was 22.1675% and after accounting for the 13% increasment of the bamboringed against the hempen-roped *Gaz*, the increasement of the *Ilahi-Gaz* over the *Sikandari-Gaz* was 9.1675% in terms of *bighas*. Thereafter, the adjustment of this difference thus caused in the size of the *bigha* was effected not only for assessment purposes but even for the pre-Ilahi *Gaz* land-grants. As such, of the latter, which were later confirmed from reign to reign, bear it out.

13. *Ibid*, fol. 148b; *Ibid.* p. 296.

14. Dr. P. Saran, in his *'Provincial Government under the Mughals'*, Moreland in *'Agrarian System of Moslem India,'* and Dr. I.H. Qureshi in his article

on the 'Pargana Administration under Akbar' (*Islamic Culture*, Vol. XVI., No. I., pp. 87-93), do not make any mention of the *tappahs* as a fiscal unit in the *pargana*.

15. '*Raqba-bandi*' documents of Akbar's reign, fols. 2a-76b.
16. This is clear from various original Chaknamahs with Khadims of Darga-Sharif, Ajmer.
17. Makhzan ul Ihetsab, Ms. O.R. fol. 217, Berlin, fols. 24a-24b.
18. *Ain*, Hamilton, Berlin, fol. 121b; *Akbar Nama*, Br. M.Add. 27, 247, fol. 332a puts the terms as '*Sihaya-i-Zabt*'.
19. *Ain, Ibid. Diwan-i-Pasand*, fol. 10b.
20. This is clear from the detailed description of the *qasbas* and their *mauzas* given for the *tappahs* in the above *Raqba-bandi* documents.Such an analysis is equally confirmed by the later documents viz. Delhi *Bedehi Subshjjat-i-Deccan* (Delhi Jhara) No: 1184 *Darftar-i-Diwani*, Hyderabad, fols. 19a-183a and the uncatalogued *pargana* documents in Rajasthan Archives, for the region of Aurangzeb.
21. An 18th century land revenue Persian Dictionary, Br. M. Add. 6603, fol. 55b, correctly defines *tappah* as a combination of few *mauzas*, and would be named after the largest of the *mauzas* under its jurisdiction. It puts this as an old practice introduced by the revenue experts for the covenience of flscal administration. As against this, Wilson's *Glossary* p. 817, gives too general a picture of the *tappah* as, 'Small tract or division of country smaller than a paragraph, but comprising one or more villages. In some parts of North West, it denotes a tract in which there is one principal town or a large village with lands and villages acknowledging the supermacy of one amongst them and forming a sort of corporate body, although not otherwise identical".
22. *Mirat-i-Sikandari*, Ms. Orient, Quart 1151, Berlin, fols. 309a, 359b, refer to the territorial divisions of *tappahs* in Gujrat before the annexation of the province of Gujrat.
23. *Ain*, Jarrett, Vol. II, p. 118, while giving details of the '*Dasturs*' i.e. Codes in force in the *mahals* of the *sarkar* of Lahore, *subah* Lahore, makes an incidental reference to the *tappah* Bharli, *tappah* Phulwari amongst the 16 *mahals* in the area of Punjab with one code. This proves the existences of the *tappah* as a territorial unit in Akbar's reign, which is further confirmed in details by the above *Raqba-bandi* documents. Also, Ms. No. Suppl, 482, Bibliotheque Nationale, Paris, fol. 157b,quoteş a *Parwana*, dated A.H. 991(1583 A.D.), for the rehabilitation of the village Kayara Kehra, *Tappah* Baraili, *Pargana Haveli* Baraili (*sarkar* Badaon, *subah* Delhi).
24. For the reigns of Shahjahan and Aurangzeb, various uncatalogued *Pargana* documents of R.A., Jaipur, confirm it. Besides this, various

Mss. bear it out. For Shahjahan's reign, *Padshah Nama* by Lahori, Ms. No. 565, K.B. Library, Patna, fol. 172a. *Maktubat-i-Khan-Jahan-i-Muzaffar Khan*, Br. M.Add. Rieu. 111837, Add. fols. 4a, 54b 120a; also *Makhzam-ul-Ihetsab*, Berlin, fols. 5b-6b. For Augangzeb's reign, *Malumat-Ul Ufaq* 354/124, Lytton collection, M.U. Aligarh, fol. 174a clearly quotes the divisions of the *subah* into "Sarkars, Parganat, Tappahjat and Chaklajat; also *Mirat-i- Ahemdi*, printed text, pp. 275-276.

25. R.A. Jaipur uncatalogued *pargana* documents.
26. The seat of the *tappah* and that of the *pargana* was always known as *qasba Raqba-bandi* Documents fols. 2a-76a; Also, Delhi *Bedehi Subhajat-i-Deccan*, C.R.O. Hyderabad, Ms. No. 1184, fols. 20a-187a.
27. *Makzan-ul Jhetsab*, Berlin, fol. 6a.
28. *Ibid*.
29. *Ibid*.
30. *Ibid*.

Chapter 14

Some Rare Persian Manuscripts and Documents on India (16th-18th Centuries) in the German Libraries

Dr. Rau, ladies and gentlemen,

I regard it a great privilege to have been invited to give a talk this evening at the Max Mueller Bhavan. I also want to express my gratitude to the West German Government which sponsored my visit to the German Libraries enabling me to consult Oriental Manuscripts relating to India. It is very little known to the scholars that some of the German Libraries have valuable collections of the Oriental Manuscripts in Sanskrit and Persian dealing with various aspects of the Indian Society and culture right from ancient times down to the 19th century. For my present talk, I shall confine myself to a few rare Persian Manuscripts and documents covering 16th to 18th centuries and comment on their importance.

The historians working on the medieval Indian History have so far relied on the manuscripts available in the Indian libraries, British Museum, London and other libraries in the United Kingdom. Though some use has been made of the Bibliotheque Nationale, Paris, no attention, however, has been paid to the rich collection of the Persian manuscripts available at the German libraries. At present in Germany, a good collection of the Persian manuscripts covering medieval Indian History is available at the Universitaetsbibliothek (University Libraries) of Bonn and Tuebingen, Bayerische Staatsbibilothek, Muenchen (Bavarian State Library, Munich), Westdeutsche Bibliothek (Ehemalige Preussische Staatsbibliothek) Marburg and Staatsbibliothek (State Library) Berlin East. Before the Second World War, an extremely valuable collection was made by

Max Mueller Bhavan Publications, 1964 Year Book, pp. 59-72.

the Staatsbibliothek Berlin but during the course of the war, the manuscripts were removed to two small towns, though important University centres, namely Marburg and Tuebingen.

A detailed catalogue of the Persian manuscripts in the Koenigliche Bibliothek, Berlin, published in 1888 A.D., is known in all the important libraries in Europe and India.[1] But the rich collection made after the publication of the catalogue was compiled in a comprehensive 'Handlist' which is available only in the Staatsbibliothek Berlin (East) whereas the manuscripts lie scattered at the above mentioned libraries in Tuebingen and Marburg. At present, a scholar could work on these manuscripts only after having consulted the 'Handlist' in Staatsbibliothek Berlin (East) which involves either way the crossing of the Berlin wall.

The valuable collection in the Staatsbiblothek Berlin was made in the course of the 19th and 20th centuries before the 2nd World War. On the scrutiny of the manuscripts, I found that many of these were purchased from the English civil or military officers of the East India Company, who while in service in India made fine personal collections and on return to England perhaps preferred to sell to the Staatsbibliothek Berlin than to the British Museum. Apart from this, many manuscripts were purchased in Bagdad and other Middle Eastern Muslim countries. Some of the valuable manuscripts having changed a few hands from India to these Muslim countries were ultimately purchased by the Staatsbibliothek, Berlin. In this paper, I would refer to just a few important manuscript throwing light on the social and economic conditions as well as the administrative system of North India from the late 16th to the late 18th centuries.

I. The first manuscript, so far unknown to any other library in Europe or India, is by some unknown writer on the *'Revaet,'* i.e. customs and social manners of the Indian people. This manuscript was written in 996 A.H./1587-88 A.D. It deals with the social manners and the religious beliefs of the various communities in Mughal India under Akbar. As such, it gives details of the various sects and the beliefs of Islam, Hinduism, Jainism, Buddhism and Zoroastrianism. In short, the manuscript narrates the social, ethical and religious life of the people of India at the close of the 16th century. As the reign of Akbar is extremely important from the viewpoint of theological discussions which took place at his court, the present manuscript, when collated with the other known sources of Akbar's reign, is bound to throw much light on the social, cultural and religious life of the people in the 16th century. I may also add that the manuscript under discussion is original and does not seem to be a transcribed copy of any other manuscript. This is an extremely important and rare unofficial source of Akbar's reign. The major portion of the manuscript is written in Persian and some parts are in contemporary Hindi.

II. The second manuscript under review is the *Ain-i-Akbari* of Abul fazl. Though the *Ain-i-Akbari* is fully known to all the Oriental libraries in India and abroad, the Hamilton Manuscript of Universitaesbibliothek Tuebingen is perhaps the earliest known to any library. The printed editions of Saiyid Ahmad (1855 A.D.) Nawal Kishore Press (Lucknow, 1869 and 1882) and Blochmann are quite well known and were not based on the best available manuscripts. Of the manuscripts of the *Ain-i-Akbari* in the British Museum, two of them (Rieu Add. 7652 and Add. 6552), copied rather accurately, belong to the late 17th century. The manuscript of Royal Asiatic Society, London (Persian 121, Morley 161), though dated 1656 A.D., is not accurately written. The other copies in the libraries of United Kingdom are either not carefully copied or belong to the 18th century.[2] In India, of the various copies of the *Ain-i Akbari* in the Tonk Collection available at National Archives of India, only one copy (No. 2011) was transcribed in the 17th century and is dated 1104 A.H./1693 A.D.[3] The Hamilton Manuscript of Universitaetsbibliothek Tuebingen is written in *Nastaliq*, i.e., a clear bold hand and the book is in an excellent condition. Before the main text of the *Ain-i Akbari*, there are two paintings attached on the leaves. The first painting is that of Akbar and Jahangir, the Mughal monarchs sitting on the thrones facing each other with two attendants standing below the thrones, the attendant in the right direction has a falcon (Baz) on his hand. The painting bears the title '*Akbar Badshah wa Jahangir Badshah*'. The second painting is that of Maharaja Birbal with a book in his left hand. The borders of the leaves and folios are in gold colour. The manuscript does not bear the name of the scribe nor does it mention the date of transcription. There is every reason to believe that the manuscript was written in Jahangir's reign and most likely belonged to the family of Maharaja Birbal which can only explain as to why the painting of Raja Birbal is affixed in the manuscript. Thus the Hamilton Manuscript of the *Ain-i Akbari* belongs to the early 17th century and, when read for the study of various aspects of Akbar's administrative system, clarifies various textual differences known from other manuscripts and helps us to interpret the text of the *Ain-i- Akbari* in a better perspective.

III. The third manuscript under reference is entitled, '*Nafaisul Muassar*' available at the Bayerische Staatsbibliothek, Munich.[4] This was written by Alaud Daula bin Hussaini in Akbar's reign in the year A.H. 973/1565-66 A.D. The author deals with miscellaneous topics. Though the manuscript is primarily a book on the poets and the writers of the age, it also gives description about some of the historical personalities of the times. At the same time, some of its portions are devoted to the political history. Apart from a narration of the political history of India, especially under the Mughals down to Akbar's conquest of Gujarat and Bengal, the author has given a brief description about the Emperor of Turkey, middle eastern Muslim countries and the Mughal relations with the Persian rulers. A copy of this manuscript is also available in the State Library of Rampur (U.P.) India.[5] The superiority and rarity of the Munich Manuscript lies in the fact that this copy was transcribed during the life time of the author and bears marginal notes on some of the folios by the author himself. Most likely, this is the original and the personal copy of the author. As such, this is the earliest and the most authentic version of '*Nafalsul Muassar*'.

IV. Fourthly, I would refer to a *Dasturulaml* of the 17th century named '*Makhzan-i-Ihetsab maaruf Dasturualml*'. This manuscript deals with the Mughal land revenue system in North India during the last years of Shahjahan's and the opening years of Aurangzeb's reigns. The manuscript was written in the 3rd Regnal year of the Aurangzeb's reign/1659-60 A. D. but the example and the drafts of revenue practices pertain to the period of Shah Jahan. The name of the author is not given but the note of the scribe shows that the manuscript was transcribed on the order of Col. Sir John Murray and the transcribed copy was completed in A.H. 1211/29th October, 1796 A.D. The author follows the usual method of giving *Dasturulaml* (code of conduct) for the daily life of a young man, for the routine of the Sultan, the functioning of the administrative departments of the state, the land revenue practices followed in various regions of North India. It may, however, be mentioned that an incomplete version of the same *Dasturulaml* is also available in the British Museum (Br. M. Rieu. 404, Add. 6599) of which a photostat copy has been procured by the Muslim University Aligarh Library.[6] The British Museum Manuscript does not contain the introductory chapter on the administrative system of the various Mughal departments. On the contrary, the Berlin Manuscript is complete and contains an extremely valuable chapter on the working of the land revenue system in the *Pargana, Tappah* and village organisations.[7]

V. Lastly, I would mention an extremely important collection of the Persian manuscripts of the 18th century dealing with the agrarian problems of Bengal, Bihar and Orissa.[8] The agrarian problems were highlighted by the British administrators when confronted with the entrenched position of the zamindars and the various other classes of assignees after the assumption of the Diwani rights in Bengal in 1765. In their well known controversy over the rights of the State versus the zamindars and other assignees, extremely divergent views were expressed by Warren Hastings, Sir Philip Frances, Mr. James Grant, Sir John Shore and Lord Cornwallis before the introduction of the Permanent Settlement in Bengal in 1793. The important portions of their respective Minutes were brought together by W. K. Firminger in his introduction to the Fifth Report from the Select Committee of the House of Commons on the Affairs of the East India Company (1812).[9] In support of their contention, each one of the above participants in the controversy tried to base his conclusions on the original position of the various assignees and the working of the land system during the Mughal age from the reign of Akbar down to the later Mughal period. Much less known hitherto, a huge analytical revenue literature in the Persian language, equally controversial in contents, was prepared by the expert Indian Munshis and revenue officials to provide background-material for the above mentioned discussion. Equally important commentaries in Persian on the working of the land system during the Mughal age were written by independent revenue experts. Most of this material produced by the Indian writers previously well preserved by the Staatsbibliothek Berlin is scattered in two libraries in Germany namely Tuebingen and Marburg and only a few copies are available in the British Museum.

The agrarian literature in Persian language by the revenue experts explains the various types of the landowners viz, the zamindars, *taaluqdars,* different categories of the *riaya* and the *muzarian* (i.e. tenants) different types of Jagirs viz. *tankhwah jagir, altambha, maafi, madad-i maash* and the types of the rent-free grants made by the zamindars. It runs into details on the question of the land rights of the State, the zamindars, *taaluqdars* and the *riaya.* Its importance is twofold, namely as a contemporary evidence of the agrarian problems of the 18th century and secondly as detailed historical analysis of the land revenue problems since the reign of Akbar. As a contemporary evidence, it is as important as the minutes of the Governor-General's Council in Bengal and the other contemporary writings included in the Firmiger's *Fifth Report* and its Introduction. For the 18th century, it quotes various Mughal Farmans and the revenue regulations enforced in the later Mughal period. However, the historical portion dealing with the late 16th and 17th centuries cannot be taken at its face value. All the same, when taken in collaboration with the contemporary 17th century source-material, it is likely to yield very important information. I have found that much information contained therein is confirmed by the 17th century documents now available for various regions of North India, especially the State Central Record Office, Bihar, Patna, State Records Office, Allahabad (U.P.) and Rajasthan Archives, Bikaner.

In the light of this source-material for the early English administrators in Bengal, the importance of some of the historical portions of the writings of the English administrators is confirmed. For example, the minutes of Sir John Shore have been criticised on the plea that he did not understand the Persian language and could not possibly understand the *Ain-i Akbari.* It is rather significant to observe that a simple working knowledge of the Persian language on the part of any English administrator so as to read the *Ain-i Akbari* would not enable him to understand the genesis of the Mughal revenue system. The *Ain-i Amal Guzar* and the chapters on the accounts of the provinces in the *Ain-i-Akbari* do not explain the entire land revenue system under Akbar in Bengal or any other province of India. Even for the analysis of the system under Akbar, we have to essentially bank on the 17th century original sources. The English administrators empolyed the most intelligent method of seeking expert advice given by the revenue experts in Persian revenue technical terminology and the system prevalent in the Mughal age. Such source material was translated in English with the help of the translators. Many manuscripts under discussion bear the translated phrases in the personal handwriting of English administrators. In this respect, I would suggest that Sir John Shore was well equipped with the knowledge of the indigenous revenue system with Sayyid Gulam Hussain as his revenue consultant.[10] Much revenue system literature was compiled for the assistance of Sir John Shore which is clearly stated in the manuscripts. A minute comparison of the Minutes of Sir John Shore and the contemporary revenue literature in Persian compiled for him shows remarkable similarity in ideas. Firminger, in his Introduction, has criticised Sir John Shore's Minutes for his notions on the pattern of Mughal revenue system and the assessment rates fixed at ½, 1/3, 2/5th, ¼, of the gross produce for the grain crops and the application of the sliding scale going as low as 1/8th for certain cash crops.[11] We know from the above mentioned revenue literature that if any fault has to be found, it would lie more with Sayyid Gulam Hussain, the revenue consultant of Sir John Shore. A scrutiny of the Bihar and Rajasthan Archives of the 2nd half of the 17th century for the territories in the Subahs of Bihar, Delhi, Ajmer, Malwa and Agra shows that the views of Sayyid Gulam Hussain and Sir John Shore on the pattern of the Mughal revenue assessment rates were perfectly correct and that Firminger's criticism is unjustified.

The revenue literature under discussion also reveals the limitations of the English administrators to understand various intricate and technical aspects of the Mughal revenue system. Sir John Shore thought that his main achievement lay in the fact of getting the recognition of the proprietorship of the zamindars.[12] Sayyid Gulam Hussain is quite clear on his analysis of the meaning of the term *malik,* i.e., proprietor when associated with the zamindar would not mean an absolute proprietor of the agrarian lands but responsible for the realisation of the revenues of his *zamindari* villages and to enjoy perquisites (*haquq* and *rasum*) in lieu thereof.[13] The right of revenue collection on behalf of the State and the entitlement to perquisites was considered a hereditary claim based on the idea of ownership (*malkiyat*). A zamindar could be divested of this right of ownership of a village only on grounds of gross negligence or recalcitrance.[14] A zamindar may be proprietor of the lands in the self-developed villages.[15] The English administrators could understand the meaning of the ownership of *zamindari* only in the English concept of the rights in property and essentially associated the hereditary ownership of the *zamindari* with proprietary right in the lands therein. Tired of prolonged discussion over *zamindari* rights, Warren Hastings conceded the right of proprietorship and inheritance to the lands on the part of the zamindars though he asserted the claim of the East India Company over the revenues of the *zamindari* lands and the power of the government to dispossess the zamindars "On any failure in the payment of their rents, not only *protempore,* but in perpetuity."[16] More than this, Philips Francis, Sir John Shore and Boughton Rous asserted the proprietory rights of the zamindars in the soil of *zamindari* lands.[17] Though all these administrators rightly repudiated James Grant's thesis of the proprietary claim of the sovereign over the *zamindari* estates,[18] none of them could appreciate the Mughal connotation of *zamindari malkiyat* (ownership) which meant the hereditary proprietary rights of the zamindars over the revenue collection and entitlement to the perquisites rather than proprietary title to the soil of the *zamindari* villages. Even Sir John Shore, who was considered to be a great expert on the Mughal land system in Bengal, could not properly comprehend the nature of the *malkiyat* (ownership) rights of the zamindars and the *ryots* of varying categories. Sir John Shore did not surrender the right of the State to regulate the terms of tenure involved between the zamindars and the *ryots* as well as the State's right to prescribe the rate of assessment to be levied upon the *ryots*. But in this context, he considered the *zamindari* lands as the partial property of the zamindars.[19] Lord Cornwallis equally asserted the State's right for the regulation of relationship between the zamindars and the *ryots* and the fixation of the rate of revenue assessment. However, in refutation of Sir John Shore's opinion, he contended that such a claim on the part of the State was not incompatible with the full proprietary rights of the zamindars over the lands of their *zamindari* villages.[20] Of course, it cannot be denied that both with Sir John Shore and Lord Cornwallis, political and administrative consideration were the guiding factors for framing the economic policy of India. Their primary consideration in recognising the zamindars as the proprietors of the lands was to ensure a stable amount of revenue for the State as well as to create a class of proprietary landlords who would in time of conflict stand by the British government. But the creation of the proprietary rights of the zamindars at the cost of the landed rights of the *riaya* and the cultivating tenants was against the canons of pre-British social structure and customary laws (*Rivaj-i Am)* of the agrarian society in Bengal, Bihar and Orissa. All this is clear from the above mentioned 18th cenury documents.

In the end, I would suggest that with the proper utilisation of all this source-material in Persian available in the above mentioned German libraries, it is possible to reconstruct the Revenue History of Bengal, Bihar and Orissa during the 18th century. This is not to belittle the importance of the already published works on the revenue history based on purely English sources.[21] The source-material in the Persian language under discussion gives a comprehensive analysis of the socio-economic structure and the land revenue problems in the prè-British era. It also makes detailed comments on the English innovations and offers a comparative study of the pre-British and post-British land revenue problems during the second half of the 18th century.[22]

References

1. Verzeichniss der persischen Handschriften der Koeniglichen Bibliothek zu Berlin, von Wilhelm Pertsch, Berlin. A.A. Sher & Co. 1888. Also, Pertsch Persische Handschriften, S. 1-674 Nr. 1-669, 1888; Pertsch, Persische Handschriften, S. 675-1283. Nr. 670, ff Register, 1888.

2. Also see comments by Dr. Irfan Habib in his bibliographical notes in *The Agrarian System of Mughal India,* p. 411. In his comparative evaluation of the Mss. of the *Ain*, Dr. Habib has not included the Hamilton Ms. Tuebingen (West Germany), the Ms. of the Bibliotheque National, Paris and the Tonk Collection of National Archives of India.

3. National Archives of India, New Delhi. In the Tonk Collection there are in all seven copies of the *Ain-i-Akbari*. Of these, Ms. no. 2011 is the earliest in transcription, dated, A.H. 1104/1693 A.D. All other Mss. belong to either 18th or 19th century.

4. Bayerische Staatsbibliothek, Muenchen, Ms. no. 3 of the published catalogue of Persian Mss.

5. State Library, Rampur (U.P. India), *Tazkra-i-Shohra-i Farsi* no. 97.

6. History Seminar Library, Muslim University Aligarh (India), Photograph no. 109, new serial no. 53.

7. The British Museum (Ms. Rieu. 404; Add 6599) has a regular introduction and has in all 132a folios. Apparently, the British Museum Ms. looks complete having been transcribed on 27th October, 1786 A.D. (vide fol. 132a). However, the introductory chapter on the administrative system available in the Berlin Ms. cannot be traced in it. It is possible that either the scribe of the British Museum Ms. omitted it or the scribe of the Berlin Ms. added it of his own from some other independent contemporary *Dasturulaml* of the 17th century.

8. Some of the important Mss. of the Staatsbibliothek Berlin (East) are, *'Nuskha Hai Bar Kafiat-in Subah Behar; Nuskha Majumauhat; Sawalat-i-Zamin Kiast az Mister John Shore; Dar Bab-i-Nuskha Sarusa Hukm, Tawarikh-i-Badhsahan-i Hind az ibtda-i Shah Timur baghayat Shah Alam; Majmuha-i Mutfarika, Akhbar ul Sadiq dar Kafiat Bengala Darj Ast.'*

9. *The Fifth Report from the Select Committee of the House of Commons on the Affairs of the East India Company,* July 1812, 2 vols. edited by W.K. Firminger, 1917 edition. Introduction, vol. 1, p. 1812, 2 vols. edited by W. K. Firminger, 1917 edition. Introduction vol. 1, pp. iii-li; Firminger's Historical Introduction to the Bengal Portion of the Fifth Report on East India Affairs, pp. CCI; James Grant's *Historical and Comparative Analysis of the Finance of Bengal,* dated 27th April 1786, vol. II, p. 170; Original Minutes of the Governor-General in Council 1776, with a plan for the settlement of the revenues of Bengal, *vide* Introduction, Chapters XXV-XXVI. Vol. I, pp. CCXViii-CCCXviii, Sir John Shore,

Minute, dated 18th June, 1789, " respecting the Permanent Settlement of the Lands in the Bengal Provinces" vol. II, *Land Revenue History of Bengal'* (Clarendon Press, Oxford, 1917), pp. 42-70. Other Minutes, *vide* Firminger, vol. II, pp. 478-510, 515-18, 734-36, 737-57; Minutes of Lord Cornwallis, *Ibid.*, Vol. II, pp. 510-15, 518-27, 527-50. Also, Bengal Permanent Settlement Regulation 1 of 1793. Also, Bihar Secretariat, Patna, Letter from Mr. Becher to the Hon'ble President, dated 24.5.1769; Letter from R. Adir, Collector, District Bhagalpur to Sir John Shore, President and Members of the Board of Revenue Nos. 35, dated 16-7-1787; 42, dated 18-8-1787; 50, dated 7-9-1787, 51, dated 9-9-1787; 55, dated 1787; B.H. Baden-Powell, 'Is the State the Owner of All Land in India?' *Asiatic Quarterly Review*, New Series - Vol. VIII, Nos. 15 and 16 July-Oct. 1894, pp. 1-20; James Mill, *History of British India*, Vol. V, Chaps. V & VI.

10. Sayyid Gulam Hussain is mentioned to be an expert revenue Munshi (official) to the Government. It is not exactly clear as to who this person was. It seems that he was the same person who was the author of *Siyar al-Mutaakhirin.*

11. W.K. Firminger, *'The Fifth Report'*, I, *op. cit.* Introduction, pp. xxviii-xxiv; Compare it with Sir John's Minute, dated 18th June, 1789, vide the Fifth Report, II, Appendix no. I; also, J Shore: Minute of April, 1788 in J.H. Harington, *'An Elementary Analysis of the Laws and Regulations'* Calcutta, 1814-15, vol. II, pp. 233-34.

12. Sir John Shore's Minute, dated 18th June, 1789 vide f.n. 11, para 8, p. 3.

13. Ms. or fol. 234, Berlin; Ms. or quart 216, Berlin.

14. For details see my Papers vide f.n. 22.

15. Ms. or Oct. 113, Berlin.

16. Vide *G.W. Forest's Selections from the State Papers of the Governor General of India*, Vol. II., reproduced from the *Fifth Report*, Introduction, p. XXXVII.

17. The *Fifth Report*, Introduction, *op. cit*, Shore's Minute, dated 18th June, 1789, Vol. II, Appendix I, *op. cit*, para 8, p. 3; C.W. Boughton Rous, *Dissertation Concerning the Landed Property of Bengal*, London, 1791.

18. James Grant, *'Historical and Comparative Analysis of the Finance of Bengal,'* dated 27th April, 1786 vide the *Fifth Report*, Vol. II, p. 170. Also see f.n. 9.

19. Sir John Shore's Minute of 21st December 1789, Para 13 *vide 'Extracts From the Proceedings of the Select Committee of the House of Commons on East Indian Affairs, 1832, Bearing on the Position of Zemindars and Cultivators Bengal; From the Records of the East India House, 1820; and From the Fifth Report of the Select Committee, 1812 (Madras)'*, pp. 264-66.

20. Views of Marquis Cornawllis, *vide Extracts (Ibid)*, pp. 265-66.

21. See S. Bhattacharya, '*The East India Company and, the Economy of Bengal from* 1704 to 1740', London, 1954; K.K. Datta, '*Survey of india's Social Life and Economic Condition in the Eighteenth Century* (1707-1813)', Calcutta, 1961; N.K. Sinha, *The Economic History of Bengal from Plassey to the Permanent Settlement,'* Vol. II, Calcutta, 1962.

22. The present author is the first writer to utilise this 18th century source material in collation with other original documents of the Mughal age from the 16th to the 18th centuries and has already written three Papers, viz. "Nature of Land Rights in Mughal India" vide *The Economic and Social History Review*, Vol. I, July-September 1963. Delhi School of Economics, Delhi, pp. 1-23; the 2nd Paper entitled, "Nature of *Dehat-i-Taaluqa* (*zamindari* villages) and the Evolution of the *Taaluqdari* System during the Mughal age" is under publication with the same Journal (Sept.-Dec., 1964 issue);'*The Evolution of the Taaluqdari System in Bengal and Awadh, during the 17th and 18th Centuries*', under publication with the University of Wisconsin (U.S.A.) in its Proceedings of a Colloquium on 'the Influence of Social Organization on Land Revenue in india', 1964.

Chapter 15

J.N. Sarkar and W.H. Moreland on the Mughal Land Revenue Administration: An Estimate

During the late 18th and 19th centuries, reflections were made by the Indian Mughals and the English administrator- scholars on various aspects of the Mughal land revenue administration but no professional historian ever dealt with the subject in a comprehensive manner. In the first half of the 20th century, the two well known scholars, the late Sir J.N. Sarkar and W.H. Moreland, worked on Mughal India.[1] As contemporaries, one was an Indian professional historian and the other initially an English civil servant posted in India ultimately developed into an historian.

In the beginning of the 20th century, Sir J.N. Sarkar assiduously devoted himself to the Mughal age and produced monumental works on the political history of the period. Sarkar also showed interest in the administrative structure of the Mughal Empire[2] but in this respect his achievment is rather little. On the revenue side, he banked on the *Ain-i Akbari, Mirat-i Ahmadi,* a few *Dasturulamals* and chronicles of the late 17th and 18th centuries. Even on the basis of this material, he could not properly analyse the Mughal land revenue terminology embodied in the Persian texts. In his book on Mughal Administration, there is no coherence in the sketchy chapters on the land revenue administration.[3] There is more of a collection of anecdotes from the contemporary manuscripts rather than a presentation of any co-ordinated picture of the agrarian system. Of the two *Farmans* of Aurangzeb's reign which Sarkar discovered from the Royal Library, Berlin, and published in the *Journal of the Royal Asiatic Society* and later on included in his book on the *Mughal Administration,*[4] the *Farman* to Mohammad Hashim had already been rightly used by Col. *Galloway,* [5] a fact not known to Sarkar. The

Persian texts of the copies of these *Farmans* and especially the commentaries thereupon are rather unreliable. Though the late 18th century revenue literature available from the Berlin Library is extremely useful for the 18th century History of Bengal and Bihar, it cannot be accepted for the 16th-17th centuries without further scrutiny.[6] Moreover, the differences in the revenue practices in Bengal and other regions of North India have to be clearly emphasised. Even though the late 18th century Indian revenue experts in Bengal did have an access to some of the *Farmans* and *Dasturulamals* of the Mughal age, not all the commentaries written by them provide a correct analysis of the revenue practices of the Mughal age. Some of the commentaries were written to suit the firm notions and predilections of the British revenue administrators who were participants to the great controversy over the land rights of the State versus zamindars prevalent in Bengal before the enforcement of the Permanent Settlement. Having laid his hand on the two widely publicized documents of Aurangzeb's reign and being completely ignorant of the other revenue literature lying in the Berlin Library, Sarkar could not go into the background of the commentaries written in late18th century Bengal and was not in a position to arrive at any conclusive truth. Notwithstanding all this, Sarkar's translation and published commentaries on the *Farmans* have been accepted by the later scholars without any further screening of the problem. Some of the late 18th century Indian *munshis* had well appreciated the main aspects of the Mughal land revenue administration but these portions of the revenue literature were not covered. Sarkar also revised and annotated Blochmann's recension of the *Ain-i-Akbari,* previously translated by H.S. Jarrett.[7] Even this is not free from serious errors. The revenue terminology included in the third chapter of Abul Fazl's *Ain-i Akbari* is mostly inaccurate. The definitions are are based more upon the foreign Islamic practices and the already written glossaries rather than upon the Mughal revenue documents. This has consequently given rise to various controversies and imaginary surmises reflected in the modern historical writings on the Mughal land revenue system.

In fact W.H. Moreland was the first scholar to undertake an intensive study of the Mughal agrarian system and his pioneer works have laid the students of the Indian economic history under lasting gratitude for having shown considerable enthusiasm for providing an overall picture of the Mughal age. However, his verdict is not final. Moreland was a keen student of economics and a trained English civil servant posted in the United Provinces in India. In his early work on *The Revenue Administration of the United Provinces,* [8] he made a genuine attempt to trace the legacy of the Indian land revenue system since the earliest times and its evolution under the British rule in the 19th and early 20th centuries. Moreland's approach was essentially didactic. This general historical sketch served the purpose of showing some continuity of the agrarian problems inherited from the earlier times. Apart from it, the technique of comparing the land revenue system of the medieval age with the 19th-20th centuries revenue system in India and the emphasis on the improvement brought by the British administration upon the former in various respects with historical illustrations was motivated by the keen desire to show the superiority of the British revenue administration over the past Indian revenue administration in the country. This book was also intended to serve as a handy guide for the English revenue officials in dealing with the 20th century agrarian problems relating to the landlords and the cultivators, especially when these problems were visualised in the historical perspective. However, it is doubtful if Moreland at this stage could clearly comprehend the clearcut changes which had occurred during the course of the 18th century and had sufficiently blurred the main features of the Mughal land revenue administration. Despite all his shortcomings in the proper analysis of the 16th-17th centuries Mughal revenue administration, Moreland cut the gordian knot by undermining the mere narration of the political and the military history of India. He emphasised the primary role of the economic forces in the Indian history. He stressed the fact that agriculture formed the main occupation of the people in the rural society and was the chief source of revenues of an Indian state. This was a determinate economic factor in the past Indian society. An emphasis on this aspect permeates all his subsequent writings.

The evolution of Moreland from the role of an administrator to that of an economic historian is a gradual one. By the time Moreland and Yusuf Ali published their joint paper on *'Akbar's Land Revenue System on the Basis of the Ain-i Akbari,* Moreland had developed a genuine interest in the Mughal land revenue administration. As a follow up, *India at the Death of Akbar, India From Akbar to Aurangzeb* and the *Agrarian System of Moslem India* were essentially based on historical research and Moreland was par excellence an economic historian.[9] He gradually discarded the moral tone and comparisons of the condition of the peasantry during the British rule with the Mughal age. He ultimately developed the technique of historical research but even to the last he never shook off his leaning for looking for only such source-material which he could interpret so as to suit his predilections and imperialist outlook. As an expert revenue officer, Moreland possessed considerable practical knowledge to steer through the difficult aspects of the problems in hand. Apart from it, he took to the comparative study of the different texts of the *Ain-i Akbari* available to him, contemporary chronicles, accounts of the foreign travellers, a few Mughal *Farmans* and *Dasturulamals*. All the same, Moreland's technique of historical research was circumscribed by his narrow concept of interpretation. The reading of the technical passages of the *Ain-i- Akbari* is by no means an easy one. There is no denying the fact that when Moreland wrote, practically no archival revenue source-material of the 17th century was available and it is both very difficult and risky to formulate theories without understanding the correct meaning of the revenue terminology. In the absence of contemporary documents, a technical historian is obliged to be less rigid in his interpretation.

The fact that Moreland had vast revenue experience of the modern times in a way also proved a partial handicap as in the interpretation of the ambiguous passages, he was greatly tempted to rely on imagination. This can be well illustrated with a few examples. While interpreting *Jama Deh Sala* (Ten Year Settlement), Moreland considers that the word *Jama* in the passage does not stand for an assessed demand but refers only to the problem of the fixation of new valuation.[10] When the tables of the cash schedule rates *(Dasturs)* immediately follow the description of the *Jama Deh Sala,* Moreland gets involved in a difficulty. He finds that the passage starting with the problem of price commutation further narrates the procedure of the fixation of valuation and surprisingly ends with the tables of the cash schedule rates. Moreland does not consider the possibility of reading *jama* both as a valuation and an assessed demand (based on assessment schedule rates) to be interpreted in the context of the passage and still insists that the text of the passage stands for valuation. He gets disgusted with Abul Fazl and wriggles out with the solution that the *Ain-i Akbari* is defective and the text must be corrupt. Here is an example of an overconfidence on the part of a revenue expert who takes liberty with the technique of historical research. As regards the incidence of the State demand in Aurangzeb's reign, the royal *Farman* to Rasik Das Karori (of Bihar) underlines the assessment to be enforced at the varying rates of 1/2, 1/3 and 2/5 (of the gross produce) according to the situation (dependent on the classification of land). Moreland contends that the aforesaid *Farman* made only a theoretical enunciation of the variation in the assessment rates whereas the actual demand was made nearer the maximum than the minimum.[11] Even though Moreland had no contemporary documentary evidence to reject the statement made in the *Farman,* he did so relying purely on his revenue experience for looking after the increase in the State revenues from the official viewpoint. The original *pargana* documents now available at the Rajasthan Archives, Bikaner, putting the above mentioned variation in the State demand [12] show Moreland was completely wrong in his presumption. Moreland did not understand as to how the revenue demand based on a detailed classification of the soil and the crops was levied under the Mughal regulations. His reliance on the general statements embodied in the *Ain-i Akbari* and Aurangzeb's *Farmans* fixing the incidence of revenue demand at 1/3rd and 1/2 of the gross produce under Akbar and Aurangzeb respectively[13] as uniform rates regardless of the nature of the land and the crops is rather misplaced. In fact, these rates represent the highest pitch of the revenue demand for the grain crops but the detailed sliding scale schedule rates were governed by the nature of the soil and the crops in a particular region and the variation in the demand could exist even within a single village. The schedule rates of the cash crops *(Jins-i-Kamil)* were comparatively much less, though based on the same principles of the classfication of the land and the nature of the crops. This is ultimately bound to affect our estimate on the economic impact of the revenue demand on the condition of the peasantry during the Mughal age. Moreland's analysis of the methods of assessment of the *Zabti* and the *Nasa* based on the reading of the *Ain-i-Akbari* are far from accurate.[14] Moreland has wrongly defined the *Nasa* as 'group assessment' or 'lump sum' assessment on the village or a *pargana* by agreement with the Headmen while leaving to the latter the distribution of the assessed demand on the holding of the peasants. He also takes a very rigid view about the scope and extent of the prevalence of the above mentioned methods of assessment during the Mughal age. He thinks that the most favoured method of assessment under Akbar was the *Zabti* and that the *Nasa,* comprising 'village group-assessments' and 'annual summary assessments' had become the working rule during Aurangzeb's reign. The two fixed poles for his study are the *Ain-i Akbari* and Auragzeb's *Farman* to Rasik Das Karori. He forgets that revenue practices do not disappear in such a sudden manner at the discretion of the monarchs. The *Zabti* method continued to operate throughout the Mughal rule and it co-existed with other methods of assessment.

Moreland was quite conscious of the generality of the terms like the zamindars and *riaya* and preferred to put the term peasants for the agricultural *riaya.*[15] He correctly refused to be drawn in the theoretical and legal versions about the land ownership-a controversy which had engrossed most of the writers ever since the late 18th century.[16] But he was unable to run into the details of the various classes of the agriculturists connected with the land. He did not understand the varying nature of the land tenures in the *zamindari* and the *riayati* villages during the Mughal age.[17] He looked upon the question of ownership of the land simply as vesting the peasantry with occupancy rights and beyond this he had no contemporary data to throw any light on this issue. He left this important problem unsettled. Despite his reluctance to be drawn in an abstract discussion, whether the Mughal system was based on the *zamindari* or *ryotwari* principles, his rough analogical association of a few features with either of the patterns[18] is rather too vague. The obsession of finding intermittent periods during the Muslim era, when the state either directly dealt with the peasants or through the Headmen and the village 'group assessment' method (especially after the mid-17th century),[19] smacks of lack of clear understanding of the working of the Mughal revenue administration and the role of the landed intermediaries during the Mughal age. His worst error was the conformation to the traditional three-fold division of the Mughal territories into *khalisa, jagir* and the semi -independent or automous Chieftainships.[20] Moreland could not properly comprehend the scope of the Mughal land revenue operations in the territories of the Hindu Chiefs *(zamindaran-i-umda* etc.), the demarcation of the *amli* and *gairamli* areas and the extent to which they were assignable to the Mughal state officials or to the Chiefs *(*zamindars*)* themselves in lieu of their services to the Mughal state. [21]His belief that a Hindu Chieftainship *(zamindari)* like the Mewar continued to run revenue administration on purely traditional Hindu notions of goverance uninfluenced by the Mughal System[22] is not confirmed by the documentary evidence. Moreland failed to realise the change in the position and the internal revenue organisation of the territories of the Hindu Chiefs which had occurred during the Mughal age. If the territories of the Hindu Rajput Chiefs of varying degrees *(zamindaran-i-umda,* zamindars etc.) are not considered a part of the Mughal revenues, it belies the entire understanding of the Mughal pattern of the land revenue administration. Moreover, Moreland's main thesis that the concept of the Mughal state like the earlier Muslim governments failed to provide political and social environment for the agricultural development and annual production of the country[23] is completely fallacious. His assertion that the high pitch of the revenue demand, the constant conflict between the administration and the peasants, the depopulation of the agricultural areas in one locality or another, repression of the individual energy strained the existing revenue system to the breaking point and brought about general economic collapse[24] after the middle of the 17th century are all questionable surmises which are not essentially borne by the contemporary archival evidence. All these problems need a further probe based on a scientific study keeping in view the political as well as the sociological and ethnological backgrounds of the various regions of the Mughal Empire. Equal consideration has to be paid to the concepts of the agricultural production on the part of the State and the peasants, the ratio in availability of the land for further tillage vis-a-vis population , the incidence of the revenue demand based on a detailed classification of the land and other socio-economic factors which played dominant role during the Mughal age.

Moreland's reliance on the testimony of the foreign traveller for an account on the life of the peasantry [25] is partial. The foreign travellers did not understand the concept of the land ownership in India and found institutional differences from their own countries. They asserted that unless the land ownership be vested in the hands of the nobility, the agrarian evils were bound to occur.[26]They suffered from European complexes and made contradictory remarks about the people of India. Bernier's account of the hardship and the widespread flight of the peasantry[27] is definitely exaggerated. Bernier had a motive to present deliberately an inaccurate picture of the patterns of the agrarian societies in the Asian countries in order to humour the French government about the superiority of the European and especially the French landed structure and civilisation which was the apex of European culture during the 17th century. Unless the accounts of the travellers are subjected to scrutiny on the basis of their motivations and their limitations to understand the Indian way of rural life are borne in mind, a reliance upon them for the analysis of Mughal India is extremely risky. This was Moreland's greatest shortcoming. Moreland did not try to understand the ethnic and sociological background of medieval India. He has not dealt with the *zamindari* settlements based on tribal and clannish structure - a fact which gives a real clue to the understanding of the rural society and the agrarian history of Mughal India.[28] Moreland did not try to go beneath the *pargana* level. Even his account of the machinery of the revenue collection is too sketchy.[29] He made no attempt to analyse the socio-economic factors which affected the life of the people in the villages and *qasbas,* which in many a region came to be vitally connected with the cities.[30] The spread of trade and commerce had tremendous impact upon the cultivation of the cash crops and role of cash nexus in the collection of the State revenues. Moreland's main merit was that he explained the land revenue system under the Mughals in the background of the ancient and the early medieval periods of Indian history so as to give a co-ordination picture of the agrarian features through the ages. But he failed to realise the momentum of the socio-economic forces at work during the 17th century. Many a view and conclusion of Moreland on the agrarian problems during the Mughal age need radical modification.

References

1. For the biographical sketch and works of Sarkar, see details vide *Sir Jadunath Sarkar Commemoration Volume,* published by the Punjab University, Hoshiarpur (India), 1958. For Moreland, see J.B. Harrison, 'Notes on W.H. Moreland as Historian', vide *Historians of India, Pakistan and Ceylon,* edited by C.H. Phillips, London, 1961, pp. 310-318.
2. J.N. Sarkar, *Mughal Administration* , Calcutta, 1920 (4th edition, 1952); only book on the Mughal Administration. The other book, which narrates some of the administrative problems, is translation of *Ahkam-i-Alamgiri* entitled *Anecdotes of Aurangzeb.* Also see, *Studies in Aurangzeb's Reign.*
3. *Ibid.* pp. 65-90, 146-160, 177-198, 246-254.
4. J.N. Sarkar, 'The Revenue Regulations of Aurangzeb', *Journal and Proceedings of the Asiatic Society of Bengal,* New Series, Vol. II, 1906, pp. 223-237. The Journal also includes the Persian texts of Aurangzeb's *Farmans* to Muhammad Hashim and Rasik Dass Karori reproduced from a manuscript of the Royal Library, Berlin. Also, *Mughal Administration.*
5. Col. Galloway, *Observations on the Law and Constitution of India of the Nature of the Ceded Tenures and the System of Revenue and Finance as Established by the Moohummudun Law and Moughal Government with an Enquiry into the Revenue and Judicial Administration and Regulations of Police in Bengal,* London, 1825. Also, Aurangzeb's *Farman* to Mohammad Hashim, printed in *Mirat-i-Ahmadi,* Vol. I, pp. 268-270.
6. See detailed comments vide my Paper in 'Some Rare Persian Manuscripts and Documents (16th-18th Centuries) in the German Libraries', *Max Mueller Bhavan Publications, 1964 Year book,* pp. 59-72.
7. *Ain-i- Akbari,* Vol. II, translated into English, H.S. Jarrett, 2nd ed., corrected and further annotated by Sir J.N. Sarkar, Calcutta, 1949.

8. W. H. Moreland, *The Revenue Administration of the United Provinces*, Allahabad, 1911, *Notes on the Agricultural Conditions and Problems of the United Provinces*, (revised upto 1911), Allahabad, 1913.

9. W.H. Moreland and Yusuf Ali, 'Akbar's Land Revenue System as Described in the *Ain-i-Akbari*', *Journal of the Royal Asiatic Society of Great Britain and Ireland (JRAS)*, London, 1918, pp. 1-42; W.H Moreland, *India at the Death of Akbar*, London, 1920, reprinted, Delhi, 1962; *Akbar to Aurangzeb*, London, 1923; *The Agrarian System of Moslem India*, Cambridge, 1929, reprinted Allahabad (heretofore *The Agrarian System)*; Moreland and Chaterjee, A.C., *Short History of India*, London. For the other papers contributed by Moreland, see 'The Agricultural Statistics of Akbar's Empire', *Journal of the U.P. Historical Society*, Lucknow, June 1919, Vol. Part I, pp. 1-8; 'The *Ain-i-Akbari*-A Possible Base-line for the Economic History of Modern India',*Indian Journal of Economics*, Allahabad, I, 1916, pp. 44-53. 'Prices and Wages under Akbar', *JRAS*, 1917, pp. 815-825; 'The Value of Money at the Court of Akbar', *JRAS*, 1918, pp. 375-385; 'The Development of the Land Revenue System of the Moughal Empire', *JRAS*, 1922, pp. 19-35; 'Akbar's Land Revenue Arrangements in Bengal, *JRAS*, 1926, pp. 43-56; 'Sher Shah's Revenue System,; *JRAS*, 1926, pp. 447-59; 'The *Pargana* Headman (Chaudri) of the Moughal Empire', *JRAS*, Oct. 1938, pp. 511-521. For Moreland's translation of the accounts of the foreign travellers and editiorial comments on the Mughal land revenue system, see *The Remonstrantie, Franscisco* Pelsaret (in Dutch-1626 AD), tr. Moreland and Geyl. *Jahangir's India.* Combridge, 1925; *Wellebrand Geleynssen de Jongh, Verclaringe ende Bevinding, etc.*, extracts translated, *Journal of Indian History (JIH).* IV, 1925-26, pp. 69-83; *Peter Floris, His Voyage to the East Indies on the Globe, 1611-15*, Hakluyt Society, 2nd Series, LXXIV, London, 1934; *John Van Twist, A General Description of India* (in Dutch-1638 AD) extracts translated, JIH, XVI, Madras, August 1937; 'Indian Exports of Cotton Goods in the Seventeenth Century', *Indian Journal of Economics*, Vol. V, pp. 63-77.

10. Moreland, *The Agrarian System*, pp. 248-49, 251-54; Moreland and Ali, 'Akbar's Land Revenue System' vide fn. 9; for original text, see *Ain-i-Akbari*, Br. M. Add. 6552 for 145a, Ms. Hamilton, Berlin, fol. 136a; *Akbar Nama*, Br. M. add 26, 207, fol. 119a, Ms. Br. M. OR. 27, 247, fol. 304a.

11. Moreland, *The Agrarian System*, p. 135; For Aurangzeb's *Farman* to Rasik Das Karori, See Ms. or. Quart. 259, Berlin, fols. 56a-56b; Ms. or.Oct. 113f, fol. 2a; *Nigar Nama-i-Munshi*, Ms. Pers. e I. Bodlein, Oxfd. fol. 127a.

12. Rajasthan Archives, Jaipur(now at Bikaner), See Pargana Documents of Aurangzeb's reign relating to *Malio-Jihat wa Sair-Jihat* and *Yaddasht-i Haqiqat-i Arazi wa Uftada.*

13. Moreland, *The Agrarian System*, pp. 113, 135; also Moreland and Yusuf Ali's paper vide fn. 9; for original texts, see *Ain-i-Akbari*, Br. M.Add. 7652, fols 148-150a; Ms. Hamillton, Berlin, fol. 125a-b; *Dastur ul aml-i*

Navsindgi, Br. M. Add. 6641, fols 182b-184b; *Khulasatu-s Siyaq,* Ms National Archives of India, pp. 25-27.

14. *Ibid.,* pp. 86, 97-98, 110-117, 120-121, 148-150, 235-36, 248-49, 251-54; also Moreland and Ali (vide fn. 9) pp. 24-25, 28-30; Moreland, *Land Revenue Arrangement in Bengal* (vide fn. 9).
15. *Ibid.,* pp. 2-3, 189-200.
16. See details vide my paper on 'Nature of Land-Rights in Mughal India', *The Indian Economic and Social History Review,* Vol. I, No. I, July-September, 1963, pp. 1-23, f.n.s. 1-4.
17. See details vide my paper 'Nature of *Dehat-i Taaluqa (zamindari* villages) and the Evolution of the *Taaluqdari* System during the Mughal Age', *The Indian Economic and Social History Review,* Vol. II, No. 2, April 1965, pp. 166-177; Vol. II No. 3, July 1965, pp. 269-288.
18. Moreland, *The Agrarian System,* pp. 4-6, 205-07.
19. *Ibid.* pp. 113, 122, 135-38, 160-68, 175-79, 203-07.
20. *Ibid.* pp. 13, 118-23, 141-204.
21. See details vide my paper, 'Nature of Land-Rights in Mughal India', (vide fn. 16), pp. 10-14, f.n.s. 60-70.
22. See fn. 20.
23. Moreland, *The Agrarian System,* pp. 207-08.
24. *Ibid.* pp. 144-50, 207-08.
25. *Ibid.* pp. 130-32, 144-50; For criticism of Moreland, also see a review of *The Agrarian System* by Beni Pershad, *The Modern Review,* January 1921; Brij Narian, *Indian Economic Life,* Lahore, 1929, pp. 1-54.
26. *Eulogy of Father Jerome Xavier, S.J. A Missonary in Mogor,* tr. Rev. Hosten, S.J., JASB New Series. Vol. XXIII, Letter from Agra, dated 14 September 1609, pp. 121-22; Bernier Francois, *Travels in the Moughal Empire,* tr. Constable, London, 1891, pp. 204-05, 211-12, 220-26, 233-34. See Geleynssen de Jough, Palseart, Van Twist vide fn. 9.
27. Bernier, *Ibid.*
28. See details in my papers, 'Nature of *Dehat-i Taaluqa (zamindari* villages)....' vide f.n. 7; 'The Concept of Village Society during the Mughal Age and pre-British Era' under publication in the *Proceedings of the Social and Economic History Seminar,* 1966, Institute of Advanced Study, Rashtrapati Niwas, Simla.
29. Moreland, *The Agrarian System,* pp. 100-117, 132-38. Also, *Journal of Indian History,* Madras, Vol. VI, Part II, 1927; *JRAS* 1938 vide f.n. 9.
30. See fn. 28. Also see my paper, 'An Integrated Pattern of the Commercial Life in the Rural Society of North India during the 17th-18th centuries', vide *Proceedings of the Indian Historical Records Commission,* Delhi, Session 1966 (under publication).

Index